More Praise for *Reading for Understanding, Second Edition*

Reading for Understanding is a monumental achievement. It was a monumental achievement when it came out as a first edition in 1999, bringing years of rigorous reading research together in a framework for teaching that made sense in actual secondary school classrooms. Now, just thirteen years later, Schoenbach and Greenleaf have several randomized clinical trials and multiple on-going studies at their fingertips to demonstrate the effects of this approach for developing the reading and thinking of young people in our nation's middle and high school classrooms, as well as in community college classrooms. Their careful work on developing disciplinary literacy among all students represents a passion for and commitment to supporting students—and their teachers—in reading for understanding, which translates to reading for enjoyment, self-awareness, learning, and for purposeful and informed action in our society.

—*Elizabeth Moje, Arthur F. Thurnau Professor and Associate Dean for Research,*
School of Education, University of Michigan

Reading Apprenticeship has proven to be an inspiration to Renton Technical College faculty and students alike. They have learned together to view themselves as readers in transformative ways, as they embrace powerful techniques to increase reading comprehension. The ideas and strategies in *Reading for Understanding* anchor this new and broad-based energy around reading and an enthusiasm among our faculty to model effective reading strategies for our students.

—*Steve Hanson, President, Renton Technical College, Renton, Washington*

In my work coaching teachers, I want the learning to continue when the coaching conversation ends. *Reading for Understanding* has the finest blend I have seen of research, strategies, and classroom vignettes to deepen teacher learning and help them connect the dots between theory and practice.

—*Curtis Refior, Content Area Literacy Coach,*
Fowlerville Community Schools, Fowlerville, Michigan

Schoenbach, Greenleaf, and Murphy have developed a second edition of Reading Apprenticeship that gives voice to the concrete and inspiring experiences of teachers and students LEARNING TOGETHER in a wide range of contexts. Their design for inquiry-based learning in academic literacy extends from college classrooms in the suburbs of Los Angeles to rural high schools in Utah. Highlighting the critical nature of equitable opportunity for increasingly diverse students, the authors use their powerful framework to engage students in the rigor of disciplinary learning demanded by the Common Core State Standards. It is this challenge that makes Reading Apprenticeship indispensable for all those committed to creating a career-and-college-ready future for all students.

—*Dr. Christelle Estrada, Ph.D., Secondary English Language Arts Specialist,*
Utah State Office of Education

At last count, more than 150 instructors, enough to reach a critical mass in our students' educational experience, have been trained in Reading Apprenticeship. This new edition of *Reading for Understanding* will be an important support as we continue to help our students use a problem-solving approach to decipher dense textbook information, build reading stamina, and improve their classroom participation.

—*Mary S. Spangler, Ed.D., Chancellor,*
Houston Community College, Houston, Texas

In concrete, specific ways, *Reading for Understanding* builds on the rationale behind Reading Apprenticeship to assist teachers in their efforts to scaffold student learning so all students may become more engaged, strategic, and independent readers.

—*Mary M. Katona, Assistant Superintendent, Twin Valley School District,*
Elverson, Pennsylvania

Other books on Reading Apprenticeship from WestEd and Jossey-Bass:

Building Academic Literacy: An Anthology for Reading Apprenticeship

Building Academic Literacy: Lessons from Reading Apprenticeship Classrooms, Grades 6–12

Rethinking Preparation for Content Area Teaching: The Reading Apprenticeship Approach

SECOND
EDITION

Reading for Understanding

How Reading Apprenticeship Improves
Disciplinary Learning in Secondary
and College Classrooms

Ruth Schoenbach
Cynthia Greenleaf
Lynn Murphy

JOSSEY-BASS
A Wiley Imprint
www.josseybass.com

WestEd.org

Published by Jossey-Bass
A Wiley Imprint
One Montgomery Street, Suite 1200, San Francisco, CA 94104-4594—www.josseybass.com

Cover design and images by Christian Holden.
Cover design managed by Michael Cook.
Author photos courtesy of WestEd.

Jossey-Bass books and products are available through most bookstores. To contact Jossey-Bass directly call our Customer Care Department within the U.S. at 800-956-7739, outside the U.S. at 317-572-3986, or fax 317-572-4002.

Wiley also publishes its books in a variety of electronic formats and by print-on-demand. Some material included with standard print versions of this book may not be included in e-books or in print-on-demand. If the version of this book that you purchased references media such as CD or DVD that was not included in your purchase, you may download this material at http://booksupport.wiley.com. For more information about Wiley products, visit www.wiley.com.

Library of Congress Cataloging-in-Publication Data has been applied for.

ISBN 978-0-470-60831-9 (pbk); ISBN 978-1-118-22071-9 (ebk); ISBN 978-1-118-23452-5 (ebk); ISBN 978-1-118-25900-9 (ebk)

Printed in the United States of America
SECOND EDITION

PB Printing   10 9 8 7 6 5

Contents

Foreword

IN 1999, I had the privilege of writing a foreword for the first edition of *Reading for Understanding*. I was delighted, indeed honored, to do so because the four authors (Ruth Schoenbach, Cynthia Greenleaf, Christine Cziko, and Lori Hurwitz) had provided the field with a resource that enabled subject matter teachers to do what so many find so difficult—help middle and high school readers cope with and learn from disciplinary texts. Too often, these texts and these subject matter classes had taught students that they were incompetent, not up to the challenge of learning from tough texts. But the four of them, in describing the experiences they lived through in creating and refining their academic literacy course, told a different story—one in which these same sorts of students learned that they were competent, that they possessed the intellectual capital (knowledge), collaborative resources (their peers and teachers), toolkits (strategies), and personal attributes (stamina and self-efficacy) to stand up to the very texts that defeat so many adolescent learners.

When asked to write a foreword for the second edition, I jumped at the chance. I had followed the advances they had made in professional development and research over all of the intervening years, so I knew that there would be new developments to talk about. But I knew that much of the pedagogical model had remained intact. So I wondered, at least to myself, as I reflected on the pedagogy of the first edition, *How could they ever improve on that?* Well, they have!

In the second edition of *Reading for Understanding*, Ruth and Cyndy have been joined by a new coauthor, Lynn Murphy (Christine and Lori are both pursuing new but highly related ventures) to give us another great gift—a revised and enhanced framework for teaching literacy in disciplinary settings that is as elegantly practical as it is theoretically elegant. It is a guided tour, as one examines the tools of expert teachers as they engage students in a journey that is aptly dubbed Reading Apprenticeship—learning how to become a savvy, strategic reader under the tutelage of thoughtful, caring, and demanding teachers.

Written for secondary and college teachers of classes in science, history, math, health, geography, and the like, it is practical in providing good advice for shaping classroom pedagogy and activity. But its usefulness is enhanced by its strong grounding in socio-cognitive theories of teaching and learning (how teachers and students build supportive and intellectually rigorous communities of practice) and the rich body of empirical evidence that documents its effectiveness. This is a proven program, not just an appealing set of teaching practices.

Blessed then by the forces of practice, theory, and research, the Reading Apprenticeship framework is triply trustworthy. Subject area and literacy teachers will find a rich resource for transforming their classrooms from lecture-laden settings in which disengaged students fail or merely get by into collaborative learning environments in which students are guided on a journey of success. The transformation that this approach nurtures is truly startling. The Reading Apprenticeship framework gives us hope that classrooms that typically breed nothing but boredom, cynicism, and low self-esteem among today's adolescents can become places where students learn how to (a) cope with the inherent complexity of challenging disciplinary texts, (b) use their knowledge and their peers as resources to enhance that knowledge, and (c) convey confidence about their capacity to learn on their own.

A few specifics and highlights in the second edition.

The second edition of *Reading for Understanding* **is based upon a complete model of student learning.** As in the first edition, the core approach is metacognitive. Ultimately students develop a toolkit of monitoring and fix-up procedures that they can use on their own to blaze a trail of understanding as they make their way through the jungle of complex text and difficult concepts they encounter in content area classes. That metacognitive and cognitive toolkit students develop is highly contextualized within the Reading Apprenticeship model that also includes a personal, a social, and a knowledge-building dimension. So students are not just applying strategies for strategies' sake, as we often see in what the authors call the *skills in a box* solution that many publishers offer. They use strategies for purposes of acquiring knowledge (that is itself multidimensional), and they do it in a collaborative social context that brings its own set of affordances. The social context, the knowledge acquisition, and the effective deployment of cognitive tools all shape a set of personal dispositions and attitudes students develop. These attributes include self-efficacy, stamina, and agency—all dispositions that feed back into a virtuous cycle of success and personal mastery. Thus everything we know about motivation and engagement and self-efficacy are a part of the learning cycle. Contrast this with the vicious cycle of failure breeding defeat breeding disinterest breeding failure, and we have a very different story to tell—about the core pedagogical stance that Reading Apprenticeship promotes. And of course, the very naming of the framework and the use of the apprenticeship metaphor signals a fundamental relationship between teacher and student—teachers are NOT tellers of information who "give it" to students but are coaches and facilitators who arrange conditions (personal, social, and cognitive) so that students can "get it" for themselves. So learning in Reading Apprenticeship is not just skill acquisition; instead, it is skill, will, and thrill!

The examples in this second edition are even more compelling than those in the first. One of the virtues in the first edition was the compelling set of examples provided, examples that gave teachers a clear sense of how this approach might actually work in their classrooms. The second edition continues and expands that tradition: (a) there are a lot more examples, (b) they are from a much more diverse set of age and disciplinary settings, and (c) both the materials (what students and teachers have in their hands) and the pedagogical routines are even more explicit. As a person who has worked in this arena of comprehension strategy instruction for over thirty years now, I saw a lot of ideas I worked on come alive in more vivid ways than I had ever been able to enact them. In particular, the examples demonstrate that the Reading Apprenticeship team has really figured out how to handle the difficult task of gradually releasing responsibility to students who often struggle when left to their own devices—what lifelines to offer when and for how long.

The research base is more compelling. When the first edition came out, there were a few "data-rich" studies of Reading Apprenticeship, some more qualitative and descriptive (What does it look like and how does it work in a few selected classrooms?) and others more quantitative (What sort of growth on conventional measures of achievement do students experience over time?). But now the data are piling up in both the quantitative and qualitative bins. And the news is all good! We know more about what the approach looks like in more different disciplinary settings and with students in a wider band of age levels, both younger and older. And we have evidence of its positive impact on student achievement in efficacy studies and even "gold-standard" randomized field trials. Both kinds of research should give us greater confidence and will to implement Reading Apprenticeship in a broader range of age and disciplinary settings.

The second edition of *Reading for Understanding* is itself contextualized by a broader range of resources. Not only do the Reading Apprenticeship folks know more about how to make it work in classrooms, they also know more about how to conduct effective professional development to help teachers figure out how to make it work in their own classrooms—and how to sustain the initiative over time in a school setting. So how to enact relevant professional development, engage professional learning communities, and maintain program continuity—all deep concerns of school and district leaders—are now a part of the world of Reading Apprenticeship. In a companion volume, *Reading Apprenticeship Leaders' Guide*, school leadership folks will find much to help them in their efforts to initiate and sustain the effort.

So What? A major question to ask of any consequential intervention (by that I mean one that takes time, resources, and commitment to implement) is, So what? Is it really worth the time, effort, energy, and commitment? Will it make a difference in the lives and learning of students who otherwise would be left to the whims of indifferent, undifferentiated instruction? For me, the answer is an unwavering, YES! And it's nice to know, with the publication of this second edition, that theory, research, and practice are on my side. And yours!

P. David Pearson
University of California, Berkeley

Preface

When you read, there should be a little voice in your head like a storyteller
is saying it. And if there's not, then you're just looking at the words.
—LaKeisha, grade 9 student

LAKEISHA'S classmates, gathered in a back room of the school library, compete to add their assessments of this new approach to reading that LaKeisha is describing. They are students of the first teachers ever to use Reading Apprenticeship, and they boisterously agree that they are reading in new ways.

Jason describes how his reading of the history textbook has changed:

I understand the book more now. Because I read differently. Like when you're reading, if it doesn't make sense, you can try to restate it in your own words, or you can make questions so you can understand it better. Now I read in between the lines. I basically get into the heart of it—like reading deeper into what it is saying.

Students also agree that they are reading more. Michael couches his comments as a mock complaint about his Reading Apprenticeship teacher:

Man, she's tryin' to be sneaky! She wants you to pick a book that you are interested in so you will read it more. She makes you find a book that you *like* so that you have to read it. Because you like it.

More than a decade ago, in the first edition of this book, we described piloting the Reading Apprenticeship framework in an "academic literacy" course required of LaKeisha, Jason, Michael, and the entire ninth grade at San Francisco's Thurgood Marshall Academic High School. By the end of that pilot year, reading scores for those two hundred students had jumped more than two grade levels on a nationally normed reading test. Student gains were consistent across ethnic groups and in the classrooms of the four teachers who taught the course. During the next school year, students held on to what they had learned: their reading achievement continued to grow at an accelerated rate, as measured by a standardized reading test.

Since that time, Reading Apprenticeship has become familiar to the students of almost one hundred thousand middle school, high school, and college teachers who have read the first edition of *Reading for Understanding*, participated in Reading Apprenticeship professional development, and used Reading Apprenticeship approaches in subject area classes and academic literacy classes. We have published two companion books and a two-semester curriculum in response to requests for additional support for the academic literacy course described in the first edition: *Building Academic Literacy: An Anthology for Reading Apprenticeship; Building Academic Literacy: Lessons from Reading Apprenticeship Classrooms, Grades 6–12;* and *Reading Apprenticeship Academic Literacy Course.*

Also since the first edition, our colleague Jane Braunger convened a faculty research group of teacher educators interested in using the Reading Apprenticeship framework with pre-service teachers. Members of this group worked with Jane to publish a book about this work, *Rethinking Preparation for Content Area Teaching.*

Jane was also the catalyst for developing work with community college educators interested in exploring and adapting Reading Apprenticeship for use in their classes. Currently, Reading Apprenticeship is active on over thirty campuses across the country in developmental, general education, and transfer-level courses.

During the past decade, Reading Apprenticeship has also been the focus of much research (see Chapter One). Three federally funded randomized controlled studies have found statistically significant benefits for students in Reading Apprenticeship high school classrooms—gains in comparison with control students that include improved attendance, course completion, and attitudes and confidence about reading, as well as higher achievement on reading comprehension and subject matter standardized tests.

In another major study, researchers found that even modest amounts of the right kind of instructional support transformed classrooms and benefited students. In a two-year case study of middle school and high school classrooms, teachers who were rated "moderately" skillful implementers of Reading Apprenticeship, as well as the highest-rated implementers, produced benefits for students in changed approaches to complex reading, reading engagement and academic identity, and scores on standardized tests.

Evaluation of the impact of Reading Apprenticeship in community college is also promising. A multicampus faculty research group and an evaluation by the Research & Planning Group for California Community Colleges have documented classroom instruction that markedly increases students' confidence and engagement in learning. In classrooms where achievement and persistence data have been collected, increased student grades, rates of course completion, and retention in school are typical.

As we go forward, Reading Apprenticeship continues to reach more and more teachers and to be part of major new research initiatives. As a framework offering teachers a coherent yet adaptable approach to literacy learning, Reading Apprenticeship has been an important force in the field of adolescent literacy and more recently in literacy at the college level. The first edition of this book has been a touchstone all along the way.

Why We Wrote a Second Edition

In this new edition of *Reading for Understanding*, the core principles that drive Reading Apprenticeship are still in place. They have turned out to be very sturdy over the years (see the Reading Apprenticeship framework in Chapter Two). But, over time, Reading Apprenticeship has attracted a more diverse audience and much new experience that is not reflected in the first edition.

This second edition (and a companion volume, *Reading Apprenticeship Leaders' Guide*) includes many examples from community college classrooms and a much broader set of examples at the middle school and high school level—across a variety of academic subject areas and from classrooms serving learners with diverse instructional needs.

It also includes the many arresting voices of teachers and students who are making the Reading Apprenticeship framework their own in a broad range of rural, urban, and suburban classrooms across the country.

Acknowledgments

Open-hearted students, a talented Reading Apprenticeship staff, smart and dedicated teachers, and our earliest colleagues at Thurgood Marshall Academic High School have contributed in their unique ways to the scope and spirit of this book.

We have changed the names of the students who populate these pages, but their words are true. We thank them pseudonymously, with admiration and best wishes.

Staff members of the Strategic Literacy Initiative at WestEd in the years since the first edition was published have contributed their collective knowledge, patience, and sense of humor to keep the work honest and fresh. The considerable professional expertise and energetic contributions of current and past colleagues—Jana Bouc, Jane Braunger, Will Brown, Irisa

Charney-Sirott, Gayle Cribb, Pamela Fong, Gina Hale, Rita Jensen, Marean Jordan, Margot Kenaston, Diane Lee, Cindy Litman, Kate Meisert, Faye Mueller, Tamara Taylor Reeder, and Diane Waff—are represented in all the pages that follow.

Teachers, and especially those quoted in this book (and named in the following list), have not only taught us but also inspired us. They allowed us into their classrooms for observations and documentary videotaping, made time for research interviews, and reported back to us about ways their instruction was changing. Members of the Community College Literacy Research Group even conducted their own research about using Reading Apprenticeship approaches, and are quoted liberally. We thank as well the administrators whose comments and reflections add an important perspective to the book and our thinking.

Two people made enduring contributions to this book and to the design of the original Reading Apprenticeship Academic Literacy course. Christine Cziko and Lori Hurwitz were coauthors of the first edition of *Reading for Understanding* (along with Ruth Schoenbach and Cynthia Greenleaf). Their classroom experience, savvy, and thoughtfulness were essential to our initial work and continue to inform this second edition.

Five trusted colleagues read and gave us feedback on late drafts of this book. Our thanks to Nika Hogan, Sue Kinney, Cathleen Kral, Bill Loyd, and Curtis Refior.

We would also like to acknowledge and thank the leadership of our parent organization, WestEd. The Strategic Literacy Initiative has received strong and consistent institutional support over the years as we have developed, refined, and tested the Reading Apprenticeship framework. In addition, the intellectual and personal encouragement of Gary Estes, Glen Harvey, Paul Hood, and Aída Walqui have kept us on our toes in the very best way. We are fortunate to have such colleagues. Finally, we want to offer personal thanks to our nearest and dearest—Lynn Eden, Paul King, and Peter Shwartz.

Contributing Teachers and Administrators

Anne Agard: Instructor of English as a Second Language, Laney College, Oakland, Calif.

Ann Akey: Teacher of Science, Woodside High School, Woodside, Calif.

Muthulakshimi Bhavani Balavenkatesan: Teacher of Biology, Logan High School, Union City, Calif.

Luke Boyd: Teacher of Grade 9 English, Louis Dieruff High School, Allentown, Penn.

Alec Brown: As cited: Teacher of Grade 9 World Literature and Reading Apprenticeship, ASPIRA Early College, Chicago, Ill. Currently: Teacher of Contemporary Issues/Reading and Writing I, Instituto Health Science Career Academy, Chicago, Ill.

Linda Brown: As cited: Reading Specialist, Howard County Public Schools, Howard County, Md. Currently: Developmental English Adjunct Faculty, Carroll Community College, Westminster, Md.

Will Brown: As cited: Teacher of Chemistry, Skyline High School, Oakland, Calif. Currently: Professional Development Associate, Strategic Literacy Initiative, WestEd, Oakland, Calif.

Yu-Chung Chang-Hou: Assistant Professor of Mathematics, Pasadena City College, Pasadena, Calif.

Janet Creech: Teacher of Science, Woodside High School, Woodside, Calif.

Gayle Cribb: As cited: Teacher of History and Spanish, Dixon High School, Dixon, Calif. Currently: Professional Development Associate, Strategic Literacy Initiative, WestEd, Oakland, Calif.

Christine Cziko: Coauthor of the first edition of *Reading for Understanding.* As cited: Teacher of English and Academic Literacy, Thurgood Marshall Academic High School, San Francisco, Calif. Currently: Academic Coordinator, Multicultural Urban Secondary English (MUSE) Master's and Credential Program, University of California, Berkeley, Graduate School of Education.

Charla Dean: As cited: Teacher of Academic Literacy, Ben Lomond High School, Ogden, Utah. Currently: Teacher of Reading, Mount Ogden Junior High School, Ogden, Utah.

Jill Eisner: Reading Specialist, Centennial High School, Ellicott City, Md.

Jordona Elderts: Teacher of Social Studies, John Muir Middle School, San Leandro, Calif.

Laurie Erby: Teacher of Grade 7 Social Studies, Saline Middle School, Saline, Mich.

Monica Figueroa: Teacher of Social Studies, Oak Grove Middle School, Concord, Calif.

JoAnn Filer: Teacher of English, Gloucester Township Campus, Camden County Technical Schools, Sicklerville, N.J.

Janet Ghio: As cited: Teacher of English and Academic Literacy, Lincoln High School, Stockton, Calif. Currently: Professional Development Consultant, Strategic Literacy Initiative, WestEd, Oakland, Calif.

Laura Graff: Associate Professor of Mathematics, College of the Desert, Palm Desert, Calif.

Gina Hale: As cited: Teacher of Grade 7 Core (English Language Arts and World History), John Muir Middle School, San Leandro, Calif. Currently: Professional Development Associate, Strategic Literacy Initiative, WestEd, Oakland, Calif.

Cindi Davis Harris: Instructor of English, Grossmont College, El Cajon, Calif.

Linda Hart: Adult Basic Education/GED Instructor, Renton Technical College, Renton, Wash.

Andrew Hartig: Teacher of English, Hillsdale High School, San Mateo, Calif.

Karen Hattaway: Professor of English, San Jacinto College North, Houston, Tex.

Cindy Hicks: As cited: Instructor of English, Chabot College, Hayward, Calif. Currently: Emeritus.

Monika Hogan: Associate Professor of English, Pasadena City College, Pasadena, Calif. In her role as Community College Coordinator for the Strategic Literacy Initiative, Nika interviewed several of the community college instructors who contributed to this edition.

Heather Howlett: Teacher of Grade 8 Science, Three Fires Middle School, Howell, Mich.

Lori Hurwitz: Coauthor of the first edition of *Reading for Understanding.* As cited: Teacher of English and Academic Literacy, Thurgood Marshall Academic High School, San Francisco, Calif. Currently: Deputy Director of Programs, San Francisco Education Fund.

Rita Jensen: As cited: Teacher of English Language Development, John Muir Middle School, San Leandro, Calif. Currently: Professional Development Associate, Strategic Literacy Initiative, WestEd, Oakland, Calif.

Tim Jones: Teacher of Algebra and Pre-Calculus, Arsenal Technical High School, Indianapolis, Ind.

Dorothea Jordan: As cited: Teacher of Grade 7 Pre-Algebra, Oak Grove Middle School, Concord, Calif. Currently: Retired.

Michael Kelcher: Associate Professor of Chemistry, Santa Ana College, Santa Ana, Calif.

Cathleen Kral: As cited: Instructional Leader for Literacy K–12 and Director of Literacy Coaching in Boston Public Schools. Currently: International consultant in education and Multi-Sites Coordinator for the Reading Apprenticeship Improving Secondary Education (RAISE) Project, Strategic Literacy Initiative, WestEd, Oakland, Calif.

Lisa Krebs: Teacher of English, Dixon High School, Dixon, Calif.

Deborah Leser: Principal of George Washington Community High School, Indianapolis, Ind.

Michele Lesmeister: Adult Basic Education/GED Instructor, Renton Technical College, Renton, Wash.

Anthony Linebaugh: Teacher of English and Academic Literacy, Ninth Grade Academy, John McCandless High School, Stockton, Calif.

William Loyd: As cited: Literacy Coordinator, Washtenaw Intermediate School District (WISD), Ann Arbor, Mich. Currently: Michigan Statewide Coordinator, Reading Apprenticeship Improving Secondary Education (RAISE) Project, WISD.

Walter Masuda: As cited: Professor of English, Contra Costa College, San Pablo, Calif. Currently: Dean of Fine Arts and Language Arts, Yuba College, Marysville, Calif.

Missie Meeks: Instructor of English and Basic Skills, Jones County Junior College, Ellisville, Miss.

Lisa Morehouse: Teacher of English, Balboa High School, San Francisco, Calif.

Holly Morris: Professor of Biology, Lehigh Carbon Community College, Schnecksville, Penn.

Pam Myette: Teacher of Special Education Services, Oakland Mills High School, Columbia, Md.

Nicci Nunes: As cited: Teacher of Physics and Chemistry, Thurgood Marshall Academic High School, San Francisco, Calif. Currently: Educational consultant.

April Oliver: Teacher of AP Literature and Composition, World Literature, and Dance, Los Altos High School, Mountain View, Calif.

Chris Paulis: As cited: Coordinator of Secondary Language Arts, Howard County Public School System, Howard County, Md. In this role Chris supported a number of the teachers whose Reading Apprenticeship practices are cited in this book. Currently: Educational consultant.

Caro Pemberton: As cited: Teacher of Humanities, Oceana High School, Pacifica, Calif. Currently: Principal, Oceana High School.

Allie Pitts: Teacher of Social Science, Hillsdale High School, San Mateo, Calif.

Lisa Rizzo: Teacher of Language Arts, Ben Franklin Intermediate School, Colma, Calif.

Keren Robertson: Teacher of English, Los Altos High School, Los Altos, Calif.

Cindy Ryan: Reading Specialist, Dreher High School, Columbia, S.C.

Teri Ryan: Teacher of Mathematics, Vintage High School, Napa, Calif.

Trish Schade: As cited: Instructor of Developmental English, Merced College, Merced, Calif. Currently: Associate Professor of Developmental Reading, Northern Essex Community College, Haverhill, Mass.

Ericka Senegar-Mitchell: Teacher of Biotechnology, AP Biology, and Honors Biology, Junipero Serra High School, San Diego, Calif. Founder and Director of Science in the City Outreach Program.

Patti Smith: Instructor of English and QEP Director, Jones County Junior College, Ellisville, Miss.

Stacy Stambaugh: As cited: Teacher of Academic Literacy, South High School, Omaha, Neb. Currently: Curriculum Specialist English and Special Education, South High School.

Michelle Stone: Teacher of Academic Literacy and AP Literature and Composition, Hayward High School, Hayward, Calif.

Kathleen Sullivan: Teacher of AP Chemistry and General Chemistry, Central High School, Bridgeport, Conn.

Tammy Thompson: Teacher of Academic Literacy and English, Lincoln High School, Stockton, Calif.

Tim Tindol: Teacher of Science, Lincoln High School, San Francisco, Calif.

Stacey Tisor: As cited: Teacher of Biology and Science, Irvington High School, Fremont, Calif. Currently: Beginning Teacher Support and Assessment (BTSA) and Intern Coordinator, San Mateo County Office of Education, Redwood City, Calif.

Francisco Valdiosera: Vice Principal, George Washington Community High School, Indianapolis, Ind.

Chris Van Ruiten-Greene: Teacher of English, Lincoln High School, Stockton, Calif.

Pam Williams-Butterfield, RN: Nursing Assistant Instructor, Renton Technical College, Renton, Wash.

Jane Wolford: Instructor of History, Chabot College, Hayward, Calif.

Sandy Wood: Chair of Department of Anthropology, Sociology, and Women's Studies, Santa Ana College, Santa Ana, Calif.

Nancy Ybarra: Instructor of English, Los Medanos College, Pittsburg, Calif.

CHAPTER ONE

Engaged Academic Literacy for All

Usually, in a regular history class, the teacher would say, "Read from page so-and-so to so-and-so, answer the red-square questions and the unit questions, and turn them in." And it wasn't like you had to *read* it. . . If the red-square question was here, you knew the answer was somewhere around that area right there. It was something that you could like slide by without them knowing. I don't know if they cared or not, but that's the way everybody did it.

—Rosa, grade 9 student

Most teachers, if I talk to them, they'll be like, "What, are you serious—this is college, you're asking me how to *read*? I can't help you. You should have learned that in eighth grade."

—Kalif, community college student[1]

AS A NATION and as educators, what do we expect of our middle school, high school, and college students? What messages do we send students about their academic abilities and promise? If we believe that all students should be able to think and read critically, to write and talk knowledgeably about historical, literary, scientific, or mathematical questions, we need to provide richer learning opportunities than the "red-square question" routine that Rosa describes. We need to better prepare and support students like Kalif.

This book presents an approach to improving students' ability to read critically and to write about and discuss texts in a range of disciplines—an approach that builds their academic literacy. The framework for this approach, Reading Apprenticeship, starts from the premise that engaging students like Rosa and her peers affectively as well as intellectually is key to developing the dispositions and skills required for becoming confident, critical, and independent readers and thinkers.

Like Kalif, many students feel overwhelmed by the high level of literacy expected of them in college courses. Standards for high-level literacy, such as those embodied in the Common Core State Standards for K–12 students or in the "gatekeeper" exams that determine college admission and placement, outpace many students' preparation. Teachers feel similarly overwhelmed by the distance between these ambitious literacy goals and their students' experience engaging with academic texts. When students are unaccustomed to carrying out rigorous literacy tasks, it is a daunting prospect for teachers to find new ways to engage them in the satisfaction of unlocking texts and the learning it makes possible.

Many educators express the belief that students who struggle with academic texts "just aren't motivated." Yet we see ample evidence that by helping students find their own reasons and entry points for reading challenging texts, we can support them in developing both their affective and their intellectual engagement with academic texts. When a teacher at a high-poverty high school with a majority of English learners tells us her students are "suddenly finding that the economics textbook is more interesting," and they are eager to read and discuss the ideas in it, it seems clear that the students rather than the text have changed. By learning to work through challenging passages and to collaboratively make sense of them, these students have developed a different *affective* relationship with the text and with economics concepts they previously found "unengaging."

Our work over the years with thousands of middle school, high school, college, and pre-service teachers has been the subject of multiple research studies demonstrating that teachers can successfully apprentice their students into becoming readers of academic texts. When teachers listen closely to students' thinking, probe their thinking respectfully, and help students listen to and probe each other's thinking about texts, classrooms can become lively centers of discussion about *how,* as well as what, students are reading. In such classrooms, students begin to see themselves differently and to feel more empowered as readers and thinkers. Time and again, this change in students' sense of themselves as readers and learners—their academic and reader identity—results in striking changes in how they engage and comprehend a wide range of academic texts.

What we have learned from teachers and students is consonant with a deep reservoir of knowledge developed by scholars in the areas of cognitive science and sociocultural learning theory; psychological research on motivation, engagement, achievement, and identity; and educational research on pedagogy and disciplinary literacy in core subject areas.

The Reading Apprenticeship instructional framework presented in this book combines this scholarly research with practitioner experience. This framework, described in Chapter Two, is not a program or a curriculum that teachers or schools "adopt." It is an organizing paradigm for subject area teaching, one that enables students to approach challenging academic texts more strategically, confidently, and successfully.

The Context for Change

> Reading, and its role in promoting achievement, is fundamentally an equity issue.
> —William Loyd, district literacy coordinator,
> addressing superintendents of the
> Washtenaw, Michigan, intermediate school district

Secondary and post-secondary education in the United States reflects a society that does not equitably educate people living in poverty, members of racial and ethnic minorities, those whose first language is not English, and those whose learning differences call for special education services. Problems of inequitable opportunity and outcomes do not originate in schools and cannot be addressed through schooling alone. However, strong evidence suggests that schools can either reinforce these inequities or, like the schools in the Washtenaw district and others, push against them.[2] The following look at the state of literacy in secondary school, college, and beyond makes clear the extent of the problem.

Literacy in Middle and High School

According to the National Assessment of Educational Progress (NAEP), two-thirds of U.S. high school students are unable to read and comprehend complex academic materials, think critically about texts, synthesize information from multiple sources, or communicate clearly what they have learned. Only a small minority of eighth and twelfth graders read at an advanced level. Many high-needs students have been demoralized by years of academic failure and do not see themselves as readers or as capable learners. Achievement gaps are stubbornly persistent along racial, ethnic, and socioeconomic lines. By some estimates, half of the incoming ninth graders in a typical high-poverty urban high school read two or three years below grade level.[3]

The traditional response to low literacy achievement has been to take a remedial approach to addressing skill deficits. At the middle and high school levels, low-achieving students are often required to take several remedial classes a day. Yet research has shown that isolated, skills-based instruction in reading may perpetuate low literacy achievement rather than accelerate literacy growth.[4] At the same time, a renewed policy focus on "college and career readiness" driven by concerns about global competitiveness has highlighted the importance of increasing the number of students who can read critically and make sense of complex texts.

As awareness of literacy needs in secondary school and college has grown, an increasing number of research and policy documents are highlighting the importance of a more integrated and student-centered approach to building literacy—one that addresses both academic rigor and academic engagement. Recent literacy research has identified the instructional characteristics necessary to meet the unique needs of low-achieving adolescents: treat all students as capable learners, create a collaborative climate of inquiry, build on students' interests and curiosity, tap into students' knowledge and experience, and harness their preference for social interaction to serve academic goals.[5]

However, policies instituted in accordance with the No Child Left Behind act run counter to these research findings. Narrow compliance measures typical of No Child Left Behind continue to push schools to use remedial curricula, pacing guides, and test preparation to produce "adequate yearly progress" (AYP) on state standardized tests. Schools serving the least-well-prepared students are the most constrained by test-score pressures, but high-stakes tests push teachers everywhere to promote the rote learning practices—Rosa's "red-square questions"—that have long characterized teaching in U.S. secondary schools.[6]

Low academic literacy is by no means an issue only for underperforming students. Even among students who do relatively well in class and score reasonably well on standardized tests, teachers can point to those who have difficulty comprehending and interpreting class texts, who fail to complete reading assignments, and who seem unlikely to become independent, lifelong readers. "You can't rely on the students to read," explains one high school teacher. "They will engage in projects, but they don't seem to read or understand the source materials or texts."

The momentum behind the Common Core State Standards and the accompanying development of more sophisticated literacy assessments offer hope that richer literacy learning across subject areas may become a goal against which students, schools, and teachers measure themselves and are measured by others. These new standards and assessments can also provide direction for teachers' professional learning, if they are accompanied by sustained support for teachers to develop knowledge and skills for embedding advanced literacy practices into their subject area teaching. Otherwise, the inequalities these standards and assessments have the potential to address may merely be replicated.

Literacy in College and the Workplace

Without substantial improvement in advanced literacy proficiencies such as those identified by NAEP, students will be unable to handle the quantity and complexity of assigned reading in college.[7] They are likely to struggle in the workforce as well; even for entry-level jobs, the ability to read, write, and think critically is increasingly a minimum requirement. At issue are the competencies that allow or limit full participation in our increasingly complex and diverse society.

Students enroll in college with the expectation that this continued education will help prepare them for more satisfying futures. In the United States, 44 percent enroll in a community college, either as a gateway to further education or with the goal of earning an associate degree or technical license. However, between 70 and 90 percent of these entering students are placed in remedial, or developmental, English language arts or mathematics classes, or both.[8] Success rates in these classes vary, but campuses that have tracked the progress of students who enroll in lower-level developmental courses find that only a small number of them (usually around 10 percent) ever make it to credit-bearing or transfer-level courses. Many, if not all, of these students are weak in the essential academic skills related to high-level literacy.[9]

In community college classes more generally, faculty report that students in credit-bearing classes ranging from geology to anesthesia technology also struggle with literacy. Many students seem unable to read and understand the course texts independently and rely instead on lecture notes. These same students are likely to become the future employees who have difficulty working either in teams or independently with complex instructions, open-ended problems, and multiple texts.

Community colleges are not alone in facing this challenge. Recent reports point to a dismaying literacy problem in four-year colleges as well: close to 50 percent of entering students are not prepared for the literacy tasks expected of them.[10]

The Literacy Ceiling

When students have difficulty reading and understanding subject area texts, they hit a "literacy ceiling" that limits what they can achieve both in the classroom and in their lives outside of school. Naturally, the literacy ceiling also limits what teachers can achieve in their classrooms. To the degree that students cannot independently access the knowledge and information embedded in their books and other curriculum materials, teachers try to find alternative ways to help them "get the content."

Middle school, high school, and college teachers often express frustration with students' limited academic literacy preparation, sometimes asking, "Why didn't somebody do a better job earlier of preparing these students to read what they need to read to succeed at this grade level?" Others express a sense of inadequacy and bewilderment: "What am I supposed to do when they can barely get through a page in the textbook on their own? I'm a subject area teacher, not a reading teacher!" Perhaps most disconcerting is the resignation of teachers who conclude, "It's too late for these students to catch up."

Teachers are not the only ones worried about the literacy ceiling. Students have an even more immediate and personal cause for concern. Many find reading mystifying. Faced daily with the difficulty of making sense of unfamiliar texts and literacy tasks, they have come to believe that they are "just not cut out" to be readers. With a mounting sense of exasperation, they "read" the words but cannot begin to make sense of sentences, paragraphs, and longer texts.

Students respond to their reading difficulties in a variety of ways, often avoiding a reading task entirely and waiting instead for a teacher to *tell* them what they need to know. Some students attempt invisibility, silently sliding lower in their seats in hopes they will not be called on. Others act out in class, creating distractions when they fear their errors or inadequacies might otherwise be exposed. Still others adopt a stance that clearly says, "I don't care about any of this school stuff at all." The most dedicated among them—or, perhaps, simply those with the most stamina—struggle through each new text in a painful, word-by-word attempt to string meaning together. None of these responses, of course, provides a way to break through the ceiling restricting them from higher-level learning.

"Solutions" That Don't Solve the Problem

I knew that just telling them to reread the essay or to summarize the main points wasn't enough.

—Walter Masuda, community college English 1A professor

When students are unprepared for the academic literacy demands in their courses, many teachers, like Walter Masuda, feel frustrated by their own unsatisfying "solutions" for helping them, or find themselves turning to a handful of defaults that serve only to postpone or compound students' problems. For the lowest-testing students, remediation interventions that reteach at the most basic level or packaged programs that drill students in discrete skills may be called upon. More generally, teachers may try to teach "around" the text altogether with lectures and PowerPoint presentations, or they may try to "protect" students from dry or difficult texts with alternatives that never challenge them or help them grow as readers and learners.

Instead, as Walter came to understand, effective academic literacy instruction for all levels of students must involve them in practicing higher-level thinking with complex texts precisely so that they can further develop those abilities:

Now, through the use of Reading Apprenticeship routines, I feel that the low- to average-performing students are beginning to acquire *the kind of thinking* so necessary for their academic success in my classes and beyond.

Remediation Restart

Supporting students' development as active, engaged, and independent learners is a key goal of education. Yet a common response for helping low-performing readers is a remediation approach to literacy—an approach that is more likely to take students into a remedial dead end that many never escape.

In middle school and high school, remediation may take students all the way back to decoding and the beginning of the learning-to-read process. A decision to support struggling readers by reteaching them to decode is based on a belief that students' difficulties with reading are rooted in a lack of successful phonics instruction.

The idea that early reading instruction has failed to equip middle and high school students with adequate decoding skills is pervasive. Yet most adolescents whom teachers might initially describe as "not able to even get the words off the page" are far less likely to have problems with decoding than they are to have difficulties with comprehension, unfamiliar vocabulary, limited background knowledge, and reading fluency or engagement.[11] Usually these students have been asked to do little reading in school and have very little stamina or persistence when they encounter difficulties with texts. Being sent "back to the beginning" of reading instruction can be worse than nonproductive for these students. It can reinforce their misguided conceptions that reading is just "saying the words." Nor does going back to phonics help them understand and use the complex comprehension processes or the knowledge about texts and the world that good readers rely on. In addition, by simply reteaching decoding, educators ignore some of students' most powerful assets for reading improvement: the knowledge and cognitive resources they already use throughout the many nonschool aspects of their lives.

A very small percentage of students may actually need help with decoding skills. These students, however, require intensive, precisely targeted, individualized support specific to their carefully assessed needs, provided by highly skilled teachers, and lasting no longer than necessary. Moreover, such decoding instruction need not displace meaningful literacy engagement, as numerous literacy programs for English learners and adults attest.[12]

Remedial, or developmental, literacy classes at the community college level can tie students to a sequence of from four to six semesters before they are eligible to enroll in credit-bearing English and other general education courses. For the lowest-testing students, these remedial sequences may begin with a course on sentence-level grammar, followed by a course on paragraphs, followed by a course on essays or longer works. The counterproductive effects of this compartmentalized, step-by-step structure have been well documented, with students dropping out in discouragement at various "exit points" on the path from one non-credit-bearing course to another. Research on the length of these sequences indicates that completion rates in community college English and math programs drop with each additional level of remedial coursework required of students.[13]

Searching for Skills-in-a-Box Solutions

When students are ill prepared for the literacy challenges of the classroom, it is natural to want a quick fix to bring them up to speed. We have been asked repeatedly about any intervention packages that have shown proven results. In fact, there are a few programs that do a reasonable job of supporting students who need to catch up. But these programs require skilled implementation to build students' personal engagement, develop social supports for reading, and engage students in the extensive reading of extended text—probably not the quick fix that educators may be hoping for.

Instead, the quick-fix or "skills-in-a-box" programs commonly promoted as suitable for solving a range of reading difficulties feature discrete skills practice and decontextualized reading of short paragraphs or passages. Some of these programs focus on word-level exercises and vocabulary drills; others divide comprehension into a suite of skills such as find-the-main-idea, sequence sentences, draw conclusions—all with decontextualized snippets of text. Some other skills programs put students through batteries of test preparation exercises: read a paragraph and answer "comprehension" questions, read another paragraph and answer questions, and so on. These, too, fail to help students gain the kind of deeper comprehension skills and practice that are needed for high-level literacy demands.

Simply put, there is no quick fix for reading inexperience. Decades of research have shown that reading is a complex cognitive and social practice and that readers develop knowledge, experience, and skill over a lifetime of reading.[14] In building reading aptitude, there is no skills-only approach that can substitute for reading itself. On the contrary, repeated studies have demonstrated that isolated instruction in grammar, decoding, or even reading comprehension skills may have little or no transfer effect when students are actually reading.[15]

If these were not reasons enough to avoid skills-in-a-box programs, there is also the issue of how decisions are made to place students in such programs. Inexperienced readers are often placed into skills programs based on scanty assessment information and limited understanding of their real learning needs. When placed into courses that do not fit with what they actually need or can benefit from, not only are students frustrated by the experience, but often, because of scheduling conflicts, they are prevented from participating in other, more productive learning opportunities. Instead of catching up, these students find themselves stuck in courses that only produce further delays and discouragement.

Teaching Around the Text

Many middle school, high school, and college teachers see their primary responsibility as teaching the important ideas and knowledge base of their discipline—the "concepts and content" of mathematics, chemistry, literature, history, and so on. When their students seem either unwilling to tackle or unable to understand course texts on their own, many teachers, like the history teacher speaking here, make a strategic decision to provide students with alternative means of accessing the ideas and content of the curriculum—that is, to teach "around" reading:

> I'm doing back flips in the classroom to get the content across without expecting them to read the textbook. I've stopped assigning reading. The text is almost supplementary.

To engage students in the important ideas of a text that many have not read or understood, teachers find ways to provide the entire class with some common understanding of what is in the text. They may do so by reading to students, lecturing with bullet points projected in the front of the room, or showing a video related to the content. Another teacher explains,

> Because you can't rely on students to read, I feel like I'm constantly summarizing the history textbook so kids don't miss the main points. I wish I didn't have to assume that role as much, but I find I do.

Such compensatory practices are so common that many students regard them as normal. One student's description of how reading is handled in her science class could as easily apply to any number of other classrooms:

> Usually, the teacher just writes stuff on the overhead. Then we copy it down and she gives us lots of labs to do. I don't remember using the book. We probably only used it a couple of times to look for stuff.

The strategy of teaching content without having students read—or of reducing what students are asked to read to only a small amount of text—becomes a self-defeating practice with its own domino effect. Because students are unprepared to carry out reading assignments independently, many teachers give up any thought of holding them accountable for reading. And because these students do not have to read in some of their subject area classes, they resist expectations for doing so in other classes. One result is that other teachers begin to give up their own expectations that students read academic texts independently. In this way, even with the best intentions, teachers inadvertently enable students to progress up the grades and even through college courses with very limited reading experiences and abilities. Students remain dependent on someone else to convey curriculum content.

Perpetuating students' dependence on teachers denies them opportunities— and successes—they can gain only through the extensive, independent reading of texts. Without being encouraged and supported to expand the limits of their reading, many students may never be prepared to independently read the gatekeeper texts that stand between them and their future educational, economic, civic, and cultural opportunities—texts such as the SAT exams, entry-level reading tests for jobs, college or job applications, textbooks and other reading material for postsecondary education or training, and even the directions to apply for a student loan or home mortgage.

Protecting Them from Boredom

Many students' literacy lives outside of school are decidedly digital. There is no denying the appeal of digital media for developing and validating social identity, for self-expression, and for locating rich information and entertainment resources. There are enormous opportunities for learning, interaction, research, and creativity in the digital worlds at students' fingertips. In comparison, printed or even electronic textbooks and other primarily text-based materials can seem hopelessly stodgy and old-fashioned. Nonetheless, especially for students who have yet to develop the dispositions required for concentrated literate attention, digital media can encourage coasting on the surface of text rather than slowing down to dig into it. The concentration required to sustain attention on a long or challenging text, or the persistence and confidence needed to read across multiple texts on a related topic and compare ideas in each of them, is very different from the kind of "browsing reading" that most Internet readers employ.[16]

As teachers struggle with authentic ways to build bridges between students' digital literacies and the literacies needed for this kind of focused academic endeavor, many also feel an obligation to "protect" students from dull or dreary print materials. Anyone who has read a range of secondary school and college textbooks knows that many are neither well written nor engaging.

Why, some well-meaning teachers argue, should students be subjected to these "inconsiderate" texts? Why make students plow through an encyclopedic history textbook? Why assign Shakespeare? Such objections to having students read assigned course texts arise from the valid argument that students need engaging texts to be more able and likely to actually read and understand them. We don't disagree.

In fact, we strongly encourage teachers to supplement textbooks with varied and engaging texts, to build text sets that expand students' opportunities to read about and understand important content, and to include digital sources in their search for such texts.[17] But more engaging texts are not necessarily more accessible. Primary source documents used in a history class or scientific studies found on the Internet can be more challenging than textbook explanations.

If students are to keep their future options open, they must develop the confidence and the will to approach—as well as the ability to make sense of—a range of texts, including the many gatekeeper texts that will not be inherently fascinating or well composed. When taken to the extreme, an emphasis on finding perfectly engaging and considerate texts can turn into never asking students to read anything they cannot already comfortably read or to learn about anything that they are not already familiar with or interested in.

Instead, by building bridges between students' out-of-school and in-school literacy knowledge and by expanding the range of texts students read, teachers can help them learn strategies for persisting with and understanding texts they may initially perceive as boring or inaccessible. We have a responsibility to help students learn to approach these texts as informed, critical thinkers. Armed with appropriate strategies and mental habits, students can then make their own decisions about which texts they will or will not work their way through, depending on their own goals.

In contrast to the delays and discouragement of ineffective "solutions" such as those just described, which do little to bring students into an active relationship with texts they encounter in school, we have seen more promising ways to proceed. The experiences of many teachers demonstrate that once students are helped to comprehend complex texts, of varied academic disciplines, they often find them curiously "more interesting," as did the high school economics students described earlier. Students do like to learn; they do want to become competent and knowledgeable. As we once heard a courageous young woman tell a roomful of high school teachers,

> We know we aren't very well educated. We know there are things we
> should know by now that we don't. But we're not stupid. Most of us are
> really smart. You just need to show us, break it down for us, work with us,
> and expect us to do it.

The Case for Optimism

> Reading Apprenticeship gave me the language and strategies to use with students that helped to "unlock" doors for them . . . I felt like a better teacher and that the time . . . put into the process was given back in outcomes.
> —Middle school teacher, Washtenaw, Michigan, district survey

At the heart of our approach to reading instruction is a conviction that the most powerful resources for improving student reading exist within teachers and their students. Some policymakers and administrators hold the view that secondary and college teachers are not open to pedagogical change. However, we have repeatedly seen that engaging teachers at the heart of their professional interests—on the basis of their disciplinary expertise and classroom practice— often results in teachers like this middle school teacher, who feel more effective and who see improved student learning.

Teachers' Untapped Resources

We see a strong case for optimism in the numbers of secondary and college teachers who are stepping up to address their students' reading needs by learning how to put more of the responsibility for comprehension back into students' hands. Teachers whose education has prepared them to teach history, science, math, English, technical, and other courses have a great deal of knowledge they can share with students about how to make sense of and use information from the various texts characteristic of their subject areas. This knowledge helped teachers to be successful in their own education, and they continue to draw on it as they read in their field and prepare lessons in their discipline. However, most teachers—and most fluent readers generally—have not spent much time thinking explicitly about the mental processes by which they make sense of texts in their fields. In fact, few middle, high school, or college teachers see their own abilities to read subject area texts as a powerful resource for helping their students approach these texts.

The Reading Apprenticeship approach to improving student literacy asks teachers to tap into that knowledge. More specifically, it relies on teachers working with other teachers to become conscious of their own disciplinary reading and thinking processes—the perhaps unrecognized knowledge and strategies that each uses to read effectively. When teachers become more aware of the complexity of how they themselves make sense of text, they gain new appreciation for the reading difficulties students may face. Teachers can then begin to apprentice their students to the reading craft by making their invisible comprehension processes visible to their students. As apprentices, students, in turn, become empowered as readers, able to tap and expand their own knowledge. In the course of doing so, they begin to own and improve their reading processes.

Students' Untapped Resources

In the classroom, teachers often view students through the narrow lens of academic competency. Teachers frustrated by students' inability or unwillingness to read academic text often allow this "literacy problem" to define their view of students as learners. The experiences, affinities, and skills in reading, writing, and problem solving that students gain outside school are frequently invisible to teachers and unappreciated by students themselves, who might otherwise draw on them to support the work they are asked to do in school. Nimbleness in everyday language, skills in translating from a first language to English, creativity in navigating search engines, persistence in mastering video games, even a propensity for "reading" the moods and behaviors of others—all have applications in making sense of text.

In our Reading Apprenticeship work, we have come to see students as individuals who bring powerful resources that can be tapped in a learning environment that is safe, respectful, and collaborative. As teachers work with—rather than against—some of their students' common characteristics, teachers and their students can begin to build a reading inquiry partnership, or apprenticeship.

When the learning environment is carefully constructed to promote social collaboration and make explicit connections between literacy proficiencies and students' assets and aspirations, students' social and personal concerns can serve the academic goals their teachers hold for them. Students' keen interest in themselves and their classmates can be turned toward supporting the effort and risk-taking needed to develop new skills as readers. Adolescents, who are particularly focused developmentally on trying out and forming new identities, can be encouraged to try on new reader identities, to realize that who they will become and what they will do in their lives is to a great extent in their own hands. For older students, too, a need for social connection, self-expression, and competence can serve academic goals.

In a Reading Apprenticeship classroom, students are invited to become partners in a collaborative inquiry into reading and thinking processes. The aim is to help students become better readers by making the teacher's and other students' reading processes "visible," by helping students gain insight into their own reading processes, and by helping them develop the dispositions to put these insights and problem-solving strategies to work. As students gain practice in making their own reading processes visible, additional valuable information becomes more available to their teachers—information about the social and cultural contexts, strategies, language practices, knowledge base, and understandings students are bringing to the task of making sense of texts. A reading apprenticeship is, at heart, a partnership of expertise, drawing on what a subject area teacher knows and practices as a disciplinary reader and on students' unique and often underestimated strengths as learners.

Signs of Success:
Changes in Students' Literacy, Learning, and Identities

Results from multiple studies, including three recent experimental research studies, show that in high school classrooms where teachers integrated core Reading Apprenticeship routines to invite students into text-based, problem-solving ways of working, students made statistically significant gains in reading comprehension and content knowledge.[18] Importantly, in addition to these comprehension and knowledge outcomes, students in the Reading Apprenticeship classrooms showed increased motivation for and success in tackling challenging disciplinary texts. One of the experimental studies looked as well at measures of student behavior and found that students in the Reading Apprenticeship intervention classrooms were far less likely to receive referrals or suspensions from school compared to students in the control group, both in the year they took the course and in the following year.

Through these studies we have been able to demonstrate that changes for students are the results of changes in the classroom practices of their teachers. As teachers begin to hold students responsible for doing course readings, turn the work of comprehending text over to students, and ask them to be meta-cognitive about their reading processes and share their confusion and problem solving, the classroom quickly transforms into a setting where students can gain reading experience and skill.

Looking across the recent experimental studies and other studies conducted in previous years, we see strong evidence that students gain far more from Reading Apprenticeship than a set of reading comprehension strategies.[19] They learn to direct their own learning, engage in the academic enterprise, expand their identities as readers and learners, and form new relationships to school.

In addition to studies of the impact at the high school and middle school level, a set of complementary research studies have documented changes in classroom practice and student outcomes when college faculty implement the Reading Apprenticeship framework and routines.[20] These studies present a promising picture of changes in community college classroom instruction leading to improvement in students' active engagement with texts, depth of interpretive and analytical reading and writing, and, in most instances where measured, in their grades and course completion rates.

■ ■ ■

In contrast to typical secondary and college instruction for struggling readers, which reinforces low levels of achievement for students who are already behind by steering clear of rigorous course work based on the assumption that students are not capable of performing at appropriate levels, the Reading Apprenticeship framework and approaches are based on research showing that most students *are* capable of complex thinking and carrying out disciplinary inquiry but have not been given the skills or self-confidence to approach these tasks effectively.[21]

We argue that to reach higher levels of literacy for all of our students, we need to embrace a vision of intellectually and personally engaged academic literacy for the inexperienced but capable students we serve. To move toward making this vision a reality, we must strengthen students' view of themselves and their capacities as readers and learners—while helping them build their skills in high-level literacy. We must transform subject area classes into collaborative, inquiry-oriented learning environments that intellectually engage, challenge, and support students. Chapter Two describes the model we propose for achieving these goals: the Reading Apprenticeship framework.

Notes

1. Kalif is one of dozens of students interviewed in *Reading Between the Lives,* produced by The Making Visible Project at Chabot College. Retrieved from http://www.archive.org/details/ReadingBetweenTheLivesPart1.mp4

2. Langer, J. (2001). Beating the odds: Teaching middle and high school students to read and write well. *American Educational Research Journal, 38,* 837–880.

3. National Assessment of Educational Progress. (2009). *NAEP 2008 trends in academic progress* (NCES 2009–469). Washington, DC: National Center for Education Statistics; Snipes, J., & Horwitz, A. (2008). *Advancing adolescent literacy in urban schools 3* (Research Brief). Washington, DC: Council of the Great City Schools.

4. Barton, P. (2003). *Parsing the achievement gap: Baselines for tracking progress.* Policy information report of the Educational Testing Service. Princeton, NJ: Educational Testing Service.

5. Lee, C. D., & Spratley, A. (2010). *Reading in the disciplines: The challenges of adolescent literacy.* New York: Carnegie Corporation of New York.

6. Cuban, L. (1993). *How teachers taught: Constancy and change in American classrooms 1890–1990* (2nd ed.). New York: Teachers College Press.

7. ACT. (2006). *Reading between the lines: What the ACT reveals about college readiness in reading.* Iowa City, IA: ACT. Retrieved from http://www.act.org/research/policymakers/reports/reading.html

8. Bailey, T., Jeong, D. W., & Cho, S.-W. (2010). Referral, enrollment, and completion of developmental education sequences in community colleges. *Economics of Education Review, 20,* 255–270.

9. Ibid.

10. ACT, *Reading between the lines.*

11. Biancarosa, C., & Snow, C. E. (2006). *Reading next—A vision for action and research in middle and high school literacy: A report to Carnegie Corporation of New York* (2nd ed., p. 11). Washington, DC: Alliance for Excellent Education.

12. Walqui, A., & van Lier, L. (2010). *Scaffolding the academic success of adolescent English language learners: A pedagogy of promise.* San Francisco: WestEd.

13. Hern, K., with Snell, M. (June 2010). Exponential attrition and the promise of acceleration in developmental English and math. *Perspectives.* Berkeley, CA: Research and Planning Group.

14. See Chapter Two notes 1 and 3.

15. Fielding, L. G., & Pearson, P. D. (1994). Reading comprehension: What works. *Educational Leadership, 51*(5), 62–68; Cartwright, K. D. (Ed.). (2008). *Literacy processes: Cognitive flexibility in learning and teaching.* New York: Guilford.

16. Carr, N. (2010). *The shallows: What the Internet is doing to our brains* (pp. 63–65). New York: Norton.

17. See Chapter Two notes 16 and 17.

18. Greenleaf, C., Litman, C., Hanson, T., Rosen, R., Boscardin, C. K., Herman, J., & Schneider, S., with Madden, S., & Jones, B. (2011). Integrating literacy and science in biology: Teaching and learning impacts of Reading Apprenticeship professional development. *American Educational Research Journal, 48,* 647–717; Greenleaf, C., Hanson, T., Herman, J., Litman, C., Rosen, R., Schneider, S., & Silver, D. (2011). *A study of the efficacy of Reading Apprenticeship professional development for high school history and science teaching and learning.* Final report to Institute for Education Sciences, National Center for Education Research, Teacher Quality/Reading and Writing, Grant # R305M050031; Somers, M.-A., Corrin, W., Sepanik, S., Salinger, T., Levin, J., & Zmach, C., with Wong, E. (2010). *The enhanced reading opportunities study final report: The impact of supplemental literacy courses for struggling ninth-grade readers* (NCEE #2010–4021). Washington, DC: National Center for Education Evaluation and Regional Assistance, Institute of Education Sciences, U.S. Department of Education.

19. Research studies of Reading Apprenticeship, from case studies through randomized controlled studies, are reported on the Reading Apprenticeship website, http://www.wested .org/cs/ra/print/docs/ra/rr.htm.

20. Shiorring, E. (2010). *First three years of Reading Apprenticeship in the community colleges: Summary of evaluation findings.* Berkeley, CA: The Center for Student Success, Research & Planning Group, California Community Colleges; Braunger, J. (Ed.). (2011). *Learning from teacher inquiries: Reading Apprenticeship in community college.* San Francisco: WestEd.

21. Lee, C. D., & Spratley, A. (2010). *Reading in the disciplines: The challenges of adolescent literacy.* New York: Carnegie Corporation of New York.

CHAPTER TWO

The Reading Apprenticeship Framework

At the beginning of the year, a lot of students didn't understand. "Why are we doing all this reading stuff in science? I don't get it. It's science. It's not reading." And I tried to explain to them, "Well, reading is the most important thing you can do, no matter what subject area it is. If you can't read and understand, you're going to struggle."

—Heather Howlett, grade 8 science teacher

THE CONCEPTIONS educators hold about the nature of reading naturally shape their approaches to helping students improve their reading abilities. As we noted in Chapter One, some current approaches to supporting students' reading improvement address word-level reading problems as a precondition for working on advanced literacy proficiencies. The Reading Apprenticeship approach takes a different route toward building high-level literacy because our understanding of the nature of reading and the capacity of adolescent and adult learners is different. For example, the students in Heather Howlett's science classes will learn academic reading along with science precisely because that is the most powerful way to learn.

We first present a brief summary of what we have learned about reading from existing research and our own observations and studies.

What Is Reading?

Reading is not just a basic skill. Many people think of reading as a skill that is taught once and for all in the first few years of school. In this view of reading, the credit (or blame) for students' reading ability goes to primary grade teachers, and subsequent teachers or college instructors need teach only new vocabulary and concepts relevant to new content. Seen this way, reading is a simple process: readers decode (figure out how to pronounce) each word in a text and then automatically comprehend the meaning of the words, as they do with their everyday spoken language.

This is not our understanding of reading.

About Reading

The need to continue to teach reading as students move up the grade levels and encounter increasingly complex academic material and tasks is now widely recognized. Box 2.1 lists important understandings *about* reading that are described in the sections that follow.

BOX 2.1

About Reading

Students often confuse reading with saying the words on a page. Reading is actually a complex problem-solving process that readers can learn. The following characteristics of reading are described in this section:

- Reading is a complex process.
- Reading is problem solving.
- Fluent reading is not the same as decoding.
- Reading proficiency varies with situation and experience.
- Proficient readers share some key characteristics.

Reading Is a Complex Process

Think for a moment about the last thing you read. A student essay? A school bulletin? A newspaper analysis of rising conflict in another part of the world? A report on water quality in your community? A novel? If you could recapture your mental processing, you would notice that you read with reference to a particular world of knowledge and experience related to the text. The text evoked voices, memories, knowledge, and experiences from other times and places—some long dormant, some more immediate. If you were reading complex text about complex ideas or an unfamiliar type of text, you were working to understand it. Your reading was most likely characterized by many false starts and much backtracking. You were probably trying to relate it to your existing knowledge and understanding. You might have stumbled over unfamiliar words and found yourself trying to interpret them from the context. And you might have found yourself having an internal conversation with the author, silently agreeing or disagreeing with what you read.

As experienced readers read, they begin to generate a mental representation, or gist, of the text, which serves as an evolving framework for understanding subsequent parts of the text. As they read further, they test this evolving meaning and monitor their understanding, paying attention to inconsistencies that arise as they interact with the text. If they notice that they are losing the meaning as they read, they draw on a variety of strategies to readjust their understandings. They come to texts with purposes that guide their reading, taking a stance toward the text and responding to the ideas that take shape in the conversation between the text and the self.[1]

While reading a newspaper analysis of global hostilities, for example, you may silently argue with its presentation of "facts," question the assertions of the writer, and find yourself revisiting heated debates with friends over U.S. foreign policy. You may picture events televised during earlier wars. Lost in your recollections, you may find that even though your eyes have scanned several paragraphs, you have taken nothing in, so you reread these passages, this time focusing on analysis.

Reading Is Problem Solving

Reading is not a straightforward process of lifting the words off the page. It is a complex process of problem solving in which the reader works to make sense of a text not just from the words and sentences on the page but also from the ideas, memories, and knowledge evoked by those words and sentences. Although at first glance reading may seem to be passive, solitary, and simple, it is in truth active, populated by a rich mix of voices and views—those of the author, of the reader, and of others the reader has heard, read about, and otherwise encountered throughout life.

Fluent Reading Is Not the Same as Decoding

Skillful reading does require readers to carry out certain tasks in a fairly automatic manner. Decoding skills—quick word recognition and ready knowledge of relevant vocabulary, for example—are important to successful reading. However, they are by no means sufficient, especially when texts are complex or otherwise challenging.

Yet many discussions about struggling readers confuse decoding with fluency. Fluency derives from the reader's ability not just to decode or identify individual words but also to quickly process larger language units.[2] In our inquiries into reading—our own and that of our students—we have seen that fluency, like other dimensions of reading, varies according to the text at hand. When readers are unfamiliar with the particular language structures and features of a text, their language-processing ability breaks down. This means, for example, that teachers cannot assume that students who fluently read narrative or literary texts will be equally fluent with informational texts or primary source documents.

Fluency begins to develop when students have frequent opportunities to read texts that are accessible for them because the vocabulary, the concepts, or both are reasonably familiar. English learners rapidly gain new English vocabulary when reading about familiar situations in the new language. Similarly, readers with dyslexia can tackle complex texts about topics in which they are avidly interested and about which they are knowledgeable. Multiple rereadings of more difficult, less accessible texts help broaden a reader's fluency—as can, perhaps surprisingly, slowing down by chunking a text into smaller units. Of even more importance, fluency grows as readers have opportunities, support, and encouragement to read a wide range of text types about a wide range of topics.

Reading Proficiency Varies with Situation and Experience

Literacy practices—how one engages with text, the type of texts read, the outcomes expected—are shaped by social purposes. As we move from one social situation to another, we learn varied ways of reading and distinct literacy practices linked to specific social activities. Moreover, our experiences vary from one person to another. A person who understands one type of text is not necessarily proficient at reading all types. An experienced reader of mathematical proofs may be perplexed when asked to make sense of a metaphor in a poem. A nursing student may be able to decipher the meanings conveyed by complex anatomical diagrams but feel completely at sea when trying to read a legal brief. A good reader of a motorcycle repair manual can make sense of directions that might stump an English literature professor, but she may be unable to comprehend her son's chemistry text. And a chemistry teacher may feel completely insecure when trying to understand some of the primary sources on a history colleague's course reading list.

In other words, reading is influenced by situational factors, among them the experiences readers have had with particular kinds of texts and reading for particular purposes. And just as so-called good or proficient readers do not necessarily read all texts with equal ease or success, a so-called poor or struggling reader will not necessarily have a hard time with all texts. That said, researchers do know some things about those readers who are more consistently effective across a broad range of texts and text types.

Proficient Readers Share Some Key Characteristics

Different reading researchers emphasize different characteristics of good or proficient readers. However, widespread agreement has emerged in the form of a set of key habits (see Box 2.2).[3]

BOX 2.2

Good Readers Are . . .

The following key habits of good readers are widely recognized by literacy researchers.

Good readers are

- Mentally engaged
- Motivated to read and to learn
- Persistent in the face of challenge
- Socially active around reading tasks
- Strategic in monitoring the interactive processes that assist comprehension:
  - Setting goals that shape their reading processes
  - Monitoring their emerging understanding of texts
  - Reasoning with texts in valued and discipline-specific ways
  - Coordinating a variety of comprehension strategies to control the reading process

Social Support for Learning

Our apprenticeship approach to teaching reading in subject area classes is grounded in our view of learning as a social-cognitive interactive process. In this view, which is based in the work of Russian psychologist L. S. Vygotsky, cognitive development is seen as "socially mediated"—that is to say, people learn by participating in activities with "more competent others" who provide support for the parts of the task that they cannot yet do by themselves. These more competent others—parents, siblings, peers, and teachers, for example—gauge their support of the learner's participation, encouraging the learner to take on more of the task over time. In doing this—often unconsciously or spontaneously— these guides help learners carry out valued activities (talking, cooking, playing ball, reading) with increasing independence over time. ("Scaffolding" is a term often applied to this careful gauging of "enough" support, but not too much, at the "right" time, but for not too long.)

The learning environment created by these more knowledgeable others in collaboration with learners during activities like reading or puzzle solving both supports learners and challenges them to grow. Learners begin to internalize and appropriate (make their own) the varied dimensions of the activity: for instance, its goals and functions, the actions necessary to carry it out, and the kinds of cultural tools necessary or fitting to the task. Through this social learning process, learners' cognitive and affective structures—the ways in which learners think and value tasks—are shaped.[4]

Cognitive Apprenticeships

This view of socially mediated learning applies not only to activities with observable components, such as changing bicycle tires, knitting, or skating. It applies equally, and significantly, to activities that are largely cognitive, taking place inside the mind and hidden from view. Researchers working in a social-cognitive tradition have described a variety of cognitive apprenticeships, in which the mental activities characteristic of certain kinds of cognitive tasks—such as computation, written composition, interpreting texts, and the like—are internalized and appropriated by learners through social supports of various kinds.[5] Learning to read academically complex material is yet another task that requires a cognitive apprenticeship.

Reading Apprenticeships

One literacy educator describes the idea of the cognitive apprenticeship in reading by comparing the process of learning to read with that of learning to ride a bike. In both cases a more proficient other is present to support the beginner, engaging the beginner in the activity and calling attention to often overlooked or hidden strategies.[6] From the beginning, reading apprentices must be engaged in the whole process of problem solving to make sense of written texts, even if they are initially unable to carry out on their own all the individual strategies and subtasks that go into successful reading. The hidden, cognitive dimensions in particular must be drawn out and made visible to the learner.[7] For students encountering challenging academic materials and tasks, being shown what goes on behind the curtain of expert reading is especially powerful in helping them gain mastery.

Demystifying Reading: Making the Invisible Visible

If students are to employ increasingly sophisticated ways of thinking and of solving a variety of cognitive problems, they need to interact with more knowledgeable others from whom they can learn how to carry out these complex activities. Much of what happens with texts in classrooms gives students the mistaken impression that reading comprehension happens by magic. To begin to build a repertoire of activities for reading comprehension, students need to have the reading process demystified. They need to see what happens inside the mind of a more proficient reader, someone who is willing to make the invisible visible by externalizing his or her mental activity.

Text-Based Discussion: Collaborative Meaning Making

Making the invisible processes of strategic sense-making visible to the learner must take place during reading itself. For students to approach reading expecting to comprehend what they read, and so to work to comprehend texts as necessary, they must experience reading as an inquiry into meaning and a purposeful engagement with ideas. Very little authentic discussion takes place in typical classrooms, yet for all students and particularly for English learners, talking with others is a powerful way to work out one's ideas and articulate them.[8] Text-based discussion helps readers clarify what seems clouded as well as critically question the ideas in a text. In discussions among readers, different viewpoints arise, and the diverse resources that exist among different students can help them in tackling a problem or engaging a set of ideas. To build a repertoire of text-based problem-solving strategies and stamina for thinking deeply about the meaning of what they read, students need abundant experiences of working to comprehend text in the company of others. They need ongoing opportunities to consider and reconsider—through text-based discussion—what texts may mean and how they know what they mean.[9]

Developing Engaged, Strategic, and Independent Readers

In short, our approach to teaching literacy skills is based on the idea that the complex habits and activities of skillful academic readers can be taught. But we do not believe they can be taught by a transmission approach—in which students are shown strategies, asked to practice them, and then expected to be able to use them on their own. Rather, we see the kind of teaching and learning environment that can develop students' confidence and competence as readers of various kinds of challenging texts as one that requires the interaction of students and teachers in multiple dimensions of classroom life. It is the orchestration of this interactive teaching and learning environment in classrooms that we call the Reading Apprenticeship approach to developing strategic readers.

In the rest of this chapter we briefly present the multiple dimensions of classroom teaching and learning that make up the Reading Apprenticeship instructional framework, giving an overview of students' learning opportunities in Reading Apprenticeship classrooms.

Dimensions of the Reading Apprenticeship Classroom and Framework

The following model describes the four key dimensions of classroom life that are necessary to support reading development:

- *Social Dimension:* Community building in the classroom, including recognizing the resources brought by each member and developing a safe environment for students to be open about their reading difficulties

- *Personal Dimension:* Developing students' identities and self-awareness as readers, as well as their purposes for reading and goals for reading improvement

- *Cognitive Dimension:* Developing readers' mental processes, including their problem-solving strategies

- *Knowledge-Building Dimension:* Identifying and expanding the kinds of knowledge that readers bring to a text and further develop through interaction with that text

These dimensions exist in the context of *extensive reading* and share the reading practice of internal and external *metacognitive conversation* (see Box 2.3).

Extensive Reading as the Context for Reading Apprenticeship

Surrounding the social, personal, cognitive, and knowledge-building dimensions of classroom life is reading itself. Teachers extend students' reading experiences and opportunities, making it a key enterprise of their instruction to talk together about making meaning with academic materials. When reading and collaborative work with texts becomes a key part of academic learning in the classroom, teachers provide support for students to grow as readers. Texts and talk about texts infuse the learning that students engage in and provide the context for their ongoing reading apprenticeship. Providing more focus on reading and talk about reading during classroom lessons gives teachers the opportunity to mentor students in the reasoning and problem-solving skills they need to master. More reading, more text-focused discussion, and more talk about reading and problem-solving processes—these distinguish Reading Apprenticeship classrooms from content area classes in which students are expected, but not taught, to handle complex reading tasks.

Metacognitive Conversation at the Center

At the center of the Reading Apprenticeship approach, and linking the four dimensions of classroom life, is an ongoing conversation in which teacher

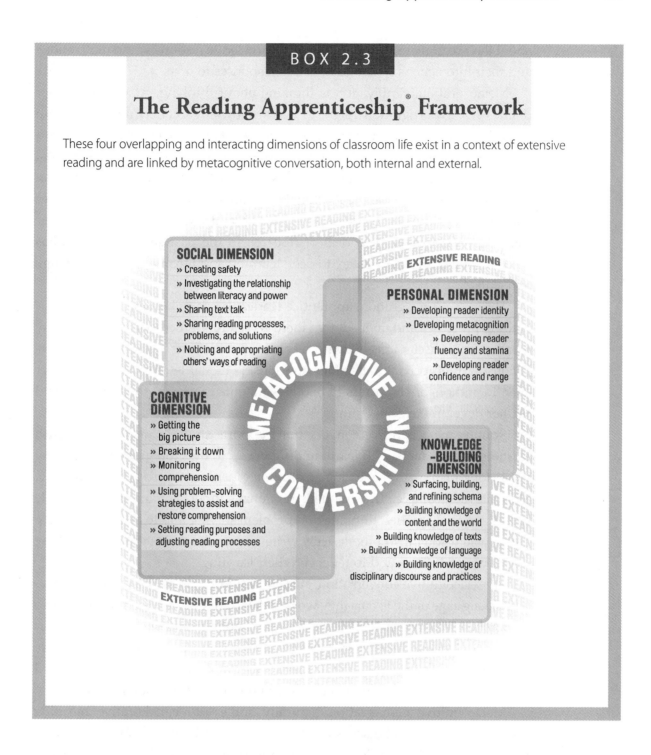

BOX 2.3

The Reading Apprenticeship® Framework

These four overlapping and interacting dimensions of classroom life exist in a context of extensive reading and are linked by metacognitive conversation, both internal and external.

SOCIAL DIMENSION
» Creating safety
» Investigating the relationship between literacy and power
» Sharing text talk
» Sharing reading processes, problems, and solutions
» Noticing and appropriating others' ways of reading

PERSONAL DIMENSION
» Developing reader identity
» Developing metacognition
» Developing reader fluency and stamina
» Developing reader confidence and range

COGNITIVE DIMENSION
» Getting the big picture
» Breaking it down
» Monitoring comprehension
» Using problem-solving strategies to assist and restore comprehension
» Setting reading purposes and adjusting reading processes

KNOWLEDGE –BUILDING DIMENSION
» Surfacing, building, and refining schema
» Building knowledge of content and the world
» Building knowledge of texts
» Building knowledge of language
» Building knowledge of disciplinary discourse and practices

METACOGNITIVE CONVERSATION

EXTENSIVE READING

and students think about and discuss their *personal* relationships to reading, the *social* environment and resources of the classroom, their *cognitive* activity, and the kinds of *knowledge* required to make sense of text. This metacognitive conversation is carried on both internally, as teacher and students individually read and consider their own mental processes, and externally, as they talk about their reading processes, strategies, knowledge resources, and motivations and their interactions with and affective responses to texts.

Metacognition, simply put, is thinking about thinking. As one researcher defines it, "Metacognition refers to one's knowledge concerning one's own cognitive process and products or anything related to them."[10] In metacognitive conversation, then, participants become consciously aware of their mental activity and are able to describe it and discuss it with others. Such conversation enables teachers to make their invisible cognitive activity visible and enables teachers and students to reflectively analyze and assess the impact of their thinking processes. A great deal of research in the past several decades has identified metacognition as key to deep learning and flexible use of knowledge and skills.[11]

Through metacognition, apprentice readers begin to become aware of their reading processes and, indeed, that there *are* reading processes. Through many means—class discussions between teachers and students, small group conversations, written private reflections and logs, personal letters to the teacher or even to authors or characters in books—students can begin to know, use, and further develop their own minds.

Routine metacognitive conversation supports students, including English learners and students with learning differences, to develop greater proficiency in all four of the language domains: *reading, writing, speaking,* and *listening.* Students read complex texts with instructional support accompanied by ample discussion to share their thinking and problem solving and to hear the thinking and problem solving of others. They write to describe their thinking processes, to interact with texts, and to reflect on their learning.

In metacognitive conversation, students build vocabulary by using the academic language of the text as they work collaboratively with their peers to solve comprehension difficulties. They listen to and appropriate the language of their teacher and peers through frequent peer, small group, and class discussion. Students are supported to learn academic discourse, using conventions of civil exchange and academic language to respond to the ideas of their classmates.

Metacognitive conversation naturally spills into collaborative meaning making and text-based discussion as students grapple with complex academic texts. But it is central to Reading Apprenticeship that the discussion is always metacognitive—a conversation about not only *what texts mean* but also *how you know* what they mean.

Such conversations and reflections, if they become routine, offer students ongoing opportunities to consider what they are doing as they read—how they are trying to make sense of texts and how well their strategies are working for them. Internal and external conversations about reading processes and the relationships they make possible between and among teachers and students are key to the Reading Apprenticeship approach.

Each dimension of classroom life—the social, personal, cognitive, and knowledge-building—has its own metacognitive component, as described in the following sections.

The Social Dimension

Establishing a Reading Apprenticeship classroom begins with the work of nurturing a social environment in which students can begin to reveal their understandings and their struggles as well as to see other students, and their teacher, as potential resources for learning.

Creating Safety

To begin developing the social dimension of the classroom, teachers work with students to create a sense that they are part of a safe community of readers. Developing this sense of safety is fundamental to the activity of investigating reading. To help students become more active and strategic readers, we need to hear from the students themselves about what is going on in their minds while they are reading. Therefore, they must feel comfortable expressing points of confusion, disagreement, and even disengagement with texts. They need to feel safe enough to talk about where they got lost in a text, what was confusing, what they ordinarily do when they have these kinds of comprehension problems, and how well these strategies work for them.

Some students may be embarrassed by reading comprehension difficulties, believing these difficulties mean they are not as skilled at reading as they should be. Making it safe for students to discuss reading difficulties mitigates students' potential embarrassment. The following classroom activities help establish a safe culture for students to take on the role of reading apprentices:

- Discuss what makes it safe or unsafe for students to ask questions or show their confusion in class.

- Agree on classroom rules for discussion so that all students can share their ideas and confusions without being made to feel stupid.

- Discuss what makes it safe or unsafe for students to engage in classroom learning.

- Agree on classroom norms that allow all students to engage in learning without being made to feel uncool.

Investigating the Relationship Between Literacy and Power

Motivation to read and to work on improving reading is affected by myriad factors, including the ways instruction builds on learners' out-of-school identities and literacies and leverages their interests and desires to learn, do, and communicate. Students' understanding of the likelihood of success and of learning itself mediates how much effort they will expend on learning tasks—that is, it influences their motivation. Motivation is also intimately related to students' cultural and peer group identity as well as their prior experiences in school.[12]

The degree to which students see doing well academically as a means of gaining status with their peers can vary. For some students, there may be a stigma attached to reading better than others in their social group. For others, school uses of literacy seem far away from the literacy practices they value. Students who are underprepared academically for the challenge of academic literacy are often perceived as resistant to learning when they are actually aspiring to achieve. For many students, experiences in academic settings have not offered the kinds of learning opportunities they need to see how purposeful engagement with academic literacy may affect their future ambitions. Engaging students in asking questions about reading (and literacy) and its relationship to academic, economic, political, and cultural power has the potential to reframe reading as a more valued activity. The following classroom activities help position reading as a universal value:

- Investigate and talk about the people who read in our society, what they read, why they read, and how reading affects their lives.

- Investigate and talk about the people who do not read in our society and how not reading affects their lives.

- Read and talk about the role played by lack of literacy in the historical disenfranchisement of particular groups of people in society.

- Talk about the relationships between literacy and power of various kinds, including academic, economic, political, and cultural.

Sharing Text Talk

Particularly when students resist engagement in reading because they have devalued it, have had little experience reading, or are embarrassed by their relative reading competence, sharing books and other texts on topics that appeal to young people is an important way of generating interest in reading. Intrinsic motivation to read can flourish in a classroom where everyone has a chance to talk about and hear about each other's interesting or important reading experiences; for example:

- Share the texts that teachers and classmates have found exciting, fun, interesting, or important.

- Share the ways in which teachers and classmates choose books they will both enjoy and be able to finish as recreational reading.

- Share teachers' and classmates' responses to the ideas, events, and language of texts.

Sharing Reading Processes, Problems, and Solutions

Teachers and students must build a sense of collaborative and respectful inquiry into each other's reading processes. This is key to establishing the conditions for successful reading apprenticeships. Once students are safe to engage in classroom reading activities and share their reading processes and difficulties, the classroom community of readers can offer its members crucial resources in the diversity and breadth of interpretations, experiences, and perspectives that different readers bring to different texts. Activities in which students have access to a variety of social resources for dealing with reading comprehension problems are another way to establish and maintain the social dimension of a Reading Apprenticeship classroom; for example:

- Talk about what is confusing in texts.

- Share how teachers and students deal with comprehension problems as they come up in class texts.

- Participate in whole- or small-group problem-solving discussions to make sense of difficult texts.

Noticing and Appropriating Others' Ways of Reading

Students possess a variety of strengths, including diverse background knowledge and experiences. Each student can have times when he or she becomes the more knowledgeable other, helping peers gain comprehension of particular texts and acquire strategies and knowledge for the comprehension of a range of texts.

Teachers act as expert resources for reading strategies, disciplinary reasoning, relevant background knowledge, and experience with particular kinds of texts and how they work. In a classroom environment where sharing one's reading processes, comprehension difficulties, and attempts to solve comprehension problems is the norm, teachers have many opportunities to share their expertise. They also can draw students' attention to the fact that different readers in the classroom bring different valuable resources that influence their interpretations of texts. The point of such activities is for students to notice and appropriate successful ways of reading and solving problems of reading comprehension; for example:

- Notice the different kinds of background knowledge and experience different readers (teachers and classmates) bring to texts and how that affects the way they interpret what they read.

- Notice the ways different readers think aloud and respond to texts as they work to make sense of them.

- Notice the different reading strategies different readers use to make sense of texts.

- Try out the different strategies and approaches other readers use to make sense of texts.

The Personal Dimension

The personal dimension of a Reading Apprenticeship classroom focuses on developing individual students' relationships to reading. Classroom activities support students in developing increased awareness of themselves as readers, inviting them to discover and refine their own goals and motivations, likes and dislikes, and hopes and potential growth in relationship to reading. This work develops within and in turn adds to the development of the social context of the classroom. As individual students gain a sense of themselves as readers, they add to the classroom community their descriptions of their varied reading processes, their responses to texts, and their questions and interpretations, all of which provide rich content for classroom discussions.

Developing Reader Identity

The activity of reading—the ability to use a variety of metacognitive and cognitive strategies to make sense of texts—is closely tied to the will to read.[13] When students feel they are not good readers, frustration, embarrassment, or fear of failure can prevent them from engaging in reading. Without confidence in themselves as readers, students often disengage from any serious attempts to improve their reading.

Learning to independently read unfamiliar types of texts and complex texts is hard work. Unless students begin to see reading as related to their personal interests and goals and as something they can improve, they are unlikely to expend the necessary effort. For poor achievers to become more motivated and persistent, the key is seeing that their effort really does lead to success. We have found that when we can convincingly frame the hard work of improving reading as an avenue toward increased individual autonomy and control, as well as toward an expanded repertoire of future life options, we have won more than half the battle.

In developing the personal dimension of a Reading Apprenticeship classroom, teachers and students work together to develop new identities as readers, awareness of their own reading processes, willing persistence in the hard work of building stronger reading skills, and increased confidence for tackling new and unfamiliar kinds of texts.

Reading researchers have found that having a sense of who one is as a reader and learner is an important aspect of motivation.[14] Especially for students who think of themselves as nonreaders or poor readers, developing a sense of reader identity is crucial. Teachers can create classroom routines or periodic activities that help students see themselves as readers, come to know what texts they like and don't like, identify where their strengths and weaknesses as readers lie, and articulate and monitor their own goals as developing readers. The following activities can help students see themselves as readers:

- Write and talk with others about previous reading experiences.

- Write and talk with others about reading habits, likes, and dislikes.

- Write and talk with others about reasons for reading.

- Set and periodically check in on goals for personal reading development.

Developing Metacognition

Gaining metacognitive awareness is a necessary step to gaining control of one's mental activity. Consciousness of their own thinking processes allows learners to "reflectively turn around on their own thought and action and analyze how and why their thinking achieved certain ends or failed to achieve others."[15] Moreover, knowledge of one's own thinking is like other kinds of knowledge in that it grows through experience (that is, through the metacognitive activity itself) and becomes more automatic with practice.[16]

Students find becoming conscious of their mental processes unfamiliar yet often intriguing. Here are examples of classroom activities that assist students in thinking about their thinking:

- Notice what is happening in your mind in a variety of everyday situations.

- Identify various thinking processes you engage in, in a variety of everyday situations.

- Notice where your attention is when you read.

- Identify all the different processes going on while you read.

- Choose what thinking activities to engage in; direct and control your reading processes accordingly.

Developing Reader Fluency and Stamina

One of the paradoxes that struggling or disengaged readers face is that in order to become more confident readers and to enjoy reading more, they need to become more fluent readers. Yet it is difficult to develop fluency without feeling confident and interested in reading. Our colleagues in secondary and college classrooms have developed a variety of ways of approaching this very difficult area:

- Demonstrate that all readers, including the teacher, are developing readers and that everyone has room to grow during a lifetime of reading.

- Identify the role that effort plays in the growth of reading comprehension over time; notice that effort pays off in becoming a stronger reader.

- Notice and celebrate progress as a developing reader; increase patience with yourself as a reader.

- Persist in reading even when you are somewhat confused or bored with a text.

- Build stamina for reading longer texts and for longer periods of time.

Develop Reader Confidence and Range

Another paradox that teachers face in developing students' personal relationships to reading is that readers who do not feel confident about their abilities are less likely to take the risks involved in approaching new kinds of texts. Extending the range of what they can read, however, is an important way that students can build their confidence as readers. Students (and their teachers) are often unaware of just how much reading students do daily. The skills, strategies, and knowledge students bring to making sense of such daily reading as notes from friends or parents, websites, movie and music reviews, song lyrics, and electronics manuals are valuable resources teachers need to invite into the classroom.[17] Convincing students that they have already mastered many text types helps build the kind of confidence they need to approach less familiar texts.

Our colleagues have used a number of activities to build such confidence and expand the range of texts students read:

- Bring the huge variety of different kinds of texts students read in their daily lives into the classroom.

- Investigate how students approach and make sense of these different kinds of texts.

- Connect the competencies that students demonstrate in approaching these texts to the resources students will need to approach unfamiliar texts.

- Have students read, with class support, short pieces representing a wide range of unfamiliar types of texts.

- Draw attention to what students *do* understand when reading unfamiliar texts.

The Cognitive Dimension

The cognitive dimension of the Reading Apprenticeship framework focuses on increasing students' repertoire of mental tools—cognitive strategies for making sense of texts. Through personal and social activities that engage students and teachers in thinking about and sharing their reading processes, the different ways in which readers approach reading begin to emerge. This sets the stage for learning new and perhaps more powerful ways to read. The goal of classroom work in the cognitive dimension is to expand the repertoire of strategies that students can use independently to control their own reading processes and, thereby, their comprehension.

A great deal of research on the reading process has identified and detailed many different cognitive strategies used by good readers to puzzle through a difficult text and to restore comprehension when they lose it. We discuss a number of them in this section. The research shows that these cognitive strategies can be taught to students who do not use them spontaneously on their own.[18] And once students learn these strategies and use them for their own reading purposes, they gain confidence and a sense of control over their reading processes and comprehension. It is important, however, to integrate this strategy teaching and strategy practice into the reading of subject area texts precisely where these strategies will come in handy for students who find such reading difficult. Teaching students a disembodied set of cognitive strategies—separate from the texts that necessitate their use and without support for independent use of these strategies—will not develop students' strength and independence as readers.

Getting the Big Picture

To begin with, strategies such as skimming, scanning, and reading ahead all give students a view of the whole text, even though particular aspects of it may need later clarification. Part of a strategic approach to texts is helping students live with ambiguity and confusion and helping them understand that they do not have to comprehend everything immediately. They can return to work on problem spots in the text, perhaps with some problem-solving strategies, after they get a glimpse of the whole. These strategies enable students to approach texts they may otherwise feel are too difficult to jump into. Teachers can model and guide students in practicing these ways of approaching difficult texts:

- Identify text types and sources.

- Skim or scan texts.

- Read through ambiguity and confusion.

- Read ahead to see whether the confusion clears up.

- Review the big picture to check comprehension.

Breaking It Down

Researchers have also found that proficient readers break texts into comprehensible units, using a variety of strategies. Breaking down the text is a particularly useful reading strategy when comprehension fails. By rereading the problematic segment of the text, readers can often identify the chunk in need of closer attention and focus on just that part to restore comprehension. Our colleagues have incorporated into their classrooms some of these strategies for breaking down the text:

- Chunk texts into small segments: for example, a section of a textbook, a caption and illustration, or a complex sentence or even a clause.

- Identify or clarify pronoun references and other textual connections that aid comprehension.

- Employ close reading of texts (linking interpretations to specific textual evidence).

Monitoring Comprehension

Reading research has shown that stronger readers monitor their reading, checking in with themselves to see how comprehension is progressing. Weaker readers are frequently unaware of how well they are understanding a text, but numerous intervention studies demonstrate that this critical awareness, and then control, of comprehension can be taught.[19] Here are some activities that teachers can model and guide students to carry out so they can monitor their comprehension while reading difficult texts, becoming increasingly self-regulated readers and learners:

- Check to see whether comprehension is occurring.

- Test understanding by summarizing or paraphrasing the text or by self-questioning.

- Decide whether to clarify any confusions at this time.

Using Problem-Solving Strategies to Assist and Restore Comprehension

Researchers have found that to help developing readers make sense of what they read, it is important to help them maintain their mental engagement with texts while reading.[20] Students' engagement with and comprehension of texts is increased by activities that help them understand that reading is an active, problem-solving process to make meaning. They must draw on all their knowledge and experiences, because a good reader's whole self is involved in reading.

All of the following strategies are used by proficient readers as ways of consolidating and refining their understanding as they read and when comprehension founders:

- Question texts, authors, and yourself about the text.
- "Talk" to the text through marginal annotations.
- Visualize what is described in the text.
- Make meaningful connections between the text and other knowledge, experiences, or texts.
- Reread sections of the text to clear up confusions.
- Summarize, retell, or paraphrase texts or parts of texts.
- Represent concepts and content of texts in graphic form.
- Represent concepts and content of texts through metaphors and analogies.
- Organize and keep track of ideas in a text through graphic organizers, outlines, response logs, and notes.

Setting Reading Purposes and Adjusting Reading Processes

Proficient readers read texts differently depending on their purposes for reading. Purposes drive reading processes. You may blitz through the television guide to find the time of a particular show; you know what you want to watch. On the other hand, if you are undecided, you may look at the offerings on every channel, even consulting the movie summaries and reviews in order to choose what to watch. Similarly, disciplinary perspectives and purposes shape the work readers do with texts.[21] Reading a political speech to analyze uses of rhetorical devices will require different reading and reasoning processes from those used in reading the same speech to decide whether to vote for a candidate.

In the beginning, students will need to consciously set their own purposes for reading particular texts, even when those texts are assigned. Then students can begin to notice, through classroom inquiry and sharing, how purposes affect the ways readers approach particular texts.

Teachers can help students learn to let reading purposes drive their reading processes by modeling, guiding, and giving students the following kinds of practice:

- Set goals or purposes for your reading whenever you approach a text.
- Read the same text for different purposes.
- Notice how reading purposes affect reading processes.
- Vary reading processes depending on the purposes for reading.

In a Reading Apprenticeship classroom, students are engaged not only in practicing a variety of strategies for controlling reading processes and restoring reading comprehension but also in assessing the effects of these strategies on their own reading and reading development. Students share what they are doing to make meaning of texts. They also share how they are doing so, becoming more aware of their own reading strategies and serving as resources to other students in the classroom.

The Knowledge-Building Dimension

Like many other factors in reading, knowledge—whether about the world of ideas in a text, the ways particular texts work, or discipline-specific ways of thinking and using language—supports reading comprehension and also develops as a result of reading.

For students to become proficient at reading to learn, they need to know something about the topics they will encounter in the text if they are to make connections to the ideas and elaborate their prior understandings. For students to access different types of texts, they need to recognize that texts have various and distinctive structures and genres. When encountering the language of texts, students need to know how to read academic versus everyday language and to use the language signposts that direct the reader through the author's ideas. To make sense of disciplinary texts, students also need to know about the customary ways of thinking, and therefore of reading, that constitute the practice of a particular discipline.[22] These different types of knowledge—knowledge about content, about texts, about language, and about disciplinary ways of thinking and communicating—are vital resources supporting comprehension.

Surfacing, Building, and Refining Schema

Research on proficient readers' mental processes has led to some key modern understandings about how the mind works, about how people think, even about what we think with. Studies have demonstrated how readers interact with texts, bringing their own stores of knowledge into play as they attempt to shape possible text meanings.[23] Readers do not passively absorb information from the text; rather, they actively mobilize their own knowledge structures to make meaning in interaction with the text.

Readers call up whole worlds of knowledge and associations as they read, triggered by particular ideas, words, or situations. These knowledge structures are known as schema. Schema for particular networks of knowledge and information are activated as individuals read and add to their existing schema as they encounter new information.[24] In addition, their existing schema influence the ways they approach and make sense of texts.

Schema—stores of knowledge about texts and about the world—are organized as networks of associations, which can be triggered by a single word. For example, the word "ball" may call up images of baseball diamonds, backstops, and bases, as well as the pitchers, batters, catchers, umps, fielders, and even sports commentators who take part in the game. Innings, errors, random statistics about particular players, and even the smells and sounds of baseball stadiums may quickly and automatically come to mind as such images and ideas flood into consciousness. For another reader, the same word, "ball," may call up competing schema: images of fancy gowns, corsages, tuxedos, limousine rides, and the blushing self-consciousness felt at a first prom. Proficient readers know they must relinquish schema that prove inappropriate as they encounter further information from the text, but less experienced readers will often hold onto inappropriate images that block meaningful connections with the text.

Knowledge can be stored in other ways as well; for example, as grammars for particular kinds of texts. Proficient readers of children's stories will have a story grammar that enables them to predict what will unfold after "Once upon a time."[25] Knowledge can also be stored as a script for an event with a well-known and predictable structure, such as a birthday party or eating in a restaurant.[26] From experience ordering meals, individuals have a script for the routine of getting the host or hostess's attention, being seated and given menus, and so forth. They are therefore not surprised when a person approaches with a small pad of paper and asks, "Have you decided yet?"

In a Reading Apprenticeship classroom, to help students not only to activate appropriate schema for particular texts but also to recognize that texts trigger whole networks of associated knowledge and experiences, teachers use activities such as the following:

- Recognize the different schema that can be triggered by a single text.
- Share the schema individual readers bring to mind while reading a particular text.

- Identify the schema appropriate for making sense of particular texts.
- Relinquish competing but inappropriate schema for particular texts.

Building Knowledge of Content and the World

Many studies have shown that students with prior knowledge of the topics they will encounter in a text comprehend more of the text and also recall more information from it than students who lack this knowledge.[27] Because prior knowledge is such a powerful resource for comprehension, many kinds of pre-reading activities—such as learning experiences to build conceptual understandings, pre-reading guides, and even brief text summaries before students read the text, have been developed as ways to build schema, thereby increasing student comprehension and retention of information. In addition, educators have developed many ways to activate the knowledge students already have about topics they are going to read about. Finally, many studies have shown that in the face of new and competing information, students relinquish their previous conceptions or ideas with great difficulty.[28] Strategies for articulating and challenging misconceptions are important if teachers are to counter the strong but incorrect theories students hold about many topics.

Teachers can use activities like these to prepare students to learn new information:

- Brainstorm and share knowledge or information about the topic.
- Identify conflicting knowledge or information about the topic.
- Imagine yourself in situations similar to those that will be encountered in the text.
- Explore conceptual vocabulary that will be encountered.
- Take positions on a topic before reading about it.
- Evaluate the fit between your prior knowledge or conception of a topic and the ideas in the text.

Building Knowledge of Texts

Knowledge about the ways different kinds of texts are structured and the ways these structures reveal the organization and interweaving of the author's ideas has also been shown to influence comprehension and memory.[29] Proficient readers use their awareness of text structures to understand the key points of a text, and when they report what they recall, their summaries reflect the text organization. Less-experienced readers, apparently unaware of text structures, have difficulty organizing and prioritizing text information. In our work we often see students who can follow a typical narrative but are bewildered by the text structures in informational text. Yet ample research shows that when students are taught to identify text structures through the use of such supports as graphic organizers or text previewing, their comprehension increases.[30]

Teachers can assist students with activities that focus on texts' underlying structures:

- Identify the ways particular texts are structured.

- Notice patterns in structure across texts of given genres.

- Preview a text to build a schema for it; notice structural features such as headings, subheadings, and illustrations.

- Use text organization and structure to assist in comprehension of particular texts.

- Notice and use the interconnections between visuals and text to build comprehension.

- Use signal words and phrases to aid comprehension and to predict the direction particular texts will take next.

Building Knowledge of Language

Knowledge about language and how it works to inventively convey meaning in everyday and academic discourse is key to unlocking the meaning of texts. Students need to develop both fascination and facility with words, acquiring word-learning strategies they can apply when faced with the variable and rich vocabulary presented in texts. Similarly, they need to develop facility for disentangling the complex sentences and ideas presented in academic texts. Subject area texts often rely on academic discourse, characterized by complex sentences containing multiple embedded clauses, verbs that have been turned into nouns standing for large disciplinary concepts, and Latin- and Greek-derived vocabularies. By engaging students in inquiry into word and sentence construction and meaning, teachers can help develop the metalinguistic awareness and skill that students need to bring to bear in becoming academic code-breakers.[31] The following activities assist all students but are especially valuable for English learners:

- Identify the particular kinds of language used in particular kinds of texts.

- Use contextual clues from the text to define unfamiliar words.

- Recognize when familiar words are used in unfamiliar ways, and use context to understand the new meaning.

- Identify roots, prefixes, and suffixes of Latin- and Greek-derived words often encountered in expository texts.

- Create word families associated with particular ideas or subject areas.

- Break complex sentences into component clauses to identify the ideas and relationships expressed.

Building Knowledge of Disciplinary Discourse and Practices

Recently literacy research has begun to focus on identifying effective ways to integrate knowledge about customary ways of thinking and using language that characterize discourse in particular academic disciplines into literacy and learning in the subject areas.[32]

Students need to understand the specific "habits of mind" characteristic of particular academic disciplines in order to make sense of academic texts and use them to carry out valued inquiry tasks in particular domains.[33] We have observed how important it is for students to know how particular texts are functioning in the world, what enterprise these texts serve, and what social practices the texts are contributing to.

Knowing about topics, text structures, and language alone does not help students who are bewildered by the larger sense of a text and its uses in a disciplinary enterprise. For example, students are often unaware that scientific activity is motivated by the enterprise of explanation or discovery, or that history is an enterprise devoted to interpretation and explanation of events, or that the study of literature can be understood as an aesthetic exploration of the human condition.

Discipline-specific knowledge is related to the more general idea of communicative competence—competence in producing and comprehending particular forms of language, or discourse—that develops in particular social settings. In the past few decades, research in the varied fields of linguistics, social psychology, cognitive science, anthropology, and education has illustrated how proficient readers and writers of particular texts acquire not just the component skills or processes needed to read and write but also the ways of participating in literacy activities valued by particular communities of readers and writers.[34] They learn specific "ways with words"[35] by actively participating in reading or writing in the company, and with the guidance, of more skilled practitioners.

Authors who write within the practice and language conventions of a particular discipline often assume that readers have an appreciation and understanding of that discipline's ways of thinking. Specialized ways of thinking have associated specialized ways of using language, which we might call disciplinary ways with words. In our work with secondary and college teachers, we have been exploring ways to help students build their knowledge of text structures and of the ways with words and ways of thinking that are characteristic of different disciplines. These types of knowledge are particularly important when educators hope to apprentice student readers to academic reading, yet they have rarely been included in subject area teaching. We believe that teaching students about the text structures of disciplinary text and the disciplinary enterprise these texts mirror will enable students to "crack the codes"[36] of academic texts in order to become more successful and ultimately more independent learners.

Teachers can help students acquire disciplinary and discourse-specific knowledge by making their own disciplinary habits of mind visible to students through thinking aloud and class discussion, helping to demystify the hidden codes—the ways of using language, the conventions of form, and the larger questions and standards of inquiry and evidence—that count in particular disciplines. Moreover, they can engage students in classroom activities such as these:

- Identify the possible purposes that the authors of particular texts may have had in creating these texts.
- Identify the possible audiences that particular texts seem to be addressing.
- Identify the functions that particular texts serve in particular circumstances.
- Explore the large questions, purposes, and habits of mind that characterize specific academic disciplines.
- Inquire into the ways in which texts function in particular disciplines.
- Identify the particular ways of using language associated with particular academic disciplines.
- Use valued reasoning practices of the disciplines to inquire into text meanings.
- Use texts to carry out valued disciplinary inquiries and tasks.

■ ■ ■

In the next several chapters, we bring the Reading Apprenticeship approach to life through portraits of classroom practice illustrating extensive reading, metacognitive conversation, and each of the four dimensions. We also present lessons and specific assignments from classrooms of our colleagues in middle school, high school, and community colleges around the country. Because these are real classrooms, their activities resist neat categorization into one or the other of the interacting dimensions of the Reading Apprenticeship approach— though we try, for the sake of exposition, to do so. Nevertheless, the fact that the dimensions overlap in our approach is an important part of the picture we want to illustrate. Areas of classroom life overlap, activities serve multiple purposes, and good teachers are always doing more, as they construct teaching and learning in the classroom, than may at first be obvious. We hope that what emerges in these portraits of practice is a vision of classrooms in which learners are engaged, motivated, and clearly gaining power, knowledge, and independence as readers.

Notes

1. Alexander, P. A. (1997). Mapping the multidimensional nature of domain learning: The interplay of cognitive, motivational, and strategic forces. In M. L. Maehr & P. R. Pintrich (Eds.), *Advances in motivation and achievement* (Vol. 10, pp. 213– 250). Greenwich, CT: JAI Press.

   Moje, E. B., Dillon, D. R., & O'Brien, D. G. (2000). Re-examining the roles of the learner, the text, and the context in secondary literacy. *Journal of Educational Research, 93,* 165–180.

   Ruddell, R., & Unrau, N. (1994). Reading as a meaning-construction process: The reader, the text, and the teacher. In R. Ruddell, M. Ruddell, & H. Singer (Eds.), *Theoretical models and process of reading* (pp. 996–1056). Newark, DE: International Reading Association.

   Scribner, S., & Cole, M. (1981). *The psychology of literacy.* Cambridge, MA: Harvard University Press.

   Street, B. (1995). *Social literacies: Critical approaches to literacy in development, ethnography and education.* London: Longman.

2. Kuhn, M. R., Schwanenflugel, P. J., & Meisinger, E. B. (2010). Aligning theory and assessment of reading fluency: Automaticity, prosody, and definitions of fluency. *Reading Research Quarterly, 45*(2), 230–251.

   Kuhn, M. R., & Stahl, S. A. (2003). Fluency: A review of developmental and remedial practices. *Journal of Educational Psychology, 95*(1), 3–21.

   Valencia, S. W., Smith, A. T., Reece, A. M., Li, M., Wixson, K. K., & Newman, H. (2010). Oral reading fluency assessment: Issues of construct, criterion, and consequential validity. *Reading Research Quarterly, 45*(3), 270–291.

3. Guthrie, J. T., & Alvermann, D. E. (1991). *Engaged reading: Processes, practices, and policy implications.* New York: Teachers College Press.

   Paris, S. G. (2005). Reinterpreting the development of reading skills. *Reading Research Quarterly, 40*(2), 184–202.

   Paris, S. G., Wasik, B. A., & Turner, J. C. (1991). The development of strategic readers. In R. Barr, M. L. Kamil, P. Mosenthal, & P. D. Pearson (Eds.), *Handbook of reading research* (Vol. 2, pp. 609–640). Mahwah, NJ: Erlbaum.

   RAND Reading Study Group. (2002). *Reading for understanding: Toward an R&D program in reading comprehension.* Santa Monica, CA: RAND.

   Rapp, D. N., & van den Broek, P. (2005). Dynamic text comprehension: An integrative view of reading. *Current Directions in Psychological Science, 14*(5), 276–279.

   Schoenbach, R., & Greenleaf, C. (2009). Fostering adolescents' engaged academic literacy. In L. Christenbury, R. Bomer, & P. Smagorinsky (Eds.), *Handbook of adolescent literacy research* (pp. 98–112). New York: Guilford Press.

4. Vygotsky, L. S. (1978). *Mind in society.* Cambridge, MA: Harvard University Press.

   Vygotsky, L. S. (1986). *Thought and language* (Rev. ed). A. Kozulin (Trans. & Ed.). Cambridge, MA: MIT Press.

5. Bransford, J. D., Brown, A. L., & Cocking, R. R. (Eds.). (1999). *How people learn: Brain, mind, experience, and school.* Washington, DC: National Academies Press.

Brown, J. S., Collins, A., & Newman, S. (1989). The new cognitive apprenticeship: Teaching the craft of reading, writing, and mathematics. In L. B. Resnick (Ed.), *Knowing, learning and instruction: Essays in honor of Robert Glaser* (pp. 453–494). Hillsdale, NJ: Erlbaum.

John-Steiner, V. (1985). *Notebooks of the mind: Explorations of thinking.* Albuquerque, NM: University of New Mexico Press.

Lave, J., & Wenger, E. (1991). *Situated learning: Legitimate peripheral participation.* Cambridge, MA: Cambridge University Press.

Rogoff, B. (1990). *Apprenticeship in thinking: Cognitive development in social context.* New York: Oxford University Press.

6. Rose, D. (1995). *Apprenticeship and exploration: A new approach to literacy instruction* (Literacy Research Paper 10). New York: Scholastic.

7. Baker, L. (2008). Metacognition in comprehension instruction: What we've learned since NRP. In C. C. Block & S. R. Parris (Eds.), *Comprehension instruction: Research-based best practices* (2nd ed., pp. 65–79). New York: Guilford Press.

Kamil, M. L., Borman, G. D., Dole, J., Kral, C. C., Salinger, T., & Torgesen, J. (2008). *Improving adolescent literacy: Effective classroom and intervention practices: A practice guide* (NCEE #2008–4027). Washington, DC: National Center for Education Evaluation and Regional Assistance, Institute of Education Sciences, U.S. Department of Education.

Kucan, L., & Beck, I. L. (1997). Thinking aloud and reading comprehension research: Inquiry, instruction, and social interaction. *Review of Educational Research, 67*(3), 271–299.

Vacca, R. T. (2002). Making a difference in adolescents' school lives: Visible and invisible aspects of content area reading. In A. E. Farstrup & S. J. Samuels (Eds.), *What research has to say about reading instruction* (3rd ed., pp. 184–204). Newark, DE: International Reading Association.

8. Atwood, S., Turnbull, W., & Carpentale, J.I.M. (2010). The construction of knowledge in classroom talk. *Journal of the Learning Sciences, 19,* 358–402.

Goatley, V. J., Brock, D. H., & Raphael, T. E. (1995). Diverse learners participating in regular education "book clubs." *Reading Research Quarterly, 30,* 352–380.

Langer, J. (2001). Beating the odds: Teaching middle and high school students to read and write well. *American Educational Research Journal, 38,* 837–880.

Rex, L., & McEachen, D. (1999). If anything is odd, inappropriate, confusing, or boring, it's probably important: The emergence of inclusive academic literacy through English classroom discussion practices. *Research in the Teaching of English, 34,* 65–129.

Walqui, A., & van Lier, L. (2010). *Scaffolding the academic success of adolescent English language learners: A pedagogy of promise.* San Francisco: WestEd.

Wilkinson, I. A., & Son, E. H. (2011). A dialogic turn in research on learning and teaching to comprehend. In M. L. Kamil, P. D. Pearson, E. B. Moje, & P. P. Afflerbach (Eds.), *Handbook of reading research* (Vol. 4, pp. 359–387). New York: Routledge.

9. Applebee, A. N., Langer, J. A., Nystrand, M., & Gamoran, A. (2003). Discussion-based approaches to developing understanding: Classroom instruction and student performance in middle and high school English. *American Educational Research Journal, 40*(3), 685–730.

McConachie, S., Hall, M., Resnick, L., Ravi, A. K., Bill, V. L., Bintz, J., & Taylor, J. A. (2006). Task, text, and talk: Literacy for all subjects. *Educational Leadership, 64*(2), 8–14.

Soter, A. O., Wilkinson, I. A., Murphy, K., Rudge, L., Reninger, K., & Edwards, M. (2008). What the discourse tells us: Talk and indicators of high-level comprehension. *International Journal of Educational Research, 47*(6), 372–391.

10. Flavell, J. H. (1976). Metacognitive dimensions of problem-solving. In L. B. Resnick (Ed.), *The nature of intelligence.* Hillsdale, NJ: Erlbaum.

11. Baker, Metacognition in comprehension instruction (see note 7).

Baker, L. (1991). Metacognition, reading, and science education. In C. Santa & D. Alvermann (Eds.), *Science learning: Processes and applications* (pp. 2–13). Newark, DE: International Reading Association.

Cartwright, K. B. (2008). Cognitive flexibility and reading comprehension: Relevance to the future. In C. C. Block & S. R. Parris (Eds.), *Comprehension instruction: Research-based best practices* (2nd ed., pp. 50–64). New York: Guilford Press.

Donovan, S. M., Bransford, J. D., & Pellegrino, J. W. (Eds.). (1999). *How people learn: Bridging research and practice.* Washington, DC: National Research Council.

Kamil, Borman, Dole, Kral, Salinger, & Torgesen, *Improving adolescent literacy* (see note 7).

Parris, S., & Block, C. C. (2008). The impact of flexibility on vocabulary and comprehension development. In K. D. Cartwright (Ed.), *Literacy processes: Cognitive flexibility in learning and teaching* (pp. 257–278). New York: Guilford.

12. Benard, B. (2004). *Resiliency: What we have learned.* San Francisco: WestEd.

Dweck, C., & Molden, D. (2006). Self-theories: Their impact on competence motivation and acquisition. In A. Elliot & C. Dweck (Eds.), *Handbook of competence and motivation* (pp. 122–140). New York: Guilford Press.

Duym, V. K. (2006). Academic literacy in the English classroom: Helping underprepared and working class students succeed in college. *Teaching English in the Two Year College, 33*(3), 313–315.

Hall, L. A., Burns, L. D., & Edwards, E. C. (2011). *Empowering struggling readers: Practices for the middle grades.* New York: Guilford Press.

Harris, A. L. (2011). *Kids don't want to fail: Oppositional culture and the black-white achievement gap.* Cambridge, MA: Harvard University Press.

Lewis, C., & del Valle, A. (2009). Literacy and identity: Implications for research and practice. In L. Christenbury, R. Bomer, & P. Smagorinsky (Eds.), *Handbook of adolescent literacy research* (pp. 307–322). New York: Guilford Press.

Mahiri, J., & Godley, A. (1998). Rewriting identity: Social meanings of literacy and "revisions" of self. *Reading Research Quarterly, 33*(4), 416–433.

Maloney, W. H. (2003). Connecting the texts of their lives to academic literacy: Creating success for at-risk first-year college students. *Journal of Adolescent & Adult Literacy, 46*(8), 664–673.

Orellana, M. F., Reynolds, J., Dorner, L., & Meza, M. (2003). In other words: Translating or "para-phrasing" as a family literacy practice in immigrant households. *Reading Research Quarterly, 38*(1), 12–34.

Smith, M., & Wilhelm, J. (2006). *Going with the flow: How to engage boys (and girls) in their literacy learning.* Portsmouth, NH: Heinemann.

Tatum, A. W. (2006). Engaging African American males in reading. *Educational Leadership, 63*(5), 44–49.

13. Committee on Increasing High School Students' Engagement and Motivation to Learn, National Research Council. (2004). The nature and conditions of engagement. In *Engaging schools: Fostering high school students' motivation to learn* (pp. 31–59). Washington, DC: National Academies Press.

Ferguson, R. F. (2008). *Toward excellence with equity: An emerging vision for closing the achievement gap.* Cambridge, MA: Harvard Education Press.

Guthrie, J. T., Wigfield, A., & Von Secker, C. (2000). Effects of integrated instruction on motivation and strategy use in reading. *Journal of Educational Psychology, 92*(2), 331–341.

Jiménez, R. (1997). The strategic reading abilities and potential of five low-literacy Latina/o readers in middle school. *Reading Research Quarterly, 32,* 224–243.

Kamil, Borman, Dole, Kral, Salinger, & Torgesen, *Improving adolescent literacy* (see note 7).

Lee, C. D. (2007). *Culture, literacy, and learning: Blooming in the midst of the whirlwind.* New York: Teachers College Press.

Litman, C., & Greenleaf, C. (2007). Traveling together over difficult ground: Negotiating success with a profoundly inexperienced reader in an introduction to chemistry class. In K. A. Hinchman & H. Sheridan-Thomas (Eds.), *Best practices in adolescent literacy instruction* (pp. 275–296). New York: Guilford Press.

Murie, R., Collins, M. R., & Detzner, D. F. (2004). Building academic literacy from student strength: An interdisciplinary life history project. *Journal of Basic Writing, 23*(2), 70–92.

Smith, M. W., & Wilhelm, J. D. (2002). *Reading don't fix no Chevys: Literacy in the lives of young men.* Portsmouth, NH: Heinemann.

14. Alvermann, D. E. (2001). Reading adolescents' reading identities: Looking back to see ahead. *Journal of Adolescent & Adult Literacy, 44,* 676–690.

Buley-Meissner, M. L. (1993). Reclaiming personal knowledge: Investigations of identity, difference, and community in college education. *College English, 55*(2), 211–221.

Christenbury, L., Bomer, R., & Smagorinsky, P. (Eds.). (2009). *Handbook of adolescent literacy research.* New York: Guilford Press.

Gambrell, L. B., Marinak, B. A., Brooker, H. B., & McCrea-Andrews, H. J. (2011). The importance of independent reading. In S. J. Samuels and A. E. Farstrup (Eds.), *What research has to say about reading instruction* (4th ed., pp. 143–158). Newark, DE: International Reading Association.

Greenleaf, C., Schoenbach, R., Cziko, C., & Mueller, F. (2001). Apprenticing adolescent readers to academic literacy. *Harvard Educational Review, 71*(1), 79–129.

Gutierrez, K. D. (2008). Developing a sociocritical literacy in the Third Space. *Reading Research Quarterly, 43*(2), 148–164.

Hull, G., & Rose, M. (1989). Rethinking remediation: Toward a social-cognitive understanding of problematic reading and writing. *Written Communication, 8,* 139–154.

McCarthey, S. J., & Moje, E. (2002). Identity matters. *Reading Research Quarterly, 37*(2), 228–238.

Moje, E., & Luke, A. (2009). Literacy and identity: Examining the metaphors in history and contemporary research. *Reading Research Quarterly, 44*(4), 415–437.

Pacheco, M. (2010). English-language learners' reading achievement: Dialectical relationships between policy and practices in meaning-making opportunities. *Reading Research Quarterly, 45*(3), 292–317.

Penrose, A. M. (2002). Academic literacy perceptions and performance: Comparing first-generation and continuing-generation college students. *Research in the Teaching of English, 36*(4), 437–461.

Rose, M. (1989). *Lives on the boundary.* New York: Penguin Books.

Schunk, D. H. (2003). Self-efficacy for reading and writing: Influence of modeling, goal setting, and self-evaluation. *Reading & Writing Quarterly, 19*(2), 159–172.

15. Shulman, L. S. (1986). Just in case: Reflections on learning from experience. In J. Colbert, P. Dresberg, & K. Trimble (Eds.), *The case for education: Contemporary approaches for using case methods* (p. 210). Needham Heights, MA: Allyn & Bacon.

16. Baker, L., & Beall, L. C. (2009). Metacognitive processes and reading comprehension. In S. E. Israel & G. G. Duffy (Eds.), *Handbook of research on reading comprehension* (pp. 779–812). New York: Routledge.

Bransford, Brown, & Cocking, *How people learn* (see note 5).

Flavell, Metacognitive dimensions of problem-solving (see note 10).

Greenleaf, Schoenbach, Cziko, & Mueller, Apprenticing adolescent readers to academic literacy (see note 14).

Kingery, E. (2000). Teaching metacognitive strategies to enhance higher level thinking in adolescents. In P. E. Linder, E. G. Sturtevant, W. M. Linek, & J. R. Dugan (Eds.), *Literacy at a new horizon: The twenty-second yearbook* (pp. 74–85). Commerce, TX: College Reading Association.

Nist, S. L., & Simpson, M. L. (2000). College studying. In M. L. Kamil, P. Mosenthal, P. D. Pearson, & R. Barr (Eds.), *Handbook of Reading Research* (Vol. 3, pp. 403–422). Mahwah, NJ: Erlbaum.

Pressley, M. (2002). Metacognition and self-regulated comprehension. In S. J. Samuels & A. E. Farstrup (Eds.), *What research has to say about reading instruction* (3rd ed., pp. 291–309). Newark, DE: International Reading Association.

17. Alvermann, D. (2011). Popular culture and literacy practices. In M. L. Kamil, P. D. Pearson, E. B. Moje, & P. P. Afflerbach (Eds.), *Handbook of reading research* (Vol. 4, pp. 541–560). New York: Routledge.

Alvermann, D. (Ed.). (2002). *Adolescents and literacies in a digital world.* New York: Lang.

Cohen, D. J., & Snowden, J. L. (2008). The relations between document familiarity, frequency, and prevalence and document literacy performance among adult readers. *Reading Research Quarterly, 43*(1), 9–26.

Coiro, J., & Dobler, E. (2007). Exploring the online reading comprehension strategies used by skilled sixth-grade readers to search and locate information on the Internet. *Reading Research Quarterly, 42,* 214–257.

Coiro, J., Knobel, M., Lankshear, C., & Leu, D. J. (2008). *Handbook of research on new literacies.* New York: Erlbaum.

Dalton, B., & Rose, D. (2008). Scaffolding digital comprehension. In C. C. Block & S. R. Parris (Eds.), *Comprehension instruction* (2nd ed., pp. 347–362). New York: Guilford.

Gee, J. P. (2008). Games and comprehension: The importance of specialist language. In C. C. Block & S. R. Parris (Eds.), *Comprehension instruction* (2nd ed., pp. 309–320). New York: Guilford.

Hull, G., & Schultz, K. (2001). *School's out: Bridging out-of-school literacies with classroom practice.* New York: Teachers College Press.

Mellard, D., Patterson, M., & Prewett, S. (2007). Reading practices among adult education participants. *Reading Research Quarterly, 42*(2), 188–213.

Xu, S. H. (2008). Rethinking literacy learning and teaching: Intersections of adolescents' in-school and out-of-school literacy practices. In K. A. Hinchman & H. Sheridan-Thomas (Eds.), *Best practices in adolescent literacy instruction* (pp. 39–56). New York: Guilford.

18. Beck, I. L., & McKeown, M. G. (2006). *Improving comprehension with Questioning the Author: A fresh and expanded view of a powerful approach.* New York: Scholastic.

Block, C. C., & Duffy, G. G. (2008). Comprehension strategies and direct explanation of strategies: Where we've been and where we're going. In C. C. Block & S. R. Parris (Eds.), *Comprehension instruction* (2nd ed., pp. 19–37). New York: Guilford.

Brown, A. L., Palincsar, A., & Armbruster, B. (1994). Instructing comprehension-fostering activities in interactive learning situations. In R. Ruddell, M. Ruddell, & H. Singer (Eds.), *Theoretical models and processes of reading* (pp. 757–787). Newark, DE: International Reading Association.

Conley, M. W. (2008). Cognitive strategy instruction for adolescents: What we know about the promise, what we don't know about the potential. *Harvard Educational Review, 78*(1), 84–108.

Duke, N. K., Pearson, P. D., Strachan, S. L., & Bilman, A. K. (2011). Essential elements of fostering and teaching reading comprehension. In S. J. Samuels and A. E. Farstrup (Eds.), *What research has to say about reading instruction* (4th ed., pp. 51–93). Newark, DE: International Reading Association.

Fisher, D., & Frey, N. (2008). Comprehension instruction in action: The secondary classroom. In C. C. Block & S. R. Parris (Eds.), *Comprehension instruction* (2nd ed., pp. 258–270). New York: Guilford.

Gavelek, J. F., Raphael, T. E., Biondo, S. M., & Wang, D. (2000). Integrated literacy instruction. In M. L. Kamil, P. Mosenthal, P. D. Pearson, & R. Barr (Eds.), *Handbook of reading research* (Vol. 3, pp. 587–608). Mahwah, NJ: Erlbaum.

Palinscar, A. S., & Brown, A. L. (1984). Reciprocal teaching of comprehension-fostering and comprehension-monitoring activities. *Cognition and Instruction, 1*(2), 117–175.

Paris, S., Lipson, M., & Wixson, K. (1994). Becoming a strategic reader. In R. Ruddell, M. Ruddell, & H. Singer (Eds.), *Theoretical models and processes of reading* (pp. 788–810). Newark, DE: International Reading Association.

Raphael, T. E., Highfield, K., & Au, K. H. (2006). *QAR now: A powerful and practical framework that develops comprehension and higher-level thinking in all students.* New York: Scholastic.

Rueda, R., Velasco, A., & Lim, H. (2008). Comprehension instruction for English learners. In C. C. Block & S. R. Parris (Eds.), *Comprehension instruction* (2nd ed., pp. 294–307). New York: Guilford.

19. Baker, Metacognition in comprehension instruction (see note 7).

Garner, R. (1994). Metacognition and executive control. In R. Ruddell, M. Ruddell, & H. Singer (Eds.), *Theoretical models and processes of reading* (pp. 715–732). Newark, DE: International Reading Association.

Greenleaf, Schoenbach, Cziko, & Mueller, Apprenticing adolescent readers to academic literacy (see note 14).

Palincsar, A. S., & Brown, A. L. (1989). Instruction for self-regulated reading. In L. B. Resnick & L. E. Klopfer (Eds.), *Toward the thinking curriculum: Current cognitive research* (pp. 19–39). Alexandria, VA: Association for Supervision and Curriculum Development.

Scardamalia, M., & Bereiter, C. (1985). Fostering the development of self-regulation in children's knowledge processing. In S. F. Chipman, J. W. Segal, & R. Glaser (Eds.), *Thinking and learning skills: Research and open questions.* Hillsdale, NJ: Erlbaum.

Schunk, Self-efficacy for reading and writing (see note 14).

20. Baumann, J. F., & Duffy, A. M. (1997). *Engaged reading for pleasure and learning: A report from the National Reading Research Center.* Athens, GA: National Reading Research Center.

Bristow, P. S. (1985, December). Are poor readers passive readers? Some evidence, possible explanations, and potential solutions. *The Reading Teacher,* 318–325.

Lent, R. C. (2006). *Engaging adolescent learners: A guide for content-area teachers.* Portsmouth, NH: Heinemann.

Mathewson, G. (1994). Model of attitude influence upon reading and learning to read. In R. Ruddell, M. Ruddell, & H. Singer (Eds.), *Theoretical models and processes of reading* (pp. 1131–1161). Newark, DE: International Reading Association.

Mellard, Patterson, & Prewett, Reading practices among adult education participants (see note 17).

Nist & Simpson, College studying (see note 16).

Wigfield, A., Guthrie, J. T., Perencevich, K. C., Taboada, A., Klauda, S. L., Mcrae, A., & Barbosa, P. (2008). Role of reading engagement in mediating effects of reading comprehension instruction on reading outcomes. *Psychology in the Schools, 45*(5), 432–445.

21. Bakerman, C. (1985). Physicists reading physics: Schema-laden purposes and purpose-laden schema. *Written Communication, 2*(1), 3–23.

Blanton, W., Wood, K., & Moorman, G. (1990). The role of purpose in reading instruction. *The Reading Teacher, 43,* 486–493.

Cohen & Snowden, The relations between document familiarity, frequency, and prevalence and document literacy performance among adult readers (see note 17).

Darvin, J. (2006). On reading recipes and racing forms—the literacy practices and perceptions of vocational educators. *Journal of Adolescent & Adult Literacy, 50*(1), 10–18.

Rapp & van den Broek, Dynamic text comprehension (see note 3).

22. Alexander, P. A. (2003). The development of expertise: The journey from acclimation to proficiency. *Educational Researcher, 32*(8), 10–14.

Brent, D. (2005). Reinventing WAC (again): The first-year seminar and academic literacy. *College Composition and Communication, 57*(2), 253–276.

Curry, M. J. (2004). Academic literacy for English language learners. *Community College Review, 32*(2), 51–68.

Heller, R., & Greenleaf, C. (2007). *Literacy instruction in the content areas: Getting to the core of middle and high school improvement.* Washington, DC: Alliance for Excellent Education.

Langer, J. (2011). *Envisioning knowledge: Building literacy in the academic disciplines.* New York: Teachers College Press.

Lea, M. K., & Street, B. V. (1998). Student writing in higher education: An academic literacies approach. *Studies in Higher Education, 23*(2), 157–172.

Lee, C. D., & Spratley, A. (2010). *Reading in the disciplines: The challenges of adolescent literacy.* New York: Carnegie Corporation of New York.

Moje, E. (2008). Foregrounding the disciplines in secondary literacy teaching and learning. *Journal of Adolescent and Adult Literacy, 52,* 96–107.

Norris, S. P., & Phillips, L. M. (2003). How literacy in its fundamental sense is central to scientific literacy. *Science Education, 87,* 224–240.

Pearson, P. D., Moje, E. B., & Greenleaf, C. (2010). Literacy and science: Each in the service of the other. *Science, 328,* 459–463.

Shanahan, T., & Shanahan, C. (2008). Teaching disciplinary literacy to adolescents: Rethinking content-area literacy. *Harvard Educational Review, 78*(1), 40–59.

Yancey, K. B. (2009). The literacy demands of entering the university. In L. Christenbury, R. Bomer, & P. Smagorinsky (Eds.), *Handbook of adolescent literacy research* (pp. 256–270). New York: Guilford.

23. Anderson, R. (1994). Role of the reader's schema in comprehension, learning, and memory. In R. Ruddell, M. Ruddell, & H. Singer (Eds.), *Theoretical models and processes of reading* (pp. 469–482). Newark, DE: International Reading Association.

    Hull, G., & Rose, M. (1990). This wooden shack place: The logic of an unconventional reading. *College Composition and Communication, 41*(3), 287–298.

    Kintsch, W. (1988). The role of knowledge in discourse comprehension: A construction-integration model. *Psychological Review, 98,* 163–182.

    Martinez-Roldan, C. M., & Franquiz, M. E. (2009). Latina/o youth literacies: Hidden funds of knowledge. In L. Christenbury, R. Bomer, & P. Smagorinsky (Eds.), *Handbook of adolescent literacy research* (pp. 323–342). New York: Guilford.

    Smagorinsky, P. (2001). If meaning is constructed, what's it made from? Toward a cultural theory of reading. *Review of Educational Research, 71*(1), 133–169.

    Williams, J. P. (2007). Literacy in the curriculum: Integrating text structure and content area instruction. In D. S. McNamara (Ed.), *Reading comprehension strategies: Theories, interventions, and technologies* (pp. 199–219). Mahwah, NJ: Erlbaum.

24. Anderson, Role of the reader's schema in comprehension, learning, and memory (see note 23).

    Bransford, J. (1994). Schema activation and schema acquisition. In R. Ruddell, M. Ruddell, & H. Singer (Eds.), *Theoretical models and processes of reading* (pp. 483–495). Newark, DE: International Reading Association.

    Cunningham, A., & Stanovich, K. (1998, Spring/Summer). What reading does for the mind. *American Educator,* 815.

    Learned, J. E., Stockdill, D., & Moje, E. B. (2011). Integrating reading strategies and knowledge building in adolescent literacy instruction. In S. J. Samuels and A. E. Farstrup (Eds.), *What research has to say about reading instruction* (4th ed., pp. 159–185). Newark, DE: International Reading Association.

    Rapp & van den Broek, Dynamic text comprehension (see note 3).

    Simonsen, S., & Singer, H. (1992). Improving reading instruction in the content areas. In J. Samuels & A. Farstrup (Eds.), *What research has to say about reading instruction* (2nd ed., pp. 200–217). Newark, DE: International Reading Association.

    Sinatra, G. M., & Broughton, S. H. (2011). Bridging reading comprehension and conceptual change in science education: The promise of refutational text. *Reading Research Quarterly, 46*(4), 374–393.

    van den Broek, P. (2010). Using texts in science education: Cognitive processes and knowledge representation. *Science, 328,* 453–456.

25. Idol, L. (1987). Group story mapping: A comprehension strategy for both skilled and unskilled readers. *Journal of Learning Disabilities, 20*(4), 196–205.

Goldman, S. R., & Bisanz, G. (2002). Toward a functional analysis of scientific genres: Implications for understanding and learning processes. In J. Otero, J. A. Leon, & A. C. Graesser (Eds.), *The psychology of science text comprehension* (pp. 19–50). Mahwah, NJ: Erlbaum.

Pearson, P. D., & Camperell, K. (1994). Comprehension of text structures. In R. Ruddell, M. Ruddell, & H. Singer (Eds.), *Theoretical models and processes of reading* (pp. 448–468). Newark, DE: International Reading Association.

Reutzel, D. R. (1985). Story maps improve comprehension. *The Reading Teacher, 38*(4), 400–404.

Reznitskaya, A., Anderson, R. C., Dong, T., Li, Y., Kim, I., & Kim, S. (2008). Learning to think well: Application of argument schema theory to literacy instruction. In C. C. Block & S. R. Parris (Eds.), *Comprehension instruction* (2nd ed., pp. 196–213). New York: Guilford.

26. Anderson, Role of the reader's schema in comprehension, learning, and memory (see note 23).

27. Bower, G. H. (1976). Experiments on story understanding and recall. *Quarterly Journal of Experimental Psychology, 28,* 511–534.

   Bransford, Schema activation and schema acquisition (see note 24).

   Dochy, F., Segers, M., & Buehl, M. M. (1999). The relation between assessment practices and outcomes of studies: The case of research on prior knowledge. *Review of Educational Research, 69*(2), 145–186.

   Kintsch, The role of knowledge in discourse comprehension (see note 23).

28. Dochy, Segers, & Buehl, The relation between assessment practices and outcomes of studies (see note 27).

   Donovan, M. S., & Bransford, J. D. (Eds.). (2005). *How students learn: History, mathematics, and science in the classroom.* Washington, DC: National Academies Press.

   Roth, K. (1991). Reading science texts for conceptual change. In C. Santa & D. Alvermann (Eds.), *Science learning: Processes and applications* (pp. 48–63). Newark, DE: International Reading Association.

   Simonsen & Singer, Improving reading instruction in the content areas (see note 24).

   Sinatra & Broughton, Bridging reading comprehension and conceptual change in science education (see note 24).

   Tippett, C. D. (2010). Refutation text in science education: A review of two decades of research. *International Journal of Science and Mathematics Education, 8*(6), 951–970.

   van den Broek, P., & Kendeou, P. (2008). Cognitive processes in comprehension of science texts: The role of co-activation in confronting misconceptions. *Applied Cognitive Psychology, 22,* 335–351.

29. Akhondi, M., Malayeri, F. A., & Samad, A. A. (2011). How to teach expository text structure to facilitate reading comprehension. *The Reading Teacher, 64*(5), 368–372.

   Berkowitz, S. (1986). Effects of instruction in text organization on sixth-grade students' memory for expository reading. *Reading Research Quarterly, 21,* 161–178.

   Britt, M. A., & Sommer, J. (2004). Facilitating textual integration with macro-structure focusing task. *Reading Psychology, 25,* 313–339.

   Cohen & Snowden, The relations between document familiarity, frequency, and prevalence and document literacy performance among adult readers (see note 17).

   Haas, C., & Flower, L. (1988). Rhetorical reading strategies and the construction of meaning. *College Composition and Communication, 39,* 167–183.

Meyer, B.J.F., & Poon, L. W. (2001). Effects of structure strategy training and signaling on recall of text. *Journal of Educational Psychology, 93*(1), 141–159.

Reznitskaya, Anderson, Dong, Li, Kim & Kim, Learning to think well (see note 25).

Taylor, B. (1992). Text structure, comprehension, and recall. In J. Samuels & A. Farstrup (Eds.), *What research has to say about reading instruction* (2nd ed., pp. 220–235). Newark, DE: International Reading Association.

30. Akhondi, Malayeri, & Samad, How to teach expository text structure to facilitate reading comprehension (see note 29).

Fang, Z., & Schleppegrell, M. J. (2010). Disciplinary literacies across content areas: Supporting secondary reading through functional language analysis. *Journal of Adolescent & Adult Literacy, 53*(7), 587–597.

Goldman, S. R., & Rakestraw, J. A. (2000). Structural aspects of constructing meaning from text. In M. L. Kamil, P. Mosenthal, P. D. Pearson, & R. Barr (Eds.), *Handbook of reading research* (Vol. 3, pp. 311–335). Mahwah, NJ: Erlbaum.

Kendeou, P., & van den Broek, P. (2007). The effects of prior knowledge and text structure on comprehension processes during reading of scientific texts. *Memory & Cognition, 35*(7), 1567–1577.

Lemke, J. (1998). Multiplying meaning: Visual and verbal semiotics in scientific text. In J. R. Martin & R. Veel (Eds.), *Reading science* (pp. 87–113). London: Routledge.

Mitchell, J., & Erickson, G. (2004). Constituting conventions of practice: An analysis of academic literacy and computer mediated communication. *The Journal of Educational Thought, 38*(1), 19–42.

Pearson & Camperell, Comprehension of text structures (see note 25).

Waldrip, B., Prian, V., & Carolan, J. (2006). Learning junior secondary science through multi-modal representations. *Electronic Journal of Science Education, 11*, 87–107.

Williams, Literacy in the curriculum (see note 23).

31. Bear, D. R., Invernizzi, M., Templeton, S., & Johnston, F. (1996). *Words their way: Word study for phonics, vocabulary, and spelling.* Upper Saddle River, NJ: Prentice-Hall.

Bos, C. S., & Anders, P. L. (1990). Effects of interactive vocabulary instruction on the vocabulary learning and reading comprehension of junior-high learning disabled students. *Learning Disability Quarterly, 13*(1), 31–42.

Carlisle, J. F. (2010). Effects of instruction in morphological awareness on literacy achievement: An integrative review. *Reading Research Quarterly, 45*(4), 464–487.

Dean, D. (2008). *Bringing grammar to life.* Newark, DE: International Reading Association.

Fang, A., & Schleppegrell, M. J. (2008). *Reading in secondary content areas: A language-based pedagogy.* Ann Arbor: University of Michigan.

Kasper, L., & Weiss, S. T. (2005). Building ESL students' linguistic and academic literacy through content-based interclass collaboration. *Teaching English in the Two Year College, 32*(3), 282–297.

McCutchen, D., & Logan, B. (2011). Inside incidental word learning: Children's strategic use of morphological information to infer word meanings. *Reading Research Quarterly, 46*(4), 334–349.

Nagy, W., Berninger, V. W., & Abbott, R. D. (2006). Contributions of morphology beyond phonology to literacy outcomes of upper elementary and middle-school students. *Journal of Educational Psychology, 98*(1), 134–147.

Schleppegrell, M. J. (2009). Grammar for generation 1.5: A focus on meaning. In M. Roberge, M. Siegal, & L. Harklau (Eds.), *Generation 1.5 in college composition: Teaching academic writing to U. S.-educated learners of ESL* (pp. 221–234). New York: Routledge.

Scott, J. (1993). *Science and language links: Classroom implications.* Portsmouth, NH: Heinemann.

Short, D. J., & Fitzsimmons, S. (2007). *Double the work: Challenges and solutions to acquiring language and academic literacy for adolescent English language learners: A report to Carnegie Corporation of New York.* Washington, DC: Alliance for Excellent Education.

Sternberg, R. J. (1987). Most vocabulary is learned from context. In M. G. McKeown & M. E. Curtis (Eds.), *The nature of vocabulary acquisition* (pp. 89–105). Hillsdale, NJ: Erlbaum.

Walqui, A. (2006). Scaffolding instruction for English language learners: A conceptual framework. *International Journal of Bilingual Education and Bilingualism, 9*(2), 159–180.

32. Chin, C., & Osborne, J. (2010). Supporting argumentation through students' questions: Case studies in science classrooms. *Journal of the Learning Sciences, 19,* 230–284.

Courts, P. L. (1997). *Multicultural literacies: Dialect, discourse, and diversity.* New York: Peter Lang.

De La Paz, S., & Felton, M. K. (2010). Reading and writing from multiple source documents in history: Effects of strategy instruction with low to average high school writers. *Contemporary Educational Psychology, 35,* 174–192.

Kuhn, D. (2010). Teaching and learning science as argument. *Science Education, 94,* 810–824.

Lee, P., & Ashby, R. (2000). Progression in historical understanding among students ages 7–14. In P. N. Stearns, P. Seixas, & S. Wineburg (Eds.), *Knowing, teaching, and learning history: National and international perspectives* (pp. 199–222). New York: New York University Press.

Moje, E. B., Peek-Brown, D., Sutherland, L. M., Marx, R. W., Blumenfeld, P., & Krajcik, J. (2004). Explaining explanations: Developing scientific literacy in middle school project-based science reform. In S. Strickland & D. E. Alvermann (Eds.), *Bridging the literacy achievement gap, grades 4–12* (pp. 227–251). New York: Teachers College Press.

Rabinowitz, P. (1987). *Before reading: Narrative conventions and the politics of interpretation.* Ithaca, NY: Cornell University Press.

Scott, *Science and language links* (see note 31).

Temple, C., & Hinchman, K. A. (2008). Fostering acquisition of official mathematics language. In K. A. Hinchman & H. Sheridan-Thomas (Eds.), *Best practices in adolescent literacy instruction* (pp. 229–245). New York: Guilford.

Their, M., with Davis, B. (2002). *The new science literacy: Using language skills to help students learn science.* Portsmouth, NH: Heinemann.

33. Appleman, D. (2000). *Critical encounters in high school English: Teaching literacy theory to adolescents.* New York: Teachers College Press.

Borasi, R., & Seigel, M. (2000). *Reading counts.* New York: Teachers College Press.

Curcio, F. R., & Artzt, A. F. (2011). Reading, writing and mathematics: A problem-solving connection. In D. Lapp, J. Flood, & N. Farnan (Eds.), *Content area reading and learning: Instructional strategies* (3rd ed., pp. 257–270). New York: Erlbaum.

De La Paz, S. (2005). Effects of historical reasoning instruction and writing strategy mastery in culturally and academically diverse middle school classrooms. *Journal of Educational Psychology, 97*(2), 139–156.

Hillocks, G., Jr., & Ludlow, L. H. (1984). A taxonomy of skills in reading and interpreting fiction. *American Educational Research Journal, 21*(1), 7–24.

Kuhn, D., Cheney, R., & Weinstock, M. (2000). The development of epistemological under-standing. *Cognitive Development, 15,* 309–328.

Langer, J. (2011). *Envisioning literature: Literary understanding and literature instruction* (2nd ed.). New York: Teachers College Press.

Lee, P. J. (2005). Putting principles into practice: Understanding history. In M. S. Donovan & J. D. Bransford (Eds.), *How students learn: History, mathematics, and science in the classroom.* Washington, DC: National Academies Press.

Newell, G., Beach, R., Smith, J., & VanDerHeide, J. (2011). Teaching and learning argumenta-tive reading and writing: A review of research. *Reading Research Quarterly, 46*(3), 273–304.

Osborne, J. (2002). Science without literacy: A ship without a sail? *Cambridge Journal of Education, 32*(2), 203–218.

Saul, W. E. (Ed.). (2004). *Crossing borders in literacy and science instruction: Perspectives on theory and practice.* Newark, DE: International Reading Association.

Voss, J. F., & Wiley, J. (2006). Expertise in history. In K. A. Ericsson, N. Charness, P. Feltovich, & R. R. Hoffman (Eds.), *The Cambridge handbook of expertise and expert performance* (pp. 569–584). Cambridge, UK: Cambridge University Press.

Wineburg, S. S. (1991). Historical problem solving: A study of cognitive processes used in the evaluation of documentary and pictorial evidence. *Journal of Educational Psychology 83,* 73–87.

34. Bartholomae, D. (1985). Inventing the university. In M. Rose (Ed.), *When a writer can't write: Studies in writer's block and other composing process problems.* New York: Guilford.

   Courts, *Multicultural literacies* (see note 32).

   Lemke, J. L. (1990). *Talking science: Language, learning, and values.* Norwood, NJ: Ablex.

   Rabinowitz, P., & Smith, M. (1998). *Authorizing readers: Resistance and respect in the teaching of literature.* New York: Teachers College Press.

   Rex, L. A. (2001). The remaking of a high school reader. *Reading Research Quarterly, 36*(3), 288–314.

   Scribner & Cole, *The psychology of literacy* (see note 1).

   Street, *Social literacies* (see note 1).

   Wineburg, S. (2001). *Historical thinking and other unnatural acts: Charting the future of teaching the past.* Philadelphia: Temple University Press.

35. Heath, S. B. (1983). *Ways with words: Language, life and work in communities and classrooms.* New York: Cambridge University Press.

36. Cope, B., & Kalantzis, M. (1993). *The powers of literacy.* Pittsburgh, PA: University of Pittsburgh Press.

   Courts, *Multicultural literacies* (see note 32).

   Delpit, L. D. (1995). *Other people's children: Cultural conflict in the classroom.* New York: New Press.

   Gee, J. (1996). *Social linguistics and literacies: Ideology in discourses* (2nd ed.). London: Falmer Press.

   Godley, A. J., Carpenter, B. D., & Werner, C. A. (2007). "I'll speak in proper slang": Language ideologies in a daily editing activity. *Reading Research Quarterly, 42*(1), 100–131.

   Gutierrez, Developing a sociocritical literacy in the Third Space (see note 14).

   Kynard, C. (2008). "The blues playingest dog you ever heard of": (Re)positioning literacy through African American blues rhetoric. *Reading Research Quarterly, 43*(4), 356–373.

   Lemke, Multiplying meaning (see note 30).

The Social and Personal Dimensions

Building a Foundation for Engaged Learning

It seems like in other classes, if you make a mistake, everybody is whispering, "He sucks" or "Omigod, he missed *that* word." [In here] it's kind of a warm atmosphere, and like everybody understands what they're doing. You're just relaxed, and you can read.
—Brian, grade 10 student

WHETHER CONSCIOUSLY or not, all students experience the social and personal dimensions of classroom life. For many students, like Brian above, this experience is a painful exposure of what they take to be their own inadequacy. The result is that students shut down and are shut out of learning opportunities because they conclude that they aren't *able* to read. For students to gain new perspectives on themselves as readers and learners, classroom norms and values have to change. The tables have to turn—from valuing correctness to valuing struggle, from valuing right answers to valuing the process of coming to know, and learning how to learn. The personal and social dimensions of the Reading Apprenticeship framework are the foundation for reconstituting more productive and hopeful classrooms, so that all students can, as Brian says, "relax and *read.*"

The mission of educational equity embedded in the Reading Apprenticeship framework begins with establishing a classroom community that promotes all students' evolving sense of themselves as competent learners. With support and repeated opportunities to experience academic success, they will come to see themselves as people who can take control of their reading and learning.

Starting from Day One

What I discovered was that even though you can introduce Reading Apprenticeship after the semester has started, when Reading Apprenticeship routines and values define reality for students from the first day of the course, the class atmosphere is more positive and student retention and success are much more impressive.

—Karen Hattaway, community college composition teacher

Teachers often ask, "How do I start?" Sometimes it may seem more comfortable to start by cherry-picking a few discrete cognitive strategies like questioning or summarizing. But as Karen Hattaway found in her community college course, establishing Reading Apprenticeship routines for making thinking visible from the first day of the semester meant that she could create a classroom culture in which collaboration felt safe and inquiry was expected from day one.

Building a classroom community may look different depending on a teacher's style, course content, and the educational context. In addition, the population of students in each class—their attitudes and previous school experiences—will necessarily shape the way a teacher builds community. Successful students usually know to ask for help when they need it and feel empowered to do so; students who struggle may not. Establishing a community characterized by inquiry—where all are able to value and build on what they bring to the class, and where support as well as academic expectations are equally high for all students—is vital to address longstanding educational inequities. Thus, as we will see in visits to a number of classrooms, in addition to creating a sense of shared norms and safety for collaboration, Reading Apprenticeship teachers demonstrate an important focus on nurturing students' thinking and relationships to literacy.

On the first day of school in Will Brown's Introduction to Chemistry class, students are immediately immersed in an academic community designed to build the social and personal dimensions of the classroom (see Classroom Close-Up 3.1 and the related Box 3.1). Will's students find that the knowledge they bring with them will always be engaged, an openness to inquiry will always be expected, collaboration with classmates is a given, and they will learn the disciplinary discourse and practices of chemistry as well as important chemistry content.

Starting Reading Apprenticeship from day one means beginning with the social dimension of the classroom to create a safe and collaborative learning environment, and tapping into the personal dimension by building connections to students' knowledge, experience, creativity, and curiosity. Over time, this learning environment, which will be driven by metacognitive conversation, supports students' engagement with subject area reading and helps students build needed dispositions and skills to become increasingly independent learners.

CLASSROOM CLOSE-UP 3.1
Developing Dispositions for Engagement

It is the first day of the school year in teacher Will Brown's Introduction to Chemistry class. Forty percent of the students have scored below the 10th percentile on the state's standardized reading test. Introduction to Chemistry counts toward the district's graduation requirements in science but covers only half the material of regular college preparatory classes in chemistry. Most of the students in this class have been unsuccessful in science classes previously and are taking the course simply to be able to graduate.

The computer monitor at the front of the room welcomes and orients students. As they find their

---

Welcome to Introduction to Chemistry

Please take your assigned seat. See seating chart on front table.

Preamble #1: *Write 1/3 page and keep.*

What do you know or think about mixtures and solutions?

What do you want to learn about mixtures and solutions?

---

way to nine round tables labeled with team names such as Kinetic Kids and Solubility Stars, Will explains to the class that every day begins with a short writing activity—the preamble.

Before inviting volunteers to read their responses, Will introduces norms for classroom discourse. "Let's all turn so we can see the person who's talking. And I'm going to go to the side of the room, to help train you to talk to the class. Everyone here needs to hear what you're saying to be part of that learning process."

As three students share what they know or think about mixtures and solutions, Will acknowledges, validates, paraphrases, frames, and elaborates students' contributions in ways that demonstrate his undivided attention and his respect for student thinking.

Hani, an English learner from the Sudan, offers, "I think it's something that you can make or something like that. I don't really know."

"So we can *make* solutions? That's a good thing to know about," Will responds. "We can, and we *will* make them."

The preamble discussion leads to a hands-on investigation and observation of mixtures and solutions, with students immediately immersed in active science inquiry and sense making.

Building the Social Dimension

> It was as if all the energy they had put into hiding their sense of failure could now
> go into trying to understand what they were reading—or at least into understanding
> where they were getting lost or what it was that confused them.
>
> —Christine Cziko, high school academic literacy teacher

When we first worked with teacher colleagues to design and field test the model for Reading Apprenticeship, it was clear that students needed to let teachers know what was going on in their minds when they were reading—where they got stuck, what was confusing, what seemed easy, and what did

Sample Day-One Practices for Establishing a Reading Apprenticeship Classroom Community

The Classroom Close-Up of day one in Will Brown's Introduction to Chemistry class includes a number of practices that immediately immerse students in a Reading Apprenticeship community. These practices structure Will's class across the year.

SURFACING STUDENTS' KNOWLEDGE AND INTERESTS

- Students think and write to open-ended questions that invite metacognition:
  - What do you know or think about _____?
  - What do you want to learn about _____?
- Students share their thoughts with the class.
- The teacher models norms for listening attentively.
- The teacher responds to student contributions by making connections to the lesson, linking their questions to the science investigation to follow.

INTRODUCING NORMS OF STUDENT-TO-STUDENT INTERACTION

- The classroom is set up in table groups.
- The teacher models giving attention to the speaker by turning to look at the student and telling the class what he is doing and why.
- The teacher removes himself from center stage and explains why.
- The teacher demonstrates that students' ideas have value by asking students to share their thoughts and by responding without evaluation—instead extending, making connections, and acknowledging their contributions.

APPRENTICING STUDENTS INTO DISCIPLINARY LANGUAGE AND PRACTICES

- Class begins with a discipline-based metacognitive task.
- The teacher signals expectations for students through the language of chemistry in the preamble prompt and table group names.
- The teacher immerses students directly into inquiry through preamble prompts and discussion, as well as science investigation.

not. Without this input, teachers could not know how best to help them become more competent readers.

Yet many students, particularly those who had felt unsuccessful with reading in the past, felt ashamed to reveal any difficulties. To gain students' trust and active participation it would be necessary to create the sense that students and teacher formed a community of readers, committed to a collaborative inquiry aimed at understanding and improving their reading. This meant making sure students felt that their classmates, as well as their teacher, valued their participation. To buy into this community effort, students first had to feel safe.

Over the years, as teachers have implemented Reading Apprenticeship—first in secondary schools and now also in colleges—building relationships among students has proven to be key to developing students' trust and participation, their willingness to take an active role in their own learning and contribute to the learning of their peers. The students described earlier by teacher Christine Cziko, who learned to exchange defensiveness for collaboration, walked into the very first Reading Apprenticeship classrooms[1] in the fall of 1996; a safe learning community remains just as central to students today.

Building Relationships and Norms for Classroom Collaboration

In middle school, many but not all teachers make sure that students know each other. In high school, it's far from universal for students to know even the names of everyone in their classes. By the time students are in college, building classroom relationships is often a very low priority. As the demands for subject-specific instruction increase, teachers may feel uneasy dedicating time to anything "nonacademic." However, if students are to collaborate in reading and understanding text, then taking time to build classroom relationships and develop norms for interaction is crucial—and pays off academically. Regardless of the age of students and the pressures to cover course content, teachers need simple ways for class members to get to know each other and establish the norms that make collaboration possible.

Building Relationships

Two simple activities are offered as examples of how taking a few minutes for students to share information sets the tone that in this class we expect to get to know each other and work together.

Having students share information from an interests-and-reading survey is an obvious but effective way to begin building classroom relationships. After completing the survey, partners choose a few questions or topics to ask each

BOX 3.2

Interests and Reading Survey Excerpts

One way to help students get comfortable with the norms and goals of a Reading Apprenticeship class is with a survey about students' interests and reading experiences. Students respond to the survey, answer a partner's questions about their responses, and introduce the partner to the rest of the class based on the conversation the two had about the survey. The teacher collects and reviews the surveys for a more in-depth introduction to the new class.

These questions are excerpted from the Interests and Reading Survey in the Assessment Appendix.

PART 1: GETTING TO KNOW EACH OTHER

1. What is your favorite subject in school?

2. What is your favorite pastime or hobby?

3. What obligations do you have besides school?

7. What is your favorite movie?

9. Name one of your favorite musicians/musical groups.

PART 2: GETTING TO KNOW EACH OTHER AS READERS

16. Does your family read in a language other than English?

19. What does someone have to do to be a good reader? (Check **only** the three most important ones.)

31. What kinds of books do you like to read? (Check **all** the ones you like to read.)

38. In general, how do you feel about reading?

PART 3: FINAL REFLECTIONS

39. Write any comments or concerns you have about this class.

40. What do you hope to achieve in this class?

other more about and then decide how to use what they have learned to make introductions to the rest of the class. In this way, students learn many things about one other person and also at least *something* about everyone in the class. Even in a lecture hall, students can turn to a partner nearby to begin a conversation about reading and their lives.

Box 3.2 provides an excerpt from such a survey (which is reproduced in full in the Assessment Appendix).

A walkabout bingo game can loosen up a classroom of strangers *and* make connections to content themes. In a nutrition class, for example, students search for classmates with particular health-related attributes listed on a bingo card: are you a vegetarian, do you know someone with diabetes, do you know your

BMI, do you skip breakfast, and so on? In a five-minute debriefing, students share information they have learned about their classmates and find out what they may have in common. Students laugh to learn that only three of them prefer salad to French fries. Students who have family members with diabetes give each other a sidelong glance. A student who recently started running every morning explains his new understanding of BMI. Two boys grin and acknowledge that they like to cook. (See a sample walkabout bingo card in Box 3.3.)

BOX 3.3

Walkabout Bingo Sample

Directions: Write your name in one of the boxes that describes you. Then walk around the room and talk to as many people as you can to complete the bingo card (the card must not leave your hands). Write in each box the name of a person who fits the description. You can write a name only once. When you finish, sit down. Be prepared to share your findings!

Writes poetry	Writes e-mail	Writes notes to family members	Reads in a language other than English	Has someone in the family who reads in a language other than English
Reads the sports section of the newspaper	Reads the comics section of the newspaper	Has a favorite magazine, titled _____ _____	Has a favorite book, titled _____ _____	Has a favorite website, titled _____ _____
Favorite subject is math	Favorite subject is is music	Favorite subject is is art	Reads science fiction	Reads true-life drama
Reads about video games	Reads how-to books or magazines	Reads computer manuals	Reads cookbooks	Has a favorite author, named _____ _____

CLASSROOM CLOSE-UP 3.2

"I Prefer a Name with Encourage Meaning"

Community college teacher Anne Agard wondered whether the Reading Apprenticeship routines she had been using productively with her upper-level ESL students would work for students at a considerably lower level: students with English vocabularies of no more than a few thousand words. She decided to find out. One of her first assignments involved these "high beginning" ESL students in reading and discussing author Sandra Cisneros's musings about her name and then in writing accounts of their own names, to share with classmates.

"I gave students time to write in their journals about their own names: what their names meant, how they got their names, and how they felt about their names. After about twenty minutes, I had them sit in groups of three, exchange journals, read two other students' writing, and ask each student at least one question about something they would like to know more about. The students then had another ten minutes or so to write more, and they completed the writing for homework."

Here are some unedited excerpts from the class:

Sui Wei: My name is Sui Wei. In Chinese, first name means little flower that belong in the orchid family. It has light yellow flowers and blooms in the fall.

I don't understand all the meanings why my father gave this name to me. I think that it's a beautiful name for a little girl. But it isn't apopiate for a woman. I prefer a name with encourage meaning.

Galina: My name is Galina. That name came into Russia from Greece. In Grecian it means quiet and calm. In Russia it is an ordinary name and doesn't mean nothing. In Byelrussian is sounds like a branch of tree. I didn't like my name until 15 years old. Later I got accustomed to myself name and didn't nervous more.

Anne calls the "My Name" activity "extremely effective in beginning to build a sense of community in the class." Her only adaptation has been to devote *more* time to it, so that every student in the class has a chance to interact with every other student. As the semester progressed, she became increasingly convinced that many Reading Apprenticeship routines in modified form were effective for these lower-level ESL students and "led to comprehension of more challenging texts and the production of more interesting and complex writing than I have generally seen at this ESL level."

Community college ESL teacher Anne Agard gives her "high beginning" ESL students opportunities to get to know each other with a focused writing assignment, "My Name," which simultaneously introduces students to each other and to a process writing approach involving multiple drafts, group work, and peer feedback. In Classroom Close-Up 3.2, Anne describes the first steps of the activity and the richness it brings to her class.

Is sharing this kind of personal information worth the class time it takes? In classrooms where students will work together every day, spending relatively few minutes in activities like these can accelerate students' responsiveness to each other, their willingness to view each other empathically, and their ability to collaborate to understand challenging texts.

For teachers, knowing about students' interests and goals helps in several ways, including to forge connections to the curriculum and to reading, to draw students' interests and experiences into classroom conversation, and to take the role of a more informed mentor. Teachers are able to use this knowledge of individual students fluidly, as students engage in a range of whole class and small group interactions.

Rita Jensen heard from her middle school students that they want their opinions to be known. They were eager to tell her that they want to have choices, they want to talk and share ideas, they want teachers to ask them whether they understand and to help them if they are struggling. As one of Rita's students revealed, it feels important to be asked:

> I have a million things going on inside my head, but no one ever asked
> me about them before.

Developing Class Norms

As students begin to collaborate, a set of student-developed class norms can be a valuable touchstone. For students whose past experiences have made them skeptical that their ideas, and not the teacher's, are the ones that matter, it can be especially important to see that the norms are student-driven—the authentic result of their ideas about what they need to engage in challenging learning. Walter Masuda, who is in the habit of developing "classroom standards" with his community college English 1A students, finds there is an important difference when students feel that the standards are theirs to uphold:

> I have always attempted to create a safe space in my classroom for students to express their thoughts without fear of ridicule or harsh judgment. At the beginning of all my classes, the students and I generate a list of classroom standards that we feel will result in the most productive atmosphere for learning and discussion.
>
> Invariably, the students themselves will suggest that everyone needs to listen to others and to respect differences of opinion. I have found that students are more likely to refer to the course standards during moments of tension when they are the ones who established those standards to begin with.

When posted, as in Walter's classes, norms help students share the responsibility of creating a productive learning environment, and they provide a set of agreements to which students can hold themselves accountable. (Box 3.4 outlines a procedure for involving students in setting class norms.)

Teaching Student-to-Student Academic Conversation

A hallmark of classrooms where Reading Apprenticeship has taken hold is the collaboration students exhibit when talking with each other about texts.

BOX 3.4

Setting Norms for Learning

PURPOSE

Norms are a set of agreements you and your students make so that everyone can invest in learning. Let students know that this class will involve them in sharing their ideas and experiences. What will help them feel safe and supported to share not only what they are confident about but also what confuses them?

PROCEDURE

- You might ask students to brainstorm answers to questions such as these:
  - What makes you feel comfortable in a classroom?
  - Uncomfortable?
  - What are some things the teacher can do to support your learning?
  - Not do?
  - What are some things classmates can do to support one another's learning?
  - Not do?
  - What would get in the way of your learning?
- Offer students time to think individually, or to work in pairs, to gather their thoughts about these questions.
- Have students share their ideas by posting sticky notes on a common poster or by reporting ideas from their partners.
- Begin from students' ideas of things that support or undermine their learning and develop with the class a preliminary set of "norms" for how everyone will support one another's learning in the class.
- Post a large version of the norms and have students add to them as needed.
- Periodically, as issues arise, you may need to return to the norms to remind students of their agreements or to add to the norms.

Because many students will have had little experience engaging in student-to-student academic conversation, they need explicit instruction. High school English teacher Chris Van Ruiten-Greene takes the time to establish a routine of courteous, engaged, student-to-student exchange. She aims for a comfortable social context in which students can easily move into more academic conversations. She also credits the peer collaboration required in these academic conversations with changing students' commitment to learning.

> We begin with what "civilized" discourse looks like. So the first couple of months, that's huge. It's very important. I've slowed down. I've done less. I'm very explicit: Stop, let's greet each other and talk about what you did

on the weekend. I want you to practice being an active listener. You turn toward the person, you have eye contact, you nod when they speak. You ask a question back. Those are things we do.

You have to convince students that asking them to practice those things that don't look like memorizing vocabulary counts in this classroom. They have to know that this too is curriculum.

It is an investment that builds: It is safe, I'm expected to share, I have to share because it counts. If I have to share, it feels better when we are civil.

The key is, they own the text differently in their commitment to the discussion. It is one thing to not turn work in to me, but it is another thing to come to class and have nothing to say. "I feel peer pressure," one of my students said. "I know Macbeth."

Box 3.5 describes additional ideas for scaffolding student-to-student conversation that takes an academic turn. These ideas fall into four categories: be explicit in modeling good listening, be interested rather than evaluative, promote student-to-student conversation, and know how to encourage participation.

With her high school history students, teacher Allie Pitts uses mini-lessons and sentence frames to promote small group, student-to-student conversation:

As I see the need for the growth of particular skills, I try to develop a mini-lesson around those skills. I do activities about the importance of body language and tone of voice, and I do mini practice conversations in which I provide students with sentence starters. For instance, one that tends to come up around midyear is how to effectively invite other students [in your group] to participate. I try to get students to move from "What do you think?" to "What do you think about X's idea that _____?" Kids can be overly corny when they first start using the sentence starters, but they do use them and it does facilitate more effective conversation. Over time, students end up using the language of the sentence starters without realizing it.

Rita Jensen also provides sentence frames, which her middle school students can use to carry out class and peer discussions (see a sample of these discussion supports in Box 3.6). These can be especially valuable as scaffolds for English learners, like Rita's students, but all students benefit from these models of building on each other's ideas and giving evidence for their ideas.

By week six in Rita's class, the results of establishing and working with student-defined norms and scaffolding academic discussions about text are evident in the way "squirrelly" middle school students work in groups productively, learning to use each other as resources, pooling their knowledge, and negotiating shared understandings. Classroom Close-Up 3.3 is a glimpse of this classroom as

BOX 3.5

Scaffolding Academic Conversation

Many students need explicit instruction and support to learn how to carry out academic conversations. Through modeling and reinforcing student behavior during class discussions, you teach students how to participate. You also actively demonstrate that each student's ideas, experiences, and thinking processes are valued and contribute to the learning of the whole group.

EXPLICITLY MODEL GOOD LISTENING

Show interest in student remarks by listening carefully, asking students to make connections between different students' ideas, and acknowledging contributions with a simple but encouraging "Thank you," "Hmmm," or nod. If appropriate, ask a follow-up or clarifying question. Ask students what they notice about the way you listen and respond to comments and how they think it makes the speaker feel; let them know you expect the same behaviors from them—in class discussions and in their partnerships and small groups.

ACCEPT ALL CONTRIBUTIONS

Avoid correcting students *or* praising them for being correct. Instead, be encouraging without setting up a dynamic in which some students' contributions will be seen as more valuable than others': express interest in their ideas, thank students for contributing, or invite classmates to comment on what another student has said.

MOVE TO THE SIDELINES

Encourage students to talk directly to each other when they are responding to each other's thinking. Some teachers find that when they move away from the front of the room or take a seat, students are better able to direct their attention and their responses to their classmates.

ENCOURAGE PARTICIPATION

To encourage all students to participate in class discussions and exchanges of ideas, you can use a variety of ways to call on students equitably without intimidating those who are reluctant to speak up in the whole class setting.

Name cards. Calling on students randomly removes the sense that they are being tested rather than encouraged to offer their ideas. Use name cards made from the class roster to call on individuals, pairs, or groups.

Spokesperson. Speaking for others is often easier for students than speaking for themselves. Ask students to share an idea they heard from someone else or to speak on behalf of their group.

Quick writes. Jotting down ideas sometimes helps students gather their thoughts before sharing something with a partner, small group, or the class. Quick writes also work well as a way to enforce "wait time."

Wait time. Give students time to think. Don't be tempted to fill silences with your own talking—these silences help spur students to speak up. Tell students you will wait for them to think a moment (or finish their quick write) before they respond—and then wait! Let them know they can use this same strategy in their partnerships and group work.

> ### BOX 3.6
>
> # Sentence Frames
> # That Support Academic Conversation
>
> Sentence frames support students to participate in thoughtful, relationship-building academic conversation. These scaffolds are particularly important for English learners, to help them begin the process of getting their ideas expressed.
>
> ASKING QUESTIONS
>
> - When I read . . . on page xx, I wondered . . .
> - After I read . . . on page xx, I got confused about . . . because . . .
> - On page xx . . . I could not understand why . . .
> - Do you think it makes sense for . . . to do . . . after what happened on page xx?
>
> OFFERING EVIDENCE
>
> - I think one reason is on page xx, where it says . . .
> - I don't think . . . could be true because on page xx it says . . .
> - If . . . is true, then that is a good reason to believe that . . . is true.
> - Even though . . . is true, on page xx, . . . is stronger evidence for the opposite idea.
>
> BUILDING ON IDEAS
>
> - I agree with your idea that . . . and I would like to add . . .
> - I like your idea that . . . Do you think that means . . . ?
> - I have a different idea. To me, the evidence . . . on page xx means . . .
> - Would you agree that there is a connection between . . . and . . . ?

a collaborative community in action. Students have the sense that they can solve reading problems, either individually or together.

Building Safety: It's Cool to Be Confused

It's no secret that students will go to great lengths to hide what they perceive as their own inadequacies and to avoid potential humiliation in front of their peers. By the time they are nearing adulthood, students have developed compensation strategies to avoid tasks they do not do well, yet these very tasks can stand in the way of advancement in college and the workplace. To help students become self-directed, strategic readers, teachers must find a way for them to feel safe voicing confusion about what they are reading.

CLASSROOM CLOSE-UP 3.3

"Amidst Familial Gatherings"

Students in Rita Jensen's grade 7–8 English language development class have read a poem by Ricardo Sanchez, "Old Man," made notes on copies of the poem with all their questions and connections, talked with their small groups about their ideas, and now are checking in with the whole class.

Rita opens the discussion. "What are some things that we need to air out in the whole group, to try and find some answers, some things that you're still not sure of? Confusions?"

Hector volunteers, "This one right here, 'amidst familial gatherings.' I had to look it up because none of my . . . anybody in my group couldn't figure out what it meant."

Rita lights up at the opening Hector has provided, "Amidst *familial* gatherings? Oh, this is a great example of a word that looks like another word, isn't it? Okay. What's that middle word, familial? What does that sound like?"

"Familiar," a few students offer.

"Familiar," Rita repeats. "What else does it look like?"

More students chime in, "Family."

"Family," Rita agrees. "So familiar is—you know everybody, right? And a family is people who are close to you, okay? Amidst familial gatherings. What's a gathering?"

Martin says, "Like when people get around?"

Rita restates Martin's idea, "People get together, okay. So what's the problem, still?"

"Amidst," Rita hears from several directions.

Seeing that Vin wants to answer, Rita says, "Vin, what's *amidst*?"

"I looked in the dictionary," he explains, "and it says 'in the middle of.'"

Rita nods and repeats, "In the middle of. So now we can say 'in the middle of family gatherings.' Does that make sense?"

Students murmur agreement.

"Okay," Rita says, then turns back to Hector. "You see how you worked that out? You know, first, you asked your partners. And then they didn't know, so you went to the dictionary. Right? That still didn't really solve it for you, did it?"

"No," Hector says.

"Okay, so what did you do then?"

"I talked it over with the whole class."

Many students believe, often based on their experiences in school, that *already knowing* rather than being confused or wondering is the only thing of value in an academic setting. Students come to believe that knowledge about something is acquired whole: you either have it or you don't. Teachers have the important job of turning this intellectually crippling misconception around, so that students understand that confusion is the perfect starting place for learning.

In Reading Apprenticeship classrooms, teachers emphasize the value of talking about what one does not understand. To develop students' belief in the value of this kind of exchange, some teachers are quite direct: credit for class participation includes sharing reading confusion and questions. Students understand that the more explicit they can be about where in a text they got lost or why they thought something was difficult for them to understand, the more credit they receive. These teachers report that as this idea takes hold and students are acknowledged for discussing their reading difficulties, a noticeable change occurs for many of them.

One Reading Apprenticeship teacher says, "This class values thinking. The more you think, talk, and write about your thinking, the better your grade will be. There may be wrong answers, but there are no 'wrong ideas.'" Another teacher we know posts "It's cool to be confused!" in large print at the front of her classroom.

As a matter of course, most Reading Apprenticeship teachers begin class discussion about a text by soliciting students' confusion or questions. In Will Brown's high school chemistry class, for example, it's not uncommon for students to be called on to explain what *questions*—not necessarily what answers—they have (see Classroom Close-Up 3.4).

Investigating Relationships Between Literacy and Power

Supporting the social dimension of a Reading Apprenticeship classroom is not only about creating a sense of comfort for students to express confusions and have productive academic conversations. Supporting the social dimension also means making room for discussion and analysis of the relationship between literacy and different types of power in society (as appropriate to each subject area), including the role of literacy and learning in students' current and future lives and in the lives of people around them.

Exploring Life Goals

Students may rarely have a chance to consider why they are learning particular skills or gaining knowledge about particular topics. One way teachers introduce an investigation between literacy and power is to ask students to identify individuals in their community whom they admire or whose jobs they might like to do. What kind of education has been valuable to these people? How did they acquire it? Students can interview these individuals to find out what education and training prepared them for their current work, collecting, if possible, a few examples of the texts they must read to be successful—including emails, memos, technical reports, manuals, visual illustrations, and the like. They may also ask questions about the more personal side of literacy in the lives of people they interview—does it make you feel more powerful in your life? How so?

Similar conversations can take place, early in varied content courses, about why it may be of particular value to learn science, to gain math skills, to read literature, to know history. These conversations can be referenced throughout a course to link students' learning efforts to personal and social power.

Other conversations about literacy and power might have an economic thrust. Teachers might ask students to read and discuss a few simple texts highlighting the relationship between levels of schooling, potential jobs or careers,

CLASSROOM CLOSE-UP 3.4

"That's Cool. You're Isolating What You Don't Know."

In Will Brown's Introduction to Chemistry class, students are reading the first section of an introduction to an acids and bases lab. Will invites students to mark down their questions and anything that is not clear.

Later, Will calls on students, one table at a time, and records their questions on the board.

Durrell reads from the text, "'One excellent way to tell whether an acid-base reaction has occurred is to use an indicator in the reaction mixture.'" He then asks, "Is there more than one way?"

Raymond refers to a sentence in the text and asks, "Why do an acid and a base neutralize one another?"

Michael adds, "I also have a question about the neutralizing part. Like he was saying *why*. Mine is, *How long* would it take for them to neutralize each other?"

Mario reads aloud, "'Any acid will react with any base.' Is that true?" he wonders.

Lizzi's question is about a color test for whether a substance is an acid or a base. "Like, how do you know what colors are acids and what colors are bases?"

"Ah, that's one of the big issues of this lab," Will comments as he continues recording students' questions.

When it is Hani's turn to share something she wondered about or did not understand, she identifies a difficult passage and freely admits, "I didn't get this sentence. It says, 'One of the produce [products] of acid and base reactions is always water.' I don't get what that means."

"So how did you mark it?" Will probes.

"I just wrote, 'I don't get it.'"

"That's really cool that you're isolating what you don't get," he says.

Then he tries again to help Hani be more specific about what is causing her confusion. "Is there a word or something?"

"No, it's not a word," Hani says. "I just don't get this sentence."

Will accepts her response and notes that they will work on the sentence later.

Finally, Durrell offers the puzzling word *calorimetric*, which Will and the class help him tease apart.

Reading back over the recorded questions, Will makes some observations. First, he refers to questions such as How do they neutralize each other? and How long does it take? He points out that "you had to understand the text to ask that. The text isn't giving you an answer. Maybe it will. Or maybe you're going to figure it out in lab."

Then he focuses on a different kind of question students had, when they did not understand the text. "I saw a couple of things where you're getting into the issue of clarifying. Hani, [you] had identified a sentence where you weren't sure of what it meant. Durrell had identified a word that he wasn't sure about."

Will emphasizes the importance of clarifying in being able to read science productively. If a reader of science doesn't "get" something, Will explains, that point of confusion needs to be investigated. "Being aware of when you don't know—and really making sure you mark it—that prompts you to fix it." It's important to know when you don't know, he repeats.

and income (see, for example, the data in Box 3.7). For many students, the prospect of economic independence is highly motivating.

Having such discussions about literacy and power can be part of creating a shared context for the effort the class will engage in to read and understand a variety of challenging texts.

Building Relevance with Essential Questions

To support ongoing exploration of literacy and power, some Reading Apprenticeship teachers use thematic "essential questions" and cycle back to

Research About Education and Economic Power

Even a simple investigation of research showing relationships between literacy and financial life trajectories can build motivation and create a shared context for the effort the class will undertake as they engage with challenging texts. Students might be interested in the following research linking education and earnings.

Today's jobs demand greater literacy skills than ever before. By 2018, 63 percent of all jobs will require some college.

Reading and writing proficiency is a key to success in higher education and the workplace. Over 85 percent of jobs in four of the fastest growing occupations will require postsecondary education.

Source: The Georgetown Center on Education and the Workforce, 2011.

■■■

Education pays off in higher median yearly wages:

$22,900 high school dropouts

$32,700 high school graduates

$38,300 some college or an A.A. degree

$54,000 bachelor's degree

$69,800 professional degree

Source: U.S. Bureau of Labor Statistics, 2010.

■■■

Across a working lifetime (age twenty-five to sixty-four), a person's earnings increase dramatically with education level. Earning a four-year college degree is almost twice as valuable as earning a high school diploma, for example.

$ 973,000 high school dropouts

$1,304,000 high school graduates

$1,547,000 some college/no degree

$1,727,000 A.A. degree

$2,268,000 bachelor's degree

$2,671,000 master's degree

$3,252,000 doctoral degree

$3,648,000 professional degree

Source: The Georgetown Center on Education and the Workforce, 2011.

these regularly during a unit of work. Essential questions that support students in reflecting on the role of literacy in various contexts can build motivation and engagement by helping students discover authentic reasons for persevering in challenging academic work. In Box 3.8, for example, one set of essential questions invites students to investigate power relationships in texts related to people's human and civil rights; a second set of questions focuses on the power of being informed about healthy diet. Essential questions are not limited to inquiry into the power of literacy, of course. In Chapter Five, we consider essential questions again, in their more general role of helping students sustain an inquiry across multiple texts and synthesize information that essential questions elicit.

BOX 3.8

Sample Essential Questions to Build Motivation and Engagement

For students exploring a set of history texts about the topic of human and civil rights, the following essential questions deepen their understanding of the role and power of literacy for securing and extending people's human and civil rights:

> What rights are important to people?
>
> How have people used their First Amendment rights to secure and extend these rights?
>
> How has literacy affected people's ability to secure and extend their rights?

For students reading a selection of science and social science texts focused on nutrition and national obesity trends, especially as these trends affect young people, the following essential questions focus on the power of literacy as it relates to the health of people they care about, including themselves:

> What factors are contributing to the epidemic increases in obesity and diabetes?
>
> How do these factors relate to me, my family, my friends, and my community?
>
> What can people do to reverse the alarming trends in obesity and diabetes rates?
>
> How does literacy affect people's ability to take charge of their own health?

In academic literacy or English classes, students might consider what literacy has meant to authors whose writing has been personally meaningful or what literacy has meant to groups of people and their role in society:

> How do people's experiences shape their attitudes toward reading?
>
> Why do people read?
>
> How does literacy open and close doors in people's lives?

Source: These and other essential questions organize students' reading in the three units of the *Reading Apprenticeship Academic Literacy Course.*

Building the Personal Dimension

> I was scared of picking up books. I didn't even want to pick up a book. I was petrified of English. Now I'm there going, "Cool, I can understand this." Actually picking up books now, I like picking up books. It's thumbs up.
>
> —Greg, grade 9 student

One of the most striking changes we see in Reading Apprenticeship classrooms is in how students view their relationships to literacy and learning. The power and agency acquired with even the most modest improvements can motivate students' renewed efforts toward increased mastery of academic literacy.

Greg, the ninth grader just quoted, had been in "resource" English, not freshman English, at the beginning of the school year. A few weeks into the semester, he joined a regular English class where students were "Talking to the Text," using "big words" like "metacognition" and working collaboratively. By the end of the year, even though Greg is still reading below grade level, he is thrilled to report, "I can pick up a book and just read it." One of the biggest differences for him, he says, "is actually knowing how good I am at reading." And he intends to keep getting better:

> I want to get up to the most good books. Like I had kids in some of my classes say, "Oh, yeah, this is a cool book. You should read it." Once I get going on more reading, then I'm going, "Okay, I'll pick out that book."

Why Read? Setting Authentic Purposes

For Greg, the social motivation of being able to read the books his classmates value is an authentic reason for becoming a better reader. In addition to other reasons he may have, Greg wants to be able to respond when people in his classes say, "Oh, yeah, this is a cool book."

In Nancy Ybarra's developmental English class, where most of her community college students are English learners, many students are motivated to take advantage of the opportunities that brought their families to the United States. They know that reading well is the key. Early in the semester, Nancy has the class read and discuss a newspaper article about a group of immigrant students who get together on Saturday mornings to read and discuss Dante's *Inferno*. "Why would they do that?" Nancy asks. It turns out that her students can relate (see Classroom Close-Up 3.5).

Not all students, of course, approach the opportunity of becoming a better reader with authentic reasons for reading. Some deny the value of reading entirely. Michele Lesmeister, for example, was used to hearing from her Adult

CLASSROOM CLOSE-UP 3.5
"I Want to Be a Teacher"

Community college teacher Nancy Ybarra passes out a copy of a newspaper article titled, "Dante's devotees meet eagerly each Saturday." She asks her developmental English students to read the article and talk about it with a partner. "I want to see what you think of it," she says, somewhat mysteriously. In each pair, at least one of the students is an English learner.

As partners talk over their ideas about a group of immigrant high school students who get together at a coffee shop every Saturday to read and discuss Dante's *Inferno* with their teacher, Nancy moves around the room, listening in. Then she brings the class together for discussion about why the students in the article would get together on the weekend to read a very difficult text. Her students appear to make connections to their own reasons for showing up in Nancy's class.

Teacher: Why on earth would these kids be motivated to do that?

Jorge: In the summer program, all the other students knew the Greek gods and all that other stuff, and they didn't. They felt outcasted. So I guess that motivated them to learn more. So they want to study harder, and I guess that's why they're doing this little club thing at a coffee shop.

Tomas: Probably because their parents come from different countries, third world countries, so they just feel motivated to learn more. My mom comes from El Salvador. She came here when she was like twenty and she's never gone to school here.

One of her biggest goals for me is go to school. That's all she wanted, you know. And like for me, I've never really enjoyed school, but I can relate to those kids that once they start learning, it becomes pleasant to you. It gives you a good feeling. Not only that, it gives you confidence.

Teacher: So you think those kids are getting some kind of good feeling inside from what they're doing.

Tomas: Of course. If not, they wouldn't be doing it.

Teacher: Actually, I talked with Tan about it. Can you share what you were saying, Tan?

Tan: When I come here my English is not very good. So I must practice more. I went to a dance school [where] I have some friends. We make a group. After that time we talk together and some people ask me, I can answer. Because I want to practice my English. Because I study but normally I cannot answer directly. [If] somebody ask me, I must think of how I answer. Of how it is. But when I practice every day, my English is improve a little bit.

Teacher: A lot, a lot. Did you want to say something, Jessica?

Jessica: I think people that are born here don't appreciate that they could get things easily. Like people who come from other countries, they know they have to work hard to get where they want to get, and they want to get farther. Like my mom has been working since she was ten, selling fruits. And I'm like, I don't want to do that. I want to be a teacher. So, I don't know. They want to become something more.

Basic Education/GED students, "Why should I read when I can get the information some other way?"

Michele was determined to break through her students' resistance. When she first tried Reading Apprenticeship, one of her early moves was to help students brainstorm authentic reasons to read. Initially, students' responses were brief, and the resulting list was limited. But in the days that followed, a student asked if Michele would add a new reason to the list. Another reason came up in class conversation. Eventually, someone hung a marker on a length of yarn next to the chart so anyone could contribute to the list, at any time. Someone else added blank lines as a reminder that the list was still in process. (See Classroom Close-Up 3.6 for the list Michele's students created.)

Michele reflects with satisfaction on the way students appropriated the list, once they saw that it really was their own:

> I think when I opened the class with this activity, students were waiting for the "right" answer to be given. There was no right answer; all answers were right. The final poster has several blank lines waiting for others to contribute. This is yet further proof to me as a classroom teacher that students yearn for a sense of community when they come to school.

The "Why do we read?" document is an important part of Michele's classroom. It is written in students' own words and has been instrumental in answering students' increasingly less frequent complaint, "Why are we learning this?" The list reminds students of their individual reasons for being in this class—their short- and long-term goals; it invites them to incorporate new goals suggested by others; and it documents that they are members of a community of people who have reasons to support and take each other seriously. An apparently simple list, it is in fact a powerful recognition of students' legitimacy as learners.

CLASSROOM CLOSE-UP 3.6
Why Do We Read?

When Michele Lesmeister's Adult Basic Education students gave it some thought, they found a surprising number of important reasons *they* read, even though most had never really thought of themselves as "readers."

- Helps us learn
- Gain new knowledge
- Become better readers
- Explore the world (from wherever we are)
- Being able to read protects our civil right
- Improves communication skills in speaking and writing
- Reading allows us to find our way in this world
- Gives us options for being a better parent
- Is one way to relax and rest or sleep
- Helps us have a superior relationship with others
- Improves my vocabulary

- Shows me how to do certain things like make a recipe or fix something
- Gives us a way to feel better
- Encourages us to receive a better education
- Helps us be informed about current events and local happenings
- Provides some fun and pleasure
- Gives us something to discuss with our family and friends
- Reading is a way to get a job or job improvement
- Makes our lives easier
- Improves brain function
- Keeps us young
- Allows us to be respected by others
- _____
- _____

Building Reader Identity

By asking students to learn something new, we are, in effect, asking them to become someone new.[2] For many students, the sense of fixed identities ("I'm not a reader," "I'm not a good student," or "I don't have that kind of brain") is a powerful barrier to learning. When teachers are able to provide consistent support for students to try on new ways of acting, thinking, and interacting, we have seen evidence of significant shifts in academic identity over the course of an academic year and sometimes within a single semester. In Reading Apprenticeship classroom studies, where students had yearlong opportunities to be mentored in the reading and thinking processes of the disciplines, case study interviews revealed profound shifts in students' conceptions of reading, reading practices, and their identities as readers and students. In the classes overall, the shifts represented in the interviews were frequently accompanied by improved course grades, decisions to take additional academic classes, and score increases on standardized tests of reading comprehension.[3]

The importance of helping even the most discouraged students to reinvest in themselves as learners cannot be overstated. Even the smallest increments of success build momentum for the persistence and the stamina that will continue to build students' reading success and reshape their reader identities.

Negotiating Success

Eduardo, an inexperienced reader in Will Brown's Introduction to Chemistry class, is an example of the many students who need small, but consistent, invitations to build a new academic identity. Over time, Eduardo's initial stance of disinvestment and resistance shifted to one of interest and participation as it began to dawn on him that his teacher was on his side. Will persistently focuses his instructional moves and interactions with Eduardo through a single criterion: *Will this encourage or discourage this student from investing himself in the learning process?* Classroom Close-Up 3.7 recounts how Will and Eduardo were able to shift Eduardo's learner identity from the bravado of failure toward well-supported success.

At the college and adult education level, issues of reader identity remain salient. Although college students have made a choice to continue their education and to pursue personal academic goals, many are underprepared for college level courses and may carry with them a negative view of their academic abilities. But when students of any age are supported to succeed, and do so, they feel better about themselves and what they can accomplish. Students in Michele Lesmeister's Adult Basic Education/GED class answered a question at the end of the semester about how their understanding of reading had changed since their attendance in her class. Students' responses might also be understood as commentary on how their academic identities had changed since attendance in the class:

"I am understanding so much more . . . we practice in class and that helps me a lot because I can understand what I am reading. I want to explore the things I have in my mind and I think this will help me."

"My understanding changed about 80 percent. Now I feel more comfortable in my reading."

"In other classes, I felt blindfolded. My reading a lot has helped me have contact with other people, and the free talking style has helped my reading get bigger and in many different books."

"Feeling better while I read after I attended class."

CLASSROOM CLOSE-UP 3.7
Choosing Not to Fail

In September when we first meet Eduardo in Will Brown's high school chemistry class, he is uncooperative and unmotivated. He keeps up a steady stream of negative patter, and when Will reminds the class to work quietly, Eduardo replies, "We don't have to." In a class discussion, Eduardo announces that he does not care if he fails.

At the same time, however, Will notices that Eduardo enjoys being part of the classroom discussions, even if only to tell a classmate that he can't hear her or to piggyback on another student's idea with an offhand, "Sounds good."

When called on, however, Eduardo often declines to participate or claims that his idea has already been given. Will encourages him, nonetheless. "It's important to hear different voices," Will reminds Eduardo, as he persists in calling on him.

Likewise, during group work, Will focuses on Eduardo's potential contribution rather than his misconduct, asking an idle Eduardo, "How are you contributing to the group?" When the reply is that he has no book because of a library fine, Will's focus is on solving the problem rather than laying blame. The following day, Eduardo's resistance softened, he comes into class on time and signals to Will that he is taking his hat off as part of his new willingness to join the class.

During the ensuing weeks, Eduardo expresses concern that the class materials are too difficult, and Will expresses confidence in Eduardo's capabilities. Will shares strategies he uses to make science reading more interesting and comprehendible, and students discuss what is easy, hard, interesting, and confusing for them. Eduardo's confidence increases both by the realization that reading science requires effort of everyone, including expert readers like Will, and by the metacognitive reading routines (see Chapter Four) that help him identify his areas of confusion and provide support for solving reading problems.

In addition, through metacognitive conversations, Eduardo's conceptions of schooling surface and are thus on the table for negotiation. His idea that reading proficiency is a fixed trait and that collaboration is cheating both are challenged by his experience of his own improving reading proficiency and the amount of learning he is able to benefit from and contribute to as a member of a collaborative group in Will's class.

Finally, seeing his efforts pay off is a crucial factor in Eduardo's turnaround. In late November, after getting back a corrected test, he serenades the room: "I . . . got . . . a . . . B . . . and . . . I'm . . . so . . . happee."

Despite his real progress, Eduardo has so many incompletes that he is in danger of failing the semester. Will's grading policy, which allows up to 80 percent credit for late assignments, means that Eduardo can make the choice *not* to fail, and he does.

In the second semester, Will continues to encourage and guide Eduardo, and each success contributes to the next. Eduardo goes on to earn an A.

In an interview in June, Eduardo notes that he is no longer the student who was willing to fail. He has a new academic identity. Now, he says, "Science seems interesting to me. So I like to read."

Investigating Personal Reading Histories

Transforming one's identity, seeing oneself in a new light, is often initiated by reflecting on the experiences that have shaped that identity. An assignment that involves students in exploring their personal reading histories gives them an opportunity to identify events or individuals in their lives that have helped or hindered their growth as readers. In such a "personal reading history" assignment, students are asked to think back over their reading experiences and identify key moments in their development as readers.

Teachers have used variations of the personal reading history assignment to draw out students' positive and negative experiences in particular subject areas as well, tailoring the prompts to focus on experiences of reading and learning in science or math, for instance. *What supported your reading and learning in science? What discouraged it? Think of times you felt like an insider in math, and times you felt like an outsider.*

By pairing up with another student to share their reading experiences, students can begin to build the social connections that will support the collaborative work ahead, when they will grapple together with academic texts and tasks. By also sharing with the whole class their supportive and discouraging experiences in their growth as readers, students can start to see how the types of readings they and others find appealing, as well as those they avoid, are related to experiences around such texts in the past. In the case of negative reactions to particular texts or subject areas, they can begin to uncouple their emotional reactions from the reading they need to do. (See Box 3.9 for a description of the personal reading history assignment.)

In Walter Masuda's English 1A course, his community college students create and share personal reading histories as one of their first assignments. Walter believes this assignment has two important benefits—personally for the students and to help him achieve his goals for students' reading and writing:

> Certainly the kind of reflection that I want students to conduct as they attempt to understand difficult texts was enhanced by having them think about their own challenges and successes as readers. Then, too, knowing that their peers also had similar concerns about their reading, and were willing to share those personal concerns with others, helped to build a sense of trust and camaraderie among the students. Although students did not rate this activity at the top of their lists when surveyed about its usefulness in helping them to write better papers, I feel that it set the stage for the kind of reflective dialogue that would serve them well as they engaged in other Reading Apprenticeship routines more directly related to the educational goals I set for the class.

BOX 3.9

Personal Reading History

PURPOSE

Everyone has a "reading history." For some students, reading has had mostly positive associations, with supports from which to build an even stronger identity as a reader. For others, being able to reshape a negative reader identity often depends on reflecting on personal moments or experiences that created reading barriers. When students reflect on and share their personal reading histories, they have an opportunity to view themselves and their classmates more generously, as "readers in progress," with reader identities they can understand and change.

PROCEDURE

TEACHER MODEL

- Create your own personal history of some key moments or events in your development as a reader. Respond to the following prompts, being sure to include both positive and negative experiences:

    - What reading experiences stand out for you? High points? Low points?

    - Were there times when your reading experience or the materials you were reading made you feel like an insider? Like an outsider?

    - What supported your literacy development? What discouraged it?

- Read your personal reading history to the class, and invite students to interview you about your reading history.

STUDENT ACTIVITY

- Provide students with these same reading prompts and ask them to use the prompts to create their own personal reading histories.

- Have partners share their histories. Explain that the listening partner must not interrupt, but that after both partners have shared, their job is to discuss what they learned about each other. What were some similarities in the barriers and supports they experienced? What were some differences or surprises?

WHOLE CLASS ACTIVITY

- Bring the class together and invite volunteers to share what they learned were similarities and differences in reading experiences and what made them feel like insiders or outsiders.

- Record these ideas for everyone to see.

- Review these ideas in view of the class norms. Add any new norms that students think will further contribute to maintaining a safe inquiry community.

One outcome of conversations about personal reading histories can be for students to recognize the variety and range of texts that "count"—for example, in science or math—triggering a broader appreciation for reading in a field. A class brainstorm of what counts as reading in science might include such texts as articles on personal health, technology articles and websites, mechanics manuals, environmental simulations, chemistry simulations, science fiction, topographical maps, collections, biographies, news about NASA projects, science museum exhibits, field guides to plants and animals, and so forth.

Such brainstormed lists help to enlarge students' concept of themselves as potential readers of science. Students who may have proclaimed that they don't like reading science and never understand what they are reading may realize that there are science texts they read, enjoy, and learn from—that their reader identity is more nuanced than they had been allowing and likely has room for further growth and elaboration.

Building Agency, Confidence, and Dispositions for Learning

Students whose long school histories are filled with largely passive learning experiences may have lost any sense of academic agency. They may be puzzled and even angry about being asked to think for themselves. To marshal and focus the effort required for academic work, they will need support for developing key dispositions for approaching and engaging in challenging tasks. They will need to develop dispositions to be interested and critical learners—curious, able to tolerate ambiguity, and expecting to construct understanding—not simply to carry out prescribed procedures.

Building Agency

Community college anthropology teacher Sandy Wood believes that faculty and students have colluded in what she calls the "accommodation dance" and must work toward other ways of interacting that help students find their own agency as learners:

> We have lowered our expectations of student learning, and students have come to expect to be taught via lecture—and with little reading on their own—the content of the tests they will take.
>
> I strongly feel that a central issue in my course is trying to engage students in "seeing" themselves as readers and lifelong learners. The reader and learner identity issues that emerged from our journals and class discussion were the most fruitful, and many students told me that this was the first class where these issues were discussed *in their student lives*.

In Classroom Close-Up 3.8, Sandy's students respond in their journals to her efforts to incorporate Reading Apprenticeship reading and thinking routines into her introductory anthropology course.

Cindy Ryan greets her grade 9 academic literacy students on the first day of school with the information that they have been "handpicked" for her course. "There was something in your file that caught someone's attention," she says. In effect, she tells them they are in her academic literacy class because they have been selected to succeed. And that is how she treats them, as capable students invested in their own learning. At the end of the year, students write reflections about their ability to take increasing control of their reading, in some cases to actually enjoy reading:

> "As a reader from the beginning of the year to today, I can read longer. I actually get interested in the book that I am reading. I also notice that I use more thinking, for example like I really think about what I read to try to understand it."

> "I feel that every one should take this class in freshman year. All of what I have learned in this class has and is helping me in all of my other classes. I am the first out of six kids [in my family] to make it on an honor roll (A/B)."

> "When I first started this class I was scared. I have discovered that I have courage to read stuff that I couldn't read. I'm more confudent. Also I need to work on spelling."

Fostering a Code-Breaking Stance

As Cyndy Ryan's academic literacy students reflect at the end of the year, students need to develop the disposition to remain confident in their own abilities and to value persistence—for example, through motivating

CLASSROOM CLOSE-UP 3.8

"Does It Really Matter What I Think?"

Students' journal comments about community college teacher Sandy Wood's attention to whether they can read and understand their assigned anthropology textbook range from annoyed to grateful. Although the dissenters are a minority, their resistance reflects, in part at least, the passivity they have developed over their years in school:

> "Does it really matter what I think the author is saying or means? Isn't the issue *what we are expected to know . . . what you want us to know for the test?*"

Most students, however, appreciate that they are being encouraged to confront the challenges of reading college-level texts and the reality of what it means to be academically literate. The average reading level at Sandy's community college is grade 8; her

anthropology students' average reading level is grade 10; and her course materials are written at grade 13:

> "I never understood before about academic reading and that it is different from just plain old reading. Why didn't anyone ever tell me before?"

> "It is great to have a teacher that truly cares about whether or not we learn."

> "It's very hard for me to comprehend and understand what I am reading. Instead of filling myself with frustration, it's just better to ask for help if needed and other resources that can help comprehend what is being read and use it as a key to improve and get to the point where it'll just become easy and I will want to keep reading."

self-talk—while struggling through challenging text. It can take time for students who have not read extended text in many years, perhaps in their whole lives, to build up stamina for the challenge of reading long passages or for long periods of time, especially when they lack knowledge about a topic. They will need to learn to approach unfamiliar text with a *code-breaking stance,* trusting that they have analytic skills and can use strategies to solve problems of comprehension, rather than giving up at the first difficulty they encounter.

Teachers have a crucial role in supporting students to negotiate a transition from disengagement and alienation to more positive engagement and self-investment. To help students appreciate what they *do* read, and to make it clear that they are not the only people who have difficulty with particular texts, many Reading Apprenticeship teachers invite students to bring to class any texts they feel confident reading but think might confuse others. Many students bring song lyrics or computer or technical manuals of some kind, but the sheer range of texts they read outside school can be surprising—and can help to redefine what counts in their minds as reading.

This assignment has multiple benefits. It is an early and important step in building a community in which students know each other's interests and strengths, share their reading processes, and present themselves as competent readers in their own right. Students who have thought of themselves as "non-readers" when limiting this term to school-assigned texts come to see themselves as competent readers of particular materials, topics, and genres.

Students' sense of competence is further bolstered when a teacher is willing to share his or her efforts to comprehend these student-owned texts. Students "own" these texts because they bring to them relevant experience and background knowledge. Listening to teachers try to make sense of texts like gaming directions or technical manuals by "thinking aloud" (verbalizing their process of trying to make sense of texts) in front of the class often results in predictable hilarity; at the same time, this kind of modeling also underscores the point that successful reading requires an understanding of how language is used differently and conveys different content in different contexts. It should also signal students that they probably have more reading expertise—with certain types of texts whose language, content, and "rules" they already know—than they might think. (Box 3.10 provides a few guidelines and suggestions for an eye-opening "stump the teacher" introduction to thinking aloud.)

Thinking aloud with out-of-school texts demonstrates to students that in the course of school, professional, and recreational lives, all individuals encounter texts that they find easy to understand, and all also encounter texts that confound them. Despite what students believe, it is important for them

BOX 3.10

Modeling Thinking Aloud with Out-of-School Texts

PURPOSE

This informal introduction to the "think aloud" process puts the teacher in the public role of a reader who must try to unlock the door to a difficult text—with a limited set of keys. Students, on the other hand, may recognize and enjoy their own expertise at reading the particular types of text that stump a teacher but not themselves.

PROCEDURE

- Bring in a few examples of out-of-school texts (street map, restaurant menu, advertisement, bus route) that you can project (or copy) for all students to see.

- Ask students to take notes on what they notice you saying or doing as you try to understand the texts.

- Model thinking aloud with one or two of the texts:

  - Preview the text. Take a look at its parts and any graphics. Out loud, tell yourself what you do or do not know by looking the text over quickly.

  - If you are able to make any connections to your background knowledge or experience, describe what they are, out loud to yourself.

  - Start reading aloud, and stop when you get confused by a word, phrase, or sentence.

  - Out loud, identify the problem and ask yourself questions to try to solve it. Out loud, describe the problem-solving process you are going through as well as your reactions to the text.

  - Agree with yourself that you may have to "tolerate ambiguity," maybe having only a guess about the meaning of the roadblock you identified.

  - Continue reading to see whether the roadblock clears itself up, and let yourself know how, out loud, if it does.

- Ask students what they saw you doing as you worked to understand the texts.

- Invite students to bring to class texts that they feel confident and capable reading but that they think might be difficult for others (you, especially) to understand.

- Project or distribute copies of these for the whole class.

- Take the classroom challenge and model thinking aloud with one or two texts nominated by your students.

to understand that reading is not a magic skill that they either have or do not have. Rather, reading, as we understand it, is an ongoing process of problem solving, and some of the problems posed by a text will be greater than others. Developing social norms and discourse routines to support collaborative problem solving helps to assure students that working together with each other and the teacher, they can solve problems of understanding as they read. They can learn strategies, skills, and habits that will help them become more engaged, fluent, and competent readers.

Students carry with them into the classroom a wealth of proficiencies and dispositions that can be drawn upon to support their reading development. They live in complexly structured social worlds that they "read" with considerable skill. They can interpret what a facial expression, tone of voice, and style of clothing predict about how a peer will behave. They may avidly explore the meaning of song lyrics, movies, and other mass media. Many first- and second-generation immigrant youth function as culture brokers and language interpreters for their families, interacting with considerable agency and skill with social service bureaucracies, health professionals, and others. Often, young people are earning money for themselves or their families.

From many years in diverse classrooms, we have come to see secondary and college students as having powerful resources that can be tapped in a learning environment that is safe, respectful, and collaborative. In such classrooms, inviting students' self-awareness, strategic problem solving, knowledge, and experience serves instructional ends. We have also seen that when teachers invite students to reflect on the social competencies and strategic abilities they display outside the classroom and share them with others, it helps students to make connections between these capabilities and those required by academic reading tasks.

Students of all ages want to feel skillful and in control of a widening arena of their own activities, capable of making decisions and taking action to influence their experiences. To draw on this desire for agency and competence, teachers must put students in the driver's seat. Teachers cannot know how their students experience a reading task: to provide well-targeted instructional support, teachers must rely on students as authorities about their own experiences as readers. By inviting students to share what they like and dislike, what they read outside of school, how they go about reading, what problems they encounter, and what they know about making sense of texts, teachers engage students as partners to promote students' own growth as readers.

In an interview at the end of her first year using Reading Apprenticeship approaches with her students, Lisa Krebs, a grade 10 English teacher, put it this way:

> It's interesting, all the benefits of reading. You never really connect reading with the litter on campus, or reading with attendance. Even my desks were cleaner, like there wasn't time to doodle. There's physical evidence that they were more mentally engaged. It starts with reading, but it's really about how kids feel about themselves, and their own abilities and their own power.

In one grade 9 classroom, featured in Classroom Close-Up 3.9, almost every student faced challenges that are often equated with an unpromising future; instead, a Reading Apprenticeship approach and unusually strong teacher support revealed to these students a new understanding of their very real academic abilities and power.

Throughout this book we necessarily take on one topic at a time: one chapter, one dimension, one aspect of one dimension, one example, one quote. But an important understanding of Reading Apprenticeship is the perpetual interaction of the dimensions and the fluidity with which they influence any particular classroom moment. It is not the case, for example, that the personal and social dimensions are addressed early in the year with some community-building activities and *then* the learning can start. Yes, they are addressed early because they *are* foundational, but their importance never wanes. Rita Jensen, whose middle school ESL students taught her much of what she knows about Reading Apprenticeship, offers this bit of advice:

> Teachers get confused that doing particular activities at the start of the year to set a classroom culture is the extent of how the social and personal dimensions operate in Reading Apprenticeship. If you're paying attention to the social and personal dimensions, building safety in your classroom takes more than a getting-to-know-you activity or norm building or personal reading history. These are important, no question, but they're just the beginning of what it means to build a classroom that feels safe. And students do need to feel safe if you're asking them to talk about being confused about something you asked them to read.
>
> It's also important to keep in mind how all the dimensions keep interacting, all the time. Maybe the next time students are reading something really hard, you ask them to stop and reflect with a partner. They're going to need to be metacognitive, they're going to need to collaborate, they have an opportunity to develop stamina and to use cognitive strategies, they're probably going to learn something—all from a three-minute Think-Pair-Share—if the social and personal dimensions are being tended. The more experience you have with Reading Apprenticeship, the more you will appreciate the genius of how the dimensions are always interacting and the social and personal dimensions are always instrumental to the learning. They make the learning possible!

Assessing Effort and Growth

Grading and assessment policies are an important signal to students of what is valued in any class. When a teacher is working to establish a learning environment that fosters new relationships to reading and learning and collaborative interactions among students, grading policies that reward individuals

CLASSROOM CLOSE-UP 3.9

Becoming a Student

In this unusual classroom, a special education teacher and an English teacher, Pam Myette and Jacqueline Dzubak, work with twenty ninth graders who have been selected for a double English period in which they receive extra support to engage with the regular—and challenging—freshman English curriculum. Many of these students are classified for special education; two are English learners. They have never seen themselves as readers or as college bound, and only two had been consistently productive in middle school.

During the class visited below, students are reading chapter 9 of *To Kill a Mockingbird*.[4] They have been asked to Talk to the Text and locate and highlight a quote that describes Atticus's bewilderment regarding Maycomb County. The instructions include a question about the author's intent: What do you think Atticus is implying and why did Harper Lee include it?

Text-Based Class Discussion

Teacher 1: All right, let's hear some feedback. What do you think?

Cab: (*Referring to highlighting he has made on his text, boxed below*) Atticus is saying that he knows how to face his children when they ask him a question, but the one thing he probably *doesn't* want is them to ask questions around the town and get *their* opinion.

> You know what's going to happen as well as I do, Jack, and I hope and pray I can get Jem and Scout through it without bitterness, and most of all, without catching Maycomb's usual disease. Why reasonable people go **stark raving mad** when anything involving a Negro comes up, is something I don't pretend to understand . . . I just hope that Jem and Scout come to me for their answers instead of listening to the town. I hope they trust me enough.

Teacher 1: Why doesn't he want them to ask other people questions?

Cab: Probably their life would change from that.

Teacher 2: (*Checking that students understand why Atticus is concerned for Jem and Scout*) What is Atticus discussing with Uncle Jack? What is the context of this discussion? What is happening in Maycomb County all of a sudden?

Nola: Atticus is defending the Negro, which is like now people are changing their mind when the Ewells, when before they were for them.

Teacher 1: (*Looking over Cab's highlighted text*) Cab pulled out some good language here, the whole town has gone "stark raving mad" when anything involves a Negro. In the line before that, what's some other language [Atticus] uses to describe Maycomb's problem?

Teacher 2: Go back to the text.

James: Bitterness.

Teacher 1: Right . . . What did he call it?

Sandor: Disease.

Teacher 1: Disease, he's calling it disease. Why does he call it that?

Vincent: I have a question. I don't think it says it's a disease.

Teacher 1: Is he talking about a real illness? A physical illness?

Jason: No, like mental.

Vincent: I thought he was talking about always sometimes always happens each year.

Teacher 1: Okay, it's around. It's contagious.

Awele: He means everybody around seems to be catching this rumor that's going around and so they're saying metaphorically it's a disease, and he doesn't want Scout and Jem to get caught up in that.

Teacher 1: Right, so it's a contagious thing—metaphorically. Woo. Good job. Metaphorically. Okay, so metaphorically, the disease is not really a physical illness, but it is a disease of thinking, a way of thinking, the prejudiced way. Did everyone get that?

Text-Based Small-Group Questioning

Following the discussion, students move into small groups, where they share the questions, clarifications, and visualizations they prepared for homework the previous night. Pam reminds students that they are collaborators: "Help each other out. Some people are going to have some good questions. You may discuss those. Other people may need some help figuring out the chapter. Give them some help. Give them some support. Discuss the chapter. Discuss what is really, really going on, what's important, and what you want to remember and discuss with the whole group."

The questions students share in small groups vary in sophistication, but many are those any teacher could appreciate:

> Why did Atticus think it was so important to defend Tom Robinson?
>
> How does the fact that Scout's dad is helping a black man affend [affect] the town and the Finch family?
>
> Why is it so hard for Scout to restrain herself from hitting her cousin Francis?
>
> Why did Scout refuse to fight that mean kid in school? And why is this important?

Small-Group Theme Discussion

In another group, students discuss the themes the class is focusing on in the novel. Clark claims he can squeeze all four themes out of a single paragraph, and his partners check his reasoning.

Awele: Okay, go ahead, explain.

Clark: (Reading from the text) "Because I could never ask you to mind me again. Every lawyer gets at

least one case in his lifetime that affects him personally. This one's mine, I guess." That's like she's *coming of age,* learning new stuff.

Awele: Okay.

Clark: And then, "You might hear some ugly talk about it at school, but do one thing for me if you will—"

Awele: That's *prejudice.*

Clark: "You just hold your head high and keep those fists down. No matter what anybody says to you, don't let them get your goat." That's like *courage.*

Awele: Yeah . . . okay.

Clark: The next one's *justice-injustice.* "Try fighting with your head for a change . . . it's a good one, even if it does resist learning." That's it.

Awele: (Unconvinced) How is that justice versus injustice, though?

Agreeing with Awele at this point, the third student in their group proposes a different paragraph, and the three continue their discussion.

When these previously inexperienced readers graduated from high school, their two ninth-grade teachers held a farewell party for them. Almost all were going on to college, many the first in their families to do so. At the party, students talked about how the class reading routines and the way their teachers respected and worked with them had helped launch them as students and readers. Four years later, they held onto the belief that they had become students that year.

---

for right answers and mastery will very quickly undermine student engagement in risk taking and problem solving. Subject area teachers are necessarily concerned that students acquire a body of thought, skills, and content in their courses. However, thoughtfully aligning grading and assessment to focus on effort, progress, and growth, at least in the literacy components of the class, will be key to fostering the personal and social foundation for engaged learning that is so vital to Reading Apprenticeship.

Equally important will be involving students in assessing their own progress, developing further insight into their own reading and learning processes, weighing for themselves how well particular strategies and actions support their comprehension of academic texts, and setting goals for their own growth.

Early on, monitoring student participation and effort will be helpful in signaling to students that investing effort will pay off in deeper comprehension and learning.

■ ■ ■

As we further describe the Reading Apprenticeship framework over the next several chapters, we also introduce Student Learning Goals, which teachers and students alike can use to monitor growth. The goals are organized into categories that parallel the dimensions of the Reading Apprenticeship framework. So, for example, student goals for the social and personal dimensions reflect much of the content of this chapter. They can help students anticipate, direct, and track their classroom interactions and reading behaviors related to a new classroom focus on collaborative problem solving and reader engagement. (Student Learning Goals and suggestions for using them appear in the Assessment Appendix.)

In Chapter Four, we will see how metacognitive conversation—the heart of the Reading Apprenticeship framework—supports students in developing and appreciating their abilities and power as students and readers.

Notes

1. There are two models of Reading Apprenticeship: the *Reading Apprenticeship Academic Literacy Course* and a model for integrating Reading Apprenticeship approaches into disciplinary courses. Originally, Reading Apprenticeship was developed as a framework for a two-semester grade 9 course; this course now includes professional development, a full curriculum, and *Building Academic Literacy: An Anthology for Reading Apprenticeship*. Reading Apprenticeship professional development is also available for teachers of all disciplinary courses and from middle school through college; in this model, teachers incorporate Reading Apprenticeship approaches into their own courses, with their own materials.

2. Feldman, A. (2004). Knowing and being in science: Expanding the possibilities. In E. W. Saul (Ed.), *Crossing borders in literacy and science instruction: Perspectives on theory and practice.* Newark, DE: International Reading Association.

3. Greenleaf, C., & Litman, C. (2004). *Reading Apprenticeship classroom study: Linking professional development for teachers to outcomes for students in diverse subject area classrooms.* San Francisco: WestEd. A chapter based on the study of one chemistry teacher's implementation of Reading Apprenticeship, and its impact on his diverse, urban students, has also been published: Greenleaf, C., Brown, W., & Litman, C. (2004). Apprenticing urban youth to Academic Literacy. In D. Strickland & D. Alvermann (Eds.), *Bridging the literacy achievement gap, grades 4–12.* New York: Teachers College Press.

4. Lee, H. (1960). *To kill a mockingbird.* Philadelphia: Lippincott.

CHAPTER FOUR

Metacognitive Conversation
Making Thinking Visible

The most important thing I do is begin an ongoing metacognitive conversation about making sense of text. Initially, I model, articulating my own processes as a reader as I read aloud. My students and I begin looking at specific places in the text where we have problems understanding, where we have to slow down, where we are uncertain. We talk about what we might do to figure things out; we test various strategies. We talk about whether or not a particular strategy worked and, if so, what we understand as a result. A lighter tone develops as reading becomes less of a mystery and more of a project that we work on together in class.

—Gayle Cribb, high school history teacher

AT THE HEART of the Reading Apprenticeship classroom is metacognitive conversation: an inquiry into how readers make sense of text. The conversation is both internal, as individual readers observe their own minds in actions, and external, when readers discuss what they are noticing, what they are stumped by, and how they are solving reading problems. In a Reading Apprenticeship classroom, metacognitive conversation about reading is an integrated, ongoing topic of study in a discipline: *How* do we read U.S. history, or biology, or calculus, or Shakespeare?

As teacher Gayle Cribb describes, she and her students become very curious about how their minds are working as they read history. Gayle models by articulating her own reading processes, describing her observations about where she needs to figure something out as well as what she does to resolve confusions. Her students take up this investigation, applying it to their own reading processes and discussing what they are learning, sometimes in pairs or small groups, and sometimes as a class.

In Gayle's experience, metacognitive conversation serves to demystify the reading process for her students. When students learn to be metacognitive about the mental and affective processes they are going through as they read, as they hear and observe how their peers and teacher work through challenging texts, they begin to notice when and where their concentration lapses or their comprehension breaks down. From there, they learn to be strategic about using cognitive tools to refocus or solve reading problems, becoming active agents of their own learning. Through such talk, members of a classroom community naturally make their thinking visible to each other—available for reflection, reappraisal, and appropriation by others.

Reading Happens in Your Mind

> You just stop and be like, "Hey, what does it mean? Wait, let me think. How does it work? What is this sentence trying to tell me." I don't think I've always done that. I think maybe this year, you could say.
>
> —Hani, grade 10 student

The speaker, Hani, has just reached the point of realizing that when she reads, sentences are trying to tell her something. Hani is not anomalous. A surprisingly large number of students have never realized that reading is not the same as tracking and saying the words on a page. Comments such as the following reveal just how common it is for students to be unaware that text is supposed to have meaning. They relate "reading" with their experience of learning to read in the primary grades—decoding.

> "Well, it's simple. Reading is saying the words you see when you look at a page." (grade 9)

> "My sister is a good reader because she can pronounce everything, even if it's hard words or big words. She can pronounce it." (grade 10)

> "I think of myself as an 'average' reader. I am pretty good at sounding out my words. It just might take me longer than others." (community college)

Even students who sense a disconnect between "reading" the words and understanding the text don't necessarily know what to do about it.

> "You know sleepwalking? I can move my eyes to the end of the page but not remember anything I read. Like sleepreading." (grade 9)

> "I was busy reading. I don't know what it was about." (grade 9)

Metacognitive conversation is a revelation for these students, an introduction to their own and others' thinking processes. But the value of metacognitive conversation extends to more experienced readers as well—to all readers, in fact. Metacognition makes it possible to take control when reading, to approach increasingly complex texts and a growing range of specialized genres with a sense of efficacy.

> ### BOX 4.1
>
> ## Exploring Students' Concepts of Reading
>
> PURPOSE
>
> Students will have different ideas of what it means to read. When these beliefs are surfaced and recorded for the whole class, they are available for revision or refinement later, as students learn more about the reading process.
>
> PROCEDURE
>
> - Record on chart paper (and save) students' brainstorming ideas about what it means to be a "good reader." Prompt students as needed:
>   - How can you tell if someone is a good reader?
>   - Who is someone you consider a good reader? Why?
>   - What do you have to do to read science well? Math? Literature? History?
> - Do not challenge or "edit" students' ideas. Record all ideas, in students' own words.
> - Later, invite students to refer to this initial list and revise or elaborate on their early ideas about reading. For example the class may modify an early idea that "good readers read fast" into a more complex understanding that "good readers ~~read fast~~ change reading speed depending on how difficult the text is for them and how much they know about the topic."

When introducing metacognitive conversation, teachers may want to invite students to surface their initial beliefs about reading, perhaps by exploring what they think reading is. Students' sometimes simple understandings or misconceptions are then available for revision over time, as students gain more experience investigating their reading process. (Box 4.1 describes an activity to help students surface their concepts and beliefs about reading.)

Introducing Metacognition

> When you read, there should be a little voice in your head like the storyteller is saying it. And if there's not, then you're just looking at the words.
>
> —LaKeisha, grade 9 student

Students quickly pick up on the concept of metacognition, or thinking about thinking. LaKeisha's academic literacy teacher introduced metacognition in September, and within days LaKeisha was not only using metacognition daily but also explaining it to others. She had learned how to look inside her mind and observe her own thinking processes.

Students' responsiveness to the idea of their own thinking is thrilling for teachers as well. Monica Figueroa, a middle school social studies teacher, was delighted with the way her students took to the practice of thinking about their thinking:

> The very first benefit [of Reading Apprenticeship], that I really saw early on, was metacognition, the idea of having them actually think about what they were thinking. It was just so great to me, to have them actually participate in their own brains. That their brains do these miraculous things and they can actually control that! Paying attention to the wheels in their head—knowing that they have wheels—I see the pride growing in them.

Anyone who has worked with adolescents knows that they can be intensely self-absorbed, consumed with questions of individual identity and of their place within their peer group and the world. When we first developed Reading Apprenticeship, we realized that we could use this self-interest to get students thinking about their own reading processes. We thought of this self-absorption as our ally: Why wouldn't adolescent students naturally be motivated to uncover how and what they thought as they read, and to want to compare their thoughts and thinking processes with those of their friends?

Over the years, we have found that most adults have the same fascination with the usually hidden inner workings of their own minds and the minds of others.

Thinking About Thinking

In the previous chapter, we describe an activity in which teachers model thinking aloud as they try to read texts that students bring into class to "stump" them. These are texts the students read comfortably in their lives outside of school, such as computer manuals or song lyrics. In addition to showing students that reading competence is not an absolute state (which their teacher enjoys and they do not, for example), the activity introduces students to a particular kind of metacognitive conversation, the Think Aloud.

Teachers often follow up this initial exposure to thinking about thinking by involving students in a Think Aloud experience that does not involve reading at all, one that allows students to focus almost entirely on metacognition. Such tasks with lower cognitive demands tend to put students at ease with sharing their thinking. (Box 4.2 presents an example of how to introduce students to thinking aloud.) Teachers have invented many other examples appropriate for their contexts and content, including having students think aloud while observing a science experiment.

BOX 4.2

Students Practice Thinking Aloud

PURPOSE

To give all members of a class a low-risk opportunity to practice thinking aloud and to see how available their thinking is to them, model and then have partners take turns describing their thinking as they engage in a nonthreatening cognitive task such as the one described here.

PROCEDURE

- Model thinking aloud metacognitively during the pipe cleaner task that follows (or another of your devising), and have a partner make notes on what you say.

- Display these notes for all to see and ask students to identify and explain examples in the notes that demonstrate metacognition.

- Give each student four or five pipe cleaners and a piece of paper. Assign partners.

- Instruct students that one partner will create a pipe-cleaner creature that can stand on two feet; the other partner will observe and record the creature creator's thinking aloud. Encourage students to be inventive with the pipe cleaners. Set a time limit of two or three minutes.

- Some ideas for the creature creator to think aloud about:

  - What do I predict will be tricky about creating a creature that won't fall over?

  - What do I want my creature to look like and why?

  - What am I thinking and feeling about each step of joining and shaping the pipe cleaners?

  - What am I going to do next and why?

- Have the partners trade roles.

- Ask the partners to choose one or two comments from their combined notes to share with the class.

- Lead a class discussion focusing on metacognitive elements of the comments.

Students also respond with interest when asked to imagine a scenario in which their thoughts are a comment to themselves on what they are doing or thinking at the time. For example, students might imagine an internal metacognitive conversation when they are pitching to a strong batter in a high-stakes game, when they're stuck on mass transit and notice an attractive stranger, when they are on the phone with someone but want to end the call, or when they need to study but are upset by a friend's behavior earlier in the day. Thinking about such scenarios, talking about them with others, or even acting them out makes it clear to students that they can tune into their internal thought processes, which means they can also work to control them. Having students describe these kinds of scenarios using cartoon thought bubbles with metacognitive conversation in the bubbles is a graphic way for students to get in touch with this perhaps strange concept of thinking about their thinking. (Classroom Close-Up 4.1 is

CLASSROOM CLOSE-UP 4.1

Metacognition "At Light Speed"

Grade 9 academic literacy teacher Cindy Ryan introduced the idea of a "metacognitive scenario" by first asking students to think about times when they have conversations with their friends and suddenly wonder, "How did we get to this point in our conversation?"

Students shared their recognition of situations like this, and Cindy asked, "What do you do when you realize this?"

Students explained ways in which they trace the conversation back to its source. Cindy explained that the class was going to do something similar, today. She then introduced an example of a metacognitive scenario: "A student has been daydreaming when the teacher calls on him or her." She showed the class a thought bubble with the student saying "Wait . . . What did she just say?"—and asked

the class to give some examples of what people daydream about in class.

Answers such as "Wondering if I'm going to get my nails done," "Thinking about my mama's paycheck," and "I'm hungry" made it clear that students understood the scenario.

So Cindy asked, "What goes through your mind when the teacher calls on you and you've been daydreaming?" Students offered ideas related to their shock at being caught and stalling to figure out what question or topic the class is on.

"How long does this take? How fast does it happen?" Cindy asked.

Students' response was unequivocal—"At light speed"—and Cindy had her opening to introduce metacognition.

an example of how teacher Cindy Ryan introduced this kind of "metacognitive scenario" activity to her grade 9 academic literacy students.)

Once students have a sense of metacognition and their ability to think about their thinking, they can benefit from a class discussion of the Student Learning Goals for Making Thinking Visible (see the Assessment Appendix). Students should understand that they will be making their thinking visible to themselves and others by monitoring and repairing their reading comprehension and by means of internal and external conversation and writing.

Capturing the Reading Process

When students have explored the general concepts of *metacognition* and *metacognitive conversation* with nonreading activities, an activity called Capturing the Reading Process can direct them from thinking about their thinking to thinking about their thinking *while reading.* In Capturing the Reading Process, students read a specific text to themselves and think about what processes they used as they worked through the text: What mental moves did they make? What exactly did they do with or to the text?

The teacher captures examples of these moves from students on a class list that makes their collective thinking visible. One student may notice, for example, that she lost focus and had to bring her mind back to the text; another may volunteer that neither his partner nor he could understand a specific sentence, so they skipped it; yet another student may offer her process of trying to picture the kind of chemical reaction she was reading about. Box 4.3 describes how Capturing the Reading Process prepares a class to build a "living" Reading Strategies List.

Building a Reading Strategies List

Many Reading Apprenticeship teachers tell us that building and continually referring back to the Reading Strategies List is one of the most important literacy routines they embed into their teaching. By probing students' thinking and reasoning and asking them to share specific examples of their reading processes, teachers help students develop a type of inquiry conversation that is metacognitive and that students can apply to any text.

The Reading Strategies List that a class begins with one particular text will continue to grow as students encounter new texts and new types of texts and so identify new reading processes. The list should be conceived of as a living document, one that remains posted and available for adding to and revising.

It is likely that the list will grow more elaborated as well as longer. For example, if students in a history class have nominated the strategy "ask questions" for their Reading Strategies List, they may at some point want to elaborate with discipline-specific strategies, such as "ask questions about the author's point of view" or "ask questions about whose point of view is not represented." In a science lab, students may elaborate "ask questions" with "ask questions to identify variables" or "ask questions to identify patterns," for example.

Likewise, if students begin with more specific examples, these can later be grouped and labeled—as examples of asking questions, or setting a purpose for reading, or visualizing, or making personal connections, and so forth. (Chapter Seven introduces a number of these umbrella cognitive strategies.)

Over time, even though the Reading Strategies List becomes a less necessary support, students will continue to refer to it when they need ideas for solving particular reading problems. The list also serves as a history of their own growing repertoire of problem-solving strategies.

Walter Masuda, who used the Reading Strategies List in his community college English 1A class, sees its development as an important contribution to students' understanding of metacognitive conversation and an important resource. "Students' high regard for the usefulness of the list," he says, "has convinced me that I should use it in all my writing classes." (Classroom Close-Up 4.2 includes the list that Walter's students developed and were able to refer to.)

BOX 4.3

Capturing the Reading Process

PURPOSE

By sharing their reading processes, students begin to appreciate the great variety in strategies and approaches that different readers bring to a text. They will also see that different people's knowledge and experiences shape the meanings they derive from texts—that meaning is constructed in the interaction between individual readers and texts, not solely in the texts themselves.

Capturing the Reading Process is students' introduction to creating a living and growing classroom Reading Strategies List.

PROCEDURE

- Choose a slightly challenging text that will be intriguing to students.
- Give students time to read silently; monitor to see when most students have finished the reading.
- Ask students to write down a few notes about what they did to make sense of the text: what reading processes they used to solve comprehension problems, stay involved in the text, or make connections from the text to other knowledge or ideas.
- Model one or two examples of your own reading processes from the beginning of the text, such as the following:
  - When I read the second sentence, about reading under the covers, I could picture that in my mind.
  - When I came to the pronoun "they," in the third sentence, I had to check back to the first sentence to be sure "they" meant Kevin's books, not his parents.
- As partners and small groups are sharing their reading processes, circulate to listen in and, as needed, model how to probe for specifics (suggestions follow).
- Invite students to share their strategies first with partners, then in small groups, and then with the class. Help students be specific by probing their reasoning and thinking:
  - What did you do?
  - How did you do that? Where in the text did you do that?
  - Can you give us an example from the text?
  - Why did you decide to do that?
  - How did that help your understanding?
- If students are having trouble articulating their reading processes, introduce some problem-solving strategies:
  - Did anyone have to reread any part? Which part? How did that help?
  - Did anyone think of something else that was related to this text? What was the connection? How did that help?
  - Did anyone have trouble with this part? How did you get through it?
  - Did anyone make a guess about the meaning of an unfamiliar word? How did you do that?
- Record students' ideas on a class list. (Save the list. It will serve as the beginning of the Reading Strategies List that the class will continue to develop.)

CLASSROOM CLOSE-UP 4.2
"Don't Freak Out"

Walter Masuda was intrigued by the support that a Reading Strategies List might offer his community college writing students. His students in English 1A were experienced with annotating text, and Walter saw the Reading Strategies List as an opportunity for students to move easily from private annotations to shared discussion of ways to approach difficult text.

To start, students read and annotated an excerpt from a challenging essay, answering these questions:

- What were some of the thought processes you used as you were reading the passage? You can include anything you were thinking just before, during, and/or after you read the passage.

- Which passages were particularly challenging for you? Why?

- What did you do to make sense of those challenging passages?

After completing the questions independently, students shared with a partner what they had written, and then the whole class engaged in a discussion of the challenges and strategies students had identified. Walter recorded their ideas as follows:

Reading Strategies List
- Imagine myself "in the reading."
- Reread or read more slowly and deliberately.
- Get meaning from context first; use dictionary later as a check on understanding.

- Read passage aloud (or have someone else read passage to us).
- Take a deep breath to quiet the mind.
- Read the last paragraphs first so we know where the reading "ends up."
- Skip to a point in the reading where comprehension is better; go back later to difficult passages.
- Summarize or paraphrase a difficult reading passage.
- Discuss challenging passages with peers.
- Break down reading into smaller chunks.
- Develop a visual (graphic) road map of the reading.
- Get a second opinion.
- Go online to do some research.
- Don't freak out if at first you don't understand something. Keep reading, because an explanation or clarification may be coming up later in the text.

In Walter's view, the power of the Reading Strategies List is that "by giving developing writers access to the thought processes of more expert readers and writers, we give students who might otherwise be at risk for failure the tools they need to succeed. It's one thing to admonish low-performing students that they need to pay more attention to their reading, or that they need to work harder on essay organization, and quite another to give them the 'habits of mind' that could actually make a difference in their reading and writing performance."

Establishing an Inquiry Culture

Students who find academic reading difficult often do not recognize that they are confused or, if they do, may not feel they can do anything about it. Bringing confusion out into the open and establishing an inquiry culture in class can help.

In Reading Apprenticeship classrooms, teachers often begin a text discussion with the assumption that students will have identified particular reading problems they want to solve: "What confusions did you have?" The teacher's question is a reminder that the class operates as an inquiry culture.

Initially, however, when students are asked about their confusions, they may feel uncomfortable exposing uncertainty or considering multiple possibilities, especially if they have learned that school rewards certainty and "right answers." Yet confusion can be a powerful starting point for learning.

To promote students' willingness to explore reading confusions, teachers may find that first they must help students recognize that they *are* confused. For example, community college developmental English teacher Trish Schade explains that she has to work with students to help them notice what they do not understand before they can even begin to articulate their reading process:

> A lot of times students would write that something was easy for them [to read], but if you looked at their summary, it was way off. So initially it was really telling to me that they didn't actually know that they didn't understand.
>
> Most of the students when they first read, it was just to get through it—it wasn't necessarily to understand it. After we started using the logs [metacognitive logs, described later in this chapter] and metacognition, then talking about it and visualizing, they started reading with a different purpose. And if they didn't understand, they would at least be able to ask questions about it. And that was a huge change.

Trish explicitly invites students to recognize what is not making sense or what questions they have as they read. She uses questions such as those in Box 4.4 to probe and facilitate discussion and to let students know they are part of a classroom that values inquiry.

As students identify and describe their reading processes and problems, they will naturally include their problem-solving processes. For many students, the "fix-up steps" in Box 4.5 quickly become automatic when they get stopped by a "roadblock" and need to clarify a point of confusion in a text. The last step, getting outside help, will become increasingly comfortable for students when the collaborative structure of the classroom begins to reveal their peers as valuable outside resources.

In the inquiry culture of a Reading Apprenticeship classroom, students articulate their reading processes with language that develops organically through the Reading Strategies List and metacognitive conversation. After students have begun to surface their reading processes in their own words, teachers can introduce the vocabulary of reading research to further develop students' precision when discussing the work they are doing as readers (see, for example, Classroom Close-Up 4.3).

BOX 4.4

Questions to Elicit Student Thinking

Because so much classroom dialogue takes the form of teacher initiation/student response/teacher evaluation (IRE), students may be unpracticed in responding to questions that invite thinking rather than retrieving information. Be transparent about how you will help students collaboratively explore their thinking and the kinds of questions they should expect.

And respond nonjudgmentally, with a nod, a thank-you, or a follow-up question. Your attentiveness will produce more conversation than your praise (or its obvious absence).

Invite Thinking. Ask questions that do not presume everyone has the same ideas.

- So . . . what do you think?
- What was especially interesting—for you?

Invite Confusion. Ask questions that encourage students to reveal their reading difficulties:

- How did you know that your understanding was breaking down?
- Can you point to certain places in the text where you lost comprehension?

Probe. As needed, help students share or uncover why they may have offered a particular answer.

- Help us understand your thinking on that.
- Can you tell us a little more?
- What in the text makes you say that?
- Can you give us an example?

Document. Record students' ideas so that they are easily available for others to respond to and to compare and connect.

Extend. Ask questions that explicitly focus students on responding to others' ideas and confusions.

- Does everyone agree?
- Did anyone else have a similar problem?
- What might be another way to look at that?

Link. Help students connect to previous learning and student thinking.

- How might this relate to . . . ?
- What connections come up for you?

BOX 4.5

Confused? Fix-Up Steps

1. Ignore the unclear part and read on to see whether it gets clearer or the unclear part turns out to be unimportant (that is, you can still understand what you are reading).

2. Reread the unclear part (more carefully).

3. Reread the sentence(s) before the unclear part.

4. Try to connect the unclear part to something you already know.

5. Get outside help (from peers, the teacher, or resource materials).

CLASSROOM CLOSE-UP 4.3

Letting Students Into the Vocabulary of Reading Research

Teachers Christine Cziko and Lori Hurwitz not only talked with their ninth-grade academic literacy students about how students would benefit from a focus on their reading processes—they also introduced students to the language of reading researchers. "We treated students like real partners, and they seemed to like knowing that we were doing what the 'experts said' would make a difference in their reading." Students in their classes kept a reading glossary that included the following terms, introduced in meaningful contexts:

text: anything that communicates using language or symbolic means (written, oral, or graphic)

engagement: active mental involvement in reading and learning

competence: skill in something

metacognition: thinking about your thinking or a conscious awareness of your thinking processes while they are happening

strategy: a plan of action

schema: knowledge or information you have about a topic that helps you make connections to new knowledge or information related to that topic

fluency: the ability to do something so quickly and easily that you hardly have to think about it

chunking: breaking up a text or sentence into pieces small enough for you to understand

paraphrasing: putting ideas in a text into your own words

summarizing: deciding what is most important in a text and putting it into your own words

Cultivating Metacognitive Conversation

> When I was told I had to "Talk to the Text," I thought it was dumb. Then I realized
> we had to do this for a purpose. This purpose was to keep our heads going and to
> make sure that we knew what the text was about. . . Now I know that I can be my
> own person and not cheat off someone just to get the answers.
>
> —Alberto, grade 9 student

In Reading Apprenticeship classrooms, metacognitive conversation is structured by particular routines that students get comfortable using on a regular
basis. Some routines, such as the Reading Strategies List or Think Aloud, are
particularly useful for introducing students to the *idea* of metacognitive conversation or to particular reading strategies. Other routines structure a way for
students to document their reading process. Alberto, the student just quoted,
learned to document his thinking with the Talking to the Text routine.

As Alberto tells it, Talking to the Text was not an instant hit. However, his
teacher, JoAnn Filer, persisted in modeling Talking to the Text and supporting
students' use of it. Alberto and his classmates settled into the Talking to the Text
routine and began to appreciate its purpose: "to keep our heads going." Alberto
found that with his head going, he understood more of what he read. And as
he came to understand more, he began to reappraise his learner identity. By the
end of the year Alberto was proud of being his "own person" (and not someone
who needed to cheat).

Theodore, one of Alberto's classmates, was also successful using the Talking
to the Text routine. Theodore reports that even his teachers other than Ms. Filer
noticed the improvement:

> When I learned to Talk to the Text, my teachers from my other classes
> started to notice my grades getting higher.

This section describes the Talking to the Text routine and two other written
routines—metacognitive double-entry journal, and metacognitive log—and
looks at the Think Aloud routine in greater detail. These forms of metacognitive
conversation structure ways for students to monitor their comprehension and
consciously interact with the text. Students come to realize that academic reading is characterized by active problem solving and that they can be successful
problem solvers.

Think Aloud Routine

Virtually all Reading Apprenticeship teachers use Think Aloud to model the
ways in which reading requires thinking of readers (including experienced
readers like themselves), what it looks like to be mentally active when reading,

and specific ways of thinking that students need to develop to be successful readers of their course texts.

In Chapter Three, Think Aloud is discussed for use with students' own out-of-school texts, when the purpose is primarily to support students' personal sense of agency and competence. Earlier in this chapter we described a low-risk cognitive task (Box 4.2) for giving students practice thinking aloud. Such warm-ups prepare students for a more text-focused use of Think Aloud as a metacognitive conversation routine.

When Teri Ryan has to convince her high school geometry students that attention to reading is appropriate in a math class, she *tells* them that math is a language, so to be successful in math they have to learn the language of math. But then she *demonstrates* with a Think Aloud—the first of many that she undertakes, and, more often, that her students undertake.

Ideally, Think Alouds are modeled as the teacher's authentic problem-solving responses to or engagement with a text. Sometimes, however, the teacher is very familiar with the text and understands it; authentic interaction with the text is not an option. In these cases, the teacher instead models *the kinds of reasoning* that students might use to unpack the text. In the following description of a Think Aloud, Teri's purpose is to demonstrate how students can unpack the language of mathematics:

> We discuss important ways that a math textbook is different from other textbooks. For example, it has fewer words, the sentences are compact, and every word is extremely important. Then I let students know that I am going to model what this kind of text density means to me as a reader.
>
> I will have chosen a descriptive paragraph in a section we are about to begin—say, "Using Inductive Reasoning to Make Conjectures"—and I ask students to follow along as I read and Think Aloud. I ask them to have a piece of paper beside their textbook so that if I do anything they want to remember, they can make a note of it. I explain that as I read, "I'm going to break this down and take very small pieces, or chunks, and really make sure we understand each word."
>
> Here's how I would start with the first sentence of a paragraph that introduces inductive reasoning. First, I would read the sentence all the way through, and then I would repeat the last clause:

> When several examples form a pattern and you assume the pattern will continue, you are applying *inductive reasoning*. *Inductive reasoning* is the process of reasoning that a rule or statement is true because specific cases are true. You may use inductive reasoning to draw a conclusion from a pattern. A statement you believe to be true based on inductive reasoning is called a *conjecture*.[1]

"'You are applying *inductive reasoning*.' Okay, *inductive reasoning* is italicized, which tells me I have to pay close attention to it. And, I realize it's a new idea. I wonder what this could mean. I know *reasoning*—I mean, it's an idea I'm familiar with—making sense of something. I'm not sure about *inductive*. Let me read the first part of the sentence again: 'When several examples form a pattern and you assume the pattern will continue . . .' Okay, you see a pattern. You make a bet—you assume the pattern is going to keep going. When you do that, 'you are applying *inductive reasoning*.' So is assuming that a pattern will continue the same as inductive reasoning? What does that really mean? Maybe it will help me to go on."

Then I would read the second sentence and make some connections between the second sentence and the first sentence:

"Okay, if 'specific cases' in the second sentence is the same as 'several examples' in the first sentence, does that mean 'a rule or statement' in the second sentence is the same as 'pattern' in the first sentence?" I might say at that point that the second sentence didn't help me too much, and ask students what they were thinking. Then I would ask students to try the third sentence (where I think we will get some clarity).

Students might end up with notes about chunking, rereading, making connections, finding synonyms, reading on and then checking back—strategies that they can start to apply in their own reading.

When introducing Think Aloud as an academic routine, the teacher's role is to model with a brief segment of text, invite students to comment on the Think Aloud, model again, invite students to comment, model again, invite students to comment, and so on. After several rounds of whole class practice, partners practice independently, and then the teacher brings the class back together to discuss what students are discovering or having trouble with. Then the process is repeated with another short text segment. Each time, the teacher limits his or her "stage time," inviting students to offer their own Think Aloud ideas.

Cindy Ryan frequently Thinks Aloud with her grade 9 academic literacy students, projecting a text for all to see and voicing the questions and comments the text brings up for her. She annotates selected phrases and sentences on the projected text with her thinking and invites students to comment on her thinking or to make their own comments, which she transcribes on the projection. Once having established this back-and-forth flow of "reciprocal modeling," it is the most natural thing in the world to turn the projector over to her students, who vie for the chance to Think Aloud and make their own notes as they exchange problem-solving ideas with classmates (see Classroom Close-Up 4.4).

Box 4.6 presents an overview of how to introduce Think Aloud as a routine for students to practice with academic text. The related metacognitive bookmark (Box 4.7) is a scaffold that students can use as they are learning metacognitive conversation routines.

CLASSROOM CLOSE-UP 4.4
Reciprocal Modeling of a Think Aloud

Cindy Ryan reads aloud from a projected text as her grade 9 academic literacy students follow along. She is reading the first few sentences of a Sherman Alexie essay, "Superman and Me," about growing up on a Spokane Indian reservation.[2] She interrupts herself to Think Aloud and write comments and questions on the projection:

"'I learned to read with a Superman comic book.' I learned to read . . . I'm thinking he must have been young.

"'Simple enough, I suppose.' I'm wondering, What's simple? Is it the comic books or reading? I'm not quite sure what he means right now."

Cindy reads, thinks aloud, and writes another comment or two, then opens the metacognitive conversation to the class. "Now, let me ask you all, what were you all thinking in these first few sentences?"

Students offer their own, reciprocal Think Aloud comments about the text, and then Tanya volunteers to take over from Cindy, who trades places with her and settles into Tanya's seat at a table with three other students.

Marker in hand, Tanya begins reading aloud from the projected text, "'We were poor by lost [most] standards, but one of my parents usually managed to find some minimum wage job or another.'" She pauses and looks back over what she has read, silently underlining the phrase *We were poor*.

"What's going through your mind?" Cindy asks.

"When he says, 'We were poor,' he doesn't mean like they were living on the streets. He means that they didn't have enough money to do what *he* wanted to do." In the margin of the projected text, Tanya transcribes this idea, and the rest of the students mark their photocopies similarly.

Cindy addresses the class: "Does anyone have something that they were processing, that maybe she didn't put up there—because, remember, we all think differently—that you would like to share with the class?"

Angel offers, "For minimum wage I had put that that's how much they gotta get paid. They can't get paid no less than minimum wage. Government says."

Tanya underlines *minimum wage jobs*, adding the label "just enough to get by."

"There you go," Cindy acknowledges. "Anyone else? I saw a couple of hands. Jonté."

"I underlined *which made us different by reservation standards* because the reservation standards are different from ours."

Cindy looks around the room. "If that's what he's processing, that's what he would put down. We're going to come back and look at this sentence [later], okay?"

Jeanette volunteers to be next at the projector. She reads to the class, "'We lived on a combination of irregular paychecks, hope, fear, and government sur—surplus food.' So that means they were on welfare?" Then she begins to answer her own question. "They didn't have enough, just enough, they was living off government money, too. They had the government paying for some of their stuff. They had help from government."

Listening to Jeanette, Dante asks, "From that little thing you just read, how do you know that they are on food stamps, like?"

Jeanette looks down at the text, then up at Dante. "Sur—government food, government . . ."

Cindy supplies the elusive new word: "Government *surplus* food."

The class continues its discussion, noting the prefix *ir-* in *ir*regular paychecks and the use of the past tense: we *were* poor, we *lived*, I *had* a brother and three sisters . . .

Suddenly Tanya asks, "So is he older and more wiser and has all the money that he needs, like he was remembering what happened and he's like, 'Thank God I'm not where I used to be'?"

"What makes you think that—'Thank God I'm not where I used to be?'" Cindy asks.

"Cause, it was like, we had to live paycheck to paycheck, welfare, government food stamps, cause he had a big family, minimum wage—so he must be older and have more money and has a big family that he can take care of and not live at minimum wage."

"Are you making a prediction?" Cindy asks.

"Yeah."

"Ah, should we write that down? That you're predicting that now he's more financially secure?"

Jeanette adds another note to the projected text: "prediction that he's financially secure."

"Good comments, you all," Cindy thanks the class.

BOX 4.6

Introducing Think Aloud

PURPOSE

Think Aloud is an important early routine to help students learn how to focus on their thinking process when they read and how to make their thinking visible.

PROCEDURE

1. Select a short passage of text that is accessible to your students but that also provides opportunities for close reading and problem solving. Plan a few (three to five) Think Aloud moves you want to model, such as those on the metacognitive bookmark (see Box 4.7). Make student copies of the passage and another copy to project and write on.

2. Demonstrate your thinking strategies by thinking aloud and simultaneously underlining and writing predictions, responses, questions, connections, and so forth on the projected text.

3. Invite students to share their observations of your thinking processes in a class discussion. Record these on the class Reading Strategies List.

4. Invite students to describe their own thinking processes during your reading of the passage.*
   If students seem reluctant to jump in, give them a chance to reread the passage first. Add their ideas to the Reading Strategies List.

5. Continue with "reciprocal modeling": you model one or two sentences and students comment on what they saw you do; then students practice Think Aloud with a partner for one or two sentences, reporting back to the class what processes they and their partner used; you model again and students comment on what they saw you do; then student pairs practice and report back. Add to the Reading Strategies List.

6. As a class, discuss and evaluate the Think Aloud experience.

*You may want to give students a copy of the metacognitive bookmark (Box 4.7) to scaffold their practice. Another option is to allow students to read silently and make notes about their thinking processes before sharing with a partner.

After students have practiced carrying out their own academic Think Alouds, teachers transition them to written routines for documenting their reading processes. Teachers, however, continue to use Think Aloud strategically, to focus on particular thinking skills or types of text. A history teacher, for example, might model identifying rhetorical devices, the point of view from which historical events are told, or the source and authoritativeness of particular texts. A science teacher might highlight comprehending data arrays or models, identifying evidence and evaluating explanations offered in science texts, or forming inquiry questions based on these texts. Think Aloud is endlessly flexible—and should always be brief and reciprocal.

For teachers who are not used to revealing their thinking processes, first attempts at Think Aloud can be challenging or uncomfortable. High school

BOX 4.7

Using a Metacognitive Bookmark

PURPOSE

When teachers first model metacognitive conversation with a Think Aloud, many give students a bookmark for keeping track of the common kinds of thinking processes the teacher will be demonstrating.

Students can use this same bookmark as a scaffold for their own metacognitive conversations when practicing with a partner.

As a scaffold, its use should fade as students become more comfortable with metacognitive conversation routines.

PROCEDURE

- Give each student a copy of the bookmark and briefly review students' understanding of the various categories and examples.

- Explain that as you Think Aloud, you will model many of these. Ask students to listen for examples.

- Think Aloud, modeling metacognitive conversation.

- Invite students to describe some of the thinking processes you used.

Let students know that they can use the bookmark whenever they practice metacognitive conversation on their own and with classmates.

Sample Metacognitive Bookmark

Predicting
I predict . . .
In the next part I think . . .
I think this is . . .

Visualizing
I picture. . .
I can see . . .

Questioning
A question I have is . . .
I wonder about . . .
Could this mean . . .

Making connections
This is like . . .
This reminds me of . . .

Identifying a problem
I got confused when . . .
I'm not sure of . . .
I didn't expect . . .

Using fix-ups
I'll reread this part . . .
I'll read on and check back . . .

Summarizing
The big idea is. . .
I think the point is. . .
So what it's saying is. . .

Note: The bookmark is a sample only. Please adapt and revise it according to your subject area and student needs.

English teacher Doug Green[3] reverted to literature instruction instead of thinking aloud—more than he is happy remembering:

> I found myself falling into explaining the short story to them rather than talking about my thinking as I read the short story. It was really hard for me to discipline myself to do that because one of the thinking strategies is making connections to other things. And as soon as I start making connections to other things, I lead myself very quickly into explaining the short story instead of talking about my thinking techniques. That was hard to resist.

The idea of modeling a Think Aloud for her adult GED students gave technical college instructor Michele Lesmeister the jitters. As she explains in

CLASSROOM CLOSE-UP 4.5

Preparing for a "Relationship with Text"

When Michele Lesmeister first decided to model Think Aloud, she was worried that her adult GED students would be bored, and she was nervous about her own performance. Instead, her students were immediately engaged, often interrupting to add their own comments.

Michele addressed her nervousness by preparing in advance.

"Modeling was, at first," she says, "very stressful because I was unaccustomed to showing others my own reading processes. I had to find a natural pace for myself, and this took practice, lots of false starts, and reworking the passages. I found that if I did a thorough text analysis first and then set it next to my clean copy under the document reader, I was much more explicit.

"When I modeled," Michele explains, "I methodically worked my way through the passage noting everything I found from specialized or new terms, to punctuation, sentence structure, and any clues like transition words to show the interplay between groups of words or ideas.

"What I realized later was that the students could identify the reading issues I had with certain passages. When I skipped over something, the students noticed and asked why.

"One day during a modeling exercise, I stopped for a moment. A student said, 'You look like you are thinking about something important—does that mean that you are having a relationship with the text?'

"'Exactly,' I said. 'I am engaging the text and this takes time and energy, doesn't it?'

"Another student said, 'So what you are doing is active, like active learning.'

"Then the first student added, 'I always thought that reading was a passive activity, and we had to be quiet, like in the library. This . . . whatever you call it, RA [Reading Apprenticeship], is helping me realize that when a writer writes something, it is a lot more than words. Yeah, before I thought it was just words.'

"This group of students was realizing what I had come to see. The power of working together to discuss the process of reading and understanding had become the class's goal: to not just 'read words' but to understand more of what they read.

"By my modeling and behavior, I gave the students permission to try to tackle harder passages and not fear challenges or stumbling blocks. If they did not know the answer, someone else might or we could all help."

Classroom Close-Up 4.5, she calmed her nerves by preparing carefully before modeling Think Aloud for her students.

Students in Yu-Chung Chang-Hou's community college developmental math classes learn to Think Aloud as part of their homework routine.[4] Yu-Chung assigns her students to pre-read the textbook before the class in which they will go over it. "Talk out loud, to yourself," she advises, as the next step is to make metacognitive notes about the text to bring to class.

> I tell them, "You will not understand everything, but you still need to do it." Some people say, "I would rather you teach us, and then I will go home and read." But I say, "No. Even though you will not understand totally and will have some frustration, when you come back to the classroom, you will understand faster than people who don't do those notes. You will pay attention when I explain, and you will know why."
>
> An unexpected thing I found was that students like to do their homework more because they know if they get frustrated, they can talk to themselves. It's very powerful.

Talking to the Text Routine

Essentially, Talking to the Text is a silent, written form of Think Aloud. Students annotate a text as they read it, documenting in writing the interactions they are having with the text: what's confusing, what seems important, what's connected to what, what questions are coming up, and so forth.

When community college GED instructor Linda Hart modeled Talking to the Text for her students, she was surprised by how many of them didn't realize that, as readers, they could take an inquiry stance to a text. As one student told her, "If *you* ask questions when you read, then it must mean it's okay for me to do that."

The sample of Talking to the Text in Box 4.8 demonstrates a number of ways a particular ninth grader thought about a single paragraph she was "talking"

BOX 4.8

Talking to the Text: Student Work Sample

Students in Alec Brown's grade 9 College Literacy class use Talking to the Text frequently and understand that they have many ways to interact with what they read. In this example, Alec's student Carmen has asked questions, made connections, commented, predicted, and paraphrased.

[Annotations surrounding text]

Does the word delegate mean something bad? in Spanish it's were you go to acuse someone of something like a police station.

In 1840, two ladies, along with their husbands, traveled to London as delegates to the World Anti-Slavery Convention. These two women were Lucretia Mott and Elizabeth Cady Stanton. Stanton met Mott at the convention for the first time. They were shocked to discover that because they were female, they could not join in the debates (nor could the British women who were there). Stanton, Mott, and the other women present were forced to sit outside the debate room. Later, Lucretia Mott wrote in her diary that the "world" convention was titled as such by "mere poetic license." The angry women sat and promised to do something about this mistreatment. Stanton poured her anger into a plan. She wrote in her own diary, "We resolved to hold a convention as soon as we returned home, and form a society to advocate the rights of women."

Why would they be shocked that they could not join the debates? I think it would be obvious because women back then didn't have many rights.

I don't understand what she is saying. I think it's saying something like that the convention is bad and many people comment on that.

I agree with what they think.

She is saying that they as women are gonna have their own convention at home. and they want something in their society for women.

Note: The text that students are reading is *Women's Suffrage: Giving the Right to Vote to All Americans,* by Jennifer MacBain-Stephens (Rosen Publishing Group, 2006), p. 9.

BOX 4.9

Introducing Talking to the Text

PURPOSE

By making notes about their thinking as they are reading, students make their thinking visible to themselves and then have written notes to discuss later with a partner or the whole class. Many students feel safer and better prepared to discuss texts and their reading process after having had time to record their thoughts on paper. Talking to the Text can be an especially effective alternative to Think Aloud for English learners.

PROCEDURE

- For use with a projector or document camera, make enlarged versions of the first paragraph or two of a text students will read, leaving plenty of space for making notes between the lines and at the margins.

- Make copies of the entire text for students, leaving generous margins. (If photocopying is an issue, provide students with sticky notes instead.)

- Review with students the types of questions and reading strategies they have practiced using in Think Alouds.

- Explain that Talking to the Text is a written Think Aloud and that by practicing Talking to the Text, students will get in the habit of Talking to the Text *in their head*—something good readers do to help them stay interested in the text and solve problems of understanding.

- At the projector or document camera, model thinking aloud, marking the text as you go with underlines, arrows, questions, comments, and so forth. Invite students' observations and questions about your annotations.

- Ask students to read silently and annotate the next paragraph with their own Talking to the Text marks and comments.

- Have partners share their Talking to the Text marks and how they cleared up or tried to clear up any roadblocks they came to.

- Invite volunteers to share with the class some of their Talking to the Text marks. Ask them to explain
  - What did you mark?
  - How did that help your reading?
  - How did talking with a partner help?

- You can add students' comments to the demonstration text and label them (for example, "asking questions," "visualizing," "predicting") to reinforce shared reading process vocabulary.

- Model again with the next paragraph, or as necessary, respond to any confusions students may have about the process.

- Have students continue to make their own Talking to the Text annotations and discuss them with partners.

- Bring the class together to discuss students' experiences Talking to the Text.

One word of warning: it is important not to turn Talking to the Text into individual seatwork. It is, after all, through their interactions with classmates that students learn new approaches for making meaning from text.

to: she makes connections to a confusing vocabulary word, predicts what some unusual language might mean, comments on the historical context, notes her emotional responses, and paraphrases a statement that was not exactly clear to her.

Because Talking to the Text documents students' internal metacognitive conversations, it makes their thinking easily available for their own reflection or review, for discussing with classmates, and for assessment. As students learn to annotate a text with their thinking, these Talking to the Text notes are explored in partner and class discussions. After students read and annotate independently, they need the opportunity to share their thinking and problem-solving strategies. (Box 4.9 describes a process for introducing Talking to the Text.)

Metacognitive Double-Entry Journal Routine

Many teachers are familiar with two-column, double-entry journals, or T-charts, and they may use them for many purposes. Students often use them to collect text-based evidence. In Reading Apprenticeship classrooms, double-entry journals are sometimes employed in this way, as a tool for grounding thinking in the text, and sometimes as a metacognitive conversation routine to alert students to how the text is causing them to respond to it. Box 4.10 shows sample double-entry formats such as I Saw/I Thought and Evidence/Interpretation. In the same box, a triple-entry journal—What It Actually Says/What We Think It Means/How We Figured It Out—guides students through a three-step process to unpack their thinking.

As with introducing any routine, the teacher models, invites students to reciprocate in a whole class setting, has students practice independently with partners or small groups, and brings the class back together to discuss what they are learning or are still confused about.

High school students in Gayle Cribb's mainstream U.S. history class use the I Saw/I Thought double-entry journal for their reading assignments, so it was natural for them to use the same metacognitive approach for "reading" a short documentary. Following the film, students' double-entry notes prime them for participation in metacognitive conversation, first with partners and then as a class. (See I Saw/I Thought student work samples in Box 4.11; an excerpt from the related class discussion appears in Classroom Close-Up 4.6.)

At the community college level, Walter Masuda and his English 1A students found that a variation of the I Saw/I Thought double-entry journal unlocked a writing assignment that had caused problems for previous classes of students: to cross-reference two texts in developing an essay asserting the validity or lack of validity of a particular sociological theory.

In this Reading Apprenticeship class (which Walter was tracking for a comparative study), students read the same texts as other classes had, one a theory of prejudice and the other an interview with someone who described the development of his own prejudice. Unlike in Walter's other classes, they also completed a Theory/Evidence double-entry journal. The excerpt here shows one student's entry for the first of several postulates in Vincent Parrillo's theory of prejudice and evidence from an interview by Studs Terkel that supports its validity.

Theory of Prejudice (Parrillo's theory)	Evidence of Validity (Terkel's interview with Ellis)
1. According to Parrillo, scapegoating is the need to blame someone else, generally a marginalized group, for one's own misfortunes. (509)	1. Ellis's economic misfortunes caused him to become bitter. He needed a specific group to hate because, in his words, "Hatin' America is hard to do. I had to hate somebody." He says that because both he and his father were members of the Klan, "the natural person" for him to hate would be the African-Americans. (517)

Previously, Walter says, students "got lost" when they had to write their own essay based on the two texts. The class using the Theory/Evidence journal did not:

> The number of essays requiring rewrites (papers earning scores of 72 or below) was only 20% for the RA [Reading Apprenticeship] class (n=30), but for the control class, more than twice as many essays required a rewrite (43%, n=21). . . A revision rate of around 43% for this assignment is typical of past English 1A classes that never had the benefit of RA instruction. Often the revision rate would approach 50%, so the unusually low revision rate of 20% for the RA class was extremely atypical for this writing assignment. Quite frankly, I was astonished by the large difference.
>
> When I asked the students later to rank the RA routines in order of usefulness, the "theory and evidence" organizer was ranked the highest, with students often commenting that it helped them to understand the ideas from the readings better and to write a more organized paper.
>
> Thus, the "theory and evidence" routine served an important organizational function as well as a metacognitive one.

BOX 4.10

Sample Metacognitive Uses of Double-Entry (and Triple-Entry) Journals

Double-entry journals such as I Saw/I Thought and Evidence/Interpretation force students to notice how they are interacting with a text, whether previewing it or reading it. Triple-entry journals can be used to focus students on *how* they solve reading problems.

PREVIEW: "Normal Regulation of Blood Glucose," pages 112–114, including diagram

I Saw (notes and quotes from the text)	**I Thought** (my questions, connections, sketches, roadblocks, clarifications, comments)

READ: "Diffusion, Osmosis, and Osmotic Pressure," pages 39–46

Evidence	**Interpretation**

READ: *To Kill a Mockingbird*, pages 1–6

Author's important ideas	**My thoughts, feelings, questions**

CLARIFY: The First Amendment

What it actually says (quote a word or phrase that is confusing)	**What we think it means** (translate the word or phrase into something we understand)	**We think it probably means this because...** (explain how we figured it out)

BOX 4.11

Metacognitive Double-Entry Journals: Student Work Samples

As part of learning about Japanese internment in the U.S. during World War II, students make double-entry notes in response to a documentary based on "home movies" made in the camps. The notes prepare everyone in the class to explore their observations and ideas in later metacognitive conversations with classmates. Journal entries of two students are presented here.

STUDENT 1

I Saw / I Heard	I Thought / I Wondered
American soldiers were standing watching the buses pull up and unload the Japanese.	Did they care, in the movie it looked sort of like they were just hanging out watch the buses
Some of the Japanese shown in the pictures were not sad but happy looking	Most of them were taken away from their house maybe without their family.
The camps were like little towns library and other stores	It was good they put in some stores so they weren't just isolated by themselves.
One man that was Japanese was in a uniform	How did he get to be in the army. Did they allow that?
The Japanese played sports and have fun together even though they were in the camps	They still tried to live their lives even in the camps which might have been hard to do
The camps were in different areas so each one was different in weather or treatment	Did certain areas mean different treatment or was it the same anywhere you went (camps)

STUDENT 2

I Saw / I Heard	I Thought / I Wondered
There were many buses	They were for moving to camps
There were a lot of houses They had a library, park	How many people did live each house?
People are laughing in front of the camera	The life in the camps was not hard?
Honor Rolls A men pointed his name	These people were working in American military?
Playing Sumo	They had a freedom to have fun.
I could find American nation flag, but not Japanese.	

CLASSROOM CLOSE-UP 4.6
"Okay, What Else Did You Notice?"

Gayle Cribb's U.S. history students, many of whom are English learners and mainstreamed special education students, have just watched and made metacognitive double-entry journal notes (see Box 4.11) responding to a documentary about U.S. Japanese internment camps during World War II.

Gayle invites volunteers' comments and also calls on nonvolunteers, because everyone is prepared for the discussion with the double-entry notes they have made; she probes students' thinking with follow-up and extension questions; and she documents their ideas on the board. At the end of the class's metacognitive conversation, Gayle asks students to consolidate their response to the discussion in writing.

As we drop in on the discussion (excerpted here), Gayle begins with an open-ended question:

Teacher: So what are some of the things you noticed?

Megan: I thought it was kind of weird that, well not really weird but ironic, that they were still in the army for the U.S. when at the same time they're in the concentration camps, like pretty much being punished, but they still felt the loyalty to the country.

Teacher: And what does that make you think?

Megan: Like that they still felt like even though they were being put in these camps, and other people were like scared they were spies, but at the same time they still felt like that they were American, that they were loyal to their country and they still wanted to help.

Teacher: Okay, what else did you notice?

Luis: They didn't seem sad. They seemed happy.

Teacher: Did that surprise you?

Luis: Yeah, cause I thought they were going to be like sad, but they were happy. Like they were playing and everything.

Teacher: Okay. And did other people notice that?

Class: Yeah.

Teacher: Okay, and what did you think about that? What are you thinking?

Jason: That it's not like the Hitler camps. The people are happy, their families weren't separated from

each other. It's not all death around them, and people are smiling and playing and all that stuff. And they're even having parades for that Japanese sergeant guy.

Teacher: Okay. Not Hitler's camps for sure. Right? What else are you thinking about this?

Scott: It was kind of like their families were kind of going on with what they had. Like they didn't know how long they were going to be there, so they didn't want to be sad the whole time. So they had to make the best of it. And they were doing the home movies, so they wouldn't be, like, sad on a home movie.

Teacher: So what do you suppose the filmmakers' purpose was? What were they trying to do? Why did they make these films anyhow?

Gracia: To show they were happy . . . like they were in their normal lives. They had normal lives in the camps.

Teacher: And who are they going to show this to?

Gracia: The future generations.

Teacher: Future generations. So we could say that's the audience for these films. Does anyone else have another idea about the intended audience for these films?

Fabian: Well, video cameras were contraband, so I think that like they wanted to kind of show that it was unjust to have them relocated in those camps because why else would they want to sneak and risk getting caught with cameras if they were contraband?

Teacher: So you want not just to show the future but to show—

Fabian: That it was like unjust.

Teacher: If they're trying to show that it's unjust, does that explain taking happy pictures?

Fabian: Not really.

Teacher: Explain.

Fabian: Well, it doesn't look as bad if they're happy, but they just wanted to show that they were relocated and they *did* lose their homes and they *were* forced to be relocated in camps.

(Continued)

Teacher: Okay. Taylor, what are you thinking about all this?

Taylor: Um, just like they're trying to be happy in a bad situation, and like showing the home movies is like one way to do it.

Teacher: Other things we haven't talked about yet? Kyle.

Kyle: They were showing American flags in the movie in the parade they were having for the Japanese sergeant. And I thought, Why would they have American flags? I was wondering what was the purpose of the American flags in there.

Teacher: What did people think of that? Allie?

Allie: I thought that if they didn't have the flags, that means that they would be mad at the U.S. for

putting them in the camps. But they had the flags so it seemed like they were not really mad at the U.S. for putting them in the camps.

Teacher: When you see that, what does it make you think?

Jason: When I see the flag? It symbolizes that they *are* American. Well, they're Japanese still, but they're mainly American 'cause they're citizens here and they should not be in the camps. They should be with everyone else. They are American citizens.

Teacher: Okay, so how many people have doubts about this situation, like whether this should have happened? Let's see a show of hands. Okay. And if you were to express that doubt? How about if everyone just write a little bit about that. What is it that you're wondering or concerned about here?

Metacognitive Log Routine

Metacognitive logs are a place for students to think and write about their own reading process with extended assignments such as textbook chapters, whole books, or the texts for a course project. Some metacognitive logs take the form of compiled metacognitive double- or triple-entry journals, others structure metacognitive responses to prompts about how students are reading, and some combine these forms, depending on student choice or teacher suggestion.

Like other Reading Apprenticeship routines, metacognitive logs can help students become more aware of their thinking as readers and give them more control over how well they learn. The logs can be a place for students to document their reading experience in preparation for sharing and problem solving in the whole class community.

To help students practice monitoring their reading with metacognitive logs, many teachers provide an initial set of prompts that students can use to get their thinking started. Prompts such as "I got confused when . . .," "I started to think about . . .," "I first thought . . . but then realized . . ." help keep students focused on responding to what happened to them as readers and what they did about it. (Use of such prompts is discussed in more detail in Box 6.5 in Chapter Six.)

Will Brown's Introduction to Chemistry students read their textbook side-by-side with a two-column metacognitive log (Box 4.12). Heather Howlett's grade 8 science students use the same routine as they read about astronomy. Both teachers grade students' logs with a rubric that rewards effort and learning.

In addition, these teachers ask students to share their logs. Students look for good ideas in each other's logs and specifically notice how someone else makes connections to the same text. Box 4.13 shows the form Heather's students

BOX 4.12

Metacognitive Reading Log Template

When students keep metacognitive reading logs in a loose-leaf binder, the individual sheets can easily be turned in for teacher assessment, as with the template shown. The log entries allow the teacher to see what students are understanding, curious about, or confused by—and respond accordingly.

METACOGNITIVE READING LOG

Name: _____   Class Period: _____

Chapter: _____   Sections: _____   Due Date: _____

Important Ideas and Information in theText (p.)	My Thoughts, Feelings, Questions

use when sharing their logs with a partner. She says that when partners talk together, she expects them to interrogate each other's thinking and learn from each other in a metacognitive conversation: "Why did you write that?" "What reminded you of this?" "What made you think of that picture you drew?"

In community college classes, many teachers and students have discovered the value of metacognitive logs. Holly Morris assigns her general biology students to keep logs as they read the textbook. She asks them to summarize

---

BOX 4.13

Metacognitive Reading Log: Pair Work

In this example, partners are responsible for reading and discussing each other's logs. They also work together to identify reading problems that either has had with the assignment. (This example is from Heather Howlett. She shares it on the U.S. Department of Education Doing What Works website, where she describes her work with Reading Apprenticeship.)

METACOGNITIVE READING LOG: PAIR WORK

Directions: Read your logs with a partner. Make sure that each of you has had a chance to read uninterrupted first. Once both people have had a chance to read, answer the following questions aloud, and then in writing.

1. How did you decide what to put on the left side of the log? What makes you think it is important?

2. Were there things in the reading that you didn't understand? How did you figure out what they meant?

3. What problems do you still have with the text or the reading log itself?

There will be an opportunity to share highlights and insights with the whole group after the pairs have had some time to talk.

Source: http://dww.ed.gov/see/?T_ID=23&P_ID=61&c1=1083&c2=1070#cluster-1

---

the author's main points in the left column and respond in the right column. Holly models for students a range of ways they can respond. Entries in the right column vary considerably, she reports:

> Some students gave examples. Some wrote comments such as, "I understand" or "I'm confused." Some clearly used the second column to reflect on what they were reading. For example, as J.R. was writing about the H+ gradient across the cell membrane in the electron transport chain, he wrote in the second column, "I guess then that the H+ ions cannot diffuse across the membrane." This comment may not seem like a big deal, but he was clearly slowing down to think about the transport process.

After a second year of assigning the logs to her General Biology 1 and 2 classes, Holly is considering expanding the use of metacognitive logs to her nutrition classes:

> Based on lecture averages [from test scores, logs, and student case studies], student comments, and my observations, I am confident that students are interacting with the textbook at a deeper level, resulting in a better understanding of the course material.

In addition to supporting students' metacognition and learning, logs also provide a record of student work that increases accountability for reading and allows teachers to gauge students' progress. As formative assessment, students' log entries are a teacher's most valuable information. Hector, for example, a seventh grader in Rita Jensen's English language development class, writes conscientiously in his metacognitive log, showing Rita how he reasons about what he reads, how he applies reading strategies the class has focused on, and how his comfort with English is evolving. Classroom Close-Up 4.7 shows Hector's log entries from three successive assignments.

CLASSROOM CLOSE-UP 4.7

Knowing What Hector Knows

Hector is a little old to be in seventh grade, but he is a newcomer to the United States and has a lot of English to learn. What he knows about life, however, keeps him tracking his thinking as he reads different pieces of fiction in Rita Jensen's middle school English language development class. As a result of his log entries, Rita learns more about how to support Hector's literacy development.

Amber brown feells blue

How come the title says Amber brown feels blue if the book says that she is having fun with her friends painting her nails and jumping on her bed the title should be Amber brown feels a little unlucky.

lamb to slaughter

I thought this story was going to be about a person traiding a lamb and got ripped off because of the title.

I think Mary's husband had a child with another lady and his job does not pay him much and he can't pay for child support for both babyie's because he said "it could efect with my job" and that is some thing that can efect his job.

While I was reading I stoped at the word sunbath [sunbather] because I did not know what it meant so I chunked it up and I thought this person means a bath as hot as the sun.

J Cob have I ♥ed

My group and I had some confusions and we clarified them. I had a confusion that one twin is three years older than the other. Then Dennis said they were twins. I had another question of how a thirteen year old can go to high school and Dennis said they have a difrent district so they can change things.

I predicted that loise will do something to Caroline so luise could be popular.

I predict that beacause loise haites Caroline and she might be capalble of doing that to Caroline.

I think this storie will get to be turning about love beacause now it says both sisters are having fights.

Cultivating Collaboration

> The most effective strategy I have used is allowing students to collaborate and discuss each other's understandings of texts. In one class period, we may move from pair sharing to small group sharing and end the period with whole group sharing. They start to take ownership of the information and are able to conduct very sophisticated conversations about science topics. I never saw this depth of knowledge and dialogue before I began integrating literacy instruction with my science teaching.
>
> —Heather Howlett, grade 8 science teacher

The emphasis on metacognitive conversation in Reading Apprenticeship classrooms means that even class discussions are collaborative. In addition, students need opportunities to work out their thoughts in more intimate conversations with peers; partner and small group structures make this possible. As teacher Heather Howlett says, she often involves students in all three collaboration structures in a single class period. "The key," she says, "is to create a safe environment in which all students feel comfortable working with any of their classmates."

It is through such collaborations that students can exchange ideas and share their knowledge, strategies, experiences, and problem-solving approaches. Ultimately, with abundant practice, these social experiences shape the cognitive habits and dispositions students will take into their individual interactions with texts.

Collaborative Class Discussion

As noted earlier, the inquiry discussions typical of Reading Apprenticeship classrooms are quite different from the recitations or teacher-student IRE (inquire-respond-evaluate) dialogues that define much classroom discussion. There is an important shift in who's talking and what's being talked about. Instead of calling on students to retrieve information and then evaluating the correctness of students' responses, teachers ask students to share even tentative thinking or their thinking about their thinking. Additionally, teachers encourage much more student-to-student discussion and limit their own participation.

Most students, however, have little experience in this kind of classroom discussion. Strategies for scaffolding students' increased participation in collaborative discussion are described in Chapter Three, Box 3.5. These include ways for teachers to explicitly model good listening, respond with nonevaluative encouragement, orchestrate more student-to-student responding in the whole class setting, and ensure equitable participation.

The importance of the teacher's role in facilitating class discussion does not mean the teacher must direct every classroom exchange. Yet even with the goal of increasing student-to-student exchanges, teachers often find it challenging to minimize their direct participation. A bit of engineering may be called for. Some teachers purposely move away from the front of the room, finding a place on the sidelines or a seat with one of the table groups. Other teachers move the furniture, rearranging rows of desks into U-shaped seating for better student-to-student communication, or organizing desks in groups of four for whole class as well as group work. Even with the teacher less obviously "in charge," most classes will still need a lot of practice arriving at classroom discussions that look more like a soccer game with distributed participation than like serial ping-pong with the teacher always involved.

To be reminded of a class discussion that fits the soccer model more than the ping-pong model, see Classroom Close-Up 4.4. Teacher Cindy Ryan is clearly facilitating the Think Aloud discussion, but her students do not necessarily address their comments only to her (nor is she the person primarily modeling at the projector). Box 4.4, Questions to Elicit Student Thinking, is another resource to be reminded of as an example of how teachers manage class discussions that focus on collaborative inquiry.

Partner Work

In collaborative classrooms, teachers frequently ask students to work with a partner—to share their internal metacognitive conversations, for example, and to learn from and help each other solve specific reading problems. Partnerships give every student in the class an intimate audience and a collaborator, while the partnership structure creates for every student an accountable opportunity to learn and contribute.

Middle school social studies teacher Laurie Erby has observed another benefit of pairing students to think together about their reading:

> One of the things that I am really starting to notice is that the students who normally would have just kind of skimmed over words that they didn't understand, get to the end, and be okay with the fact that they didn't get it, are actually taking the time to try to figure it out.

A quick partner structure—Think-Pair-Share or Think-Write-Pair-Share—can be used over and over to get all students thinking, exchanging ideas, and actively participating in the academic life of the classroom. This structure gives individual students time to think, perhaps to write (Talk to the Text notes or responses to a specific prompt), pair up with a partner to discuss their ideas, and then have the result of their conversation available to share during a whole class discussion. (Box 4.14 describes the Think-Pair-Share and Think-Write-Pair-Share process.)

BOX 4.14

Introducing Think-Pair-Share and Think-Write-Pair-Share

PURPOSE

In a collaborative classroom, you will frequently ask students to work with a partner. Think-Pair-Share and Think-Write-Pair-Share are quick participation structures that can be used over and over to get all students actively engaged and contributing academically and socially to the classroom community.

PROCEDURE

Think-Pair-Share and Think-Write-Pair-Share proceed from individual thinking to partner exchange to sharing with a small group and/or the whole class.

Think or Think-Write

- Ask students to think individually about a prompt.
  - Often it helps to have students quickly write or make notes to capture their ideas.
  - Or ask students review their individual Talking to the Text notes or metacognitive logs before pairing up with another student to talk about them.

Pair

- Ask students to take turns sharing their individual thinking with a partner. To begin with, this sharing can be very structured:
  - Tell your partner one thing the first paragraph made you think about.
  - Share one of the Talking to the Text notes you made.
- Monitor pairs as they work to make sure that students are becoming comfortable sharing ideas, confusions, and difficulties and are not merely chatting. You may need to adjust seating to encourage both comfortable and productive peer conversations.
- If students need help learning how to listen to each another, give the listener a focusing task like making a note of the partner's ideas or preparing to share the partner's ideas with the class.

Share

- In varied ways, draw partner conversations into a whole class discussion. In the beginning, you may want to call on students to report to the class what they learned from their partner. Later, you may want to foster exchanges by regrouping two pairs into groups of four before bringing students back together for whole class sharing.
- When students are sharing in small groups or with the whole class, it may be essential to give listening students a task to do while others are sharing:
  - Listen for ideas that come up more than once—that probably means they are important.
  - If you hear something repeated, let me know to put a star next to that idea on the poster we're making.
  - Listen for things that are similar and things that are different.
  - Listen for evidence from the text.
  - Listen for historical [or literary, or scientific, or mathematical] thinking.

CLASSROOM CLOSE-UP 4.8

Scaffolding Partner Work

Many students in Alec Brown's grade 9 College Reading class are English learners or designated for special education. Some of the texts Alec uses are difficult for his students. When the assignment was to read text chunks of several paragraphs at a time, Talk to the Text, and then share their connections, questions, and roadblocks with a partner, Alec found that about 20 percent of the students were off task. The task was too hard.

As Alec reported early in the school year, "I wanted to just give up on the partner work. There were always three or four partnerships that didn't do anything or they just fooled around. *I* was feeling out of control."

However, instead of reverting to the comfort of whole group instruction with the teacher in charge, Alec decided to restructure the partner task. He shortened the text chunks that partners would discuss, he partnered inexperienced readers or English

speakers with students who could help them, and he changed the Talking to the Text directions. The result was "say something."

"I think of this as scaffolding," he explains. "I give them a paragraph at a time and ask them to write down anything that comes to mind—to 'say something' about the text. Then they share this with a partner and annotate their own text with what their partner wrote. Today, every student read and wrote something, and a lot of students who never volunteered before were part of the class discussion.

"My goal is to build from here, so that we are doing at least three rounds of Think-Pair-Share per lesson."

A month later, Alec's students appeared to have made the transition. Every student could be observed reading, writing, and sharing his or her thinking with a partner. All students were on task.

With practice, many teachers move students seamlessly back and forth between class discussion and Think-Pair-Share or between independent reading and reflecting with a partner. But getting started with this important structure can sometimes be intimidating. Alec Brown, a high school teacher who, along with his students, is still new to Think-Pair-Share, admits to a moment of terror every time he is about to set partners loose. "I just always think it is going to be a management nightmare. I know it never is, but that is just my gut, my first thought when I think about trying it." What this teacher decided to do after some initial flops was limit the task and let students build from success. In Classroom Close-Up 4.8, Alec describes his experiment.

In classes like Alec's, where everyone is new to partner work, getting pairs to read chunks of text together and just "say something" can be an important first step. When students are more experienced collaborators, they can focus on creating a shared understanding of the text. In Classroom Close-Up 4.9, building on each other's thinking starts to come naturally to Gayle Cribb's history students.

Small Groups

Many learning activities in Reading Apprenticeship classrooms lend themselves to collaboration in small groups, a structure that teachers often introduce after

CLASSROOM CLOSE-UP 4.9

Partnering to Think Aloud and Get the Gist

Students in Gayle Cribb's honors U.S. history class are reading *The Grapes of Wrath*, by John Steinbeck, to amplify their understanding of the Great Depression. In the lesson excerpted here, Gayle has asked students to work in pairs reading and thinking aloud about the assigned chapter (which she has photocopied and marked in chunks). After each collaborative Think Aloud, partners write the gist of the chunk either in concert or independently. Students work together for about an hour, seemingly at ease in the give and take of their collaborations. In two short excerpts, we listen in on two partnerships, at the beginning and end of the reading assignment:

Kenya: (Reads aloud, then ponders) Hmmm . . .

Natalie: That would be explaining how the land was bad. If it was moist and fertile—

Kenya: They wouldn't have that problem. Basically, they are saying it is out of our hands, not that we are controlling.

Natalie: Where? Oh, yeah. *(Partners write)*

Natalie: (Reads aloud, then thinks aloud) So, then, that is kind of expanding on how they can't do anything anymore. How since their crops weren't good they can't do anything right. "A man can hold land . . . and pay taxes." That means poor.

Kenya: Once you borrow money from the bank, that's it.

Natalie: You are going to lose everything.

Kenya: This is about—

Natalie: How the family can't do anything to save their land, and how they will have to pay the bank. *(Partners write)*

Teacher: (To the class, much later) Can I interrupt you? You and your partner can figure out what to do so that you can finish up in the next five minutes.

Thomas: (To his partner) Let's read it [all] and write a short summary.

Andrew: Yeah. Do you want to read it silently? *(Reads aloud anyway, maintaining their interaction)*

Thomas: Have to find work for money and can't expect things to stay the same all the time.

Thomas: (Reads aloud, then thinks aloud) So if he is in charge of the means of running his property and has passion, then he is the bigger person. But if the property is the only thing between him and his money, the property owns him.

Andrew: If you are in it for the money, then you are a slave to it.

Teacher: (To the class) All right, let's pull this back together. Does Steinbeck have a few things to say?

students become comfortable working in pairs (and often by combining two pairs). As in partnerships, students share knowledge, experiences, approaches to tasks, and tentative ideas, but with more "partners" and in more diverse exchanges. The potential for growth increases, and so do the challenges.

Teachers who make group work a matter of course report a range of benefits, from the increased participation it structures for students who may be quiet or unsure of themselves to the responsibility that teammates take for each other's learning. Lisa Rizzo, who teaches middle school language arts, reports that for her students, group work is an important way for them to take responsibility and recognize that they can help each other:

It gives them a sense of power, that they have a responsibility for each other.

Will Brown, who puts his chemistry students into small groups, or teams, beginning with the first day of class, found that students came to care about their teammates in ways he would not have anticipated:

> They identified as a member of a team. Not only did they care about their own learning, they cared enough about learning to care about someone else's learning. And they also wanted someone to go through it with them, because it was hard. "Let's sit down and do our reading log together and get this done," or "I'm going to be in class, you better be in class"—that sort of really taking responsibility for each other.

Kathleen Sullivan, who only recently adopted small groups as the principal participation structure in her high school chemistry classes, decided to check with students about the benefits of group work that she was observing:

> I conducted a student survey and asked all my students how much they enjoyed chemistry, how they felt they learned best, and other questions regarding the class. Over 90 percent of my students feel they learn best working with a small group to figure concepts out. They have begun to recognize that they truly learn better when they are thinking about their thinking, working in groups, and figuring the content out together. We just finished up the hardest unit in chemistry, and normally the assessment averages are in the failing range, but the average for all my classes was an 87 percent. I'm so proud of my students, plus I see them reflecting on their own work and taking pride in it.

For teachers with little experience managing group work, any discomfort in trying a new structure may be amplified by concerns about whether students can be successful with the amount of independence (and interdependence) inherent in group work: Will students maintain a focus on the academic task? Will they know when they need help? Will they contribute equitably to group products? These are legitimate questions.

Middle school teacher Rita Jensen has some reassuring advice based on experiences with her English language development classes:

> In the beginning I encourage the sharing of ideas and collaboration in completing simple group work. This may look suspiciously like cheating, but for my purposes of wanting students to share and value each other's work, it is very successful.
>
> I change groups often and without notice. Each student brings strengths to the process, so it's important to allow those strengths to emerge. Sometimes I would orchestrate different variables, like ethnicity, gender, skill level, and attitude. Sometimes students get to pick their own groups on a special day or I'd create all-girl groups and all-boy groups, or I'd put all the quiet, reluctant students together until a leader emerged.

Sometimes I put the most vocal students together to help them practice listening.

I monitor group interactions carefully, noticing when groups are not functioning. I would sit in on that group and try to stimulate the conversation. I would encourage, prod, and model. By mid-year students become fairly independent problem solvers with enough academic language to forge into RT [Reciprocal Teaching groups; see Chapter Seven]. At this point my job is to mentor, facilitate, and guide groups of learners.

In these comments, Rita suggests two ways to think about organizing collaborative group work: the teacher's role and the structure of groups.

The teacher's role is primarily to specify expectations and define assessments and to monitor and mentor the groups. In addition, teachers collect examples of group interactions and problem solving that can inform the class discussion and debriefing of the group work (see Box 4.15).

The structure of groups involves how group membership is assigned and how student roles are determined. Teachers make these decisions, depending on their purposes (see Box 4.16). Rita, for example, changes groups often. She sees groups as a way for students to discover and experience the varied strengths each can contribute. She also moves from groups in which no roles are assigned to *reciprocal teaching*, a particular form of small group interaction in which students take turns facilitating various steps in the process (see a description of

---

BOX 4.15

The Teacher's Role in Small Group Work

As a participation structure, small groups convey the message that everyone has valuable experiences and thinking to contribute. For students to experience this message as reality, the teacher has an important role, first of all, in establishing a safe environment, and then in setting the parameters for group work and mentoring groups' interactions, as follows:

- Specify the procedures and expected products of group work.

- Monitor small group processes, and mentor students by modeling appropriate group interactions and asking probing questions that facilitate thoughtful approaches to the work.

- Listen in to group conversations and collect examples of group exchanges and ideas to bring back to the ensuing class discussion.

- Ask students to reflect on and assess their own and their group members' contributions to group products.

- Underscore students' accountability for the work and their responsibilities to one another by giving students a group grade and an individual grade.

BOX 4.16

Structuring Small Groups

The goal of group work is for group members to contribute equally to the *substantive* work—the thinking, reflecting, trying out and observing, writing, discussing, and so forth. Students will need to understand this goal, because their first inclination may be to divide up the substantive work rather than to collaborate. The following guidelines support equitable participation by group members and participation by all students in a variety of grouping arrangements.

- The size of a small group should actually be *small*. Four members is ideal, and when the groups don't come out even, three is better than five.

- Vary group membership decisions according to your purposes:
  - To increase interpersonal knowledge and community
  - To establish stable working relationships
  - To create interest groups
  - To balance skills and experiences within and across groups
  - To occasionally provide targeted support and/or independence

- When students first begin working in small groups, it is sometimes helpful to assign roles so that everyone knows what to do. Some process roles include the following:
  - Facilitator (distributes turns equitably, moves the group through assigned tasks)
  - Recorder (writes notes to record or capture group thinking, writes up group work to turn in)
  - Reporter/spokesperson (presents the group's work to the assigned audience)
  - Process observer (reports to the group on how individuals participated and how the group worked together)

- Sometimes you may want to put students into groups that become expert on particular content and then share what they learn. This sharing could be in the form of group presentations to the class or in the form of a "jigsaw," in which expert groups disperse to exchange information in "home" groups made up of one member of each different "expert" group. The content selected for such groups should be related in ways that allow students to see relationships and make important connections across topics.

- Sometimes you may want to support a particular group of students as they work with particular content or skills while other students work in independent groups. Grouping students in this way should always be temporary, not permanent. All readers, whether they are perceived to be strong or struggling, benefit from substantial opportunities to work in heterogeneous groups where students work together and share their expertise.

reciprocal teaching in Chapter Seven). For Will Brown, whose "teams" stay together for extended periods, group membership needs to be stable for students to experience each other as reliable resources in the hard work of reading and understanding chemistry. Except for specific reciprocal teaching assignments, Will's groups work informally, with no particular roles assigned.

In her high school history classroom, Allie Pitts introduces collaboration early in the year and, with Andrew Hartig, her team teacher in English, makes it a significant 15 percent of students' grades.

> I am a firm believer that students learn by talking, so I have always had students work collaboratively. I introduce group work early in the year. I begin by trying to sell students on why effective collaboration is so important: I give information from employer surveys that list effective collaboration as the most important skill for employees and statistics on memory demonstrating that we tend to remember what we *say*. I emphasize that even though the ability to work with other people is important to employers, students don't have a class on it, so we need to focus on it in our [subject area] classes.

Because students often need help understanding what is required of them in collaborative group work, Allie and Andrew provide a self-assessment rubric that students use to monitor their own contribution to collaborative group work (see the Assessment Appendix, Monitoring and Assessing Student Work).

Deepening Disciplinary Uses of Metacognitive Conversation

> Because they always made us slow down and think about our thinking, I started to realize that those things in our history book really happened, that those people were real.
> —Ramon, grade 9 student

While metacognitive conversation is about making thinking visible, its ultimate goal is not simply to make students aware of their thinking, but to foster their ability to use insights about reading processes, strategies, and motivations to interact with, comprehend, and make use of a variety of academic texts. For example, Ramon, the student just quoted, found that the process of slowing down—of learning to be metacognitive as he reads—brought him to the surprising realization that history textbooks describe things that actually happened to real people.

Even as students learn to take control over reading processes, most have no particular sense that understanding the reading materials of different subject areas requires different approaches and can offer different reading experiences. In addition, because literacy practices become increasingly specialized through the grades, students must read not only increasingly complex texts but increasingly complex texts in disciplines as different as calculus or economics or biology or anthropology. Students can be helped to recognize the different kinds of thinking they do as readers by focusing in different ways: on their thinking, on their reading, and on solving reading problems, and on disciplinary processes and practices to deepen their understanding of disciplinary texts.

For many teachers and students, the metaphor of a "metacognitive funnel" helps them think about and talk about the ways readers' attention may shift as they read any given text. The representation of the funnel in Box 4.17 shows these different areas of attention and gives examples of representative metacognitive statements that apply to each. The goal for readers is to be able to intentionally and strategically focus their attention in ways that will help them accomplish their reading purposes.

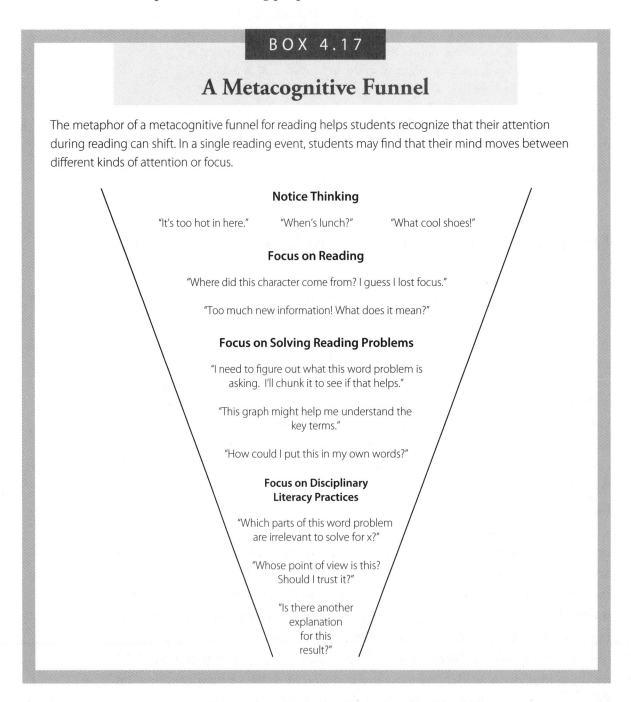

BOX 4.17

A Metacognitive Funnel

The metaphor of a metacognitive funnel for reading helps students recognize that their attention during reading can shift. In a single reading event, students may find that their mind moves between different kinds of attention or focus.

Notice Thinking

"It's too hot in here."   "When's lunch?"   "What cool shoes!"

Focus on Reading

"Where did this character come from? I guess I lost focus."

"Too much new information! What does it mean?"

Focus on Solving Reading Problems

"I need to figure out what this word problem is asking. I'll chunk it to see if that helps."

"This graph might help me understand the key terms."

"How could I put this in my own words?"

Focus on Disciplinary Literacy Practices

"Which parts of this word problem are irrelevant to solve for x?"

"Whose point of view is this? Should I trust it?"

"Is there another explanation for this result?"

The different kinds of metacognitive focus depicted in the funnel are not to be confused with *stages* of reading, as if readers start at the top of the funnel with a general awareness of where their attention is and with practice, over time, move to disciplinary approaches to reading.

Teachers who introduce the funnel to students might first model with their own reading of a disciplinary text, pointing out where they are in the funnel at different points in their reading behavior, modeling the ways readers sometimes get distracted and then refocus. To involve students in recognizing their own metacognitive processes and metacognitive focus, teachers can ask questions like the examples that follow.

Notice Thinking

Initially, to build awareness of thinking and an atmosphere in which confusion is easily shared, teachers may simply ask questions that elicit students' awareness of whether they are on or off task—questions that ask students to notice their thinking:

What are you thinking about as you "read"?

What is your mind telling you while you are "reading" this text?

What did you notice about this text?

In response, students may notice that they are watching the clock, bored, worried about their hair, frustrated, and so forth. Surfacing such mental processes in response to reading, even if these consist largely of distractions or confusions at first, is good practice for students. With the teacher's guidance, it will lead to more strategic reading.

Focus on Reading

To focus students on the source of a reading roadblock or loss of attention, teachers direct them to the text itself and ask them to focus on reading:

Where did you begin to get confused?

What part of the text caused you trouble?

Was there a particular word or sentence that got in your way?

What about Shakespeare's dialogue makes it difficult?

What was hard about keeping all these different politicians separate?

When students can identify where they encountered difficulty or where their mind started to wander, they are able to understand that reading has a problem-solving aspect. In other words, not all reading is automatic.

Focus on Solving Reading Problems

Questions that focus students on the strategies they use to solve reading problems highlight their growing agency and reinforce the notion that when they encounter reading problems, they can focus on solving them:

How did you clear up that confusion?

How could you get an overview of what this section says?

What connections did you make?

How did you figure that out?

As students learn to problem solve reading, they build and use a toolbox of cognitive strategies such as clarifying, visualizing, predicting, making connections, and summarizing, and they learn to employ these strategies in disciplinary ways.

Focus on Disciplinary Literacy Practices

Across different disciplines, students will notice differences in how text is structured and discourse is conducted. They will respond to text as historians or mathematicians or scientists, for example:

What do you know about the source of this text?

Whose voice is represented? Whose voice is missing?

What pattern are you seeing or not seeing?

What does this evidence lead you to predict?

What claims does this text make? What evidence does it present?

What would a graph of this data look like?

How does the poet use language to establish a particular tone?

By using disciplinary literacy practices, students are building the mental habits to become increasingly independent and resourceful subject area readers and to participate in, for example, scientific inquiry, mathematical problem solving, literary conversations, or historical argumentation.

The metacognitive funnel is a clear reminder that metacognitive conversation is meant to serve conceptual and content goals—disciplinary goals. For students and teachers alike, asking themselves and each other "where their thinking is in the funnel" can point to areas for further focus and learning. Based on that assessment, teachers can design their next moves to further students' apprenticeship as readers in particular disciplines. (An assessment that can help students notice their thinking and reading focus is the Curriculum-Embedded Reading Assessment [CERA] described in the Assessment Appendix.)

Reflecting on Roles in a Metacognitive Classroom

> I'm starting to notice that the classrooms are a lot less monotone and a lot less teacher centered.
>
> —Francisco Valdiosera, high school vice principal

When metacognitive conversation becomes routine, teachers learn about what students know, are learning, and are struggling with in terms of subject area content, thinking processes, and literacy strategies. In addition, because students are able to observe the many ways that teachers and peers work to understand content, evaluate their thinking and their problem solving, and approach difficult literacy tasks, students have authentic opportunities to learn and practice new ways of solving literacy problems and becoming confident and competent readers of disciplinary texts.

At the same time, many Reading Apprenticeship teachers acknowledge that the shift to a metacognitive classroom requires important reframing of their role and increased trust in students' potential. As vice principal Francisco Valdiosera observes, when classrooms are inquiry-based, students have a lot more to say.

With practice and teacher guidance, students internalize metacognitive conversation routines and apply them for their own purposes. Box 4.18 is a graphic representation of how teachers and students negotiate this transfer of responsibility. High school principal Deborah Leser, whose whole school is taking up Reading Apprenticeship, describes the classroom role changes she has noticed:

> What we're seeing more is teachers involving students in more discussion in the classroom so that students are more actively participating in their education and in talking and thinking about what they're trying to learn, as opposed to what we saw a lot of before, and what I've seen over the years that I've worked in education, which is teachers up in front telling the kids what they need to know. Now kids are discussing what they know and don't know, what they understand and don't understand. So it really gives students a chance to think through their own learning, to do that metacognitive piece and really think about their thinking.

Teachers interested in reflecting on how their own roles and classrooms may be changing as they implement Reading Apprenticeship approaches can refer to the snapshot "What Does a Reading Apprenticeship Classroom Look Like?" in the Assessment Appendix. This snapshot—which highlights a focus on comprehension, a climate of collaboration, and an emphasis on student independence—can also be a helpful lesson planning tool.

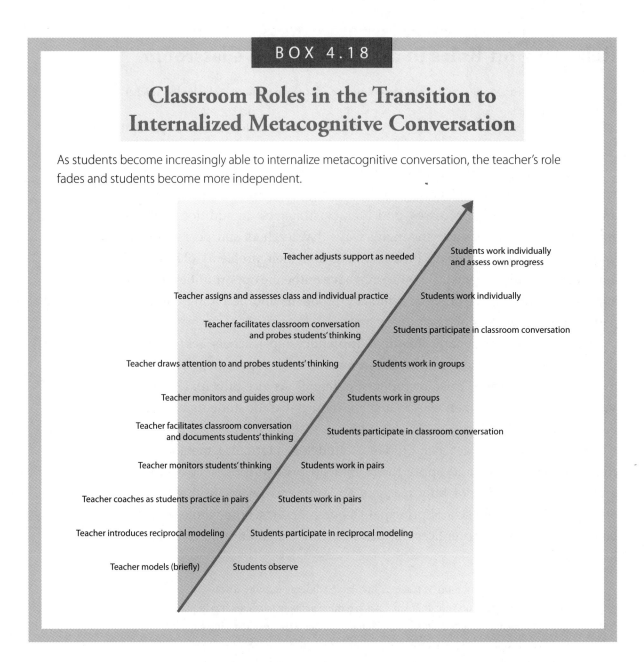

BOX 4.18

Classroom Roles in the Transition to Internalized Metacognitive Conversation

As students become increasingly able to internalize metacognitive conversation, the teacher's role fades and students become more independent.

Teacher adjusts support as needed — Students work individually and assess own progress

Teacher assigns and assesses class and individual practice — Students work individually

Teacher facilitates classroom conversation and probes students' thinking — Students participate in classroom conversation

Teacher draws attention to and probes students' thinking — Students work in groups

Teacher monitors and guides group work — Students work in groups

Teacher facilitates classroom conversation and documents students' thinking — Students participate in classroom conversation

Teacher monitors students' thinking — Students work in pairs

Teacher coaches as students practice in pairs — Students work in pairs

Teacher introduces reciprocal modeling — Students participate in reciprocal modeling

Teacher models (briefly) — Students observe

An example of disciplinary learning experiences in which other students, instead of the teacher, support students' transition to internalized metacognitive conversation is the peer analysis activity that community college composition teacher Patti Smith uses to help students improve the quality of their thinking and writing. In her Composition I course, partners respond metacognitively to each other's essays. Patti sets aside four Essay Evaluation Days per semester for students to Think Aloud and Talk to the Text about the *ideas* in each other's most recent essay. In Classroom Close-Up 4.10, she describes the process and her students' excitement about it. At a very basic level, she wants her students to be able to stop when they're reading a classmate's essay and say to the writer,

CLASSROOM CLOSE-UP 4.10

"Is That What I Wrote??"

For several years, Patti Smith has been using Reading Apprenticeship routines to help her Composition I students understand the assigned reading that they are asked to respond to in writing. In the following account, she relates what happened when her students applied those metacognitive routines to the editing of classmates' essays.

During each of the first two semesters when Patti tried out her Essay Evaluation Days, participation was voluntary (it is now required). Students had to come to the four evaluation day deadlines with a completed draft of the assigned two-page essay; in exchange, they could turn in a final draft at any time during the course. Each student interacted each day with two other students: one partner for Think Aloud and discussion and another for written commentary in the form of Talking to the Text and double-entry evidence/interpretation notes followed by discussion.

Patti describes a rough start to her experiment despite subsequent success: "The first evaluation day of the fall semester was a true dry run, not just for the students but for me as well. I made the mistake of simply trying to walk them through the processes. I had not modeled thinking aloud with my students on anything but the reading assignments in our textbook. The students were able to read aloud their partner's essay, but thinking aloud was sporadic at best. The writer of the essay was not accountable for any listening; therefore, engagement did not really occur."

Patti adjusted for the shortcomings, and students in her spring semester class benefited. They had an early opportunity to read and ask questions about the process directions, and Patti regularly modeled Think Aloud with sample student essays.

In addition, she assigned the listener (the author) the role of following along and making annotations on a second copy of the draft.

By the end of the spring semester, she was well satisfied with the value of evaluation days. Half of the twenty-two students who completed the course had attended all Evaluation Days; ten of the eleven earned A's and the other was proud to have earned a B. (Of the students who did not attend, two earned B's, eight earned C's, and one failed the course.)

The following student comments are a testament to the power of extending metacognitive conversation to writing assignments:

Sally: Evaluation days were awesome. I got to see how much my essay would keep another person's attention and how much sense it would make to someone other than me. It gave me confidence in my thinking and writing skills.

Jim: The largest benefit of attending evaluation day to me is seeing other people's writings and getting insight on different ways to express things.

Charlie: I learned so much by just listening to my writings read to me by someone else and being able to pick up on my mistakes and weak spots. I started catching myself as I was writing, thinking about the mistakes or things I'd learned about my writing on previous essays that had been evaluated.

Maggie: The revision process helped me to become a better writer because I started thinking about whether or not what I was trying to say would make sense to my classmates who would be reading my essay.

"Wait a minute: What did that mean?"—or, when hearing their own essay read aloud, ask themselves, "Is that what I wrote??"

■ ■ ■

In this chapter and the previous one, we have offered ways to introduce the social dimension, personal dimension, and metacognitive conversation separately, but in truth the described inquiries and activities are simultaneously social, personal, and metacognitive. As is true for all parts of the Reading Apprenticeship framework, the categories are organizational, not absolute.

In the next chapter, instead of moving directly to the remaining dimensions of the framework—the cognitive and knowledge-building dimensions—we take a look at the underlying premise of Reading Apprenticeship: if teachers are going to be successful apprenticing students into the reading practices and processes of their disciplines, then they need to read *with* students and *in* class. Chapter Five labels this premise "Extensive Reading."

Notes

1. Burger, E., Chard, D., Hall, E., Kennedy, P., Leinwand, S., Renfro, F., . . . Waits, B. (2008). *Holt California geometry*. Boston: Houghton Mifflin Harcourt, p. 74.

2. Alexie, S. (1997). Superman and me. In M. Dorris & E. Buchwald (Eds.), *The most wonderful books: Writers on discovering the pleasures of reading*. Minneapolis: Milkweed Editions.

3. "Doug Green" has retired from teaching and we were unable to contact him for permission to use his quote from an earlier interview. We have used a pseudonym in place of his real name.

4. Yu-Chung Chang-Hou has developed an approach to mathematics problem solving that she calls Writing and Reading Activities for Math Problem Solving (WRAMPS). She credits her experience with Reading Apprenticeship with contributing to her development of the program. A description of WRAMPS can be found at http://www.cfkeep.org/html/stitch .php?s=66561915414931&id=35258404012079

Extensive Academic Reading

Extending Opportunities and Support

When I first came to Mrs. Ryan class, I really didn't like to read. I guess because no one really pushed me when it came down to reading. As many books as I have read in Mrs. Ryan class, I just think that reading isn't bad after all. When I use to read and I didn't really understand it, I use to completely stop. Now when I don't understand the text, I think. What I like about reading is that there is so many ways to break it down.

—Harlan, grade 9 student

STUDENTS LIKE HARLAN, who used to "completely stop" when he didn't understand a text, are not beginning readers. Rather, they are highly inexperienced readers, especially at making their way through texts that demand ongoing problem solving—academic texts dense with ideas conveyed through complex sentences and novel or even technical vocabulary—subject area reading.

When Harlan became a student in Cindy Ryan's class, for the first time he was, as he put it, "pushed . . . when it came down to reading." Her academic literacy classroom brimmed with books, and her students read a range of disciplinary texts in history, science, and English language arts along with free-choice reading. Students read in class and at home. Their class embodied the features of extensive reading that translate widely: extend students' opportunities to read in class, extend the types of subject area texts students are supported to read, and increase the opportunities for students to choose texts for their own purposes (both subject area and free-choice texts). The result, from Harlan's perspective, was being able to develop the confidence, skills, and stamina to do the ongoing problem solving that academic text requires. It could even be said that as a result of his evolving reading competence, close reading to solve reading problems became pleasurable, not deadly: "What I like about reading," he reports at year-end, "is that there is so many ways to break it down."

Extensive reading, which was Harlan's experience in Cindy Ryan's class, is the "surround" in which Reading Apprenticeship happens and succeeds. Although the heart of the Reading Apprenticeship classroom is metacognitive conversation, it is only in the context of extensive reading that students have the opportunity to accelerate their development as readers and subject area learners. For students who need to move from being inexperienced to experienced readers, and from disengaged to engaged learners, there is no way around it: they must have extensive, supported opportunities to read, in class.

In this chapter we present a rationale and general guidelines for incorporating extensive reading into subject area classes. By establishing an inquiry culture and metacognitive routines such as described in Chapters Three and Four, teachers can confidently extend students' opportunities to read complex academic materials.

The Why of Extensive Academic Reading

I wanted students to become the scientifically literate citizens envisioned in the National Science Education Standards: students who read science, enjoy reading science, and even experience the passion I feel for the natural world. However, with 65 percent of incoming freshmen at my school reading below the sixth grade level, it was clear that our science curriculum, especially the textbook, did not include motivating or accessible reading for most students. To bring reading back into our science classrooms, my colleague Ann Akey and I designed yearlong literacy routines and quarterly reading projects that we use successfully with our ninth-grade students, including English language learners.

—Janet Creech, high school science teacher[1]

Janet Creech and Ann Akey had a disciplinary rationale for introducing extensive reading into their grade 9 science course: to offer students a future in which they could read about, understand, and even enjoy science and the natural world. According to Janet, the literacy routines that now anchor students' science learning—keeping metacognitive logs of their science textbook reading, regularly researching self-selected science news reports, and completing quarterly literacy projects and presentations that incorporate reading science-based books of choice—seem to make an important difference in changing students' engagement with science. With extensive reading as the context for all of students' science learning, Janet and Ann feel they are able to serve their disciplinary goals and promote students' literacy more generally. (Their course is described in more detail later in this chapter.)

Extensive reading, when practiced strategically and consistently, *serves the goals of subject area learning* and makes the following contributions to students' growth as readers:

- Academic language and subject area knowledge, as well as familiarity with text structures, genres, vocabulary, and concepts in particular subject areas, are all promoted through extensive reading.

- Fluency, stamina, and the habit of reading are powerfully boosted through ongoing and extensive opportunities to read.

- Choice of reading material, which extensive reading makes possible, contributes greatly to motivation and engagement.

- Work to comprehend academic texts with the collaboration of peers and with teacher support for modeling and metacognitive conversation helps students build text-based problem-solving skills and dispositions for engaged subject area learning. Sharing reading through book talks, presentations, text-based group discussions, and other public experiences builds excitement and interest among a community of readers.

- Increased reading experiences help students gain insight about themselves as readers and about their preferences in reading materials.

By definition, extensive reading takes time. Yet the *time* students actually spend reading and working to comprehend texts makes the single most important contribution to their reading achievement and proficiency.[2] Sadly, as teachers know, the amount of time students spend engaged in reading inside and outside of school has decreased in recent decades. Reduced reading opportunities means that students' reading competence and confidence both suffer. Without experience in making sense of academic materials, students will lack familiarity and stamina when faced with complex texts. Understandably, they will have little motivation for working their way through difficult material. Without access to the knowledge and academic language conveyed in texts, their ability to comprehend a greater range of texts will be limited. This in turn often leads teachers to lower their expectations for students' reading, thereby continuing the cycle.

Without ongoing and supported reading experiences, students stop growing as readers and even lose ground. To interrupt this downward spiral, teachers will need new and more powerful ways to bring reading back into the curriculum and the classroom.

Jane Wolford, whose community college students enroll in her history classes with little preparation for the kind of extensive reading that historians enjoy, decided to help them bear down, take on multiple disciplinary texts, and perhaps even have some fun. One of Jane's biggest challenges was students' reaction to primary sources. By taking the time in class to have students read closely and think like historians, Jane helped them build the motivation and skills to tackle and understand challenging text. She describes in Classroom Close-Up 5.1 what she and her students discovered.

CLASSROOM CLOSE-UP 5.1

Learning to Read Across Multiple Texts

Typically, the community college students in Jane Wolford's U.S. history classes were resistant and inexperienced readers of history. Most found history irrelevant. To change students' attitudes and ease them into reading like historians, Jane used reciprocal modeling of the Think Aloud to take difficult texts—especially primary sources—apart line by line. The metacognitive conversations that resulted were a revelation—to Jane and especially to her students.

"Most of my students don't know how to approach a primary source document. I didn't realize it and had been throwing them into the deep end of the pool without water wings. They were just sloughing it off: 'I can't do it, so why even try?' Now I model it, and we work through the text. They are a lot more apt to talk when you do a line-by-line reading together and show them how historians think. It leads them to think they might be able to do it.

"We were reading a famous letter by Abigail Adams to her husband, an early feminist plea— 'Remember the Ladies'—an appeal for more equitable distribution of power. One of my students, not what I call an academically minded student, stunned herself by the realization that she could understand

the letter in its historical context: 'Maybe during her time, what she said was bold. Maybe what she's saying will be important in the future.'

"To me, the key is building students' confidence. So much of it is letting them know they can go for it."

In addition to line-by-line reciprocal modeling, Jane builds students' confidence and skills by having them Talk to the Text, source texts, and keep metacognitive logs. Her students' experiences have led her to introduce Reading Apprenticeship to her colleagues.

"A lot of people question me when I describe what we do. 'You're taking forty-five minutes to cover one primary source document?' But there's much more learning going on, much deeper reading. And we don't have to do a line-by-line reading after a certain point."

In one unit essay, for example, Jane's students pull together content from four primary sources, three secondary sources, a hereditary genetics map, and their world knowledge of racial politics to argue whether or not Thomas Jefferson fathered Sally Hemings's children. For Jane's students, as history became accessible, it also became sort of interesting!

The What of Extensive Academic Reading

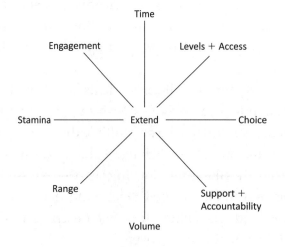

In this representation of extensive reading, the teacher and the student have different but interacting roles. Teachers extend the *time in class* for reading—and rereading—academic texts to serve subject area learning goals. By extending the reading *levels* of texts, teachers provide differentiated readings as well as a ladder of increasing challenge. Teachers also extend *access* to academic texts by using ancillary topic-related materials to add interest and varied entry points. Teachers extend students' *choice* of what to read through thematically linked texts or independent reading projects. Creating *support* for extensive reading, in terms of the classroom social and personal dimensions and a focus on metacognitive conversation, allows teachers to extend what they expect of students, to extend students' *accountability* for reading.

When students have more time for subject area reading, they are expected to extend the *volume* of reading they accomplish. With the teacher providing increased access to different levels and types of texts, students extend the *range* of what they read. As students read more and more kinds of texts, they extend their reading *stamina*. As students extend their stamina for reading longer and more challenging texts, in combination with extended opportunities to make choices about their subject area reading, they become more competent readers and, presumably, more *engaged* subject area readers.

By extending the opportunities and support for student reading, teachers see a transformation in the roles they and their students assume. High school English teacher Lisa Krebs expresses relief that now reading is a class activity and not only something students are supposed to do for homework. As a result, her goals have changed from managing and entertaining students to supporting them in their own reading, thinking, and problem solving:

> I think back to when I was early teaching, and I mean, I was doing everything. They were sitting there, sometimes with nothing on their desks the whole period. And I'm sort of telling them about the story, and showing them visual aids, and doing this, and running around, and passing out [things], and, you know, it was crazy. And they're probably thinking, "Doo da doo, I don't have to do anything."

When classrooms are places where teachers do things *for* students or *to* students, teachers are doing all of the intellectual work. When classrooms become places where teachers do things *with* students, the intellectual culture of the classroom shifts, and students have a purpose for investing in learning.

The Student Learning Goals for Building Personal Engagement (see the Assessment Appendix) make clear to students a number of ways they can think about extending their reading effort and evolving a more powerful reader identity.

Extending Time for Reading Disciplinary Texts in Class

As Lisa Krebs just described, teachers often assign reading of curriculum materials for homework and review them during class, with the result that many students avoid the reading and simply wait for the review. Depending on the class, the teacher's goals, and the time in the school year, bringing reading back into the classroom may mean any of the following:

- Students spend time reading these materials *during* class, either individually or in small groups.

- Students work together in class to make sense of key passages selected by the teacher from the core text.

- Reading may continue to be assigned for homework, but the class may work together on making sense of some or all of the assigned reading material during class time. The teacher may be actively involved but is coaching and facilitating the meaning-making process without reviewing or summarizing the text for students.

- Research and reading become an integral part of project-based learning, with the teacher choosing to spend more time actively engaging and supporting students' reading in class, and students spending more time working on projects as homework.

When students have time in class to uncover text comprehension problems and work toward solving them with the help of their teacher and peers, teachers have the opportunity to help students understand key concepts and information in the curriculum. When students are supported in reading their course texts, the texts become the resource for accessing subject matter that they are intended to be.

Early in the year, teachers may want students to spend a high percentage of class time engaged in reading and debriefing their reading of course materials. When the emphasis on reading disciplinary texts and finding ways to understand them becomes a classroom standard, teachers can become more selective about which texts or chunks of text to explore as a class or at length.

Gina Hale made decisions not only about which parts of the grade 7 history textbook to focus on, but also about how to engage a hugely diverse group of students in becoming passionate readers of history. She quickly came to appreciate that by limiting her use of the textbook to standards-based "essentials," she had time for students to read other disciplinary texts—carefully chosen with students' different needs in mind—that would bring the essentials alive. (See Classroom Close-Up 5.2.)

CLASSROOM CLOSE-UP 5.2

Supporting the Textbook with Differentiated Reading

Gina Hale admits that because she tried to "cover" the entire history textbook with her seventh graders, she had no time for extensive reading. One class changed everything.

"That year, I taught an English language arts-history core class with one-third special ed, one-third English learners, and one-third GATE [Gifted and Talented Education] students. I had nonreaders and students reading above grade level in the same class.

"At the time, I was operating on the idea that kids had to read the textbook, front to back. But that year, I needed a different plan—more kids than ever were not reading or doing homework, and way too many were failing.

"In desperation, I decided to try extensive reading. I could see that it was the only way to get my kids all reading about the same topic. I spent several afternoons with the school librarian selecting supplementary text sets at different reading levels related to my history content. At first it was a lot of work, but by the end of the year she was so excited that she created units of extensive reading for the whole seventh grade. Rather than having us sign up for library, she brought the text sets around to our classrooms. It became a real collaboration.

"Still, I didn't want to just dump the textbook, so each chapter I selected a few sections—only a few pages in the beginning, but more later—that covered the essential content standards. In pairs, students took turns reading and thinking aloud. As a class we talked about what partners discussed. It was clear that comprehension was improving, that they were reading, but I could tell from their talk that many students were not *really* engaged in the reading. I was pretty discouraged!

"The unit on medieval Europe was a turning point. The textbook had a feature on castles, so I chose that, hoping it would be interesting, perplexing. I knew students would have a lot of Disney-type schema about castles, but this section in the textbook zoomed in on how difficult and unpleasant it was to live in castles.

"After the partner work, when I asked students what they figured out about the reading, naturally their first responses were about the details selected to most appeal to a middle school audience—they enthusiastically recounted the horrors of the chamber pot. I was amused, and thrilled, by their engagement.

'Okay,' I said, 'but what did you figure out about *reading*, not castles?' Doreen, a GATE student who read well enough but typically with very little interest, responded, 'You have to really read it! It's interesting if you *read* it.'

"During that same unit, I put students into four-person research groups to support guided writing projects. They were gathering information for short stories that would take place in medieval Europe, and each student would be his or her own main character. One group included two special-ed students and two GATE students. Francisco was really smart, but a visual processing disorder made reading hard enough that he had just quit trying. Paulo read word by word, at a first-grade level. And then there were Tami and Julie, both academically successful students who nevertheless were in the habit of reading just enough to finish an assigned task.

"For resources, in addition to the textbook, they had the text sets the librarian and I had built. Paulo started with a picture book about knights, Francisco chose an illustrated encyclopedia about castles. Tami and Julie were reading a biography of Eleanor of Aquitaine and expository books about medieval court life and textiles. By the end of the unit, Paulo was reading Francisco's encyclopedia, Francisco was cross-referencing the textbook, and Julie and Tami were asking the two boys for information on knights.

"All this research and writing meant that students were rereading—to get writing ideas, check facts, or find information to share with someone else. They were building fluency, an incredible amount of schema, and stamina. And, they were engaged. Intellectually. In work.

"Over the course of that year, it became clear to me that few of my students would ever get passionate about history because of the textbook. When I decided to make more time for differentiated reading, I saw my nonreaders become readers and my good-enough readers become avid readers.

"In his end-of-year reflection, Paulo, who began the year reading at a first-grade level, wrote, 'I got better at reading. I read a book for the first time. Now I know I am not stupid. I can read.'

"*That's* what extensive reading does for students."

Extending Levels and Access for Reading

While course texts are resources for student learning, they also have limitations. The one-size-fits-all reading level of textbooks assumes a more homogeneous classroom than is often typical. Textbooks also suffer from a lack of specifics, a characteristic fault that has been called "mentioning rather than explaining."[3] To address such issues, many teachers, such as Gina Hale in Classroom Close-Up 5.2, supplement their course materials with vertical text sets that provide a range of entry points and horizontal text sets that provide more detail or different perspectives about a topic. Many text sets have both vertical and horizontal characteristics—differentiated reading levels and thematically related auxiliary texts.

Vertical Text Sets

To address the range of reading abilities in a class, vertical text sets present text about a particular topic at a range of difficulty levels. With vertical text sets, teachers can offer comfortable starting places in the curriculum to students who have different experiences and proficiencies as readers. This kind of differentiation is familiar in the instruction of English learners and in special education.

A vertical text set can serve as a ladder that allows students to progressively increase their range of reading comfort and their reading proficiency. At the same time, of course, by reading easier and then more difficult text passages about the same topic, students begin to build and elaborate subject-specific knowledge and vocabulary. Schema developed from reading a less difficult text are in place to help students in making new connections when reading a related but more complex text.

A collection of publishers' competing textbooks can be a valuable resource for creating vertical text sets. That is what Stacey Tisor realized when she was on her district's biology textbook adoption committee:

> I was teaching tenth grade biology and my students were at all different levels. I had some who were honors students—but not in science—I had general ed students, students well below grade level, and English learners who were close to being reclassified. The range meant that a single textbook was not going to work. But fortuitously, I was on the biology textbook adoption committee. Publishers were sending all these textbooks for our review, and I realized they were all written at different levels. In addition to the one we chose for adoption, I found three of the others that I used to make text sets for particular topics.
>
> Whatever the topic, everyone read the adopted text first, which was written at a level somewhat higher than tenth grade. I set the reading up with an anticipatory guide related to the lesson objective, so students

knew what to focus on. With some topics, everyone then got a second text. I put students into small groups, with the text best matched to their reading level. I had one textbook at a college level, another at a "normal" level, and a third that was low middle school/elementary.

For an evolution unit, I asked students when they finished their "leveled" text to try the next hardest text. Interestingly, it was the students reading at the lowest levels who were the most motivated to try to move up to the next level text.

Stacey is no longer in the classroom, but as a professional developer for her school district, she passes along her experience building text sets from textbooks and also shows teachers how to use the Internet to build text sets.

An activity that asks students to explore a vertical text set gives them the metacognitive experience of identifying the factors that make a text difficult or accessible, both generally and to them in particular (Box 5.1 lists a number of these factors). The activity, described in Box 5.2, asks students to rank the accessibility of texts, explore the factors contributing to their difficulty or accessibility, and set goals for moving up the ladder of text difficulty.

BOX 5.1

What Makes Text Difficult?

Readability measures provide broad indicators that can help teachers match texts to students. A readability measure, however, cannot account for a given student's ease or difficulty in reading a particular text. All of the following contribute to a student's experience of text difficulty or accessibility:

Language: Vocabulary contributes to text difficulty according to the density of unfamiliar, abstract, polysyllabic, and technical or highly specialized words. The words that will be unfamiliar in a given text vary, depending on each student's schema.

Sentence length and complexity: Long sentences are measured as harder to read than short sentences, but complex sentence structure also affects difficulty. In addition, when sentences are adapted or limited in length simply to keep them short, the loss of transition and amplifying words and phrases can actually make them harder to understand, a charge sometimes made about texts for English learners.[4]

Conceptual difficulty: Conceptually, the difficulty of a text depends on how abstract its ideas are and the amount of prior knowledge they require. Individual students bring more or less schema about particular information, ideas, or concepts.

Idea density: The density of ideas in a text and the ways in which they are embedded affect text difficulty. Textbooks, for example, pack in and relate ideas for maximum coverage, not necessarily for maximum comprehension.

Relevance: How important is this topic to the reader? Texts about motivating topics "feel" less difficult.

BOX 5.2

Exploring a Vertical Text Set

PURPOSE

When students read a set of increasingly difficult texts about the same topic, they learn to recognize the factors that make texts more or less accessible. In addition, by reading texts at different levels of difficulty, students can understand how reading multiple texts about a topic builds knowledge and fluency.

PROCEDURE

1. Collect a set of texts (four or five) on a single topic—the New Deal or prevention of diabetes, for example. The texts should represent a range of difficulty appropriate to the students in your class. In the set of texts, you might also vary the text types, choosing examples from textbooks at various grade levels, magazines, newspapers, and the Internet.

2. Give students about twenty-five minutes to work in small groups and explore the various texts. Ask students to skim the documents and take notes with the following two questions in mind. Explain that groups will then discuss their thinking about what makes text difficult and create a poster explaining their reasoning.

   - How would you rank these texts in terms of their accessibility (ease of understanding) or inaccessibility (difficulty of understanding)? Why? What features of these texts are you considering as you make these judgments? Please make a group poster that reflects the features you discussed.

   - Which texts in this set would you be most comfortable reading? Which ones do you think you could read with some support?

3. With the class, debrief students' insights and any issues they raised in their groups, and lead a discussion of the following:

   - If you and your classmates read different texts on a topic and then meet in small groups to discuss what you learned and share questions you have, how might this help you learn about the topic?

   - If you are given a choice of texts to read on a topic, how do you decide which one(s) to read?

4. Ask students to set goals for extending their academic reading range and proficiency by selecting from the text set a starting text and the order in which they will read any of the other texts.

Rita Jensen is able to increase the challenge of the texts her middle school ELD students tackle with very deliberate attention to the support available from students' interest in a topic:

> I increase the length and difficulty of the text while keeping the subject very high interest. What I expect from students increases, but support is built in.

Horizontal Text Sets

Teachers who create horizontal or thematic text sets recognize that different perspectives, supplementary content, and even different genres can be more accessible than a core text—and build schema that make the core text itself more accessible and meaningful. Horizontal text sets are a widely used way to build interest, background knowledge, and vocabulary. They can also include texts differentiated by difficulty level, combining characteristics of vertical and horizontal text sets.

In her middle school social studies class, Laurie Erby worried that her students' textbook chapter about transboundary pollution was not helping them understand the danger of global hazards like acid rain, water contamination, and nuclear fallout. To extend her students' reading, and give them a different perspective on these environmental issues, Laurie used a text set comprising interviews with survivors of the Chernobyl nuclear explosion. For students, the interview text structure was familiar and accessible, and the first-person perspectives made "transboundary pollution" concrete. The interviews had the additional advantage of varying in difficulty, depending on the subject and speaker of the narrative. Laurie describes this particular instance of extensive reading in Classroom Close-Up 5.3.

CLASSROOM CLOSE-UP 5.3
Transboundary Solution

A textbook chapter on "transboundary pollution" is not what anyone would call an inherently captivating read for seventh graders. As she explains here, Laurie Erby extended her students' reading and understanding of transboundary pollution with texts that presented first-person interviews of Chernobyl survivors.[5]

"Reading in social studies is not always high-interest reading for students. There's a lot of information in the text, and it's very dense.

"The chapter that we've been working on is on transboundary pollution... I felt that at the end of the chapter, students really didn't have a feel for the seriousness of these incidents, particularly Chernobyl.

"My goal . . . was to really give the students a better feel for what it was like for survivors of Chernobyl. The texts that I used were different survivor stories."

These interviews included descriptions of young men who repeatedly dove into radioactive water to open a valve and prevent an even more disastrous explosion, a girl's humiliation at a camp where the other children (not from Chernobyl) refused to touch her, and a scientist who measured but did not warn local people of the radiation in the milk and meat they continued to consume.

Laurie had students read their particular interview, Talk to the Text, share their ideas and questions about the text with a partner who read the same interview, and then exchange information about their interview with a group in which each student had read a different text.

"In sharing their stories," Laurie relates, "they're looking for similarities and differences . . . so they're really getting a full feel for what happened to a lot of different people and a lot of different perspectives here. The listeners are going to ask clarifying questions, and then the presenter has a chance to answer them. So if they didn't understand something that the presenter mentioned, they can ask, 'Gee, what did you mean by this?'"

Laurie's students then wrote a reflection tying in what they learned in the textbook with what they learned from the various Chernobyl stories. By reading, reconciling, and synthesizing multiple texts, Laurie's students gained a deeper understanding of transboundary pollution than reading a single textbook treatment or single survivor story could ever match.

English teacher Chris Van Ruiten-Greene's high school students are required to read core literature that many of them see as more than a little fusty. She creates horizontal text sets to build students' interest in the themes and issues that a core text raises and to clear away some of their preconceived notions about the core text's possible relevance.

With each class, before putting a text set together, Chris invites students to discuss what they know and what questions they have about the particular core text. With Alan Paton's *Cry, the Beloved Country,* for example, Chris says students typically don't know much about the book except they can see by the copyright date that it's "old." Their questions often focus on their sense of Africa as "messed up" and their puzzlement about why movement toward racial equity in South Africa was so long delayed: "Didn't they protest?" "Who was their Martin Luther King?" Then, depending on students' questions and relevant current events in South Africa and the United States, Chris creates a thematic text set of what she calls "orbiting" texts. They vary by topic, text type, and difficulty, but they are tied together by essential questions the students raise and a set of themes and potential writing topics that students generate.

> For seniors reading *Cry, the Beloved Country* in my world literature course, I extend the core reading with varied-difficulty texts for a wider view of the central themes and issues presented in the text. I choose orbiting texts to build interest, answer student questions, extend our theme discussions, and make the core reading *relevant* to postmodern concerns.
>
> Excerpts from *Guns, Germs, and Steel* really get them riled up, as do chapters from *Kaffir Boy,* racial issue articles from Johannesburg's *Daily Rand*—of which there are a plethora—and excerpts from *No More Strangers Now: Young Voices from a New South Africa.* I vary it every year, depending on students' questions and what our own American issues are in parallel to the themes we are considering. Students consistently identify themes related to the trap of poverty and its toll on human potential and dignity, the irony of achieving wisdom through enormous loss, and the shallowness of the perceived ethnic and cultural differences that set groups of people against each other—at great cost.
>
> Students respond to the orbiting texts with personal reads and logging, partner discussion, sharing out, becoming a group expert on one of the *Cry* themes, and presenting to others on topics from the orbiting texts—about AIDS or race relations, for example.
>
> The text set makes an *enormous* impact on their reading of the core text. They see why this book is still relevant and how it broadens their sense of the world and equity and raises the complexities of how to get along despite our differences. The orbiting texts make the "old" story provocative and real. They spark and fuel classroom discourse because of the issues all students connect to.

Thematic text sets might well include visual texts such as documentaries, photographs, drawings and illustrations, and physical models that extend students' understanding of text materials and vocabulary as well as the concepts under study. The same metacognitive routines students use to support their comprehension of connected text—metacognitive logs, double-entry journals, Talking to the Text, and Think Aloud—can likewise deepen comprehension of visual texts.

In Classroom Close-Up 5.4, ninth graders in Allie Pitts's history class read across a set of propaganda posters, not all of them written in English, to understand an inquiry question the posters suggest.

Textbooks as Text Sets

Textbooks themselves offer abundant opportunities for extending students' access and range as readers. A flip through the pages of a science, history, math, or English textbook will quickly reveal a variety of text types and ways of representing information. Gina Hale, in Classroom Close-Up 5.2, describes choosing sections of her history textbook for students' reading based on important content standards that students are expected to master. Teachers can also choose sections of their textbooks for class reading and focused problem solving with an eye toward "easing in" to new topics, conceptually difficult territory, or dense academic text.

With a new science chapter, for example, if students first read and Talk to the Text with the visuals, they have an opportunity to build schema for the concepts and terminology they will encounter in the chapter as a whole. Reading the visuals in this way supports students' next pass through the chapter and their close work with the connected passages of text. In small group or class discussions of the visuals they have read, students can raise questions that provide reasons to read the less immediately appealing portions of the chapter—for instance, to clarify uncertainties, to learn something that has intrigued them, to see how the textbook explains an interesting process they encountered.

Similarly, teachers can choose a particularly telling excerpt of a textbook for close reading and problem solving, ask students to work in pairs or small groups on it, and then bring the class together for further clarification, problem solving, and discussion. By breaking down long passages into manageable segments and supporting students to use Think Aloud, Talking to the Text, and partner and small group discussion to grapple with the chunks, teachers give students considerable experience with academic reading. The textbook used in this way becomes a rich resource for learning, with multiple opportunities for students to read, reread, and work their way through the challenges these texts present.

Community college mathematics teacher Laura Graff uses her textbook as a text set by having students outline chapters. Students take a first pass through with a metacognitive lens: What do I think is important here, how does it relate to other information in the chapter, and how is the text helping me understand? In Classroom Close-Up 5.5, Laura describes how students learn to use their textbook as a tool for learning, not simply as a collection of homework problems.

CLASSROOM CLOSE-UP 5.4

Disciplinary Inquiry of the Day

Students in Allie Pitts's ninth-grade history class are studying World War I. As they come into the room, the disciplinary inquiry of the day is written on the board: "How did countries use national pride to convince men to join the war?" The texts for the day are a set of primary source propaganda posters from different combatant countries.

Allie and her students work through understanding one poster in a reciprocal model, with Allie recording in two columns for the class "What We Know" and "How We Know It." Allie has students move back and forth between whole class and partner discussion.

She also encourages students to notice questions that occur to them and decide what to do about them: Is comprehension blocked without an answer, or can they work through the ambiguity or their curiosity?

Students write their questions on sticky notes that Allie collects and projects from the document camera. Yellow notes are for "crucial" questions, and orange notes are for questions whose answers students can "live without" for the moment. The class works through one student's "yellow" question and sees, along with the question's originator, that they can leave the question unanswered and still make meaning.

Students then work on a new poster with partners. Two large figures dominate: a knight and a monster. Most partners recognize that the poster is British and that the knight represents Britain.

Allie brings the class together. "Okay. The general agreement seems to be the knight is Britain. What does Britain want you to do? We are going to go back to do some historical thinking. Who is the *audience* for the poster?"

Allie then takes the class through a reciprocal model of identifying this particular text's audience, message, and purpose. When partners continue to work on the posters, they use a note taker that specifically supports this historical thinking; they also continue to keep track of "What We Know" and "How We Know It" and write their questions on sticky notes.

Ben and Pearl are partners "reading" a poster written in Cyrillic:

Ben: What do the words mean?

Pearl: I don't know

Ben: That is important.

Pearl: Could this be Britain?

Ben: This guy is ordering this guy to fight the bear.

Pearl: This seems like Britain or France.

Ben: I think it is a pretty important question: What do the words mean? (*Writes his question on a yellow sticky note.*) I think these two are in the Alliance and these are weaker. They are being forced into fighting the really scary country.

Pearl: What country does the bear represent?

Ben: I'm guessing that this guy is German because he has a pointy helmet [the teacher has told students earlier that Germans had pointy helmets].

Pearl: (*Looking at the large map on the front board*) So if this is Germany, then this is Austria or Ottoman.

Ben: I think it's Austria.

Pearl: Then the bear is Russia. Right, because it is Austria's fault and Germany just tagged along.

Ben: I'm not sure who it is trying to convince.

Pearl: Well, the poster is Russian. So they are making themselves look good.

Ben: So the audience is everyone else?

Pearl: But it is in Russian.

Ben: Why, then?

Pearl: To support themselves.

Ben: And to say that everyone else is afraid of them? I don't think that is right. Why would you make a propaganda saying everyone is afraid of us?

Pearl: To motivate them.

Ben: Oh, to motivate their soldiers. People think they are strong. They want to be part of strong armies.

Pearl: Yeah.

Partners read, discuss, and take notes about two more posters. The culminating activity is to answer the day's inquiry question, "How did countries use national pride to convince men to join the war?" It's a piece of cake for students who have already interrogated the posters with a disciplinary sourcing routine and collected the relevant evidence.

CLASSROOM CLOSE-UP 5.5
Making Textbooks Their Own

Laura Graff teaches college mathematics, but most of her courses are at a precollegiate level. Her students have struggled with math and often do not know how to read or use their textbook as an assist to understanding. As Laura describes here, she and two colleagues in the math department hit on chapter outlining as a way for students to become metacognitive about reading mathematics.[6]

"I have always thought a large problem in math and science education is reading. Students are never taught how to read technical textbooks."

Laura was not sure exactly how she had learned to read mathematics texts, but she knew it had been important to her understanding of math. She wanted her students to be able to see that the value of their $130 textbooks was for more than instructors' convenience in assigning homework problems.

When an invitation to attend Reading Apprenticeship professional development showed up in the math department mail, Laura was intrigued. She, and then two other members of the department, decided to attend. What they took away was the importance of promoting students' metacognitive conversations with the text.

To put this new understanding into practice, they designed an inquiry project to test the effectiveness of "forced metacognition." Students would be required to outline textbook chapters as a means of discovering why their math textbooks actually have *words* between the numbers.

"When outlines are first assigned," Laura says, "we are deliberately vague about what to include." What they do tell students is to think of the textbook headings as questions, to use the text to answer the questions, and to make notes of key concepts and definitions.

"The students write very detailed outlines in the beginning and evolve to skeletons of [what they think of as] 'hurried' outlines. They are actually showing how much progress they have made towards quickly picking out the key points.

"We believed that for students the process of asking questions and seeking answers to determine a hierarchy of topics—and, ultimately, produce an outline—would result in a metacognitive awakening of sorts, as they begin to build confidence and view themselves as independent thinkers.

"At the end of the inquiry, as we analyzed student outcomes, we were amazed at the positive results." Still, it was only when students spoke to a video camera about the outlining process that the instructors absorbed the full power of what students had experienced. Laura recalls it as "one of those huge 'paydays,' where you realize you have made a difference in students' lives and learning."

In brief excerpts from their videotaped interviews, three of the students who learned how to "outline" their thinking explain:

"Normally I would just look at the problems. I would completely disregard anything the book had to offer. I think being forced to do the outlines makes me realize that in every book, there is so much more information that you can notice. I apply it to every subject," Elisa reports.

For Anita, the metacognitive conversations she had with her textbook brought an immediate boost in comprehension: "As soon as I started doing the outline, I understood it a whole lot better. It took half the time for me to do the homework." She also found that outlining works out well in more than mathematics classes. "It also helped me in my physics class. I got a B—from a D to a B."

Alyce, who was repeating the developmental math course, had a wry perspective on her experience: "I've taken this exact same math class with another instructor and not had to do outlines, and he never actually asked us to open the book except for homework. So I never looked at that whole chapter itself. I only looked at the problems that were assigned for homework. That was the only time I ever opened the book—and look where it got me—in the same class with a different teacher. The fact that I'm doing [outlines now] is kind of putting it into my head so that I remember it."

Comparison Text Sets

Another form of thematic text set extends access by inviting students to compare the decisions made by authors and/or publishers. Especially revealing in history and other social sciences where interpretation necessarily varies the presentation of information and events, comparison text sets encourage students to notice differences in how texts relate similar information in different ways, focus attention through choice of photographs or headlines, and emphasize, include, or exclude different details. For example, one textbook's coverage of women's suffrage might include a photograph of men supporting the suffragist cause, whereas another might picture only suffragettes. One might describe religion as a factor in how women's rights and roles were understood; another might instead include information about Frederick Douglass's support for universal suffrage.

Students will need help making these comparisons. Keeping a log is one way for them to compare two or three texts: Is one easier to understand? More interesting? What makes it so? What is the effect of particular decisions to include or leave out certain information? Teachers also find that it is helpful for students to reflect on (1) what they know about a topic before reading, (2) what they learn from reading a first text on the topic, and (3) what they learn from reading another text on the same topic. This reflection allows students to recognize that their understanding grows the more they read about a topic.

Text + One More

A text set exists any time a topic is presented to students through more than one text. Minimally, then, adding even one ancillary text to the core text (usually a textbook) coverage of a topic means more access to the topic. Ideally, if there is only "one more" text, it is a text that offers immediate access—a photo, map, quote, short excerpt—for starting to build students' key conceptual knowledge, background knowledge, or vocabulary.

Starting small, with Text + One More, can be a worthy goal for teachers who want to experiment with text sets. (Fair warning: Text + One More has been known to morph into Text + Two More, Text + Three More, and so on. Building text sets is just like that.)

Inquiry Questions for Reading Across Texts

When students read across texts, inquiry questions serve an important role of increasing students' access to the key ideas and implicit relationships that have caused the texts to be put together in the first place.

The ninth graders reading a set of propaganda posters in Classroom Close-Up 5.4 were guided by the inquiry question "How did countries use national pride to convince men to join the war?" The inquiry question provided a purpose for reading and let students know how to focus their attention.

Chris Van Ruiten-Greene's high school seniors generate their own inquiry questions for a unit in which *Cry, the Beloved Country* is the core text. The questions they come up with are deeply thematic in nature: How does poverty trap and diminish people? Why do superficial differences between groups of people take on such import? How can loss produce wisdom?

The seventh graders in Lisa Rizzo's honors English class warm up for a lesson that entails comparing two poems with an inquiry framework that focuses them on the distinctive ways poetry communicates. Students write to the prompt "Writers might use poetry to speak to readers in a different way because _____." They then read the poems, primed to recognize and compare the poets' use of figurative language. Classroom Close-Up 5.6 drops in on a group of four students working collaboratively to understand the poems and also how the poets "speak to readers."

Extending Choice of Reading Material

Giving students some choice of reading material, even if limited, can help motivate them not only to read texts they are able to choose for themselves, but also to return to required course materials with more schema and more interest.

As described earlier, Chris Van Ruiten-Greene creates horizontal text sets that support students' reading of a core text and allow for a certain amount of student choice: in addition to the core text and certain "orbiting" texts that all students read, students choose, from among optional orbiting texts, those that will support them in becoming a group's "expert" on a particular topic or making a presentation to the class about a self-selected thematic interest. Other ways in which teachers extend choice of reading materials include subject area sustained silent reading and projects.

Subject Area Sustained Silent Reading (SSR)

SSR time has not traditionally been a part of subject area classrooms, but this is another way to provide students with multiple texts and extensive reading opportunities (see also Chapter Six for a more extended discussion of sustained silent reading).

Many subject area teachers use particular activities at the start of the class period to quiet and focus students. Sustained silent reading of topic-related materials students have chosen can become one of these regular activities. To the extent that these texts are linked to curriculum units, students are learning the content while also reading more widely and extensively in the subject area. To link the reading even more explicitly to the curriculum, teachers may occasionally facilitate conversations about what students are learning, or they may ask students to keep reading logs that address particular questions.

If teachers have classroom libraries with a variety of texts linked to curriculum topics, SSR can become part of any subject area class. High school biology and biotechnology teacher Ericka Senegar-Mitchell has created a set of eight

---

CLASSROOM CLOSE-UP 5.6
Framing an Inquiry into Two Poems

Primed with an inquiry frame, "Writers might use poetry to speak to readers in a different way because ____," the seventh graders in Lisa Rizzo's honors English class undertake multiple readings of two poems, making metacognitive notes to understand *what* the poets are saying and then to notice *how* they are saying it.

At one table, two partnerships informally work as a group of four, discussing the first poem, "The Courage That My Mother Had," by Edna St. Vincent Millay. They go back and forth between clarifying their understanding of the poem and noticing figurative language:

Bella: My reaction, I think she misses her mom. She obviously respected her mom a lot. She wants her mom??? What's granite? I want to put it like a question. Is she scared of something?

Gavin: "Courage like a rock." Is that courage solid as a rock?

Bella: It means her mom has a lot of courage.

Morris: What about "granite hill"?

Bella: Granite is a type of rock.

Gavin: This is about her mom having courage.

Lucy: Did you find other literary devices?

Bella: The brooch is like a symbol.

Lucy: I think it [the brooch] means that the courage will stay. She'll always be remembered.

Bella: Did she pass away?

Gavin: Yes. What is "courage like a rock"?

Morris: She doesn't have courage now. *(Paraphrasing the poem)* Which she has no need of but I do have need of.

Bella: I get it. She needs courage because she misses her mom. I finally understand the poem.

She needs the courage since her mom passed away.

Lucy: It also shows that she really admires her mom.

As students begin the second poem, "Mother to Son," by Langston Hughes, they do not get very far into the poem before their attention splits again between *what* the poet is saying and *how*.

Bella: It's a guy writing.

Lucy: Maybe he is putting the advice from his mom into a poem.

Bella: He is writing it down, oh, my mom told me this.

Gavin: Oh, Langston Hughes was the son and this is him from his mother?

Bella: I think that she is using the stairs as a symbol of life.

Gavin: How do you come up with that?

Lucy: What are some of the hard things that she has gone through?

Bella: Maybe her son is going through a hard time and she is giving him advice.

Gavin: What is a "crystal staircase"?

Bella: It's a symbol. Is that a symbol or metaphor?

When Lisa asks students to put the poems away until the next class and begin silent reading in *Roll of Thunder, Hear My Cry* (an assignment students will continue for homework), they petition to keep working on the poems instead. Lisa gives groups this option but points out that they will have even more *Roll of Thunder* homework if they do not get started on it now. About half the groups opt to continue their poetry inquiry, intent on solving the problems of interpretation and figurative language that they are discovering.

classroom mini-libraries that she rotates with each new biology unit. She displays her collections of journals, magazines, brochures, flyers, pamphlets, posters, and books (which she continually adds to) on two tables, one inside each of her two classroom doors. "Buffet tables," she calls them, and the metaphor is apt. Anything on the tables is available for consumption. The buffet is popular grazing before class, and students can have or check out whatever they choose. "With the right connection," Ericka explains, "they will read." In Classroom Close-Up 5.7, Ericka describes how she maintains her buffet tables and how students use them.

To promote extensive reading in U.S. history and American literature, teachers in Dixon High School's history and English departments enlisted the help of the school librarian and put together a collection of leveled books that support their combined course content. Students, including English learners and mainstreamed special needs students, chose books from the list to read during a daily twenty-minute SSR period that alternated weekly between students' history and English classes. Teachers of both courses read and responded to parts of students' metacognitive reading logs.

CLASSROOM CLOSE-UP 5.7
Biology Buffet Tables

Ericka Senegar-Mitchell introduced her biology buffet tables several years ago when she had a small grant to purchase supplementary classroom materials. She chose to buy best-selling trade books written by scientists, books to go with various curriculum units—*The Selfish Gene*, by Richard Dawkins, for her evolution unit, or *The Seven Daughters of Eve*, by Bryan Sykes, to extend students' understanding of genetics, for example. "Those fifteen books were the start," Ericka says. "I wanted my students to see science reading as not just the textbook."

Ericka gradually added more books, including reference books, children's science books (a photo book from the UK that "really shows the human body," she marvels), science magazines ("*Popular Science* is, well, really popular"), journals she subscribes to like *American Biology Teacher* and *AAAS Science* ("they may as well know what I'm up to"), and pamphlets and brochures.

About those pamphlets and brochures: "I got the collection 'bug,'" Ericka says. "I comb the city for pamphlets and brochures." She finds them in natural foods stores, a genetic counseling office, and doctors' waiting rooms. Students also

gravitate to brochures Ericka collects from the local university's science degree programs or the community college certificate programs. "I could get the same information from the Internet," she explains, "but I try to use local materials, to make it real for students. 'Omigod,' a student will say, picking up a medical brochure stamped with the name of a neighborhood doctor, 'my grandmother goes to this doctor!' Sometimes when they notice the source of a document, they laugh, 'You went *there?!*'

"I want students to be able to apply what they are learning. We had just been studying cellular transport, what the body needs for good nutrition, what it uses for fuel. One of my students was reading through a brochure from a natural foods store propounding a diet to eradicate carbohydrates. 'I don't believe that!' she snorted. 'Why would you eradicate carbs? You need them for cellular respiration.'

"That's my goal for the buffet tables. To get students to pick what interests them and then to be critical consumers. Now I get kids bringing me stuff!"

High school geometry and algebra teacher Teri Ryan, who loves to read about as well as play with numbers, has put together an extra-credit book list for her students. Her list of titles ranges from bestsellers about mathematics and mathematicians to math-related titles that are accessible to the English learners and inexperienced readers in her diverse classes. For example, her geometry students love *Alice's Adventures in Wonderland,* Teri reports. She alerts them to enjoy the many examples of similarity, congruence, and logic that relieve Alice from an afternoon in the doldrums.

Literature Circles and Book Groups

The rationale and processes that apply to "literature circles" in English courses apply to "book groups" in any subject area. College teachers as well as secondary teachers can use book groups for increasing students' choice of reading material, building engagement, and promoting students' independence as readers. As with adult "recreational" book groups, members are expected to meet deadlines and to bring their questions and ideas to the group. In student book groups, members also keep individual metacognitive reading logs.

Some teachers hesitate to try book groups because the logistics can seem intimidating, but as high school teacher Lisa Morehouse discovered, "Literature circles don't have to drive teachers crazy." After two years of teaching an ethnic literature class, Lisa decided to devote the last nine weeks of her course to literature circles. She was encouraged by the experiences other Reading Apprenticeship teachers reported, and a few additional motivators helped her past an initial fear that having four or five different novels being read simultaneously by small groups would be difficult to manage:

- My students' reading levels differed widely (grades 3–11).
- My school lacked class sets of novels for my course.
- I wanted my ninth graders to take more responsibility for their own education.
- I was given a free box of book sets for literature circles!

Because student choice is a key feature of book groups, a major consideration is whether students will feel that they actually have a choice to make. For this reason, teachers work hard to find a selection of books that vary in reading level and have potential appeal for different groups of students.

Teachers can launch students' book selection process by presenting a quick teaser about each book followed by students' hands-on preview of the different choices. Students might use the "book pass" activity described in

Chapter Six and then return to read a few pages from the books that seem most appealing.

In her literature class, Lisa Morehouse asked students to make an initial prediction about the book from its title, read for a few pages, and then respond to a set of questions. Students can use the same process to preview two or three titles before settling on one:

- After reading these pages, what do you think this book will be about?
- Pick a character introduced to you in these pages. Describe this character and what you think of him or her.
- Write at least three questions you have about the book so far.
- What is your first impression of the book?

The expectation is that teachers will have enough copies of popular titles so that all students can read their first- or second-choice book.

In Lisa's class, after students made their book selections and formed their literature circles, she gave each group a calendar on which she had indicated what days they would be able to read their books in class and the final due date. Groups set their own intermediate deadlines, and all group members signed the calendar as if it were a contract.

In Rita Jensen's middle school ELD class, students' sense of responsibility to the group is reflected in a log kept by one eighth-grader whom Rita feels was helped enormously by the social contract she entered into with her peers. Evidence to this effect, from her metacognitve reading log, appears in Classroom Close-Up 5.8.

In addition to checking students' individual metacognitive reading logs, teachers often ask literature circle groups to make connections from their book to essential questions that the whole class has been investigating, create a group book poster, stage a dramatic moment from the text, compare characters across texts they have read, and take part in other group projects in which each member of the group has a clear role and responsibility. Luke Boyd's grade 9 English students put their Facebook skills to work:

> Students in a literature circle each create a Facebook page for a different character in their novel. The project is designed to capture that character's personality in an online profile. Students have to infer how the character would present himself or herself. What kind of music would that person listen to? What books would he or she read? What Facebook groups would that character be interested in?
>
> Then the characters "friend" each other and post messages related to the plot on each other's pages, in language directly from the novel or in plausible words the student puts in the character's mouth. To review students' work, I can go online or have them turn in screen shots.

One note: It is a good idea to put "fictional character _____" or "_____ from (name of novel)" as the name of the page. That way there is no confusion about the purpose of the page. When students complete their novel, the page is taken down.

CLASSROOM CLOSE-UP 5.8
"We Decided to Read Up to Chapter 26"

Valencia is an eighth grader in Rita Jensen's English language development class who might not ordinarily finish an assigned class novel. But because she chose what book to read (*Walk Two Moons*, by Sharon Creech) with a literature circle of her peers, Valencia's commitment as a group member felt important and kept her reading. Although by the end of the book her log becomes a simple plot recitation, she does reach the end, having found in a book she earlier called "really boring" that "the last four chapters were kind of sad."

2–18

Well . . . I'm trying to catch up with my group now. I got left behind because I didn't read on Monday or Thursday. I'm at the same place as them now. So, I'm going to force myself to read up to chapter 26. We decided to read up to there.

I'm starting to think that the book is really boring though. It's not so exciting. I thought that it was going to be really interesting and exciting. Now when I read it, I'm so bored. I don't want to start reading another book though. Think that there is parts that scare me a little bit. The parts what that man keeps leaving messages at Phoebe's front door. If that happened to me I would be so scared. I would immediately tell my mom and she would probably call the police.

2–22

During the three day weekend I didn't really do that much reading . . .

Chapters to Read

2/22 tonight = chapter 19–23

2/23 tomorrow = 24–26

2/24 27–30

2/25 31–34

2/28 35–40

2/29 41–44

2–23

I stayed up until 12:30 or 1 o'clock just reading the book. I started reading at 11 o'clock. My mom kept waking up every 15 or 20 minutes, telling me to get some sleep. I was very comfortable reading last night. I was warm in my bed and there was lots of silence. I understood the story very well and I actually really enjoyed it. There were one or two words I didn't know. I was going to look them up but then I got a little sleepy. I'm surprised that I read everything I was supposed to read.

2–24

I started reading at 9:30 and got done at 10:10 PM. It was a little hard for me to understand what I was reading though. I was reading while I was watching the Grammy Awards. I did try my hardest to consentrate on my book though. I would have turned off the television but I just wouldn't. I really had to watch the awards.

2–25

Chapter 27–30

These chapters are about when Sal . . .

2–28

Last night I didn't really get a chance to read a lot.

2–29

On chapter 32 Sal thought . . .

3–2

The last four chapters were kind of sad.

Independent Projects

As a way to support choice *and* extensive reading, independent as well as group projects are a great boon. Teachers often find that when they shift more of the reading of course materials from at home to in class, independent projects are a good homework option.

In Chris Van Ruiten-Greene's high school English classes, in addition to reading the core curriculum and the horizontal text sets that support and extend the literature classics, Chris's students complete quarterly free-choice books and make presentations about them to the class:

> Everybody has to commit to a choice book once a quarter. Students are choosing their own interest avenue and that's a big deal. They have to present what they have been reading, what is floating their boat personally. They look forward to that.

Projects based on books that students choose and read independently anchor the science curriculum that Janet Creech and Ann Akey designed for their ninth grade science course. Students routinely read the textbook and keep metacognitive logs, but the curriculum also provides two streams of choice: (1) students complete monthly "Science in the News" reports about current science articles they find in print and online newspapers and magazines, and (2) they complete quarterly science book projects about science books they choose from a wide selection (see Box 5.3 for a schematic of the curriculum).

BOX 5.3

Student Choice in a Grade 9 Science Curriculum

Students in Janet Creech's and Ann Akey's grade 9 integrated science classes read required course materials and keep metacognitive logs in class but also work individually on monthly science news reports and quarterly book projects for which *they* choose the texts.[7]

Extensive Reading in Grade 9 Integrated Science Course

	First Quarter	Second Quarter		Third Quarter		Fourth Quarter	
Metacognitive Logs	Introduction	Ongoing		Ongoing		Ongoing	
Projects		Read an expository science book		Read the biography of a scientist		Read a fiction book with good science	
		Write a children's science book		Present a historical vignette		Participate in book club discussions	
Science in the News (SiN)	Intro-duction	1 Per Month	1 Per Month	1 Per Month	1 Per Month	1 Per Month	1 Per Month

"Science in the News" involves students in finding news reports in newspapers, magazines, or journals that describe scientific issues or research of interest to them. They work individually to create structured reports about their articles, then discuss them in small groups. In Classroom Close-Up 5.9, Janet describes initial challenges students had with the assignment and how they were resolved. (The assignment itself appears in Box 5.4.)

Science in the News Assignment

One way Janet Creech and Ann Akey build student choice into their grade 9 science course is with a monthly "Science in the News" assignment.[9] Students search in newspapers and magazines for science news stories of personal interest, write about the science being reported, and learn how to be knowledgeable consumers of science news.

STUDENT GUIDELINES

1. Find an article about scientific research/observations that was published in a newspaper, magazine, or journal during the assigned month. The article must be at least two hundred words long.

2. Read the article and write down what the scientists were trying to find out (what question were they trying to answer).

3. Underline, in two different colors, the following information (color in the boxes to make a key).

    ☐ The methods the scientists were using (procedure) and the type of data collected.

    ☐ What the scientists found out (results and conclusion).

4. Answer the following questions on a separate piece of paper, and staple it to this page.

5. Staple the article, or a copy of it, to this page.

QUESTIONS

1. (a) Title of the article; (b) Topic of the article; (c) Author(s); (d) Source of article (name of newspaper, magazine, or address/URL and name of Internet site)

2. (a) Write the full name and title (if given) of a person quoted in the article. (If no one is quoted, choose a different article.) (b) Why was this person quoted? What is the person's expertise?

3. How did scientists obtain the evidence on which this article is based? What steps did they follow, what types of tools did they use, and what type of data did they collect?

4. Draw a diagram of the important information explained in this article. Label your drawing with words or descriptions.

5. Write a summary of this article. Your summary must be at least four complete sentences in your own words. Do not use direct quotes from the article.

6. Do some more thinking about this article. Write at least one "on my own" question that you would like to ask the author or the scientists involved.

CLASSROOM CLOSE-UP 5.9
Science in the News Reports

Janet Creech and Ann Akey thought their carefully constructed report format was all their ninth graders would need in order to read and write about science in the news.[8] As they immediately found, however, students required explicit instruction in the process of reading science news and making the reports. Janet explains:

"To help students read, evaluate, and discuss scientific issues and findings that appear in popular media, we developed 'Science in the News' (SiN), a format to help students have an informed scientific perspective.

"We assigned the first SiN as homework, providing guidelines and a structured report format [see Box 5.4]. Looking at student work samples, however, we realized that even with relatively accessible text, such as the daily newspaper, students were not able to read and respond to the science without more help. We had to teach our students *how* to read science in the news.

"I started by finding an article to read and discuss in class. In small groups, students read the article and completed a SiN reading together, discussing *how* they approached highlighting the methods and results and *how* they constructed summaries. Teams shared their results with the whole class while I recorded their reading strategies on an overhead. Later we read anonymous student work samples, evaluating them using our new understandings of how to read SiN.

"With practice, students are able to do the SiN reading activities independently. Teams discuss the science in the reading, instead of how to read the science. Working together, students become expert readers of science in the news. More importantly, we are learning that science literacy is not a fixed object; people are not good readers or nonreaders, but evolving readers."

For the book projects that Janet's and Ann's students complete, their teachers have set parameters for the type of project students undertake each quarter, but book choice belongs to the students. During one quarter, students each become a science topic expert and then use their expertise to write a children's book. Another quarter, projects focus on science biographies, and students make class presentations in the guise of their selected scientist. The last project of the year involves students in literature circles in which group members have chosen the same piece of science-based fiction to read and discuss. Janet explains the three types of projects in Classroom Close-Up 5.10.

Janet and Ann did not expect their students to be able to complete these long-term projects without support and intermediate deadlines. Students had weekly written assignments that included metacognitive and factual notes about what they were learning. The form that students completed appears in Box 5.5.

Building science literacy is a major goal of Janet Creech and Ann Akey's grade 9 science course, so student choice is a major component. For their quarterly book projects, students have free choice of texts within the broad structure of each project, as Janet describes here.[10]

Read a science book and write a related children's book

"In the fall our classes make a trek to the school library's nonfiction science section. We give students a chart that describes where science topics can be found and let students look for a book that interests them. Once they find one, we negotiate. Because our goals for this project are to build fluency, stamina, and motivation as well as general science knowledge, our focus is helping students find books that genuinely interest them and that are not too difficult. As a result, I start to see science-based library books appearing at sustained silent reading—twenty minutes of reading a day, a school-wide policy—instead of magazines and newspapers.

"During the next four to five weeks, students complete most of their reading outside of class with the support of teacher-generated metacognitive logs designed specifically for nonfiction text. I collect and check these logs weekly to give students written encouragement on their progress. When they finish reading, students demonstrate their understanding of the topic by writing and illustrating a children's science book on the same subject.

"Tapping into students' interests produces some amazing results and encourages student engagement. One English language learner filled her book with photos and descriptions of her own beloved parrots. Another student, who produced little other work during the year, wrote a book about lizards, which he proudly shared. Many students chose their children's book projects (from their *science* class!) to include in their school-wide assessment portfolios as evidence for meeting reading and writing expectations."

Read a scientist's biography and present an interactive historical vignette

"Empowering students with personal knowledge about real scientists and the work they do is our primary goal for the biography project . . .

"When we initially introduced the biography project, we reencountered a familiar problem. We lacked motivating and accessible texts to read. Our library had a scant collection of dusty, unused volumes of 'classics.' Over the next three years, we added biographies of women scientists . . . scientists of color . . . contemporary researchers . . . and the accessible biography series *Great Minds of Science* and *Scientists Who Changed the World*.

"Once we had enough texts involving scientist biographies that students could and would read independently, students could do most of the reading outside of class. We developed new metacognitive log prompts to help students make connections to the influence of culture and society on scientific thought. Once students finish their reading, they write 250-word vignettes about a major event in the scientist's life. They dress like their scientists, bring props representing the scientists' work, and read their vignettes in small groups. The 'scientists' ask their peers in these small groups to discuss opinions about their work and discoveries."

Read a fiction book with good science content and participate in a book club

"This last project elicits raised eyebrows—popular fiction in a science class? When considering what students should read, we uncovered a closely guarded secret: Science people love to read good fiction about science. When reading fiction, we engage with the ideas of science in imaginative and enjoyable ways that we might not when reading for information.

"We wanted students to have access to this experience while providing opportunities for them to evaluate and discuss the scientific ideas they encountered. Our critical reading and discussion goals make the book clubs our most demanding project, which is why we save it for last.

(Continued)

"Book clubs are discussion groups of four to five students who have chosen to read the same book. To facilitate book choice, I bring copies of the books to class for students to look through and talk about. They rank first, second, and third choices on an individual, reading level–appropriate list. I use their choices to arrange book club groups. The book clubs meet twice a week during hundred-minute blocks, plan their own reading schedules, and discuss their books. Each student assembles and decorates a reading journal specifically designed for fiction narrative. New metacognitive log prompts help students make connections to situations or characters in the novel and analyze the science presented in the story.

"Students bring these journals with them to their book club and use them as the basis for group discussions that often lead to new insights about the far-reaching impact of science in their lives. As they contribute to scientific and literary conversations with their peers, students see themselves as successful readers of science."

BOX 5.5

Science Book Project Weekly Check-Ins

To support students' independent quarterly project work, Janet Creech and Ann Akey assigned weekly check-ins that helped students stay on track for the project deadline and keep track of their learning.[11]

READING LOG

Name_____   Due Date_____   Total pages in my book _____   Pages read this week: _____ to _____

1. Respond to two of the following metacognitive prompts. Write at least two sentences for each prompt. Try different prompts each week.

    "While I was reading"

I felt confused when . . .	I stopped because . . .
I was distracted by . . .	I lost track of everything except . . .
I started to think about . . .	I figured out that . . .
I got stuck when . . .	I first thought that . . . but then realized that . . .
The time went by quickly because . . .	I finally understood . . .
A word/some words I did not know . . .	I remembered that earlier in the book . . .

2. What was the most interesting fact that you learned this week?

3. Write down two questions that you could ask about this week's reading ("author and me" or "on my own").

4. Write down five scientific terms (terms not commonly used outside of science) from this week's reading. Explain what each one means.

5. Add the five terms from number 4 to the concept map you are keeping. Remember to label all arrows and write in a different color each week.

6. Draw a picture or graphic that shows an important idea from this week's reading. Label your drawing with words or descriptions.

7. Summarize, in a paragraph of at least four detailed sentences, the most important ideas in this week's reading. Explain as if you are talking to a person who has not read your book.

Extending Support and Accountability

When core texts are challenging, sometimes teachers resort to reading aloud from these texts to the class or having students take turns reading aloud, to ensure that students are able to access the material. *Reading for* students sometimes becomes *comprehending for* students, as well, because teachers naturally want to make sure students understand the materials being read to them. Building students' independence as readers and learners means teachers must find ways to engage students in doing the work of reading and comprehending for themselves.

Sometimes this begins with uncoupling students from their dependence on the teacher for understanding task directions. For example, science teachers may ask students to Talk to the Text of their lab instructions and clarify any areas of confusion with their lab partners. The result, teachers report, is not only fewer questions about instructions but better labs. In her history classes, Gayle Cribb realized something similar:

> One day after I had passed out written directions for a task, but students still didn't know what to do, it occurred to me that no one actually had to read the directions if I also explained them. That's when I decided to retrain all of us about the value of reading and understanding directions. Our new routine was for students to read the directions, clarify them with a partner, and then ask the class for help if they still didn't understand.
>
> Students who are less comfortable reading and had simply avoided what they thought of as "unnecessary" reading got important practice in this basic life skill. Students who formerly didn't pay attention to the reading because they knew I would explain began to take more responsibility. I was a little surprised to see, after the first couple of times we practiced this routine, how extremely efficient it was. It became the default practice in all my classes, including in my Spanish classes, where students were reading in their second or third language. It worked!

Support for extended reading that results in a savings in class time—as it can in the case of support for reading directions—is unusual. More often, support for extended reading requires a hard decision about what class time is for. Community college English teacher Missie Meeks found that when she introduced the scaffolds of having students Talk to the Text and keep metacognitive logs, it made a huge improvement in her students' success at writing research papers. But students also needed extra time to read in these metacognitive ways. In Classroom Close-Up 5.11, Missie describes how she decided to give over some of her class time to ensure that students would have the extra reading time they needed.

CLASSROOM CLOSE-UP 5.11
Making Time for What Makes a Difference

In English 1123, students conduct academic research with the goal of producing a final paper that incorporates at least ten sources to support an academic argument. Instructor Missie Meeks identified two problems that were keeping many of her community college students from being successful: particularly difficult texts and the related challenge of paraphrasing them. She hoped to address both by instituting the Talking to the Text routine and metacognitive logs.

"The vast amount of reading in the class comes from the academic literature that students use for their academic research," Missie says. "Many times these articles are written on a much higher level than students are accustomed to reading, and they become frustrated with the entire process and withdraw from the class.

"Even if the students are able to work through the text, many times they still do not have enough understanding of the text to paraphrase it. Plagiarism has always been a major dilemma in English 1123 because students do not comprehend the text well enough to summarize it."

As part of students' grades in the course, Missie made it a requirement that they add a metacognitive dimension to the highlighting they had always done on their research articles. Next to the sentences selected to support their thesis, Missie has asked students to write a metacognitive note so that she and individual students can understand the student's mental process in selecting it. "This activity," she says, "gave me a small window into the mind of the student to see if comprehension was indeed occurring."

Missie also asked students to keep a separate metacognitive log for each source. In these logs, students use the left-hand column to record statements from their reading that support their thesis and the right-hand column to paraphrase the statements. Missie found that the additional metacognitive work students did with their Talking to the Text annotations made it easier for them to comprehend and paraphrase statements supporting their argument.

Although satisfied that the new annotation and log routines were improving students' comprehension and paraphrasing, Missie noticed that the routines created a new problem. "Even though students began to understand the importance of the assignments and became aware of their thought processes, some were reluctant to commit to the time it takes to annotate a text and complete a reading log."

Given the progress students were able to make using their new metacognitive routines, Missie decided to allow more class time for students to annotate their texts and complete reading logs. "I feel that class time to complete this activity is indeed valuable . . . Average-ability students have been able to tackle these texts because the annotating and reading logs have given them tools to work through the text. Many students are no longer fearful of academic sources."

Helping students accept a shift in responsibility for reading is the focus of much of the content of this book. As already described, extending teacher support for reading includes, for example, providing text sets that include easier initial entry points or selecting segments of the text to work on as a class, reciprocal modeling through Think Aloud and Talking to the Text, breaking long passages down into manageable segments, partner and small group work to problem solve, and writing to learn through metacognitive logs and double-entry journals. Such practices, especially as they interact, represent the extended support that students need.

If students are to value this support, they must see course reading as central to the curriculum. Their assignments must signal the importance and value of reading by requiring students to *do* something public with their reading. When students are accountable to each other for their reading and preparation, when they need to read in order to complete an individual project, when they need to rely on one another's reading for joint projects and performances, when teachers collect and respond to reading logs and other evidence of student reading, reading is clearly important in the class and curriculum.

Similarly, to give reading a more prominent place in the curriculum, reading experiences and assignments should contribute to assessments of student learning. Because students have learned to value and give priority to the aspects of their course work that contribute to grades and other recognitions of achievement, reading work needs to count. When students set and reach their academic reading goals by reading course materials, their efforts should be recognized. Metacognitive logs and reflections that accompany course readings should contribute to course grades. In Will Brown's high school chemistry classes, students know exactly how their metacognitive logs (he calls them Reflective Reading Logs) will contribute to their grade. They each receive a rubric that spells it out (see Box 5.6).

A classroom culture that explicitly values reading as part of subject area learning will necessarily incorporate extensive reading. As Janet Creech reports, when she and Ann Akey redesigned their science course, they reevaluated what they wanted for their students:

> Our goals . . . were to improve student's attitudes toward science reading and give students the tools to become lifelong science readers . . . By the end of the school year, reading becomes an established routine in my classroom, and students' attitudes about reading change dramatically. When I announce the first book project in the fall, the general response is "What, we have to read the whole book?" By the time the last project rolls around in late spring, students say, "Read another book? Okay, I can do that."

Janet and Ann have extended time, access, choice, and support and accountability for reading in their science classrooms. Their students reciprocate, extending their reading volume, range, stamina, and engagement. A program of consistent, strategic extensive reading more than earns its keep.

■ ■ ■

BOX 5.6

Making Metacognitive Logs Count

When teachers have large numbers of students, the prospect of grading metacognitive logs is daunting. Experienced Reading Apprenticeship teachers have learned that structuring ways for students to *need* their logs to participate in class is the most important strategy for ensuring that students maintain their logs. Periodically collecting and spot-checking log entries is then usually enough.

Will Brown's high school chemistry students keep double-entry metacognitive logs, and he makes sure they understand what is expected, with his detailed explanation shown here.

REFLECTIVE READING LOGS AND EVALUATION RUBRIC

Throughout the year you will be asked to record notes and reflections from assigned reading using a T-table format. You will be expected to select essential information from each part of the assigned reading including text, figures, equations, and sample problems. You'll record these ideas in the left column of the t-table. With each entry, write the page number in parentheses. You are also expected to think reflectively about the text and relate the essential information to your own experiences, prior knowledge, your personal learning process and questions. You will record your reflections in the right column of the T-table. The template for making your own T-tables is on the back. Reading logs are part of your homework grade. keep all your reading logs in your chemistry binder. They are great study tools.

When I grade reflective reading logs, I look for the presence of a selection of essential ideas in the left column with page references and corresponding thoughtful reflections in the right column. I do not grade grammar or spelling, but you should work hard to make your ideas easy to understand.

I also use the reading logs' reflections as an indicator of topics requiring more in-class clarification.

Reflective reading is a personal activity. We all have unique experiences and thinking processes. So you do not share or borrow reading logs until you have completed your own reading log. In class you will have opportunities to share your thoughts and ask questions recorded in your reading logs.

The following are descriptions of the minimum criteria for each grade.

Nobel Laureate 100%	Research Scientist 90%	Lab Technician 80%	Trainee 40%
Reading log is completed on time. The left column contains plentiful essential information from each section of the text. Correct page numbers accompany each entry.	Reading log is completed on time. The left column contains most essential information from each section of the text. Correct page numbers accompany most entries.	Reading Log is turned in late. The left column contains some essential information from each section of the text. Correct page numbers accompany some entries.	Reading Log is turned in late. The left column contains little essential information from each section of the text. Correct page numbers accompany few or no entries.
The right column contains reflections for each entry that clearly show thoughtful reading.	The right column contains reflections for most entries that show thoughtful reading.	The right column contains reflections for some entries that show thoughtful reading.	The right column contains reflections for few entries that show thoughtful reading.

Upgrades		No Credit = 0%	
Students earning *Trainee* on a reading log are invited to redo reading log to meet *Research Scientist* content criteria for an upgrade to *Lab Technician*.		There are three ways to receive no credit. (1) Do not do the reading log. (2) Do not turn in your reading log. (3) Copy another student's reading log entries and turn them in as your own.	

Science Literacy Is Empowering

Additional information about extensive reading—specifically a program of free-choice sustained silent reading—appears in Chapter Six; it describes SSR as an important component of an academic literacy course.

Chapter Seven moves on to high-leverage cognitive reading strategies that, in the context of extensive reading and ongoing metacognitive conversation, help students hone their reading problem-solving skills.

Notes

1. This and following excerpts describing Janet Creech and Ann Akey's grade 9 science course are from Creech, J., & Hale, G. (2006, February), Literacy in science: A natural fit, *The Science Teacher*, pp. 22–27. Reprinted/adapted with permission from *The Science Teacher*, a journal for high school science educators published by the National Science Teachers Association (www.nsta.org).

2. Kuhn, M. R., & Stahl, S. A. (2003). Fluency: A review of developmental and remedial practices. *Journal of Educational Psychology, 95*(1), 3–21.

3. Anderson, T. H., & Armbruster, B. B. (1984). Content area textbooks. In R. C. Anderson, J. Osborn, & R. J. Tierney (Eds.), *Learning to read in American schools* (pp. 193–224). Hillsdale, NJ: Erlbaum.

4. Walqui, A., & van Lier, L. (2010). *Scaffolding the academic success of adolescent English language learners: A pedagogy of promise.* San Francisco: WestEd.

5. All excerpts in quotations are from Laurie Erby's description of using Reading Apprenticeship routines as presented on the U.S. Department of Education's "Doing What Works" website: http://dww.ed.gov/Adolescent-Literacy/Engaging-Text-Discussion/see/index.cfm?T_ID=23&P_ID=61&c1=1083&c2=1070#cluster-1

6. These compiled excerpts are from Laura Graff's discussion of her textbook outlining assignment on the Carnegie Foundation for the Advancement of Teaching website *Strengthening Pre-Collegiate Education in Community Colleges*, in the pages "Outlining Mathematics": http://www.cfkeep.org/html/stitch.php?s=14832740290866&id=34947815104339

7. Creech & Hale, Literacy in science (see note 1).

8. Ibid.

9. Ibid.

10. Ibid.

11. Ibid.

CHAPTER SIX

Sustained Silent Reading+

Dedicating Time for Independent Reading

> In order to get better at reading, you have to start reading. I'm starting to read more books than I was. Usually I wouldn't even read a book, but now I'm reading books I enjoy.
>
> —Shaunna, grade 9 student

WHY TAKE PRECIOUS class time to let students read books they enjoy? Shaunna has a pretty good explanation: The more she reads books she enjoys, the more books she reads. And the more she reads, the better a reader she becomes. As Shaunna seems to suggest, there are even reasons beyond enjoyment "to get better at reading." The more she builds reading fluency, confidence, and stamina with books she enjoys, the more books she *can* read—even books she may not enjoy but needs to understand.

When teachers first piloted Reading Apprenticeship, as the framework for the Thurgood Marshall grade 9 academic literacy course, sustained silent reading (SSR) was a crucial piece of the curriculum. It was not optional. Too many of their students had not read a book of their choice in years (if ever). The goal for SSR was to immerse students in the experience of reading—not as an all-or-nothing, succeed-or-fail proposition, but as an ongoing process of development and growth. If students could read and enjoy books they chose, they could begin to understand that all readers' abilities vary with the text, topic, and experience. With this shift in perspective, they could begin to feel more hopeful about improving their reading.

In the Reading Apprenticeship version of SSR, sacrosanct time was set aside not only for reading, but also for writing in metacognitive logs, tracking personal reading goals, and sharing book talk about the reading.

Several "generations" of student readers later, we have not changed our estimation of the value of SSR, but we call the Reading Apprenticeship version SSR+ (plus) to emphasize its distinctive metacognitive and community-building features.

Getting Real Reading Going

> I was really nervous when I came into this class. Because when I thought of Acedemic Literacy I thought reading, reading, and more reading. And some old lady that spits when she talks. . . And now I love to read. . . My favorite part of the class was S.S.R. (Silent, Sustained, Reading) . . . Some advise is don't keep reading if she is talking.
> —Sheldon, grade 9 student

In his end-of-the-year letter to the new class of ninth graders that will be entering Charla Dean's academic literacy course in the fall, Sheldon, above, has some important advice. It seems that during the year he spent in the course, his attitude toward reading took a big turn. Now, he advises the new class that although they may start the year as he did, dreading reading, by the end of the year they will need to force themselves to stop reading—especially if Ms. Dean is talking.

Teachers like Charla Dean, who incorporate SSR+ in their courses, make clear the procedures and expectations for this kind of free-choice reading, and they also make clear what students can expect to gain as a result. Box 6.1 outlines some ways to introduce students to SSR+. The Student Learning Goals, especially those for Building Personal Engagement and Collaborating in a Community of Readers and Writers, can serve as a preview for students of some specific ways that SSR+ can benefit them (see the Assessment Appendix).

For students to benefit from SSR+ practices, they must actually read. Many students prefer to diligently avoid reading. They shun books in general and express great dislike for reading. They give up easily when a book tires or bores them. To respect these students' experiences but also to disarm them, many teachers spend time right away making it safe for students to talk about negative reading experiences and types of texts they don't like to read. At the same time, teachers do some digging to find out what kind of text students may find interesting—because choosing books they want to read will be the biggest challenge of SSR+ for some students.

When Tammy Thompson first introduced SSR+ as part of her academic literacy class, she was struck by how many of her students had never learned how to choose a book they might enjoy:

> We talked a lot about reading and if they read at home, if they liked to read and why they might not like to read. Not surprisingly, most of the

kids in here didn't like to read. And so we went over the reasons they didn't like to read. One of the things that was common with most of the kids was they had never learned how to pick out a book. So one of the lessons I did was teaching them how to choose a book. We look at the cover of it, we look at the back, we talk to people to see if they've read the book, we get recommendations.

Another thing was that even if I thought a book was way too easy for them, they have permission to read it. So kids feel comfortable reading whatever book they want to read. The idea is that the more confidence they have, the harder the book they'll choose the next time.

I've learned how important it is to let students pick their own book and how important it is to teach them *how* to choose a book.

Some teachers take students on field trips to the local library or the school library. Almost all set up classroom libraries, often with much help from the school librarian. To appeal to the full range of classroom readers, classroom libraries must have great variety in reading levels and genres, including nonfiction such as biographies, historical narratives, and informational texts about topics of interest to young people. Teachers who build their own libraries report that they become expert scroungers, frequenting used-book stores, flea markets, and thrift shops. One group of teachers held a book drive in which parents, students, and other teachers solicited used books from their neighborhoods and local businesses.

Even with well-stocked libraries to choose from, students who have had little or no experience of reading for pleasure need to hear how their friends, teachers, and other people they know choose books. They need to become familiar with popular authors and with the different types of books that might appeal to them. Spending time talking about where to find books and how to choose among them is crucial for introducing inexperienced readers to the idea that they will be able to find books they will want to read and will be able to read.

Previewing Books with Book Pass

An activity that many Reading Apprenticeship teachers depend on as an orientation to choosing books is a class Book Pass. The Book Pass activity gives students an experience looking over eight to twelve books quickly, ranking a few of them for closer inspection, and making a preliminary choice of two possibilities (one to start reading and one to keep in reserve). Preliminary to the actual Book Pass, teachers can also involve students in reviewing genre options and noticing any they particularly like to read. (Box 6.2 describes the Genre Preferences activity; Box 6.3 describes Book Pass.)

BOX 6.1

Setting Up SSR+

Students benefit from understanding what is expected of them and how they will benefit from the SSR+ routines that lie ahead.

1.   Explain the ways in which SSR+ will be a regular routine throughout the year:

Reading: For example, many teachers start out with a five- to ten-minute SSR+ reading interval and gradually extend the time to twenty minutes or more. In some classes, SSR+ starts out as a daily routine and is later reduced to twice a week as students do more reading at home. On the other hand, some teachers consider SSR+ the most important thing students can do in their class and provide time for it daily, all year.

Writing: Reading in an SSR+ book is always followed with recordkeeping and writing in the student's metacognitive log.

Talking: Talking about books happens through informal classroom book talk and more formal Book Projects.

2.   Explain the reasons for doing SSR+:

Students appreciate understanding the value of SSR+. Let them know they will be setting and keeping track of goals for themselves, such as to increase the number of pages they read at a sitting (fluency), the amount of time they stay focused on reading (stamina), and even their willingness to try different kinds of books to read (agency). By keeping metacognitive logs, they will learn more about themselves as readers, and by exchanging information about books, they will expand their ideas about books they may want to read.

3.   Explain the requirements for an SSR+ book:

It must be a book (no magazines, newspapers, or comic books).

It must have more words than pictures.

It must be something you are interested in.

It must be something your parents would allow you to read, if asked.

It must not be a book you are reading for another class.

4.   Explain the SSR+ ground rules:

If you leave your book at home, choose another one from the shelf for the day.

Stay in your seat so others aren't distracted.

Do not do homework.

Do not talk.

Do your best to read for the whole time.

Write in your SSR+ metacognitive log when we finish.

Read at least two hundred pages per month, preferably in the same book.

Complete and present a Book Project for each book.

Set goals for yourself and reflect on how you are meeting them at the end of each book.

BOX 6.2

Genre Preferences

PURPOSE

Inexperienced readers may benefit from considering the variety of genres from which they can choose an SSR+ book to read. Even for students who know what genres they like to read, the Genre Preferences activity can open them to new genres they might want to consider.

PROCEDURE

1. Collect examples of some or all of the genres listed on the sample recordkeeping chart.

2. Distribute a copy of the chart to each student and go over the various categories. Invite students to explain particular genres they like or dislike and why. Show examples of the various genres and if necessary point out what is distinctive about each.

3. Model how to use the chart and ask students each to record their genre preferences.

4. Ask students each to eyeball their completed chart. What patterns do they see about what they like, dislike, and aren't sure about? Have students quickly write a response to these prompts:

   - From this chart, I can tell these things about my genre preferences:

   - One or two genres I don't know much about but would be willing to try are:

My Genre Preferences					
	?	Not at All	Not Much	Some	A Lot
Adventure/Action					
Biography/Autobiography/Memoir					
Comic Books					
Graphic Novels/Manga					
Fantasy/Myth					
Historical Fiction					
History					
Horror					
How-to-Books					
Humor					
Informational Books					
Mysteries					
Picture Books					
Poetry					
Romance					
Science Fiction					
Science/Nature					
Short Stories					
Sports					
Teen Problems					
Thrillers					
True-Life Drama					

BOX 6.3

Book Pass

PURPOSE

The Book Pass activity not only helps students who have difficulty knowing what they like to read, but also helps build community and develop students' awareness of different genres of books they might like to read.

PROCEDURE

1. Choose a range of books your students might want to read and place one book on each student's desk along with a recordkeeping sheet on which students can enter their responses to the books they preview.

2. Ask students to talk with a partner about what makes a book appealing to them. Record ideas on a class list.

3. Model how you preview a book:

   - What can you learn from the front and back covers?

   - Is this a topic that interests you? A genre you like? An author you know?

   - What is it like to read a few paragraphs? Does it seem interesting? Not too easy or too hard?

   - What is it like to skim through a few pages? Are there more than five unknown words on a page?

4. Ask students to take one minute to preview the book on their desk and jot down a quick response on the recordkeeping sheet: Author, Title, + – ?, and Notes. Invite them to use the previewing strategies you modeled.

5. Have students pass the book on their desk to the next student. Give students another minute to preview and respond to the new book. Continue so that students preview eight to twelve books. (Students will not necessarily preview all the same books.)

6. Have partners compare their lists. Did they agree or disagree about the books they previewed in common? What were the differences and why? Did either partner reconsider a book after hearing about a partner's assessment?

Author	Title	+ – ?	Notes

7. Ask students to take fifteen minutes and narrow their possible SSR+ books to two titles, making additional notes on their recordkeeping sheet to help them decide.

8. Ask each student to write a quick response to this prompt: What are the two books you chose and why did you choose them?

9. Invite volunteers to describe their choices.

10. Have students each make a final selection.

Charla Dean has a hunch that the time her academic literacy students spend at the beginning of the year *preparing* to read a book gets them itchy to actually start reading:

> All the time we spend touching, and looking at, and talking about books *before* students ever get started reading is much more effective than handing out books and telling them to read. Teasing students with the whole process of previewing and choosing a book really seems to work. When it's time to start reading, they're ready.

Giving Books a Ten-Page Chance

An important feature of SSR+ is that students can try again if they start a book and don't like it. The only condition is that they give any book they start a "ten-page chance." This is the advice Christine Cziko, Lori Hurwitz, and their Thurgood Marshall colleagues gave the first cohort of Reading Apprenticeship academic literacy students:

> What if the book you chose isn't as interesting as you had expected? If, after the first ten pages, you don't like the book, stop and find another one, either on your own or with help from friends, the teacher, or your parents. If after you've read the first ten pages you're not sure about a book, give it another ten-page chance, and then decide whether to keep it or try another book.

Stacy Stambaugh reports that the ten-page chance allows her academic literacy students to recognize that free-choice reading really is their personal opportunity to find books they like:

> We have SSR almost daily. It's a really nice way to start class, having students come in, begin reading, settle. A few students are resistant, but most are positive about SSR. They like that they really can choose, and that if they give a book the ten-page chance, they can return it.

The crucial point for students to understand is that when it comes to pleasure reading, they can choose what to read and what not to read. Abandoning a book in that context isn't the sign of a poor reader but of a discriminating reader who knows what he or she wants from reading. Good readers give a free-choice text a chance, but if it doesn't meet their interest or their needs, they trade it in for something that will.

Building Book Buzz

For some inexperienced readers, the ten-page chance begins to feel like the ten-page no-chance. Jill Eisner became concerned that a number of her academic literacy students were unable to find a book they could stick with, so she got expert help:

> Many of my students were having difficulty choosing books they enjoy. Our media specialist arranged for a person from the library to come to our school to do book talks. It was very successful.

Book talks don't only have to be done by "professionals." Peers are often students' most trusted book reviewers. In the beginning of the year in Janet Ghio's academic literacy class, once most students are reading books that have passed the ten-page chance, she throws a "book party" or two with the purpose of exposing students to new books they might want to read later and giving students practice articulating, as Janet puts it, "why someone might want to read your book." These book parties look suspiciously like adult cocktail parties, but with students holding books rather than drinks. In small groups, students stand together and talk sociably—about the *books* they are holding. Classroom Close-Up 6.1 drops in on one of Janet's book parties.

Building Stamina

Even when students have chosen books they want to read, getting students into the SSR+ habit is likely to take a few weeks of building students' stamina to stay focused on their reading. Tammy Thompson's experience with her academic literacy class is fairly typical:

> I started with five minutes. I had a stopwatch and by about four minutes and thirty seconds, they started to squirm. At five minutes, when I hit the timer, they were "Whew," so happy that they got to finish reading. Every week I increased the time. We went from five minutes to seven minutes to ten minutes. And it was interesting, when we got up to fifteen minutes, they started to squirm again, so I had to go back down to twelve, and that lasted for about a month. Currently, at the end of the year, my students are wanting to read for the entire period. But I have lessons to teach, so after twenty minutes, I hit the timer. When they hear the beep, it's "Ohhh," because they want to keep reading. Last week they actually

CLASSROOM CLOSE-UP 6.1
Book Partying

The previous week, Janet Ghio introduced her academic literacy students to what she calls a "book party." She asked them to get together in groups of three and tell each other about the books they were reading for SSR+. As students prepare for another book party, Janet asks them to meet in groups of three again, but with classmates who were not in their earlier group. She reviews the ground rules, which are also scaffolds for students who are shy or uncertain how to talk about books.

Teacher: I want you to stand. You have to have your book in your hand and your response log open. I want you each to take turns. You tell about your book title, and you can show it to everyone. And then, share your metacognitive logs, what you were visualizing [a particular cognitive strategy the class is focusing on], and maybe any other of your sentence completions [metacognitive sentence frames]. And then explain why the people you're visiting with might want to read your book. It's kind of like we're at a book party.

In a group of boys, Kent is game, but a little awkward. He shows the book cover (*Hoops*, by Walter Dean Myers), gives a two-sentence plot synopsis, and then is able to extend his presentation with something he *visualized* in the book.

Kent: So far it's about Lonnie. He wants to play basketball. But so far, his coach, Cal, left with their money for their uniforms, so they're trying to find him and get their money back. Oh, I visualized about their uniforms. They're supposed to be red and green. Not my favorite colors.

Sam goes next. He is a little brief on the plot, and, like Kent, he forgets to tell why someone might want to read his book, but he remembers to explain what he visualized and reads from his metacognitive log.

Sam: I'm reading *Stormbreaker*. And I read about how Alex Rider had to swim through an underground cave to get to an underground passage. I visualized how cold that might have been and

how dark it was. (*Reading from his metacognitive log*) "The time went quickly because it was fascinating how he could swim underwater in the freezing water and the darkness for about three minutes."

In a group of three girls, talking about books seems to come more naturally. Felicia starts, but her group members feel free to interrupt or add related ideas. When she recommends why someone else might want to read the (bestselling) memoir she is holding, Felicia's criteria for pleasure reading are apparently similar to those of millions of other readers.

Felicia: Have you read this book yet [*The Lost Boy*]? Well, the part that I'm reading, it's sad because they put him in a juvenile hall and no one believes him because they think he started a fire at the school, and it was another kid that did it. He had to go to court and everything—

Sonia: And it wasn't even his fault.

Felicia: Yeah, it wasn't his fault, but he had to go to court and stay in for another month and then he could go home. He's only twelve years old! But, yeah, you should read the book because it's like sad—

Sarah: Is that that guy that did *The Child Called It*?

Felicia: Yeah, it's the same, it's the same . . .

Sonia: Author.

Felicia: Oh, I forgot the other book. He wrote another book. What's it called? It's like *The Man* something. Yeah, you should read this book. It's sad, but it gets you mad at the same time.

When Janet calls the class back together, she invites a few volunteers to describe a book they heard about that they thought they might want to read. Janet asks the class to listen carefully:

Teacher: Keep in mind these books. You have your lists, and you're hearing from each other. How many of you are close to finishing a book? Okay, so remember that when you want to switch books, we can reserve them in the library.

talked me into letting them read the entire period. So these are students who went from squirming at five minutes to being able to read for at least fifty minutes.

Using Metacognitive Logs in SSR+

Think of yourself as a scientist. Your research subject is yourself. As a scientist, observe yourself reading. Write your observations in your SSR metacognitive log.

– Christine Cziko, high school academic literacy teacher

When SSR+ is part of a course where Reading Apprenticeship provides the framework for literacy instruction, students will spend a good deal of time participating in *external* metacognitive conversations about disciplinary reading and will have many opportunities to observe their teacher modeling *internal* metacognitive conversations. The idea that students treat themselves as "research subjects" should feel almost normal to them.

One of Christine Cziko's ninth graders, Darrell, summarized his initial understanding of SSR+ logs with an emphasis on his most basic metacognitive moves:

When we do SSR, and we have to write in our log after, it's not like, "Write about what happened in the book." It's like, "Were you looking out the window? How much of the time you were supposed to be reading were you concentrating?"

Students' observations of their own personal reading behavior include records of how long and how many pages they read during SSR+ time. Other observations of themselves as readers range from Darrell's "Were you looking out the window?" to identifying reading roadblocks, noticing what connections and questions stand out, or analyzing how a point of confusion was clarified.

To scaffold this kind of thinking and recordkeeping, most teachers provide an initial set of metacognitive prompts, or sentence frames, and ask students to choose one or more to complete. A typical format for keeping SSR+ metacognitive logs is shown in Box 6.4. Sample prompts are in Box 6.5.

The SSR+ log-keeping routine requires as little as three minutes at a time and serves two purposes. It gives students practice in reflecting on their own reading effort and processes, helping them become more aware of what they do and perhaps do not do as they read. It also allows teachers to learn about the problems students encountered and the solutions they came up with as they read.

BOX 6.4

SSR+ Metacognitive Log
Sample Template

The metacognitive logs that students keep for SSR+ can be contained in binders, spiral notebooks, composition books, or small examination booklets. The point is for the SSR+ log to be easy for students to maintain and transport. Typically, students record data about reading time and pages completed as well as their observations about their reading behavior. Some like to include a graph that allows them to chart their progress in reading time and pages completed.

Book Title _____ **Author** _____ **Total Pages in Book** ____

Date _____   Page I started on ____ and ended on ____
Minutes I was actively engaged in reading ____

Observations About *How* I Read

Date _____   Page I started on ____ and ended on ____
Minutes I was actively engaged in reading ____

Observations About *How* I Read

BOX 6.5

Sample Metacognitive Log Prompts

Early in a course, when students are new to metacognition, prompts such as the following can help them get started keeping a metacognitive log. Many teachers have students write these on a "bookmark" or the inside cover of their log.

While I was reading:	
I felt confused when . . . and so I . . .	A word/some words I did not know:
I was distracted by . . . but then I . . .	I stopped because . . . What I did next was . . .
I started to think about . . . and so I . . .	I lost track of everything except . . .
I got stuck when . . . What I did was . . .	I figured out that . . .
The time went quickly because . . .	I first thought . . . but then realized . . .
I remembered that earlier in the text . . .	I finally understood . . . because . . .

Later, students may be ready for alternative prompts, which they generate or the teacher introduces to focus them on particular reading strategies.

A reading strategy I used:	A question I had*:
An image I had in my head:	A "right there" question I went back to check:
A connection I made:	A "pulling it together" question I figured out:
I summarized . . . for myself in these words . . .	A "text and me" question I thought of:
A prediction I made was . . . because . . .	An "on my own" question I wondered about:

*These types of questions are described in the Chapter Seven discussion of QAR.

Initially, teachers model an SSR+ metacognitive log entry or two about the books they are reading during SSR+ time. They also collect examples from students' entries that serve as models for the class to talk about. Experienced SSR+ teachers find that if they respond to about five students' logs per class period, they can keep track of how the reading is going for individual students and make brief comments in the logs that let students know they have an interested audience. Many of the "While I was reading" prompts that students use in the first weeks of SSR+ suggest that it's not uncommon to be distracted or confused (or to be able to figure out something to do about it). Later, these initial prompts may give way to new ones the class comes up with, new ways the teacher wants to focus students on their reading behaviors, or no prompts at all for students who no longer need them.

Rosie, a grade 8 English learner in Rita Jensen's English language development (ELD) class, reads her SSR+ books at home. She incorporates the "I got distracted" prompt almost as a matter of course when making her metacognitive log entries, but that doesn't mean she stops reading. As documented in her log for the novel *The Contender* (see Classroom Close-Up 6.2), Rosie not only finishes this 176-page book, but she also has some opinions to share about how it was written as well as who else should read it. From Rosie's metacognitive log, her teacher gets a sense of Rosie's interests, concerns, home responsibilities, and academic aspirations.

For many students, although their SSR+ metacognitive prompts may change or drop away over time, the writing itself becomes increasingly natural and metacognitive (not to mention the shift provoked if the reading itself becomes richer). Zenaida, another grade 8 ELD student, starts the year as a fan of Christopher Pike, a horror writer popular with young adult readers. In Classroom Close-Up 6.3, Zenaida employs a number of prompts in her September, Christopher Pike, log entries. By January, she is reading Anne Frank, and her log entries reflect a marked change in her level of metacognitive engagement.

Anthony Linebaugh's academic literacy students are adept at using metacognitive prompts for writing about their SSR+ reading, but they also enjoy the opportunity to write about the situations in their books (see examples of prompts for this kind of writing in Box 6.6).

BOX 6.6

SSR+ Content-Based Writing Prompts

Write a letter to character ＿＿ giving my opinion about his or her actions.

Pretend I am character ＿＿ and write or respond to another character.

Give a character a grade or report card, with an explanation.

Make an evaluation about character＿＿ based on . . .

I think the character most like me is ＿＿ because . . .

I think the character who is the opposite of me is ＿＿ because . . .

What I would like character ＿＿ to do next is . . .

What I would like to see happen next is . . .

CLASSROOM CLOSE-UP 6.2

Rosie, Grade 8 ELD: SSR+ Metacognitive Log

Rosie's log shows how seriously she takes her SSR+ reading and writing. Her log is also a reminder that English learners' reading comprehension is independent of their mechanical mastery of English. Rosie is reading, and understanding, books at her grade level.

2–2

What I read last night was the book the Contender. I was reading the pages I was supposed to read in my room. I had plenty of light because I was sitting on my desk with a small lamp directed to the book. I read my story for about 20 minutes because I also had to write in my reading log and I had to go to sleep because my little sister (Yesnia) wanted the light of. While I was reading I got distracted by my brother asking me questions about his homework. I also got distracted when my baby sister came in and wanted me to draw a happy face. Other than that everything was cool.

2–3

What I just read so far was that Alfred is starting to get trained for boxing and he has to run every morning at 5:00 o'clock in the morning. Alfred at first did not want to go to start practice but then he realized that his trainer was right. He said that sometimes Alfred will want to quit his lessons. I read this part of the story while I was in my room helping my sister do her homework. I got distracted when my sister kept on singing songs and I had to stop reading and tell her to shut-up. But this part of the story was very interesting.

2–8

I didn't read over the weekend because I was very sick. But my goals are to finish the book so we can move on to another one. I want to end up with a *A* in ELD. Because I really want to pass on to regular classes. During the weekend all I did was in bed. My whole family went to eat dinner, and I just stayed home.

2–14

I think that my connection with this part of the story is that I don't feel good while I'm surrounded with people that don't trust me because I feel like their watching every single step I take. I think that Alfred feels the same way because one of the guys kept on looking at him by the corner of his eye.

What I think about the book

What I think about the book is that it was a nice story but they spended to much time describing something. And I also didn't like the way that they jumped from one character from another. I think that this book was mostly about how know a-days teenagers get into lots of trouble and that there is to much preasure on them like when they say that Alfred was confused and he didn't know if he should of taken drugs or not.

Recomendation

I would recomend this book to everyone. Because I think it is a great book full of peer preasure. For example if one day a big bully is after you just like Major and Alfred. You could stand up to them and show them that you are not afraid of him and that will come down the bully. I especially recomend this book to everyone that plays a sport and to see how it feels to be one day a contender and what kind of risk are you and how hard it feels.

Rating

On a scale from 1–10 I would rate this book a *10* because it wasn't a hard book to read And the good part about this book is that everyone was very happy and that it had a nice ending. Know it looks like Alfred is going to have less stress in his mind and that he is one day going to become someone important like his cousin Jeff.

CLASSROOM CLOSE-UP 6.3

Zenaida, Grade 8 ELD: SSR+ Metacognitive Log

For Zenaida, SSR+ evolves from teenage genre reading into discovering the pleasures of more sophisticated literature. English learner or not, by midyear she is completely absorbed by *The Diary of Anne Frank.*

Sept 19

I felt great and disappointed at the same time because Angela was supposed to kill monsters and she is the main character but she is now beginning to be one.

Sept 20

I was distracted because my eyes kept on drooping down and my vision is kind of blurry. I was reading but couldn't get the words to seep in my mind so I went to sleep.

Sept 21

I am intrigued right now because I am where you call "the turning point" right now is changing. I am predicting that Angela Warner is one of them already so she is going to die at the end.

Sept 22

I felt sad because Angela lost her grandfather. I also felt disgusted at the same time because Jim ate her grandfather.

. . .

Jan 10th

This story is so interesting! It gets better every page too! Because it is coming from a girl's thoughts and her feelings to her diary. It is easy to express yourself in a diary . . . I can relate to her so well. Sometimes I feel exactly what she feels and its amazing and a relief to see another teenager like me. And it doesn't matter if she's in another time . . .

Jan 12th

Again, love this book, because I can relate to the character so much. Its not what I read every day. This book is rare. I think one of the reasons that I like this book so much is because its something you can understand and its nonfiction. I feel like I'm reading a friend's diary!

. . .

Jan 24

She is so honest. And the things she talk about in her diary is so true it amazes me. Because I know what she's talking about and noticed that she actually write it out on paper but I just think it in my mind and never actually said it outloud.

Jan 25

I finished her book and kept having the feeling that I just lost a friend. I felt vulnerable because this girl, an extrordinary writer was killed and I couldn't do anything about that but share her deep feelings and thought. A part of me was angry at the world, the germans. The other part of me want to cry out how cruel and how human beings behave in this world. And I had questions: had human beings really converted into a beast? None of the family members deserved it. Even if they have their own faults in life. But that's human and they still deserved so much more.

When Anthony invites students to write about something they would like to see happen next, earnest log entries such as the following demonstrate the kind of engagement that free-choice reading promotes:

> "What I would like to happen in my book is for Ponyboy's brothers to find whoever hurt him and see why they did it. I want to see this happen because Ponyboy wasn't doing anything, just walking home from the movies."

"I would like for the main character Nick to do something to prevent the invasion. I would also like for him to try and to save the giantess from her sons because if he doesn't then Gullinda as well as the world will be doomed, and no matter how much he steals he'll never be able to live it down."

Anthony has students then use their quick writes as a scaffold for paired book talk. Conveniently, the first thing they may want to say is already written down for them when they get together with a partner.

Creating a Community of Readers

You know, I'll catch them at the back of the room, at the class library, looking at all the books they've read and talking to each other about them. I think the choice of books is what's different for them. It's not overwhelming and all the books are chosen to appeal to them, specifically. They've never had that in a library.

—Charla Dean, academic literacy teacher

At the beginning of the year, before Charla Dean's students can point with pride to SSR+ books they have read, Charla gets informal book talk going in conversations she starts up with individual students:

"Oh, you're liking that book. That's incredible." I make a point of having that conversation, of letting them talk to me about their books. As I'm walking around and kids are reading, they'll tell me, "This is SO good." I just let them talk about it. We have those conversations a lot in the beginning of the year.

Beyond the conversations a teacher can model and inspire, informal book talk between students—as in Anthony Linebaugh's class above and Janet Ghio's book parties (Classroom Close-Up 6.1)—is a form of accountability for reading that students have to each other. As well as exposing students to new books they might like to read, informal book talk promotes the idea that reading is both valued and enjoyed in their class.

In Tammy Thompson's grade 9 academic literacy class, *brief* informal book talk is a regular feature of SSR+, one that students look forward to after they complete their metacognitive logs. In the threesome that follows, Genn's partners listen attentively as she provides the latest installment from her reading. When the description is a little sketchy, they jump in because they want to know what, exactly, got the main character "really frustrated":

Genn: Well, in my book, she's following her boss around the office all day and she got really frustrated with her. So that's it.

James: Why?

Genn: Because her boss, she's rude.
James: Really.
Christine: Doesn't her boss just wear like name brand things?
Genn: Yeah, she gets mad when she doesn't wear designer clothes.
Christine: So, wait. The assistant person has to wear designer clothes?
Genn: Yeah, or she gets yelled at.

Often, Tammy chooses to follow up these partner exchanges with a quick class discussion, in which she may ask students to describe their observations about their reading as well as tell the latest news about their books' characters or plot. Discussion prompts such as those in Box 6.7 invite students to share their SSR+ reading experiences and put the work of "book talk" in their hands.

In addition to informal talk about books, students can present a Book Project for some or all of the books they read. The purpose of the Book Project activity is to build interest and excitement around books; it is not intended as a test of students' completion or comprehension of their SSR+ books. Creating and presenting a book poster is a popular Book Project. Box 6.8 presents book poster instructions for students, including those who are participating as the audience.

Charla Dean has added a few twists to the book poster activity, which she says her grade 9 academic literacy students seem to like:

> They make a book poster (half a poster sheet) that includes the title, the author, stars (one to five stars for how much they liked it), the movie rating it would get (G, PG, PG-13, and so on), at least two graphic representations, and a "golden line" (a personally meaningful quote from the book). I provide markers, colored paper, glue sticks, and a copy machine/ printer. We display the posters all around the room as advertising for the classroom library. Our favorite posters from each year join the "Hall of Fame." The Hall of Fame, by the way, is huge—it's the first impression students have of my class. I have the posters all around the room on the first day of school, and it's the one thing they all want to know about.

In Luke Boyd's grade 9 English class, students build a card catalog for the classroom library—a historical record of peers' responses to a range of books. Students use these reviews to help make their next SSR (and literature circle) selections. The book reviews are structured around a few simple objectives and suggestions:

Objectives
- Give potential readers an idea of the book's quality.
- Highlight some of the strengths and weaknesses of the book.
- Keep major plot events hidden.

Suggestions

- Rate the book from zero to five stars. You can include half stars. Justify your rating. Include a graphic symbol, too.

- Explain what you liked and/or disliked about the book.

- Don't be vague—for example, "This was cool," "This sucked," "This was stupid," "I liked this book. It was exciting."

- Don't reveal twists in the plot or the ending—who wants to read it then?

- Compare it to other books you've read—for example, "This is almost like . . ." "This is for fans of . . ."

- Keep it short and sweet—one side of an index card.

BOX 6.7

Discussion Prompts for Debriefing SSR+ Reading

Once students are familiar with these discussion prompts from whole class debriefing of SSR+ reading, give a copy to students for their use in debriefing with a partner.

DEBRIEFING OUR READING PROCESS

- Did anyone get distracted while reading? What did you do or what might you do to solve that problem?

- Did anyone get confused while reading? What did you do or what might you do to solve that problem?

- Did anyone lose interest while reading? What did you do or what might you do to solve that problem?

- Did anyone get stopped by unfamiliar words while reading? What did you do or what might you do to solve that problem?

- Did anyone get stopped by long (and complex) sentences or paragraphs while reading? What did you do or what might you do to solve that problem?

- Did anyone have a surprising experience while reading today? What did you do?

BOOK TALK

- Did anyone read something funny today? Can you tell us about it or read us a few lines?

- Did anyone read something scary or bizarre today? Can you tell us about it or read us a few lines?

- Did anyone read something sad today? Can you tell us about it or read us a few lines?

- Did anyone read anything where the language really grabbed you (like a great description)? Can you tell us about it or read us a few lines?

- Did anyone decide to "give up" on a book today or give a book another "ten-page chance"? Can you tell us why?

"Teaser strips" get Rita Jensen's middle school ELD students curious about each other's SSR+ books. On strips of paper, students write a weekly one-sentence teaser about the book they are reading and post it on the wall below a photocopy of their book cover (or a quick art piece they make of a cover for their book). During weekly gallery walks, teasers like "Will Sharon run away from her abusive father and quit school?" or "Why does everyone in Sam's family keep dying?" spark interest in the books that classmates are reading and suggest questions to ask the book's current reader. The teasers, Rita reports, really build engagement for students about what to read next.

BOX 6.8

SSR+ Book Poster Assignment

Whenever students complete a book (or about every four weeks), they may also complete a book poster (or other type of book project). The instructions to students presented here explain the responsibilities of the book poster presenter and the audience.

PART 1: CREATE A BOOK POSTER

- Include the following on your poster:
  - The book's title and author
  - A visual representation of a significant scene in the text
  - A quotation that is important to your book, with a page number
  - A statement explaining why someone might enjoy your book (or not)
- Posters will be displayed on the wall so your classmates can be reminded of your book when they consider a new one to read.

PART 2: BOOK TALK

- Introduce your book: give the author, genre, and where you are in the book so far.
- Present a brief plot summary (but don't give away the ending).
- Explain the significant scene shown on your poster.
- Read the book quotation on your poster and explain its importance.
- Explain whether you recommend the book. Why or why not?

PART 3: ACTIVE LISTENING

- Take notes during a book talk to remember the book or a question for the presenter.
- Engage in book talk with your classmates after a presentation.
- Add books that interest you to your list of potential selections.

Christine Cziko noticed that in her academic literacy class, as the weeks went on, students were trying out new authors and passing books around to each other. A girl who started out with an unbroken string of R. L. Stine teen horror novels moved on to reading the adult best-selling horror novelist V. C. Andrews. Then she discovered Stephen King. A group of Chinese American boys began the year reading and exchanging fantasy books, exclusively. By spring, however, they had expanded their range to include April Sinclair's coming-of-age novel *Coffee Will Make You Black*, which had been circulating steadily among their African American and Latino classmates.

Supporting and Assessing Students' SSR+ Reading Behaviors

> My SSR goal for last month was to increase my stamina and read longer and I think I did reach that goal because when I do MCLs [metacognitive logs] I read a lot of pages and I get the work done and I think I reached my other goal which was to be able to read for long periods of time and not get bored because I am so interested in certain books and I don't get bored I get more and more interested.
>
> —Damian, grade 9 academic literacy student

Damian's teacher, Michelle Stone, teaches open enrollment AP English as well as academic literacy for ninth graders like Damian. Michelle's expectations of students in both courses are the same: Try your best, and I will too. In her first year of teaching academic literacy, however, Michelle sometimes wondered whether her best was enough to take her students where they needed to go. Her students were not universally delighted to be in the class, and they were struggling with some of the course's core concepts. Consequently, Michelle worried that they weren't advancing as rapidly as they could. As the year went on, however, Michelle saw that her students were making steady progress. And by the end of the year, as she read the students' final reflection letters about their SSR+ books and reading goals, Michelle found herself a little teary-eyed. Here is some more of Damian's letter, for example:

> For SSR, I read *Tyrell* by Coe Booth. . . . I like Tyrell because he is independent and can carry his family even though it's difficult because he's only seventeen and he's doing what his dad should have done and his dad has been in and out of jail and he just doesn't know what in the heck to do and also he's not in school and he has two girls falling for him and gosh when does he get a break I just like this character because he reminds me of me because I help my mom with my younger brother and my dad isn't around neither and I just think that I'm him and he's me. . . .

I would recommend this book because a lot of people I know didn't have a dad always while they were growing up and they can relate and also feel what I felt about this book it has so much tension and suspense and drama and I like drama not in real life but in book's it's great to have it so you can be exited, sad, mad because those are emotions and once you get that right book you'll feel how I felt and you will want to read every book by that author. . . .

What I'm noticing about my reading is that I'm getting faster and I know a lot more words and different ways of learning and my reader identity is getting much more knowledge into it and that makes me feel like I am a smart young man who can do what ever I set my mind to and what ever people say will not hurt me because I know that I have the knowledge to school them in whatever and also thanks to Ms. Stone she has did a lot in this because reading used to not be my thing but now I love it very much.

My reading goal for the summer is to read three to four books and read all of them I'm going to try and get more books from Coe Booth because that author has inspired me to read more like drama books and also learn how to teach like Ms. Stone so I can teach my brother how to read and all my skills.

Damian's letter is the culmination of a year of SSR+ in which he regularly set reading goals and reflected on his reading processes and progress. Teachers who incorporate SSR+ into an academic literacy class or other course keep tabs on students' reading through their SSR+ metacognitive logs and brief conversations about a student's book or reading experience. They also help students set SSR+ goals and reflect on their progress toward meeting those goals.

Before asking students to set SSR+ goals, many teachers prime the pump with a class brainstorming session to elicit a range of possible goals. Goals students are likely to offer in the beginning of the year may relate to reading habits (read somewhere quiet, read every day), reading attitudes (find something I like about reading, give myself a chance), and "data"—duration of reading time (stamina) and pages completed (fluency). Later in the year, students' goals may shift to trying new reading strategies that the class is practicing, or a new genre or new authors or more challenging books.

Once a month or so, each student has a chance to meet with the teacher to review his or her work in SSR+. These reading conferences are structured by a student's monthly SSR+ reflection letter and the goals students have chosen for themselves. In these reflections, students write about the book they are reading, how their reading is going, how many pages and minutes they are able to read, and metacognitive log prompts they have used. (SSR+ assessment guidance and a number of tools such as the reflection letter are in the SSR+ section of the Assessment Appendix. In the Student Learning Goals section of the appendix, the Building Personal Engagement goals are also helpful for suggesting how students can focus their effort in SSR+ to help them grow as readers.)

To prepare for writing an SSR+ reflection letter and setting personal reading goals, students' SSR+ metacognitive logs are an important resource—hard evidence of their reading stamina, the metacognitive strategies they tried and found useful (or not), and their reading interests. Their logs will also remind students of any notes or comments written by the teacher and any new book titles or genres they added to their list of potential next choices. By reviewing all these entries, students can evaluate their past work and make plans for continued improvement.

The teacher's role in these conferences begins well before the meetings themselves. From the beginning of SSR+, the teacher has an active part in helping students find books they will want to read and then monitoring their engagement and progress. Some students invariably need intensive support in the beginning of SSR+, to find books and then to stay focused on reading them.

To keep track of students' reading behaviors, a simple scan of the room from time to time allows teachers to know which students are reading, pretend reading (by turning pages occasionally), or not reading—and to record the behavior with a simple key on a seating chart or in a grade book. Another way teachers monitor students' reading behaviors is by walking around the room at the beginning of SSR+ and recording students' reading progress and which students forgot their books or changed books. This recordkeeping allows teachers to zero in on supporting students who are having trouble engaging and to collect data for conferencing and grading purposes.

During SSR+ conferences, the teacher listens as a student reads his or her SSR+ Reflection Letter. The teacher then shares his or her records and observations about the student's reading behaviors. Together the teacher and student agree on how the teacher might help the student and about the student's proposed goal or goals. The goal-setting portion of the conference is an opportunity for teachers to help students stretch—the duration of their reading, how many pages they read, the reading strategies they use, the kind of metacognitive prompts they try, the topic or genre they take on, or the reading level or complexity of their next book. In their metacognitive log, students write the new (or continuing) goal agreed to in the conference, along with the date.

A student's SSR+ grade is also a conference topic. Part of making sure that students benefit from SSR+ means holding them accountable for their independent reading and for their growth as readers. At the same time, grades must be used carefully so they do not erode a student's reading confidence or increase an existing reluctance to read. Grades for SSR+ should reflect students' effort and progress toward meeting their goals. (Benchmarks that many teachers use in grading SSR+ are discussed in the Assessment Appendix.) Sometimes teachers extend the conference beyond the kind of check-in described and assess a student's reading growth. This might include having the student read aloud for an assessment of oral fluency, or Think Aloud or Talk to the Text as an approximation of mental engagement or facility with reading problem-solving strategies. The information that teachers gather from such assessments gives them insight into not only how the student is progressing but also what kind of support may be needed.

By the end of her first year using SSR+, Tammy Thompson knew which students had learned how to reengage with a book when they got distracted, which ones had moved themselves up the ladder to read increasingly more challenging books, who had read whole books for the first time in their lives, whose thinking about books had grown deeper, and who had started reading for her own purposes instead of fake-reading to please her father. Tammy briefly profiles five of her students in Classroom Close-Up 6.4.

CLASSROOM CLOSE-UP 6.4

Five Inexperienced Readers

SSR+ isn't only for inexperienced readers, but the ninth graders in Tammy Thompson's academic literacy class were less experienced readers than many of their peers. Tammy's pride in the way her students blossomed in a program of regular SSR+ is evident in her reflections on five particular readers:

"*Danny* had never read a whole book in his entire life. He'd never been taught how to pick out a book, so he didn't know what would interest him. A strategy that was really helpful to him that he talks about a lot is the ten-page rule. He'll read a book for at least ten pages, and if he's interested in it after ten pages, he'll keep reading it, and if not, he'll put the book down and he'll choose another book. And I think this helps him because it shows him that there are books that he'll be interested in, he just needs to continue trying. He has read three books this year, which may not seem like a lot, but the fact that he's never read a book in his entire life—it's a big deal. He's able to articulate his reading process; he can use the words *stamina* and *reading strategies* and *comprehension*. He can use these words that he might not ever have used before, if he even knew what they were. So he has benefited from learning how to pick out a book, and he has learned that he actually likes to read. And that's pretty exciting.

"*Stella* came into the class knowing how to read—she enjoyed reading—but she got distracted a lot, and when she got distracted, she would close the book and put it down. Academic literacy has really taught her how to stay engaged in a book and what she can do if she hits a roadblock, becomes distracted, or doesn't understand something. She knows

(Continued)

exactly what she needs to do to reengage in the book. The level of books that she's reading has greatly increased. She went from reading eighth-grade, ninth-grade books to college books. She takes her books home with her, and she's going through about a book a week.

"*Monica* is a very social girl. She likes to talk, and she likes to talk about what she reads. At the beginning of the year she would just give the plot, what happened in the story that day. As the year has progressed—and I think the metacognitive logs have helped her to process her thinking—she's analyzing the characters more and she's questioning them more. So this program has made her go deeper into the books. When she talks about her books now, it's a lot more poignant. There's substance to what she's saying. It's a lot more than just plot line.

"*Genn's* father came in on back-to-school night and didn't understand why she was in this class. He said she reads at home all the time and she likes to read, so he was confused. Working with Genn through the year, I learned that she used to fake-read a lot. That's what her father was seeing. He wanted her to read, so she would placate him and "read" even though she wasn't. Now she's actually really reading and she's thinking about what she's reading. You can see it in her metacognitive logs. So I think this has gotten her more interested in reading the books, and she's actually doing it.

"*Douglas* is another boy who came into this class and had never read a book before. He really benefited from the rule that said he could read whatever he wanted. David started at about a fourth-grade reading level and was reading books that were maybe twenty, twenty-five pages. And he would read one in a week, and then he would come back and read another one. So he was reading more and more, and he was also taking these books home. And when he hit book number ten, he was finding books in my bookshelves that he was asking me to put aside for him so nobody else would get them. And so I had four or five books at a time on hold for David so he could read them. It's safe to say that by this time he has read about forty books, and he's probably at grade level now."

Well over a decade ago, Rosa, a member of the first cohort of Reading Apprenticeship academic literacy students, recognized that of all the benefits of SSR+, the degree to which it builds reading confidence, stamina, and fluency had a profound effect on her reading beyond SSR+. Opportunities to read self-chosen materials, to reflect on her reading process, to learn about her preferences as a reader, and to spend an increasing amount of time in sustained silent reading built her stamina and self-regulation. When she had to read academic materials that posed more challenge, these skills and dispositions kicked in:

> The history book is really boring. But even if it is boring, [SSR] helped me pace myself. Even if you don't want to read it, you can.

■ ■ ■

Expanded reading opportunities, such as those provided by a program of free-choice sustained silent reading, help build students' fluency, confidence, and stamina to read (even "boring" books). The high-leverage cognitive strategies described in Chapter Seven help them take an active approach when reading problems arise.

The Cognitive Dimension
Assembling a Reading Toolbox

When we got into *Their Eyes Were Watching God*, I could not understand any of the talking. I had to remember back to Ms. Krebs's class and just say, "Okay, this is how I need to focus." So I went back into the book and I started going through it and started writing down, "Okay, this is probably what they meant, this is probably what they did not mean," and just ask questions and try to answer them.

—Greg, grade 12 student

EARLIER we introduced metacognitive conversation as a way for students to become aware of and articulate about their mental processes when they read. In this chapter, we introduce some of the specific cognitive strategies that teachers can embed in metacognitive routines to increase students' abilities to improve comprehension. The real power of this work comes when students, like Greg, have learned and internalized cognitive strategies sufficiently to integrate and use them flexibly while learning academic content. Learning to monitor comprehension, adjust reading processes for a wide variety of purposes, and strategically use a broad range of cognitive tools—such as making connections, clarifying, questioning, and summarizing—helps students become stronger and more autonomous readers.

How can teachers help students learn to use, with increasing independence, these tools for making sense of various texts? And what trade-offs are involved when strategy instruction must be included in an already crowded course of study?

The time invested initially in teaching students high-leverage problem-solving strategies is time that does not necessarily displace content coverage over the long haul. Because strategy instruction is most effective when embedded in authentic subject area reading tasks,[1] students in Reading Apprenticeship classrooms learn problem-solving strategies in the context of the regular subject area curriculum, not by doing worksheet drills.

It is certainly true that as students begin explicitly practicing reading strategies, they move more slowly through the course content, but their comprehension of what they are reading increases. As they gain confidence and facility in solving reading problems, this initial investment in strategy instruction begins to pay off. In effect, cognitive strategies instruction supports content learning. Students come to own the strategies, both in the context of their current coursework and down the road. As Greg says of his grade 12 encounter with *Their Eyes Were Watching God*, "I had to remember back to Ms. Krebs's class." And he did.

Making Problem Solving Explicit

> Mostly I just read in school so I can make it. But I like to build things, so I read a lot of instructions. I put together a stroller for my baby brother, and I helped my dad put together a computer. Now I'm starting to build these [skateboard] ramps for my friends. But I'm not really reading for that one.
>
> —Emerson, grade 8 student

Helping students assemble a toolbox of cognitive reading strategies often means starting from students' sense of themselves as problem solvers in areas other than academics. Sometimes this competence is tacitly recognized; for example, when parents trust students to care for younger siblings, or employers give students responsibilities that require them to solve day-to-day work problems. At other times, students may not recognize or appreciate the problem solving that they accomplish *all the time*. Emerson, just quoted, does not recognize the problem solving he does to build strollers or computers or skateboard ramps. In school, he uses his problem-solving strategies to figure out what level of reading effort will be just enough "so I can make it." By making students' mastery of these implicit or even unrecognized cognitive strategies explicit for them, teachers can help students build confidence and motivation for solving the cognitive problems that come up when reading academic texts.

Community college teacher Cindy Hicks implements Reading Apprenticeship in her basic skills English 101 course. She helps her students recognize ways they have become competent problem solvers by asking them a survey question on the first day of class: "Describe a time when you learned something well." Interestingly, students often cite an apprenticeship experience. Daniel wrote,

> At first I was afraid to drive because I thought I could crash a car. My dad taught me how to drive, and I practiced a lot to improve my driving.

The practicing that Daniel describes, to improve his driving skills (and not crash), represents paying concerted attention to particular kinds of problem solving. Daniel's focus and persistence, and his growing confidence in his ability to improve, can also serve him well in developing strategies for solving reading problems.

Cindy's student Labelle, who is working for a real estate broker as well as attending school, reports that making real estate loans is something she learned to do well:

> The broker who hired me gave me training that helped me quite a bit, and I became very good at it. My experience with learning to do loans gave me a lot of confidence.

Labelle's on-the-job apprenticeship, learning the intricacies of refinance and purchase loans, has given her the confidence to enroll in community college and to envision transferring into a bachelor's degree program.

These students and others in Cindy Hicks's classes have dispositions and competencies to build on, and their teacher takes time to make them aware of how valuable those resources are. When she then engages students in metacognitive conversations to solve reading problems, students' sense of themselves as competent problem solvers will have already been surfaced and validated.

Teaching Problem Solving in Reading

> The thing we did today I thought was great. The breaking [text] off into sections, and then summarizing it, and trying to find a meaning to it, and then like trying to find questions about it.
>
> —Lupita, grade 10 student

Students know from their own life experiences, whether getting through the hardest level of a video game or getting a sibling to school on time, that solving different problems calls for different sets of tools and strategies and the ability to use them appropriately. During the early weeks of supporting students to become more confident and independent readers in different subject area classes, teachers can introduce the metaphor of assembling a "mental toolbox for reading." Lupita is describing a set of tools that her English class is learning to use as they begin the year with *The Odyssey*: chunking the text into meaningful sections, summarizing those sections, and asking their own questions about what they have read. Lupita and her classmates will use these high-leverage strategies over and over, in widely different situations, as the need arises. They will also learn strategies that are more particularly targeted for discipline-specific use.

Lupita's teacher has settled on chunking, summarizing, and questioning as high-leverage reading strategies to start the year. The question of when to teach which cognitive strategies is a vexing one, however, because readers need to be able to use many strategies flexibly and simultaneously. We offer here examples of sequences for introducing cognitive strategies that different teachers have used; naturally, decisions about instructional sequence are best made with classroom and local contexts in mind.

In Rita Jensen's middle school ELD classroom, students learn five reading strategies in the first six weeks of school: questioning, connecting, summarizing, predicting, and clarifying. These strategies then become the basis for students' individual, small group, and whole class work to make sense of classroom readings. In Will Brown's chemistry classes, students are first introduced to a set of three comprehension strategies—clarifying, questioning, and summarizing—and they continue to explicitly practice those strategies months later, learning to use them in multiple ways, with multiple types of texts (see Classroom Close-Up 7.1).

Box 7.1 lists a number of high-leverage reading strategies for teachers to be aware of—either to choose from for explicit instruction or to seize on opportunistically. A particular text, for example, might invite teachers to introduce the strategy of listening for voice. Another text might call out for instruction in identifying cause and effect. Likewise, as students nominate new ideas for the class Reading Strategies List, teachers have important opportunities to validate and incorporate modeling and practice in student-identified problem-solving strategies.

The Curriculum-Embedded Reading Assessment (CERA) in the Assessment Appendix is a way for teachers and students to monitor students' growing use of cognitive strategies, including those they may already know and those they are learning.

In different subject areas, the same high-leverage strategies may have discipline-specific applications. Corey, a ninth grader in a school where many teachers have adopted Reading Apprenticeship practices, explains how chunking works in algebra compared to English:

> Sixth period is math, and we did a Talking to the Text to break down big, like word problems. So it's a lot different than using it in English, because you're using it to figure out what you have to do to solve the problem, instead of what do the words actually mean.

Likewise, Corey would find that in algebra he uses the strategy of visualizing most often to make the abstract symbols of mathematics concrete, in

---

CLASSROOM CLOSE-UP 7.1

"We're Going to Practice This and Get Better at It"

The first three sentences of an article students are about to read fill the chalkboards at the front of Will Brown's high school chemistry classroom. Words have been underlined and circled, and arrows point from the text to marginal notes Will has written to himself.

He has just modeled Talking to the Text, demonstrating how he asks himself questions as he reads, tries to clarify things that are confusing, and summarizes his understanding of what is most important.

Will asks students to read the rest of the assignment to themselves, practicing the cognitive strategies he has modeled. When students are ready, he moves to a clean chalkboard and records for the class some of their text annotations. He comments on those that indicate questioning and clarifying strategies, and then observes that summarizing statements have escaped students' attention. And so he engages the class in a mini-lesson on summarizing, pointing out ways that text structure can help students predict which ideas are important.

"Who can say, what are some of the big ideas you read in this first section? Anyone want to contribute?"

After long silence, Hani offers, "Understanding neutralize."

Will acknowledges her idea, and when no other volunteers are forthcoming, he asks whether anyone else thought neutralizing was one of the big ideas in the text. A few hands are raised, and finally James says that indicators for telling whether something is an acid or base seem to be important.

"So indicators are important," Will temporizes. "So, indicators, neutralize—what are some of the other big ideas?"

When no additional responses are offered, Will tells students, "Well, we're going to practice this and get better at it. One of the things you can look for when you're trying to build a summary is what idea keeps coming up and up and up. In science articles, a lot of times it's like a footprint that's left behind. So, what's the important thing that's always being talked about, spoken about, in this first section? Anyone want to make a guess at that?"

Mario is willing to take a chance. "Things about acids and stuff?"

"The things about," Will repeats. "What's a word we might use that the text was using, *the things about* acids and stuff?"

Surprising himself as much as anyone, Mario retrieves the key vocabulary word that "left its tracks" in the reading assignment. "Properties," he says.

Will continues as if he and Mario had planned this exchange, "So who would say that maybe the key summary is, 'Here are the properties of acids and bases?' You think that might be it? And then we could build a little list."

As Will had promised his students, the class worked together many more times to learn how to question, to clarify, and, especially, to summarize their chemistry reading.

---

science to make abstract processes concrete, and in English and history to "see" the scenes created by an author's words. In Chapter Eight, in which we focus on knowledge-building in different disciplines, we will take another look at how cognitive strategies are applied differently in various disciplines.

Regardless of which reading strategies students are learning, they should be learning them in the context of meaningful subject area text. For introducing a

A Sampling of Reading Strategies

Students can apply almost all of these strategies across disciplines, although discipline-specific applications may vary. The strategies in boldface are discussed in this chapter. In the *Reading Apprenticeship Academic Literacy Course,* students learn to use all of these (and more) over three units of work in English language arts, history, and science.

- Setting a Reading Purpose
- Choosing a Reading Process
- **Previewing**
- **Identifying and Evaluating Roadblocks**
- Tolerating Ambiguity
- **Clarifying**
- Using Context
- **Making Connections**
- **Chunking**
- **Visualizing**
- Listening for Voice
- **Questioning**

- **Predicting**
- Organizing Ideas and Information
- Paraphrasing
- **Getting the Gist**
- **Summarizing**
- Sequencing
- Comparing and Contrasting
- Identifying Cause and Effect
- **Using Evidence**
- Rereading
- Writing to Clarify Understanding
- Writing to Consolidate Learning

strategy and initially providing students with focused practice, it makes sense to choose short, accessible texts or to chunk a core academic text and focus on just one paragraph, a difficult sentence, or a single caption, graphic, or formula, in this way keeping a balance between the challenge of the text itself and the task that students are trying to accomplish.

After starting with a quick Think Aloud to model the meaning-making process underlying a particular strategy, teachers might then invite students to reciprocate, practicing their own beginning use of the strategy. Knowing that full acquisition of strategies develops only with practice over time, teachers then provide many opportunities for students to use the strategy in the course of regular subject area reading and to talk about it in pairs, in small groups, and in the whole class.

Over time, students gain facility making strategic use of a new strategy and applying it with increasingly difficult texts. Many of the high-leverage reading strategies discussed in the following section are reflected in the cognitive dimension of the Student Learning Goals (see the Assessment Appendix).

When students are introduced to cognitive learning goals early in a course, they have an opportunity to identify the discipline-specific cognitive strategies that are already familiar and preview the new ones they will learn. When students have more experience, later in a course, they can return to the list of goals and note which unfamiliar strategies they learned and which other ones they now understand better and use more effectively.

Applying a Selection of High-Leverage Reading Strategies

> At the same time I was reading it, I was trying to picture it. If it didn't seem quite clear, I'll go over it slowly. Sometimes I'll like analyze it, "This here, this here, this here," trying to get into my mind a picture or something. And then I'll go on, slowly, analyzing it all. Or sometimes if I get confused, I'll question myself. I'm like, "When was it? Okay, moonlight, right." So I'll get a picture of nighttime in my mind, like that. I didn't do that before. Ms. Cziko showed me how to put questions as I'm reading it to help me out, and after I'm reading a little bit, summarize it and go on. And if I need like clarification or something, if I can't do it myself, I'll just ask somebody. Just reading the book and knowing what it's about is not *understanding* the book.
>
> –LaKeisha, grade 9 student

LaKeisha was a student in the first Reading Apprenticeship class ever, at Thurgood Marshall Academic High School. In an interview midway through the school year, she talked about how her reading had changed. Like so many students, she had never thought that reading was much more than saying the words. What we can see from her interview, however, is her new recognition that reading is about *understanding*, and that she has the tools to make that happen. In her brief comments, LaKeisha enumerates many of the strategies she has learned: visualizing, rereading, chunking, using context, questioning, summarizing, and clarifying. LaKeisha's teacher, who was a coauthor of the first edition of this book, chose some powerful strategies for her students to learn.

We now describe a few of them: chunking, clarifying, making connections, visualizing, questioning, using evidence, getting the gist and summarizing, predicting, and previewing informational text.

Chunking Text

Teachers can take it for granted that many students already break complex sentences into shorter phrases to manage their comprehension as they read. However, for students who have never been able to crack the code of complex texts, chunking difficult, complex sentences into smaller, comprehendible phrases can be an especially powerful strategy. Many students cite the practice of chunking text phrase by phrase as one of the most useful reading strategies they have learned.

Students in LaKeisha's Reading Apprenticeship cohort first learned about chunking when teachers introduced it in terms of eating a pizza:

> Even if you're really hungry, you can't eat a whole pizza at once. You have to eat it a little bit at a time, in slices. Understanding text is similar to eating pizza. Though you may want to read a large amount at once, you may not be able to understand it unless you take it in bits and pieces.

In Dorothea Jordan's grade 7 pre-algebra class, when she decided she could no longer teach mathematics without teaching some key reading strategies, students found her approach to chunking particularly memorable (see her interview in Classroom Close-Up 7.2). She ascribes much of the improvement in her students' ability to solve mathematics problems to the chunking practice they got in her classroom.

Community college math professor Yu-Chung Chang-Hou takes chunking text a step further. Her students read and chunk their math problems, extract the necessary data, and then rewrite the problems before trying to solve them. For her developmental math students, she finds that chunking and rewriting a problem builds students' confidence that they can actually succeed:[2]

> I tell them, "Forget about math for fifteen or twenty minutes. Do not give me x, y, z. I just want you to enumerate in words all the pieces of information." Ten years ago I wouldn't do this. I would think it would be wasting time in the math class. But that step is huge. It's very important. If they do not analyze or list out all those things, they have anxiety up to here. But if you tell them, "Forget about math," then they will not think about math. "Try to understand the situation. Write it." That step is actually the most important.

When teaching students to chunk text, teachers may be surprised that even students who automatically use punctuation to identify meaningful phrases will realize for the first time that they can also pause in a sentence, to think, even when no comma or period tells them to stop. Instead of plowing along in uninterrupted reading, students may need to develop the habit of intentionally disrupting their reading to chunk text into smaller bits they can understand. Once they understand the individual bits, they can put them back together and reread the reconstructed text.

Students may not recognize that the size of any given chunk they need to interpret will vary according to the text and the reader: some students may

CLASSROOM CLOSE-UP 7.2

Chunking Pre-Algebra Text

Dorothea Jordan is an experienced middle school mathematics teacher, but she had never thought of herself as a reading teacher. Yet year by year, her students seemed to have increasing difficulty reading the texts of the mathematics classroom, whether word problems, textbook directions, or project descriptions. Finally, after she found herself rewriting her materials into "baby" language, she realized it was time to come to grips with what students really needed. In this interview, she reflects on how her teaching has changed.

"Years ago," she says, "we would read from the textbook, and if it said, *Tell whether a number is prime or composite, and if composite, list the prime factorization*—normally, we would read that and say, 'Okay, now do it.'

"Now, when I see students in September, they just read right through and then give up. They can't do the math, nor can they comprehend the text.

"So at the very beginning, I start to teach them the structure of word problems—using the routine of chunking.

"Chunking the problem, you start out, 'Okay, *Tell whether a number is prime. . .* What does prime mean?'

"And then they would remember.

"'Okay, *if composite . . .*, so what does composite mean?'

"'Oh, yeah,' they would remember.

"'*And if composite, list the prime factorization*. Okay, prime, we know what it means. What does factorization mean?'

"And then they make the connection, 'Oh, yeah, we can do the European version, or we can do the [factor] tree.'

"I really think they understand that by thinking and reasoning, and looking at the vocabulary, they can make connections to a solution. Before, they would just read, read, read, read, read through and say, 'I can't do it.'"

Dorothea explains how she involves the class in the chunking and problem solving. "I have volunteers read a sentence, and I say, 'Stop. Okay, what does that mean?' And I just constantly say, 'Stop. What does that mean?' I don't offer anything. I let them make the connections. We read the whole thing, and I say, 'You can take notes on the paper.' And then they are able to do it.

"They chunk the text, look for clue words, make connections, draw something.

"At the end of the year I asked for a reflection. 'What's the one thing that helped you over the year?'

"They said, 'Drawing what we read. And going back to the text, and thinking about what types of questions, that really has helped, too.'"

What students didn't name, but what they clearly remembered was revealed on the last day of school. "I let them do impersonations of teachers," Dorothea says, "and we had to pick out who the teacher was. The kid who did me said, 'Okay, read this. Stop!'"

be able to digest several sentences as a meaningful chunk of a particular text, others may prefer small chunks of each sentence in the same text. Some texts may not require any chunking, but at the other end of the spectrum, if students find they are breaking text into two- or three-word chunks, that may signal that chunking is not an effective strategy for that student with that text—either the text is too hard or, for students who comprehend syntax more readily, some other strategy such as questioning may better serve their comprehension goals.

Sometimes, however, when students are reading very dense text, teachers may want to insist that students initially break the text into two- or three-word chunks. This may be necessary if students are to accomplish the close reading the text requires. Cindy Ryan's students, in Classroom Close-Up 7.3, decipher the First Amendment in just such increments.

To give students an introduction to how text can be chunked, and the importance of reading on to see whether a confusion may be cleared up, some teachers do a quick activity in which meaning builds cumulatively as students put succeeding chunks together. Box 7.2 describes the process and provides a sample text that rewards clue gathering and perseverance.

Clarifying

The clarifying strategy can take different forms. In Chapter Four we noted that when classrooms develop an inquiry culture, students recognize that "confusion" can be a powerful starting point for learning. We introduced a five-step process they can adopt when reading confusions arise: (1) ignore the unclear part and read on to see whether it gets clearer or the unclear part turns out to be unimportant (that is, you can still understand what you are reading), (2) reread

---

CLASSROOM CLOSE-UP 7.3
Chunking the First Amendment

Congress shall make no law respecting the establishment of religion, or prohibiting the free exercise thereof; or abridging the freedom of speech, or of the press; or the right of the people peaceably to assemble, and to petition the Government for a redress of grievances.

In Cindy Ryan's ninth-grade academic literacy class, students are reading a variety of history texts in pursuit of an "essential question" about how the First Amendment has allowed people to secure and extend the rights envisioned in the Declaration of Independence. Making sense of this briefest of documents is the students' entire goal this class period. Independently, they have read and annotated the First Amendment. Now they bring their Talking to the Text notes to the small groups that will continue investigating what these forty-five words actually mean. Terrance and Jamila are chunking the text, collaborating to wrangle it phrase by phrase into clarity.

"We can petition," Terrance says, "and see, it say, 'and to petition the government for redress of grievances.'"

Jamila responds, "Oh. So, they saying that the law *can't take away* your petitioning the government."

"Yes, that's what I've been saying all this time!"

Jamila sees a pattern. "Let's take it a piece at a time. Taking away the freedom of speech. They cannot take away your freedom of speech. Or of the press. So they can't take away . . ."

"You know what freedom of press is, right?"

"Yeah, they're saying that the press can still type if they want to, right?"

"Somethin' like that."

Jamila reads out what she has been writing: "'Congress cannot make laws based on favorable religion or take away your freedom of speech, the press . . . ' So, let's see, 'your right to petition the government.'"

"They can't take away nothing is what they're practically saying."

BOX 7.2

Modeling How Text Chunks

PURPOSE

Chunking a text that is hard to understand allows students to break it into meaningful phrases and, by understanding the phrases, constitute a meaningful whole. Students may already know to use punctuation to help them chunk meaningful phrases, but for a particular text and particular reader, chunks can be either smaller or larger than would be indicated by punctuation alone.

PROCEDURE

- Find or prepare a text that explains how to do something, such as how to do laundry or assemble a clarinet. The text should not immediately make clear what process is being described. If a final line reveals the process, you may want to initially withhold it from the class. Make a copy of the text that you can project (see the sample text that follows).

- Project the text and read it aloud to the class.

- Ask students to write down the procedure they think is being described.

- Lead the class in going through the explanation and breaking it down into chunks.

- Help the class piece the component steps together to figure out what procedure is being described.

- If necessary, reveal any withheld information.

- Once students know what is being described, have them write a short description of how they figured it out: When did they understand it? What parts of the text were key?

The following text is an example that can be used for this activity.

1. Place the base or stock (the back, unsliced half) of the reed into 1/2 to 1 inch of water. The capillary action of the reed will pull water from the base to the tip, despite gravity. As the water reaches the middle of the reed, where the slice begins, take the reed out and quickly wet the end into which you blow. You should experiment with how saturated you let the reed get, and see what produces the best resonance for you. (Two minutes before band practice starts is not the best time for this experiment.) While the reed is soaking, you can complete the other steps.

2. Grease the corks if they seem dry.

   This will make your clarinet easier to put together and take apart. . . *(Do not reveal this chunk initially.)*

Source: "How to Assemble a Clarinet," http://www.wikihow.com/Assemble-a-Clarinet. All text shared under a Creative Commons License.

the unclear part (more carefully), (3) reread the sentence(s) before the unclear part, (4) try to connect the unclear part to something you already know, and (5) get outside help (from peers, the teacher, or resource materials).

In Chapter Four we also pointed out that one of students' first moves when they Think Aloud or Talk to the Text is to ask clarifying questions: What does this word mean? What does this have to do with that? Did I miss something?

A simple graphic organizer can help students take the first step in the outlined clarifying process: to decide whether or not to ignore a reading confusion. The organizer in Box 7.3 introduces students to the idea of identifying a text roadblock or confusion and deciding whether to move on or stop and clarify it. When students use this approach in a partner Think Aloud, they learn from their partner's experience as well as their own.

A related graphic organizer—a clarification chart (see Box 7.4)—can also scaffold students' clarifying practice, helping them work through the process of identifying a point of confusion in a text, deciding what to do about it, and explaining their new understanding in writing. The instructional focus is on having students practice identifying what question or confusion a specific roadblock is causing. The point of the chart is to help students slow down and notice where they lose comprehension and what they can do about it. In addition, the chart gives teachers useful insights into students' thought processes as they read difficult texts. (Box 7.5 shows a sample of student work with a clarification chart.)

Making Connections

Making connections is another of the strategies that students begin using early in a Reading Apprenticeship classroom, especially as they learn the metacognitive routines of Think Aloud and Talking to the Text. By making connections, readers draw on and add to their schema—the organized structures of background knowledge that are the mental magnets for any new learning to take hold and stick. (See Chapter Eight for a discussion of surfacing and building schema.)

Rita Jensen asks her middle school ELD students to make connections, predict, and ask questions whenever they read. When possible, she chooses texts she knows will draw on her students' background knowledge and experiences. In Classroom Close-Up 7.4, Rita's students share some of their connections from a quick scan before reading a poem and then some more connections they made while they were reading it more carefully.

The learning strategy of having students make connections before reading is familiar to teachers who use KWL and LINK (described in Chapter Eight) to have students call up everything they know or think they know about a topic about to be explored in a text. This information is then already percolating and available as students read to learn more—to make new connections.

During reading, students may automatically make connections, and they may also employ scaffolding tools like the clarification chart in Box 7.4 to stop and access background knowledge that may help them clarify a reading

BOX 7.3

Evaluating Roadblocks

PURPOSE

For students who do not understand that text is supposed to make sense (and there are more than a few), a first step may be for them to simply identify points of confusion and consciously decide what to do: clarify or move on.

PROCEDURE

- Explain that in pairs, one student will Think Aloud while the other records the roadblocks the reading partner identifies and what the person decides to do about the roadblock: clarify or move on.

- Have partners take turns Thinking Aloud or recording.

- When partners finish the reading assignment, have them trade papers so that each has the notes for his or her own Think Aloud.

- Ask students to review their decisions to clarify or move on: Were there roadblocks that they should have clarified but didn't? Were there roadblocks that were okay to ignore? What did they learn about reading from this experience?

Each partner should have a copy of a note taker such as the one shown here.

Page	Roadblock	Action	
			Clarify
			Move On
			Clarify
			Move On
			Clarify
			Move On
			Clarify
			Move On

confusion. After reading, students have opportunities to reflect on and consolidate the new connections and new knowledge they have acquired. These freshly elaborated schema can ease their next encounters with related information and allow them to make previously unavailable connections to their newly enlarged store of knowledge.

BOX 7.4

Clarification Chart

PURPOSE

A clarification chart helps students focus on where they lose comprehension in a text and what they can do about it. This graphic organizer suggests that reading is not magical, but rather a process of solving problems. The reader is in charge—of identifying roadblocks or confusions, trying problem-solving strategies, and taking a best guess at what the difficult passage may mean. For the teacher, the chart reveals where students struggle and what strategies they have appropriated for taking control of their reading. As students gain control and become increasingly metacognitive, the use of the chart should fade.

PROCEDURE

- Project a chunk of text that students will be reading. Demonstrate identifying and writing down a roadblock and filling in the other associated columns of the clarification chart.

- Have students create their own version of the chart.

- Invite students to nominate additional roadblocks and, as a class, work to complete the associated columns in the chart.

- Assign students to continue working with the text and the clarification chart, either individually or with a partner.

- Bring the class back together to discuss the roadblocks students selected to work with, what strategies they used, and what tentative meanings resulted.

- Assign a text for homework and have students practice using the clarification chart as part of the assignment.

- Go over the charts the next day in class and discuss the different strategies students used.

Clarification Chart

Roadblock (what it says)	Question (what's confusing?)	Strategy (my next step)	Clarification (what I think it means)

Visualizing and Visual Texts

Visualizing and visual texts help readers make abstract concepts or complex processes more concrete and more comprehensible. Yet inexperienced readers may not know how to use either and so benefit from explicit instruction.

Readers who visualize as they read activate schema prompted by the text but called up from prior knowledge or experience. Some readers naturally

BOX 7.5

Student Work Sample: Clarification Chart

Students have read "Seis," in *Bless Me, Ultima,* by Rudolf A. Anaya.[3] The following example illustrates how one student used a clarification chart as he moved through the text: quoting from a point of confusion, identifying the cause of the confusion, deciding what to do about the confusion, and making (or not making) a tentative clarification of the confusion.

Clarification Chart

Roadblock (what it says)	Question (what's confusing?)	Strategy (my next step)	Clarification (what I think it means)
I rushed into the melee	What does he mean?	Ignore	
I heard Ultima's owl sing	I don't understand this	Ignore	
No one knew the Vitamin Kid's name	How come no one knew the Vitamin Kid's name?	Keep reading	He never stopped long enough to talk
La tristesa de la vida	What does this mean?	Reread right before	Like sorrow or self-pity—lonely
Not even the Horse and Bones	What does he mean by this?	Got outside help	Probably their names like of friends

visualize as they read, but others may need practice constructing and clarifying images to build stronger understanding of text. Ninth grader LaKeisha, for example, reported earlier that visualization was a strategy she had failed to understand and use. Now, she says, "I'll question myself. I'm like, 'When was it? Okay, moonlight, right.' So I'll get a picture of nighttime in my mind." Then she adds, "I didn't do that before."

High school humanities teacher Caro Pemberton was more than a little surprised to find that many of her students did not try to visualize as they read. She relates a time when, after reading aloud a particularly evocative passage, she invited her students to describe what they were seeing:

> I was startled at the number of kids whose response was, "I didn't see anything." It really caught me up short, because to me whether I'm reading fiction or nonfiction, the visual process that goes along with my reading is such an integral part of the experience. When I'm having difficulty reading something, it's often because I can't really see what the person is talking about. If I'm having trouble understanding a concept, it's because I can't bring into focus what the person means. To me, visual images are a very critical part of understanding what I'm reading.

CLASSROOM CLOSE-UP 7.4

"My Name Is Ricardo, Too"

Students in Rita Jensen's middle school ELD class have been practicing Talking to the Text and the strategies of making connections, predicting, and asking questions. The excerpts that follow focus on the connections students make to a new poem, and how such connections contribute to a classroom community.

After students spend three minutes Talking to the Text and gathering ideas about the poem "Old Man," Rita calls the class together.

Teacher: What are some of the things that jumped out at you? Harris?

Harris: A Mexican guy wrote it. It says, "by Ricardo Sánchez."

Teacher: "By Ricardo Sánchez." So you know that name is probably a Hispanic name. Ricardo?

Ricardo: When I saw, "by Ricardo," I thought, "My name is Ricardo, too."

Rita recognizes that even such a simple connection as the poet's first name may help Ricardo to engage with the poem. She acknowledges the value of his personal connection.

Teacher: Okay, you made a connection to yourself. Good. Anything else?

Alejandra: I agree with Harris, 'cause, see, it's kind of Mexican 'cause it says some words like *indio* and *pueblo* in it.

Rita asks students to return to the poem and now give it a careful read. When Rita calls the class together again, Maria asks for help with a very strange word in the "first column, third line from the bottom." Jesus volunteers.

Jesus: Albuquerque.

Teacher: Say it again.

Jesus: Albuquerque.

Teacher: Albuquerque. What is Albuquerque?

Jesus: It's a city in New Mexico.

Teacher: It's a city in New Mexico. You know that. Why?

Jesus: 'Cause I go there.

Teacher: You've been there? You have family there?

Jesus: Yes.

Teacher: You see? So you have a whole connection to what they're talking about Albuquerque.

When Ruben asks a question, Rita throws it back to the class.

Ruben: Who is the old man?

Teacher: Who is the old man? Anybody have an idea about that?

Salvador: When I saw the old man, I said this guy is probably gone through a lot of stuff. I think that Mexican people go through a lot of stuff to come up to the United States, or any other place. And I think he probably had to suffer a lot to cross over.

As students continue to share their ideas and connections to the poem, the individual resources they bring to it cause their collective understanding of the poem, and their understanding of each other, to grow—as does Rita's knowledge of her students.

Consciously trying to picture what an author is describing is one aspect of the visualizing strategy, and students often need help practicing it with various kinds of text—fiction, poetry, accounts, instructions, and so forth.

In science, math, and history, and in many technical fields, reading (and writing) visual texts is key to the literacy practice of the discipline. As naïve readers in these disciplines, students often struggle with the complex images, graphs, and charts that can communicate vital information and concepts.

They often view the visuals embedded in their textbooks as merely art that can be read past and skipped over—and in some cases, they are right! But visual texts can be key to comprehending a text and to understanding the endeavors of a discipline more deeply. When students are inexperienced academic readers, they need support to learn how to make sense of the visual arrays that pepper disciplinary texts.

Students in Ericka Senegar-Mitchell's high school biology courses enjoy the benefit of their teacher's own code-breaking experience with visuals—gained when, as a college student, she determinedly deconstructed the complex scientific illustrations that stood between her and her goal of a medical school education. In describing her own experience, Ericka shows students how to tackle seemingly impenetrable illustrations and diagrams:

> "Pictures saved my life," I tell my biology students, and I explain that when I was studying for the medical school exam, I stumbled onto the magic of diagrams. The sheer magnitude of reviewing fifty-five chapters of text in a couple of weeks was just overwhelming. It felt insurmountable. But then I started looking at the diagrams as movies. There is such a story in each one. I took each diagram apart, adding my own labels, and then redrew it. Suddenly whole chapters could be understood in terms that I owned.
>
> For my students, I realized that I could recreate that deconstruction process. When I had simply asked them to look at a diagram and describe what they noticed, in some of my classes, with students who were used to being remediated and just doing what the teacher said, the reply would be "I notice nothing." But when I came up with some specific questions— "Let's look at color, shapes, where you are"—students were noticing all kinds of things. [See Box 7.6, Diagram Dialogues.] The questions slowed them down enough to actually find things to notice. And for me, nothing they noticed was too small to be significant. It became an opportunity to respect them for what they already knew, and they love that.
>
> When they felt respected, it also became an opportunity to ask them to tell what about the diagram confused them, to talk about what is missing for them, or what is implied. That's an awesome conversation, and it leads right into having them redraw the diagram, only including what was left out or what would make it better for students. When we do this, our discussions are richer, there is a tremendous difference in students' interaction with the text, and what they are learning stays with them. I still hear from students who tell me they are using Diagram Dialogues in their college courses!

Graphs are another visual form that students benefit from working on explicitly and collaboratively. In Classroom Close-Up 7.5, high school biology partners from Muthulakshmi "Bhavani" Balavenkatesan's class help each other

BOX 7.6

Diagram Dialogues

In Ericka Senegar-Mitchell's high school biology courses, she introduces students to the many visuals in their texts with a scaffolding routine for interrogating these complex illustrations. Students work with a partner to Think Aloud or Talk to the Text of a diagram related to a reading assignment and to use a set of questions that she dubs "Diagram Dialogues" to guide their discussion.

1. Location, location, location! Determine the setting of the diagram; where are you? Explain the overall scene in simple terms. What clues did you use?
2. Who are the players? What characters, parts, structures, or components are being represented or depicted? How do you know?
3. Are there special characters, symbols (such as arrows or callouts), or shapes (such as triangles or enlargements)? What do they represent? How do you know?
4. Are colors used intentionally? What do you think the use of color means? (For example, is the color intended to establish a relationship or distinction with components of the diagram?) How do you know?
5. What is the diagram intended to illustrate? Is the diagram showing a process, sequence, structure versus function (organization), categories, classification (such as a list or table), or cause and effect?

read a graph that represents information they have read about in a related article. Their collaborative cross-walk between the graph and article help them clarify their understanding of both.

In addition to visualizing and reading visual information, students benefit from producing their own visual representations, which will vary with the discipline, text, and purpose for reading. The process of visual note making gives readers in any discipline opportunities to access their own schema, to represent the text in a new form using what they know and what they are learning, and to integrate new knowledge (and sometimes confront misunderstandings) with their existing knowledge through the active construction of meaning. Visual note making can be a powerful way for readers to commit new ideas, information, and concepts to memory.

Although students' visual notes primarily serve to help them make meaning as they read, they can also be used after reading to demonstrate understanding through spreadsheets, databases, graphics, illustrations, and other forms of textual support that are common in the discipline in which they are working.

As Dorothea Jordan explained in Classroom Close-Up 7.2, her grade 7 pre-algebra students cited visual note making—"drawing"—as the one thing that

CLASSROOM CLOSE-UP 7.5

Close Reading of Visual Information

Having just read an article about how a strain of *Staphylococcus aureus* bacteria (methicillin-resistant *Staphylococcus aureus*, or MRSA) has evolved a frightening resistance to one antibiotic after another—including Vancomycin—high school biology partners Cal and Woodrow try to make sense of the following graph.

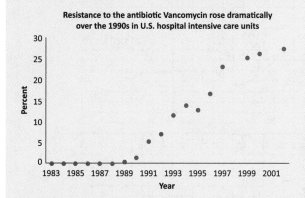

Resistance to the antibiotic Vancomycin rose dramatically over the 1990s in U.S. hospital intensive care units

Source: "Battling bacterial evolution: The work of Carl Bergstrom." Understanding Evolution. University of California Museum of Paleontology, 7 November 2011 http://evolution.berkeley.edu/evolibrary/article/0_0_0 /bergstrom_03. Reproduced with permission.

Cal: The article was talking about it [MRSA] in hospitals and this [graph] shows how it's grown in the years. I think that right here, where it goes down, is when they tried a new drug, and it might have worked for a little bit, but then it just started getting resistant to it again and just kept going. [Cal's reading of the graph aligns with the import of the article—the growth of MSRA resistance to a whole series of antibiotics—but his explanation of the graph does not jibe with the particular information in the graph, which shows only the path of MSRA resistance to a single antibiotic, Vancomycin.]

To clarify their understanding of the graph itself, the boys try to define what "percent" means on the *y* axis. Cal offers "percent of growth." But Woodrow hews tightly to the text of the graph. His precise definition for "percent" on the graph is "percent of the infection that is resistant to the antibiotic Vancomycin."

This clarification results in the boys' understanding the particulars of the graph, so Woodrow summarizes for Cal's consideration:

Woodrow: Well, in the first part where it's flat for the first five or so years, you can kind of tell that that was when they probably first introduced Vancomycin. Because those first five years, it [MRSA] really didn't have any defense against it. But you can see that after those five years, it started building up a defense.

helped them the most in her class. When students create their own graphic representations of information, the act of manipulating this information means they are seeing it in new ways that result in deeper understanding. (Box 7.7 shows notes and drawings Dorothea's students make to represent their understanding of a story problem [in Classroom Close-Up 8.4] involving a very busy nurse.) Dorothea was delighted with her students' excitement about visual note making and remarked on its particular usefulness in the collaborative work that was typical in her class:

> I realized that when students draw the problem, they are exposing their metacognition. And then, right away, their partner can see it and whether it's wrong or right.

BOX 7.7

Students' Visual Note-Making in a Pre-Algebra Class

Dorothea Jordan's pre-algebra students equate west, left, and negative on a number line as they use visual note making to figure out how many rooms are on the fourth floor of a hospital when they know the various stops a busy nurse makes to various rooms in the east and west wings.

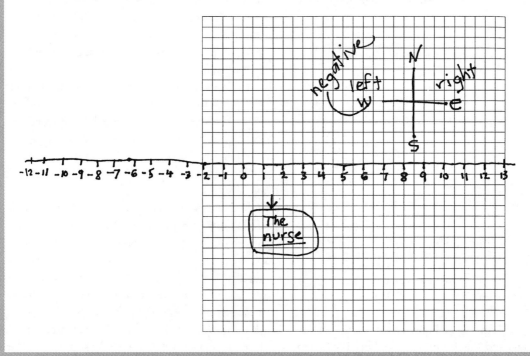

Questioning

Questions are often thought of as a way for the teacher to assess student understanding. In the inquiry culture of a Reading Apprenticeship classroom, however, students ask the questions—of the text, of themselves, and of each other. By asking their own questions, students surface their individual values, curiosities, and interests and generate their own reasons for reading.

Teaching students to ask questions as they read places the meaning-making process directly in their hands. When students ask their own content-based questions, at least two kinds of things can happen: they ask questions that deepen their engagement with a text, and they ask questions that deepen their understanding of the text. Sometimes the same question accomplishes both purposes.

The value of student questioning is multiplied when students make their questions public. Through this dialogue of questioning and answering, students are able to redefine and deepen their own understanding of the text. When they explain how they found the answers to their own or someone else's questions or why a question was interesting or important to them, they learn from each other. Questioning in these ways can be understood as contributing to the personal and social dimensions of a classroom as well as to students' facility with this important strategy.

The goal for Reading Apprenticeship teachers is to release to students the responsibility for generating the questions that drive classroom learning. Community college ESL teacher Anne Agard found that when her students ask the questions, important changes in students' reading comprehension and writing result:

> Hugely more learning occurs when students ask their own questions and discuss the answers together, in contrast to responding to questions posed by the teacher. This turn-around in cognitive processing seems to have profound and dramatic effects both on the development of reading comprehension and on the quality of subsequent writing. I have been acting on this insight and exploring its implications over the past few years, first at higher levels and now with good results at this lower level.

In addition, Anne sees that through the process of asking their own questions, her students are developing the independence that is "the most critical key to their future success as academic readers."

Similarly, Caro Pemberton found that her high school humanities students responded with increased engagement when given the opportunity to ask and answer their own questions about a text. In Classroom Close-Up 7.6, Caro describes the move to this new questioning paradigm in her classroom.

ReQuest

A simple structure for having students share the questions they have generated, ReQuest, is described in Box 7.8. Students prepare questions about a text—questions they themselves can answer—and then take turns leading the discussion of them through a hand-off process: whoever answers a question asks the next one, and no one can answer a second question until everyone has asked and answered one in the first round.

For example, when Lori Hurwitz's ninth graders in the first Reading Apprenticeship cohort read an excerpt from Frederick Douglass's autobiography in class, she asked them to think of themselves as teachers and each to come up with five questions about the text that a teacher would think

CLASSROOM CLOSE-UP 7.6

When Students Ask the Questions

Caro Pemberton has learned to entrust text to her high school humanities students, particularly by letting students' own questions drive the learning in her classroom. In the interview that follows, she describes her growing discomfort with the role of teacher as questioner, even when the questions are open-ended. The Reading Apprenticeship framework gave Caro a welcomed nudge toward shifting responsibility to her students for generating and asking the text-based questions the class would discuss. The result for students, she says, has been more and deeper engagement with the text and with their classmates.

"In the past, I've approached reading assignments by asking students to respond to *my* questions. But I was never sure whether they got there because I sort of pushed them down the path that I wanted them to take, or they were there on their own. There has always been that feeling that I'm feeding it to them or that they're responding in a somewhat stifled way to the questions because they're expecting that I'm looking for a particular answer. Even when I've tried to ask open-ended questions, there's still that feeling. We all have in our own head what we're thinking when we

ask questions. You don't know for sure whether you're getting a spontaneous answer from the kids or the kids are holding back because they're intimidated about saying what's on their mind or because they think you're looking for something in particular.

"The difference when kids come up with their own questions is that the question itself indicates how deeply they've thought about what they've read. In order to ask a question, they have to understand.

"When I first started asking students to pose questions about their reading, lo and behold, I got this absolutely incredible group of questions. Day after day, I continued to be impressed with the quality of the questions.

"The kids seemed to be much more engaged in the reading. That's part of what's exciting about it, their level of engagement. A very different dynamic happens when they're asking the questions than when a teacher does. When they're leading the discussion, leading the answers, the quality of the questions really indicates that they're thinking about what they're reading. There's no doubt in my mind that it helps students go deeper."

were important. These questions formed the basis for a round of ReQuest. Quick rounds of ReQuest soon became a classroom staple, and writing the questions a frequent homework assignment. The questions students asked and the responses they got from classmates were a useful gauge of students' understanding of what they had read. Lori also used ReQuest as an opportunity to model and ask students to reproduce questions that drew on a range of different kinds of mental processing to answer (see the discussion of QAR that follows).

QAR

Students in many Reading Apprenticeship classrooms learn to develop (and answer) text-based questions structured by Question-Answer Relationships (QAR).[4] They learn that, depending on the structure of a question, the

BOX 7.8

ReQuest

PURPOSE

ReQuest is a questioning routine that helps students practice preparing, asking, and answering text-based questions. The ReQuest turn-taking structure ensures equitable participation.

PROCEDURE

- Have each student prepare questions about a text the class reads in common. (This can be a homework or an in-class assignment.)
- Ask one student to begin by reading one of his or her questions aloud and calling on a volunteer to answer it.
- Explain that the volunteer must provide both the answer and the evidence for it.
- After a student answers, have the questioner check in with the class: Do they agree with the answer? Do they agree with the evidence? Can they add other evidence?
- Have the student who first answered the question (regardless of whether the answer was challenged) ask the next question.
- Continue until all students have asked and answered at least one question.

answer will be found in the text or in interaction between the text and their existing schema. Students become metacognitive and much more strategic about answering text-based questions—for their own purposes as well as on high-stakes tests. The four types of question-answer relationships—*Right There!*, *Pulling It Together*, *Text +Me*, and *On My Own*—are described in Box 7.9.

When Janet Ghio introduces her ninth graders to the QAR categories, she points out that different readers may successfully answer questions in different ways. So, for example, a Pulling It Together question for one student might be a Text + Me question for another. Janet makes sure students can explain *how* they got an answer. Caro Pemberton also includes this important guideline for the development and use of QAR. After asking a question, Caro's students ask a follow-up question to reinforce the idea that the type of question is defined by what you do to answer it:

> What did you have to do to get the answer to this question? How did you get the answer?

BOX 7.9

Question-Answer Relationships (QAR) Overview

When students understand the role of two variables in text-based questions—what's in the text and what's in the reader's schema or background knowledge—they can be metacognitive about finding answers to the types of relationships that result: Right There!, Pulling It Together, Text + Me, and On My Own. Each type has its own important purposes.

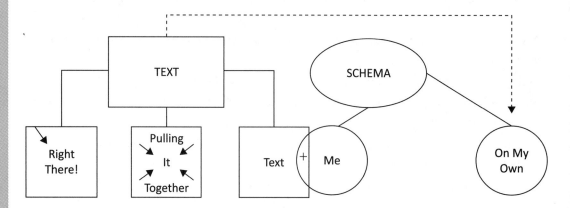

RIGHT THERE!

The answers to these questions are in the text, right in one place.

• When was the Nineteenth Amendment ratified?

PULLING IT TOGETHER

The answers to these questions are in the text, but they are not right in one place—you have to pull the answer together from different places in the text.

• What do Elizabeth Cady Stanton and Susan B. Anthony have in common?

TEXT + ME

The text has part of the answer, and so does the reader.

• What do Susan B. Anthony and our new mayor have in common?

ON MY OWN

The text prompts these questions but does not answer them. The answers depend on what the reader thinks, wonders, already knows, or can find out elsewhere.

• Why were men afraid to allow women to vote?

In Classroom Close-Up 7.7, high school teachers Christine Cziko and Lori Hurwitz describe how QAR works in their classrooms; they include a simple text and sample questions they wrote to introduce QAR.

CLASSROOM CLOSE-UP 7.7

Introducing QAR

Academic literacy teachers Christine Cziko and Lori Hurwitz were eager to have their students learn how engaging (and empowering) it could be to create their own text-based questions. To introduce students to Question-Answer Relationships (QAR), they modeled and used a variety of simple texts for students to practice with. Each student practiced writing text-based questions of each of the QAR types (which require that students know the answer and/or how to find it).

The point of students' work with QAR was not to master QAR categorization but to better understand what the reader needs to do to answer the question types, which require different interactions between text and schema. Christine and Lori considered it a bonus that QAR practice also prepares students for finding the answers to the most traditional kinds of assessment questions.

"We found that our students typically understood the Right There! and Pulling It Together questions easily, but they often had trouble with the Text + Me and On My Own questions, so we talked with them about why some question types are harder to create than others, and we provided practice with a variety of simple texts, like the one we call 'David Woke Up Late.'"

■ ■ ■

David Woke Up Late

David woke up fifteen minutes late. As soon as he saw the clock, he jumped out of bed and headed for the shower, afraid he'd miss the bus again.

He looked in the dryer for his favorite jeans, but they were actually still in the washing machine.

"Dang! I told Shelley to put my stuff in the dryer! Thanks, Sis. Now what am I gonna wear?"

After settling for baggy shorts and a polo shirt, he grabbed a bag of chips and a soda from the kitchen and searched frantically for his history book. When he found it, David stuffed it in his backpack, along with his "lunch," hat, and lucky deck of cards.

As he ran to the bus stop, he told himself firmly, "I will not stay up late watching wrestling!"

Right There!

- What did David do as soon as he saw the clock?
- What did David tell himself as he ran to the bus stop?

Pulling It Together

- Who is Shelley?
- What did David look for before he left the house?

Text + Me

- Where was David heading?
- What time of day was it?
- How nutritious is David's lunch?

On My Own

- Should teenagers watch television on school nights?
- Should parents be responsible for waking their kids up in the morning?
- Why is David taking cards to school!?

Using Evidence

In a Reading Apprenticeship classroom, students become comfortable using text-based evidence all the time—for answering questions, making assertions, and figuring out why they're confused. That's the nature of a classroom organized around inquiry, and it means that students come to expect evidence as a matter of course, from themselves as well as their classmates. Students also come to appreciate the authority that text-based evidence lends to their ideas.

Routines like evidence/interpretation journals and metacognitive logs get students in the habit of citing evidence for their own purposes. When they share evidence in classroom conversations, norms for citing evidence simplify the process for everyone.

In Gayle Cribb's history classes, for example, students know not only to cite text-based evidence, but also to wait for classmates to locate it before explaining their thinking or questions. Gayle establishes these routines in the first weeks of class:

> In my experience, basing discussions in text allows for academic rigor because we are able to tie our ideas, questions, and explorations to one thing—the text. We at least can all start "on the same page" and return to that spot. In order to do that, we need to develop norms for referring to that spot.
>
> From the beginning of the year, I ask students to reference the text. Usually, they will have noted particular evidence during their individual work by marking up the text or noting page numbers in metacognitive logs or evidence/interpretation note takers. Then, in early class discussions, I develop the routine for referencing text with a number of prompts:
>
> > "Where in the text did you see that?"
> >
> > "What in the text made you think that?"
> >
> > "Take us with you."
> >
> > "What page was that on?"
> >
> > "Could you read that part to us first?"
> >
> > "Wait until we all get there."
> >
> > "Has everyone found it yet?"
> >
> > "Cite your source."
>
> Very early, we talk about how to do this efficiently: "What would help us find the place in the text quickly?" From their answers to that question, language develops: "Page 24, first complete paragraph, in the middle," or "In the intro, lowercase Roman numeral iv, top of the page."

By October, this is all pretty automatic. Students expect to be following references in the text. They remind each other and pause for everyone to get there. It becomes an easy routine that helps to make our discussions stay focused and go smoothly.

When students learn how to cite text-based evidence in class discussions, the practice naturally spills over into partner and small group discussions. Classroom Close-Up 7.8 shows a brief example of two GED students explaining their thinking to each other in terms of textual evidence.

CLASSROOM CLOSE-UP 7.8

"Because Later in the Story It Says"

Students in Michele Lesmeister's technical college GED class have read the first chapter of a novel about a group of immigrants from diverse countries who form a community by planting a garden. The character Kim, who starts the garden, is from Vietnam, where her father was a farmer. Michele's students discuss Kim's motivation in small groups, matter-of-factly supplying text-based evidence for their assertions. The following exchange between Michael and Manuel is part of a much longer text-based group discussion.

Michael: See, it all starts right here. *(He reads)* "I stare at my father's photograph, his thin face stern, lips latched tight, his eyes peering permanently to the right. I was nine years old and still hoped that perhaps his eyes might move. Might notice me." So she's sitting there all the time staring at this picture, hoping that the eyes will just basically move, just to acknowledge her.

Manuel: Because later in the story it says, "When his spirit hovered before our altar, did he even know who I was?" *(Pointing to the text)* Right here.

Michael: Yeah, I see it.

Manuel: (Repeating from the text) "Who I was?" Because the picture cannot see her.

Michael: The reason why it says that, right there is because, it say: "I was born eight months after he died. Worse, he had no memories of me." Basically she's saying that where his spirit is around, does he know who I am? Because she didn't have a chance to meet him, really. She was born eight months after he died, so she really didn't have a chance to meet him.

Manuel: Yeah, she's looking for that chance—

Michael: She doesn't know what he's like or nothing like that—

Manuel: Yeah, that's why she is looking for chances to meet him, and then she's trying to get the chance to visit him by his spirit. And how to get that, she's going to plant the beans. She's going to plant the beans in order—because you can read it. *(He reads)* "He will watch me, watch my beans break the ground and spread and would notice with pleasure their pods growing plump." Then she says, "I will show him that I was his daughter." That's the way she's going to get him.

Getting the Gist and Summarizing

"Getting the gist" is a high-leverage reading strategy that is a particular kind of summarizing. It is a way for students to monitor their comprehension in small chunks: What is the gist of what I just read? What did this sentence/paragraph/page/diagram just tell me? Similar to paraphrasing, getting the gist lets readers know on the spot whether they understand what they just read. Getting the gist does not require an evaluative filter—deciding which information is most important—in the way that summarizing does. It is simply a systematic check on understanding. When students Talk to the Text, for example, the kind of summarizing they typically do is comprehension monitoring—getting the gist—not evaluating the relative importance of or relationships between various chunks of text as they might in summarizing.

True summarizing is one of the most complex (and frequently assigned) comprehension strategies students are expected to master. From the upper primary grades on, students are asked to write summaries of textbook chapters, novels, science lab findings, and written materials of all kinds. Yet even college students struggle to summarize their reading. To summarize well, students must first comprehend what they have read and then make decisions about what is important and not so important in a text and what kinds of relationships have been represented. We have found, through the experiences of many Reading Apprenticeship teachers, that students at all levels learn summarizing with remarkable effectiveness through structured interactions with their peers.

Jordona Elderts, a grade 7 social studies teacher who was frustrated by years of "constantly summarizing for students so they don't miss the main points," found that the peer summary analysis process she learned through Reading Apprenticeship (see Box 7.10) made a huge difference. She now spends time in the first month of the school year teaching this single comprehension strategy, so that for the rest of the year her students are doing the work of summarizing themselves:

> They would read chunks of material and write down a sentence for that chunk, have to summarize it and then compare it with their partner's, and modify it. I think one of the most thrilling things was when I asked how many people changed their sentence after reading their partner's. It was about two-thirds of the class. I find that really unusual because normally they'll just share their sentence and say, "Okay, great. Yours is great, mine's great." And they'll move on. They really kind of negotiated for meaning and negotiated the best way that they could write a summary that could encompass the main idea.

In mathematics classes, teachers have adapted the Summary Analysis by a Peer task for application to math solutions. Partners query each other's math solutions in mathematical form and as written explanations. Box 7.11 is the note taker that students complete and exchange when the task is Math Solution Summary Analysis by a Peer.

BOX 7.10

Summary Analysis by a Peer

PURPOSE

Most students have had only teachers as the audience for the summaries they are required to write. With peers for an audience, students get immediate feedback and the opportunity to negotiate meaning in a metacognitive conversation.

In this activity, distinct from some forms of peer editing, students' only attention is to meaning.

PROCEDURE

- Have students prepare a summary of a text they have read in common.

- In pairs, have students read a partner's summary, answering in writing the following questions about the summary:

    - If you hadn't read the text yourself, would you be able to understand what it was about from this summary? Why or why not?

    - Is there anything important that should be added to this summary? What is it? Why do you think so?

    - Is there anything unimportant that should be left out of the summary? What is it? Why do you think so?

- Have partners exchange their responses, read and discuss them, and make revisions to their respective summaries based on the discussion of their partner's feedback.

Two writing activities that help students hone their summarizing skills are This Is About/This Is *Really* About and the Twenty-Five-Word Abstract. In the first activity, students learn how to identify main ideas and then infer a summary. In the second, they learn precision. In both summarizing activities, students should be learning that "summaries are made, not found."

Teacher Christine Cziko created This Is About for the first cohort of Reading Apprenticeship students. They knew that a summary involved pulling together the most important parts of a text and writing them down in shortened form, but most had little idea about how to decide what was important or how to put key ideas into their own words. Initially she used This Is About to help them distinguish main ideas from details. To teach students to infer the main idea when it refers to an unstated theme or big idea, she took the activity to another level—This Is *Really* About. Both versions of This Is About are described in Box 7.12. Box 7.13 is a completed example of This Is *Really* About. It shows how students might develop a summary of what the novel *Julie of the Wolves* is *really* about.

BOX 7.11

Math Solution Summary Analysis by a Peer

This note taker is a student handout that adapts Summary Analysis by a Peer (Box 7.10) for use in mathematics classes.

- Trade your completed solution with your partner.

- Read your partner's solution. Answer the following questions about the solution.

    1. Can you follow the solution in math form? Why or why not?

    2. Can you follow the solution in written explanation form?

    3. Does the answer seem reasonable? Why or why not?

    4. Has the original question been answered completely?

    5. Is there any thing important that should be added to the solution? What is it? Why do you think so?

    6. Is there anything unimportant that should be left out of the solution? What is it? Why do you think so?

- Return solutions and these answers to your partner.

- Read what your partner wrote and talk it over.

- Make revisions to your own work based on the answers given by your partner.

High school teacher Tim Tindol wanted to help his students use summarizing to better understand science texts, and he also wanted students to understand the genre of abstracts, the formal summaries used in academic research papers. He developed the collaborative Twenty-Five-Word Abstract activity to accomplish both purposes. Students individually read and select the main idea in a science text, work in groups to clarify vocabulary and compare group members' selected main ideas, write individual abstracts based on the group discussion and consensus, and then

---

BOX 7.12

This Is About/This Is *Really* About

PURPOSE

Students work in the whole class, individually, and in groups to identify main ideas and use them to synthesize or infer a summary.

PROCEDURE

- Ask students to silently read a passage and be ready to "tell what the passage is about."
- Record all student ideas, details and main ideas alike.
- Have the class compare the ideas on the list to distinguish main ideas and details. Highlight those identified as main ideas. Some texts may require you to prompt students to make inferences about what the main idea may be.
- Have students individually decide which statements from the list capture all or part of the main idea.
- Have students work in pairs or trios to compare their ideas and agree on which to include or synthesize.
- Record groups' ideas and facilitate another class discussion about why some ideas are or are not main ideas. Edit the list accordingly.
- Depending on the affordances of the text, challenge students to capture big ideas or themes by continuing to ask, "This is about that, but what is it really about?"
- Have students return to their groups and write a summary of the passage.

---

compare abstracts and develop a collaborative abstract that represents the group's best thinking. Tim imposes the twenty-five-word limit to help students focus on being clear and concise. (Box 7.14 describes the Twenty-Five-Word Abstract process.)

Visual summaries, or posters, are another way Reading Apprenticeship teachers have students present their understanding of key ideas or concepts in a text. Working in small groups, students first discuss their ideas and develop consensus about what is most important, then decide what visual representation of the ideas will be most effective and create the poster. The important work of the group is in discussing their ideas and choosing a discipline-appropriate graphic form of communication. Some teachers have groups rate each other's posters, based on the content of the posters (not the "art").

BOX 7.13

Sample "This Is *Really* About"

Using the procedure described in Box 7.12 for synthesizing main ideas into a summary, students reading the young adult novel *Julie of the Wolves*, by Jean Craighead George, might come up with ideas like those that follow.

Their process would be to list, winnow, and combine their most important ideas; step back to decide what those ideas are *really* about; and write a summary that incorporates the text's big ideas and most salient details.

CLASS LIST

Chapter 1 is about . . .

- a girl who runs away.
- a girl who is lost on the tundra.
- an Eskimo girl.
- a girl who tries to escape a traditional arranged marriage.
- surviving the elements in an Alaskan winter.
- a girl who is unhappy about decisions being made for her.

GROUP WORK

Chapter 1 is about . . .

- a girl who runs away and is lost on the Alaskan tundra over a winter.
- an Eskimo girl who tries to escape a traditional arranged marriage.

Chapter 1 is really about . . .

- a girl struggling with cultural identity.
- a girl learning to confront difficult choices.
- a girl struggling with gender roles.

SUMMARY OF CHAPTER 1

Julie is a girl of Eskimo ancestry who is learning to confront difficult cultural choices. To avoid the Eskimo tradition of an arranged marriage, she runs away into the vast Alaskan tundra.

Predicting

Predicting, like visualizing, requires readers to access their own relevant background knowledge or schema and prepare to organize new information accordingly. Essentially, readers must summarize what they know from the text so far, put it in the context of their related schema about genre and topic, predict the flow of main ideas or thrust of a plot, and then select structures or details that

BOX 7.14

Twenty-Five-Word Abstract

PURPOSE

Limiting students to twenty-five-word summaries helps them really focus on what is important.

PROCEDURE

- Have students individually read a text and highlight main ideas and difficult vocabulary.

- Have students work in small groups, first to clarify vocabulary, using each other's thinking and other classroom resources.

- Have group members take turns presenting their highlighted main ideas as well as their reasons for selecting them.

- Ask groups to discuss and reach consensus about which are the key points.

- Have students individually write an abstract of twenty-five words or less that includes the key points selected by their group.

- Have students take turns presenting their abstract to their group members.

- Ask group members to discuss differences among their abstracts and then agree on and write a group abstract of twenty-five words or less on a poster.

- Have groups post their abstracts and rotate around the room reading the abstracts of the other groups. On sticky notes, have groups rate each poster, including their own, on the importance, clarity, and conciseness of the information in the abstract. (Alternatively, have groups rate the posters, but do not supply criteria. Instead, after all abstracts have been rated, lead a class discussion in which students surface the qualities that led them to rate an abstract as successful.)

might logically follow. Authors' use of text structure, text signals, and visual text features provide multiple clues that support meaningful prediction.

Reading Signals in the Text

In the case of text structure, students may be much more familiar with using prediction with narrative than with informational text, but prediction can be a particularly valuable strategy for navigating challenging informational text. In a narrative structure, students might predict "The girl has learned she is strong, now the horse will die"; with informational text, students might use their knowledge of text structure to predict "That was one cause of the Civil War, now it's going to tell about another one" or "This definition of molecule is going to be followed by examples that will make the definition easier to understand."

At another level, instead of predicting how text structure will contribute to meaning, readers keep track of text signals and predict where the text will go. Text signals allow readers to make predictions about how the author's use of these language markers will contribute to meaning. Text signals include punctuation and transition words such as *however, including, in other words,* and *for example* to signal the path an author has created for readers to follow. In addition, informational text includes visual text features such as subtitles, bullets, and highlighted vocabulary that provide clues for what is important and what is to come. These clues help readers predict or prepare for new ideas or information.

The author's purposes in using text structure, text signals, and text features may seem self-evident to experienced readers, but many students miss these

---

BOX 7.15

How Are My Predictions Doing?

PURPOSE

To help students learn to check and revise their predictions as needed while they read, How Are My Predictions Doing? is simple and quick.

PROCEDURE

- Provide students with reading material chunked at points that allow for prediction, such as the beginning of a chapter in a novel, or one subheading at a time in expository text.
- At the beginning of each chunk, ask students to make a prediction, an educated guess, or a hypothesis about what will follow in the text.
- At the end of their reading, ask students to check and see whether their predictions made sense and why or why not.

The following note taker can help students get used to checking their predictions and getting better at making them.

Text _____ Pages _____

1. Reread your predictions from the last entry.

   Were your predictions correct?

   If yes, what clues helped you?

   If no, what clues threw you off or what clues did you miss?

   Why did you make the predictions that you did?

2. What predictions do you have for the next section of text?

clues without explicit instruction. In Chapter Eight, as we focus on the knowledge-building dimension of Reading Apprenticeship, signal words and visual text features are discussed again, as examples of the knowledge about text and language structures that students need to build.

Building Engagement

Predicting can also serve to build students' engagement with text. When readers predict, they establish a particular purpose for reading: to see whether their predictions bear out. Sometimes students will naturally keep track of their predictions and check on how they are or are not unfolding. But if predicting is a new strategy for students, an activity like How Are My Predictions Doing? in Box 7.15 can provide effective practice.

Previewing Informational Text

When teachers ask students to preview an informational text before reading it, they are asking students to activate their schema about the text content and structure as well as to develop personal reasons for reading the particular text. Previewing helps students prepare to engage the reading task. (A discussion of previewing fiction when students are making personal selections for literature circles appears in Chapter Five. Previewing books for Sustained Silent Reading is discussed in Chapter Six.)

With practice, previewing informational text can become almost automatic, but when students are first learning to preview, they benefit from an enumeration of things to look for and questions to answer. They also need opportunities to share what they are learning. Through metacognitive conversations, students can come to appreciate that previewing helps them anticipate what will be interesting about a text or what makes them better able to approach a difficult or unappealing text.

Questions such as those in Box 7.16 can guide students, when approaching informational text, to recognize and use personal resources: their evolving learner identity and their existing schema.

Helping Students Become Strategic Readers

> I love when students seen as smart are able to articulate how they were able to figure something out and everyone follows along. You can almost hear the relief: "Oh, it's *not* magic. They're *not* just smarter than me. They just did *x*. I could do *that!*"
> —Gayle Cribb, high school history teacher

When students are learning cognitive reading strategies, some will use a variety of tools on a regular basis, and others will use two or three tools most

BOX 7.16

Sample Questions for Previewing Informational Text

When students preview a text, they give themselves a head start on understanding it. Not only do they preview what they may know about the content, but they also get a focused look at the clues embedded in the text structure and text features. Most important, they develop a sense of how they may be able to engage the text at a personal level: what demands will the text make on their perseverance and stamina, and what rewards may their effort provide?

The following list of sample previewing questions starts and ends with how the reader will make the reading task personally relevant. In between are questions that relate to the reader's schema.

- *How does reading this text relate to me personally?* Why am I reading it? How will I benefit?

- *How does the content of this text relate to what I already know?* What do I know and want to know about this topic? What concerns or questions do I have?

- *What do I need to know about the author, publisher, and* intended *audience?* Is this a reliable source? Why was this text written?

- *How does the structure of this text relate to what I already know?* What genre is this? What are its characteristics? How will the text be organized? What can I learn from the title, copyright date, table of contents?

- *How do the text features relate to what I already know?* What can I learn from the headings, subheadings, questions, bullets, illustrations, captions, etc.? How are they intended to aid comprehension?

- *How do features of the typography relate to what I already know?* Why are bold, italics, size, and color used here? How are they intended to aid comprehension?

- *What is my purpose for the reading?* Therefore, what reading processes will I use?

consistently. The goal in teaching students to use different tools is to make them strategic readers, so that when they have a comprehension problem they can choose an appropriate tool and work to solve the problem independently. The choice of tool or reading strategy would depend on the nature of this problem, the student's purpose for reading, and the student's comfort level with each of the tools. In short, students would have a variety of tools to draw on when they started to sense they were no longer making meaning of a text.

As Gayle Cribb describes, students really do learn to recognize these strategies as tools available for their own use: "*I could do that!*" To help students use these strategies with increasing flexibility, many teachers structure assignments that explicitly demand practicing with a suite of complementary strategies.

Supporting Strategy Integration

As students are learning new reading strategies, Reading Apprenticeship routines such as Talking to the Text and metacognitive logs can be structured to feature particular combinations of strategies. Students could be asked to practice clarifying and making connections, for example. I Saw/I Thought note takers could be set up so that students focus on asking questions and summarizing. When a new piece of expository text is being introduced, students could be asked to preview the text, predict what they will be learning, and think about how their purpose for reading the text will inform the way they read it. These are simple examples of how strategies can be combined for students to practice. No coordinated group work is necessary, even though students would share their ideas and questions with a partner, group, or the class.

A next step, used by many Reading Apprenticeship teachers, is to structure independent group work in which students collaborate to make meaning from challenging texts, while practicing high-leverage reading strategies. As participants in these groups, students have access to each other's thinking: they can draw on the resources of the group to solve their own comprehension problems, and they can also see how other readers use comprehension strategies to make sense of texts.

For example, in a structure commonly known as "reciprocal teaching,"[5] four students build their comprehension of a text by collaboratively practicing the strategies of predicting, clarifying, questioning, and summarizing. Reciprocal teaching of a text begins as group members independently preview the text. One student then facilitates the group's discussion of their cognitive moves to *predict* what the text will be about. Next, students individually read the text and make notes to use in the group discussion that follows. After the reading, a second student facilitates a discussion of what parts of the text were confusing and how group members tried to *clarify* them. A third student leads a discussion of *questions* that group members developed to help remember the content of the text, and the fourth student is responsible for managing the group's collaboration in developing a group *summary* from the individual summaries each group member will have written. The prediction facilitator then steps in again, to lead a discussion of the group's final prediction: what they *predict* they will learn about next, given what they know now.

Role cards can help students get started with reciprocal teaching, or "team reads" as the students in Will Brown's chemistry classes label the process. Will's role cards, in addition to explaining the role and providing sample facilitation prompts, have a particular science focus (see Box 7.17).

Reciprocal Teaching Role Cards in Science

Will Brown adapted reciprocal teaching roles for the team reads his students do in chemistry. Each student in a group of four has a particular *facilitation* role, but the whole group participates, regardless of whether the conversation is about predicting, clarifying, questioning, or summarizing.

PREDICTION FACILITATOR

Your job is to help the team members predict what they will read about next by using clues in the reading. You also help the team review earlier predictions to see why they were or were not accurate.

You might ask questions like these *before* your team reads:

- What are your predictions about what this next section will tell us?

- How were you able to guess? What information did you use?

You might ask questions like these *after* your team reads:

- What were our predictions about this section? Were any of them correct? What information or clues turned out to be the most helpful?

- What do you think we will read about next?

Good science readers make predictions about what is upcoming in the text by using text information as well as their own knowledge of science, science methods, and science genres. Predicting is a way to surface relevant schema, focus the reading, and check understanding to stay engaged.

CLARIFICATION FACILITATOR

Your job is to help team members point out parts of the reading that were not clear to them. You also ask the team to help find ways to clear up these problems.

You might ask questions like these:

- Which parts were confusing or unclear as you read?

- Can anyone explain that part?

- What strategies did you use to clarify that part?

- What can we do to try to understand this?

Good science readers look for the parts of a text that are confusing them and use fix-up strategies such as rereading, scanning ahead, thinking back, identifying unknown vocabulary, chunking words or phrases, and using their own knowledge of science topics, science methods, and science genres.

(Continued)

QUESTION FACILITATOR

Q:A   Q:??

Your job is to help the team ask and answer questions about the text. These can be questions to help remember things about the text or questions that the text makes team members wonder more about.

You might ask team members questions like these:

- What does the text make you wonder about? How can you put it in a question? What can we do to find the answer?

- What question can you ask that will help us remember something important about the text? Can someone please answer it?

Asking questions, or inquiry, is the heart of science. Good science readers ask and answer questions as they read to help build interest and stay engaged. They also ask questions to help remember what they read. These questions may be about topics, methods, claims, and evidence. Science questions can address the credibility and relevance of the ideas in the text.

SUMMARIZATION FACILITATOR

a + b + c = ?

Your job is to help each team member restate the main ideas and key facts in the reading in his or her own words. Then it is your job to help the team come up with one summary for the group.

You might ask questions like these:

- Which ideas do you have to understand to be able to summarize this text? (Which ideas could be left out and still get the point across?)

- Can you use your own words or a diagram or picture to tell the main ideas?

- How can we combine ideas into one overall summary?

Good science readers paraphrase, visualize, and summarize while reading to check for understanding, to help themselves remember, and to get the big ideas. When they write summaries, they have been thinking about what is important all along. These summaries are not found in the text, but are formed by the reader from their thinking.

When introducing reciprocal teaching, some teachers model the various facilitation roles with the whole class many times before setting groups off on their own. Janet Ghio puts the students in her grade 9 academic literacy class into a classroom "fishbowl," giving alternating groups publicly coached practice in carrying out the reciprocal teaching procedure. In Classroom Close-Up 7.9, Janet's students have just spent two class periods in these fishbowl sessions and now are working independently in groups for the first time. In a short visit with one group, students demonstrate an early but promising level of independence not only in identifying comprehension problems in the reading but also in helping each other solve them.

CLASSROOM CLOSE-UP 7.9

Nutrition-Speak: "What's Up, Apple?"

Students in Janet Ghio's grade 9 academic literacy class have been reading a set of texts about nutrition and health. They are about to read, in reciprocal teaching groups, a text from the website of the Harvard School of Public Health in which the validity of the widely promoted USDA MyPyramid* is challenged. Students have practiced reciprocal teaching with their teacher's coaching, and today groups are on their own for the first time.

We visit one group as they discuss a small section of the reading assignment. Ariana, the group's "clarifying coach," facilitates as group members' share reading questions for clarification, and then Kate takes over, as "questioning coach." The distinction between clarifying and questioning is lost on the students, but that is insignificant. They are focused on the idea that the text should make sense.

Both girls begin their facilitation with a question chosen from "role cards," scaffolds their teacher provides when her students are just starting out with reciprocal teaching.

Ariana: (Reading from her "clarifying" role card) Which parts of the text were confusing?

Kate: I thought this paragraph was confusing, and the last one. Cause like they started naming a whole bunch of organizations. It just kind of threw me off.

Ariana: Oh, right here?

Kate: Yeah,

Ariana: United Fresh Fruit and Vegetable Association, Soft Drink–

Kate: Yeah.

Ariana: Why was that confusing?

Kate: Cause I really don't know what they are. So I can't really do it.

■ ■ ■

Kate: (Reading from her "questioning" role card) What questions did you ask and answer for yourself in the text?

Ariana: Why did the USDA give two-year-olds advice about how good dietary habits can promote health and reduce risks for major chronic diseases?

Kate: I thought it said for people two and older.

Ariana: Yeah, but why give a two-year-old advice when they're not the ones—

Kate: Yeah.

Ariana:—Making their meals?

Kate: Do you guys know what nutrition-speak meant?

Shane: Oh, right there?

Kate: Yeah.

Shane: No. Nutrition—don't that mean like good food or something?

Kate: It can't be a language, but maybe it's like how nutritionists speak when they talk amongst each other, like how kids talk slang. I don't know.

Shane: Nutrition-speak.

Kate: (Modeling how a nutritionist might greet someone) What's up, apple?

Group laughter.

Kate: (Addressing the two boys) Do you guys have any questions?

Ryan: Why does the pyramid have to be revised every five years? Like why do they have to change it?

Kate: I was wondering that too.

*The USDA's MyPlate has replaced MyPyramid (which replaced the USDA's classic Food Pyramid). Accordingly, the Harvard School of Public Health now focuses its commentary on MyPlate. The text that Janet Ghio's students read is no longer online.

Orchestrating Independence

As students practice and begin to incorporate new cognitive strategies for understanding texts, teachers can ask them to evaluate how particular strategies are working for them in their problem-solving efforts. Students might share with the class what they did to create a summary, how they figured out whether they needed to clarify something in the text, how they composed a question, and ultimately, what difference these strategies made for their comprehension of class texts. In this process, individual students become more

---

CLASSROOM CLOSE-UP 7.10

"So, You Are Using a Text Clue There"

Eleventh graders in Gayle Cribb's honors U.S. history course are preparing to read the Supreme Court case *Korematsu v. United States,* which challenged the constitutionality of the Japanese internment during World War II. They have read *Snow Falling on Cedars,* a piece of historical fiction about the internment, and viewed *Something Strong Within,* a documentary about life in the camps, and they have discussed a brief timeline of the Japanese experience as immigrants in the United States.

Students are now undertaking a close reading of the parts of the Constitution that will apply to their understanding of the court case. First, they Think Aloud with partners, stopping to clarify language they do not understand, rephrase the gist of what they have read, and make notes so they can summarize each article. Partners are digging into such concepts as habeas corpus, ex post facto, and bill of attainder. Gayle moves around the room, listening to pairs and stopping to probe student thinking. Then she calls the class together to share some of the reading problems they are encountering and how they are solving them.

Sam refers to Article I, Section 9, number 3. "We were looking at the [textbook] title of that specific number, 'Unfair Punishments,'" he says, "so we're thinking that that's what ex post facto was referring to."

In response, Gayle focuses on the reading strategy Sam described, naming it to make this metacognitive move memorable for the whole class: "So you are using a text clue there to understand a little series

of words that you don't understand, that you haven't heard before."

"Jeannie," Gayle says, "I saw you doing something to solve a problem. I think you were looking at habeas corpus."

"Oh, we read the footnote at the bottom."

Gayle is pleased to reinforce a historical text feature her students are using: "So you found some footnotes. Yay, footnotes!"

She continues to draw from the pairs to enrich the understanding and potential strategic repertoire of the entire class. "In this group, you spent a long time, I believe, on the 'elastic clause,' right? Article I, Section 8, number 18?"

Laura describes the problem she and her partner were having. "The wording was rather odd. And we didn't even know 'the foregoing powers,' and it was confusing. We tried to deal with it in sentences. We went up to 'foregoing powers' and tried to figure out what it meant. And then we took the second part."

Gayle reframes the strategy for the class, "I'm seeing it's really one long sentence, and you broke it up into phrases and tried to see if you could make sense of the phrases and stick it all back together again."

Gayle's monitoring of students' reading is strategic. She is helping them build a repertoire of strategies for this kind of rigorous work with text, punctuating students' sustained work with metacognitive conversations and discussions of the text.

"Shall we move on?" she asks. "Back to the text."

aware of the specific strategies that worked for them. They develop a fuller picture of themselves as readers, coming to know in some detail what is useful for them as readers.

Students in Gayle Cribbs's U.S. history class have had a taste of this. They read as problem solvers and talk about what strategies are working for them. In Classroom Close-Up 7.10, students demonstrate that it is at least as interesting for them to describe how they figured out the meaning of *ex post facto* as it is to finally know what it means.

Eventually students will be able to skip the "making thinking visible" part of their comprehension practice. The metacognitive conversation will be both internal and internalized. Instead of saying, "Okay, now I will summarize this article or tolerate ambiguity or predict," experienced readers have a repertoire of strategies that almost automatically offer themselves up when they will do the most good. This is not to say that even the most accomplished readers don't hit roadblocks and literally "rack their brains" to come up with a useful tool, but the tools are there.

■ ■ ■

In the next chapter, we look at how the reading dispositions and strategies students are learning play out in the knowledge-building dimension of the Reading Apprenticeship framework, and how teachers can support students in building content, text, language, and disciplinary knowledge.

Notes

1. Conley, M. W. (2008). Cognitive strategy instruction for adolescents: What we know about the promise, what we don't know about the potential. *Harvard Educational Review, 78*(1), 84–108.

2. Yu-Chung Chang-Hou has developed an approach to mathematics problem solving that she calls WRAMPS. She credits her experience with Reading Apprenticeship as contributing to her development of the program. A description of WRAMPS can be found at http://www.cfkeep.org/html/stitch.php?s=66561915414931&id=35258404012079

3. Anaya, R. A. (1972). *Bless me, Ultima.* Berkeley, CA: TQS Publications.

4. QAR was developed by literacy researcher Taffy Raphael as an offshoot of the work on schema theory that revolutionized thinking about reading instruction beginning in the late 1970s. The notion that students could benefit from understanding themselves as schema builders resulted in Raphael's identification of the text-schema relationships that students use in QAR to ask and answer questions about what they read and what they know.

5. Palinscar, A., & Brown, A. (1984). Reciprocal teaching of comprehension-fostering and comprehension-monitoring activities. *Cognition and Instruction, 1*(2), 117–175.

CHAPTER EIGHT

The Knowledge-Building Dimension

Surfacing and Building Schema in the Disciplines

> I have a big goal to read all the Jackie Collins books before I'm 20, so I read a lot of that. . . . *Othello* was kind of hard. I used like a little bit of schema because last year we read *Romeo and Juliet,* and this year we read *Othello,* and they're both tragedies. Usually they're going to follow the basic outline of what Shakespeare writes as a tragedy. Like once you already read an author's work, you kind of know how that author likes to write.
>
> —Shelli, grade 10 student

KNOWLEDGE—whether about the world of ideas in a text or about the ways particular texts work—both supports reading comprehension and develops as a result of reading. To access the ideas and information in different types of texts, readers call on overlapping types of knowledge. We have chosen to categorize them in this chapter as knowledge about content and the world, knowledge about texts, knowledge about language, and knowledge about disciplinary discourse and practices.

Tenth-grader Shelli, quoted at the opening, has developed some knowledge of different kinds of texts that she applies to reading fiction. She has come to understand (and enjoy) the potboiler, a genre favored by Jackie Collins. But Shelli has also developed clues about how to read Shakespearean tragedies. As she says, her schema from reading *Romeo and Juliet* gave her a way to approach *Othello*: "You kind of know how that author likes to write."

In this chapter, we look at the ways in which teachers can support students in accessing and building on their prior knowledge, or schema, generally and in relation to specific disciplines. Yet even in a chapter focused on building knowledge, knowledge is not the end in and of itself. To help students build knowledge, the overarching goal remains that of increasing their confidence and competence as independent, critical readers and writers of academic texts. We are still talking about how to promote student agency.

Thinking Metacognitively About Schema

> The concept of schema emerges as we work with text. One of the things that keeps coming up is what individuals know—and bring to the text. I use the word "schema" to name it. Soon the function of schema in students' reading is obvious to them. Usually there is a nice moment when we notice together that the more schema you have about something, the easier it is to read about that topic, and the easier it is to learn more about it. The feeling in the room is something like, "How cool is that?!"
> —Gayle Cribb, high school history teacher

Schema is a concept that students should understand and own. They can think of schema as a personal library of knowledge—based on a lifetime of reading and experience—that they already have and can draw on, add to daily, and revise if they need to as they learn more. This information is organized, filed for future retrieval. When students encounter new information or experiences, their minds automatically try to figure out how the new information fits with schema they already have: What do I know that is like this? What pattern am I seeing? Where do I file this?

Students may find, for example, that they have lots of schema for music, filed in different ways (types, artists, instruments, last night listening to the car radio, Jerome's favorite songs), so even if they hear a Bach fugue for the first time, they recognize patterns: it's music, not sandpaper. They no doubt have considerably less (or even incorrect) schema for Daniel Webster (his cousin Noah, for example, was the lexicographer).

High school reading specialist Linda Brown found that the concept of schema makes it easier for her students to understand why they may have trouble comprehending particular texts:

> On a metacognitive level, not as an excuse, the concept of schema has allowed students to understand a reason for the difficulties some experience.

For teachers, awareness of the schema that students have and may need to develop is especially important if they anticipate a mismatch between students' schema and the texts they are expected to understand. When giving reading assignments, most teachers take it upon themselves to surface students' prior knowledge about a topic or genre or author as a jumping-off place. What teachers do less often is help students become metacognitive about schema, showing them how they can activate relevant knowledge they already have from other

CLASSROOM CLOSE-UP 8.1
"Give That Schema a Second"

When Lisa Krebs introduced her tenth graders to *Othello*, she was concerned that they would be quick to dismiss it as too hard or too boring. As she explains, she pushes students to explore their schema as a way to remind them of how much knowledge they already bring to the text if they figure out how to use it:

"I'm trying to get them to be motivated readers by showing them that they do have schema within themselves that will help them understand what's going on, on the page. I explain that the more you recognize, or the more you can bring in experience to a reading, the more interesting it is to you. And then, hopefully, the more likely you'll be to want to read it, and to want to really explore the ideas that are in it.

"For example, we did a Talking to the Text on a section from Act 2, where the messenger is telling all of the Venetians in Cyprus that it's time to party—

they've won the battle against the Turks, and also a fellow has recently married.

"Kids understand party, because Harold [the messenger] uses words like 'festivity' and he talks about keeping the kitchen open and having access to food and wine. But he also talks about how it's celebratory because of the nuptials. A lot of kids stopped on that word: 'Nuptials? What is that? I don't understand what that is.'

"I helped them see that they do know what that is, they just don't use that word as nuptials. 'Think about the term prenuptial,' I said. 'You know what a prenuptial agreement is, right?' And everybody knew that.

"And so just trying to let them in on that they do have a lot of schema there, that they just need to give it a second, to sort of sit on it a minute and not give up."

reading, discussion, or experience, and then demonstrating for students how to further develop this existing knowledge.

In Classroom Close-Up 8.1, high school English teacher Lisa Krebs describes a simple example of how she engages students in retrieving schema they already have in order to build on it.

Although not all new information presents readily discernible patterns or schema connections, as students learn to think of themselves as capable problem solvers, they consciously engage in the search for these patterns with increasing persistence and success. When they become metacognitive about the background knowledge they have, they are active agents in their own reading growth. They surface and use the schema they have to make connections between prior and new knowledge, they see when to relinquish and revise misleading schema, and they work on developing new schema to make sense of particular texts.

When teachers introduce students to the concept of schema, humor is a particular ally. The schema "collisions" that make humor humorous can immediately draw students into consideration of how their minds organize knowledge. For example, the headline "Red Tape Holds Up Bridge" makes us smile precisely because competing schema for "red tape" allow us to visualize a very unlikely piece of engineering. The headline can be understood in more than one way: it depends on what schema the reader brings or applies.

In the first Reading Apprenticeship classes, teachers Christine Cziko and Lori Hurwitz routinely challenged their academic literacy students with ambiguous headlines (and enlisted students in the search for such examples). By jointly considering the different ways of understanding these headlines, students could see for themselves the role of schema in how easily or accurately readers understand text. (Box 8.1 describes the "Ambiguous Headlines" activity.)

Political cartoons are another way to introduce students to the role of schema in understanding. Readers of the political cartoon in Box 8.2 will understand the cartoonist's basic message about gender-role reversal, regardless of their

---

BOX 8.1

Ambiguous Headlines

PURPOSE

Text that can be understood in more than one way highlights for students the role of schema in assigning meaning. Ambiguous headlines provide for an engaging exploration of how our minds relate what we already know to what we read.

PROCEDURE

- Collect a number of newspaper headlines that can be interpreted in more than one way. (For example: "Police Begin Campaign to Run Down Jaywalkers"; "Safety Experts Say School Bus Passengers Should Be Belted"; "Two Sisters Reunited After 18 Years in Checkout Line"; "Kids Make Nutritious Snacks"; "New Vaccine May Contain Rabies"; "Killer Sentenced to Die for Second Time in 10 Years"; "Miners Refuse to Work After Death.")

- Have students copy down an ambiguous headline and write what they believe to be an improbable but plausible explanation.

- Ask students to write what they believe is the probable meaning of the headline and an explanation of the schema necessary to understand it.

Here are student examples:

"Squad Helps Dog Bite Victim"

Improbable meaning: Bad people help a dog bite people.

Probable intended meaning: A group of people rescue someone who got bitten by a dog.

Schema: You have to know that groups of rescuers are sometimes called squads.

"Eye Drops Off Shelf"

Improbable meaning: The eye falls down off the shelf.

Probable intended meaning: Eye drop medicine gets removed from the store.

Schema: You have to know that headlines sometimes leave out words to save space. Eye Drops Taken Off Shelves would have made more sense. Also you have to know that when something is wrong with it, stuff gets taken out of the store so it doesn't hurt someone.

BOX 8.2

Cartoon Schema

PURPOSE

The structural features of cartoons—graphic exaggeration, easily discerned clues, and few words—allow students to focus on ways their schema "fill in" to enrich the text and graphics.

PROCEDURE

- Project the political cartoon for all to see and distribute a copy to each student.

- Ask students to Talk to the Text and discuss it with a partner:

    – What do you think the cartoon means?

    – Why did the artist create this cartoon?

    – What evidence or clues did you use?

- Facilitate a class discussion of students' ideas. What was the role of schema?

"Election Day!" was created by E.W. Gustin in 1909. The original is held by the Library of Congress.

knowledge of women's suffrage. Readers will appreciate the scene even more if they know that this cartoon was published after sixty-plus years of struggle for women's right to vote *and* a full decade before women were actually able to celebrate election day.

Working with low-risk materials like ambiguous headlines, jokes, and cartoons can help students and teachers alike recognize that an individual's schema are undeniably shaped by his or her particular experiences and background. Although class members will share a significant amount of schema by virtue of their common exposure to mass media and living in the same nation, region, state, and municipality, classrooms are nevertheless places where diverse sets of schema come into contact. When individual histories meet over a particular text, varied understandings are bound to emerge. When unexpected interpretations occur, sometimes teachers conclude that students merely lack schema. Routine invitations to think metacognitively about schema can therefore serve teachers as well as students. Both groups benefit from seeing what schema resources students can offer to the conversation and, conversely, how a perfectly understandable misreading of a text may occur due to schema differences. With new understandings of the sources of their students' misreadings, teachers can then help students refine their schema for the task at hand. In such circumstances, teachers discover that far from lacking in schema, students have warehouses of experience and information that can support them in tackling complex text.

For example, technical college instructor Michele Lesmeister was frustrated with a model of adult GED instruction that assigns students' reading material according to Lexile measures. Her students tested at the grade 5 Lexile level, and that's the level at which their textbook was written. However, when Michele introduced Reading Apprenticeship approaches, she decided to also introduce a few texts that were more challenging. She surveyed students about which classroom materials worked best for them and found that the easiest to comprehend were not necessarily preferred:

> Interestingly, the exercises selected as best by the students were the type of assignment that compelled them to participate the most, argue the most, and engage the best with the text and in a variety of ways. [To me,] this was like a permission slip to continue to toss out the leveled reading textbook materials and focus more on relevant content—and in a more meaningful way. By the end of the quarter, they were reading grade 9–10 level materials. I found that by applying the conceptual sophistication and intellectual maturity that my students possessed, I could cross such superficial boundaries in my course, leading to a much more engaged classroom.

In Michele's class, texts better matched to students' maturity, combined with collaborative participation routines, gave students a much needed opportunity to build new schema and begin the upward spiral to learning more.

The importance of background experience and knowledge in assisting comprehension is undeniable. Teachers can take advantage of what they know about their students to select texts that will evoke their experiences. This can be empowering for students who may otherwise believe their experiences and knowledge do not matter in the classroom. Yet, when taken to an extreme, starting only with what students know can result in *staying* with what students know. For students with little schema about a topic of study, not already knowing sometimes becomes a trap. In one academic literacy classroom, for example, a student dismissed the need to read a text about the Armenian genocide by asking, "Is anyone in here from Armenia?" She had learned to expect only topics and texts related to her experience and those of her peers. If not supported to stretch beyond what they already know, students may never learn to make connections between the known and the new. They may get stuck exploring what they already know. With metacognitive awareness of their schema, students can instead focus on building and refining what they know—learning to learn in the process.

Surfacing, Building, and Refining Schema

> *Teacher:* I'd like to get some volunteers to respond to today's preamble: What do you know about organic chemistry or think about it, what are some organic molecules that you know, what do you want to learn about organic chemistry?
>
> *Alma:* Organic reminds me of like organic stores, they have foods and drinks that are basically just pure, natural.
>
> *Teacher:* So you're wondering if the name "organic," you might get a meaning from that. Okay, Kyle.
>
> *Kyle:* I know some different organic molecules that's in us and some plants, like sucrose, glucose. Um, should water be in it?
>
> —Exchange in Will Brown's honors chemistry class

As part of his introduction of a new chemistry unit, Will Brown invites his students to consider a set of "preamble" questions, first in writing and then with the class, about what they might encounter in their upcoming study of organic chemistry. He is not concerned that they may have misconceptions. He is interested in students' surfacing any current schema and making preliminary or tentative connections to new information. He knows they will have many opportunities to add to and revise their schema for "organic" as it relates to chemistry, water, and even health food.

Will has an inherent trust of the inquiry process—perhaps because he is a science teacher. He understands that for students to build or revise schema, they must first surface any partial understandings or misconceptions they may have. Once these are on the table, Will's responsibility is to provide sufficient opportunities for students to evaluate and add to or revise them.

Surfacing Schema

Surfacing students' schema sometimes means tolerating their misconceptions. For teachers who are making a transition to more student-centered, inquiry-based learning, this part of the learning process can be unsettling. When students are developing any area of autonomy and competence, they will make mistakes. In Reading Apprenticeship classrooms, because so much knowledge building is collaborative, in addition to the incorrect "knowledge" that students sometimes have, there will be times when they communicate those errors or misconceptions to others during discussions or group work.

Knowing when, whether, and how to intervene in students' misunderstandings is a skill that teachers develop as a crucial part of encouraging and guiding students toward deeper comprehension of challenging texts. Some knowledge errors don't matter; some are addressed by other students. Many misconceptions get worked out naturally as engaged learning proceeds; others are significant detours or dead ends that need to be handled.

What we want to emphasize is that in Reading Apprenticeship classrooms, where teachers are negotiating long-term student success, the need to ensure that students have immediate, correct information almost never trumps building or maintaining student engagement. Given a choice of whether to simply ignore a misstatement or misconception, to set up a next learning task that explicitly counters it so students develop their own ways of refuting the error, or to step in with correct information and perhaps derail student engagement, teachers learn to make very deliberate calculations.

In Classroom Close-Up 8.2, Will describes a model he tries to follow when addressing student error. The related Box 8.3 maps this approach in a flow chart.

Will's approach, which he also uses when students expect him to give them the answer to a question, means that students come to recognize that the teacher is not the center of the classroom—*they* are. Rita Jensen labels this understanding a "huge turning point" for her middle school classes:

> Lots of times students have been "taught" that, if they wait, the teacher will provide whatever answer is required. If they don't answer, she will do it for them. It's a huge turning point when students see that the teacher won't give them the answer. Instead of keeping them dependent, you are teaching them agency.
>
> It's bigger than just not providing the answer. It is about creating a culture of curiosity and collaboration in the class. It can begin with reciprocal modeling, when the teacher says to the class, "I am wondering about this. What do *you* think?" Or when someone ventures an idea, it can get thrown back to the class or to partners or small groups. "Who has another idea?"

When students are on the wrong path, the hard part is redirecting them to other thinking without shutting them down. But if they are in the habit of asking and being asked, "Where is your evidence for that?" or "What makes you say that?" their ideas are not rejected, but neither are they accepted without sufficient evidence. Students feel the difference.

CLASSROOM CLOSE-UP 8.2

Decisions That Keep Students in Control of Their Learning

Will Brown's high school chemistry students have learned that he will rarely step in and resolve a question, error, or confusion. Will has an internalized "flow chart" that he uses in responding to students, and it is based on split-second assessments of whether the confusion is an opportunity to support student inquiry. (See also Box 8.3.)

"When I notice a student's error or misconception, my first move is to make sure that the problem is not one of communication. Sometimes what appears to be a misconception is only a miscommunication and can be cleared up with a clarifying question to the student.

"If I really am dealing with an error or misconception, I evaluate how important it is. When the error is insignificant or simply distracting, I may put it to rest with a brief response.

"But when the error or misconception has the potential to interfere with learning goals, I have to ask: What is the urgency of addressing it? Can learning progress if I ignore it?

"If learning goals and learning progress are being derailed, I have three choices: initiate an inquiry, make a mental note to initiate an inquiry later, or clear up the confusion myself.

"My preference is to get students working on clearing up the error or misconception. I make this choice when I know that with some probing on my part, the student or other students in the class have the necessary schema to work it out.

"On the other hand, if I know that the lesson or upcoming lessons address the error or misconception, I'll let students know to be on the lookout for more information, and we will return to the confusion or question once they have sufficient schema to address it.

"If there is no other option, I will provide the relevant conceptual framework and the 'correct' answer. I only do this if there are no other resources I can offer students as a basis for building the knowledge needed, or if I know there is no upcoming opportunity to address the misconception 'properly,' through inquiry. My default position is to keep students engaged and in control of their learning."

One brief example demonstrates Will's resolve to turn misconceptions over to students. Groups have been asked to come up with a definition for "substance" based on a recent lab:

Jerome: We wrote, "A particular type of constitution."

Teacher: What does that mean? What does "particular" mean?

Class: A certain one. Specific.

Teacher: If it's particular, it's one, right? And what's "constitution"?

Jerome: Isn't that like a democracy or something like that?

Teacher: Yeah, we've got the Constitution and democracy. Do you think that's what they're talking about?

Jerome: No.

Teacher: So maybe that word has different meanings whether you're talking about science or government. Does anyone else have another definition they'd like to share? Let's work from that direction.

BOX 8.3

Error Response Flow Chart

Internalized flow charts like this one articulated by Will Brown can help teachers handle student error and keep students in control of their own learning (see also Classroom Close-Up 8.2).

Notice error or misconception

Assess whether a miscommunication → Clarify communication

Ignore, learning can progress

Assess value or urgency of resolving

Confusion distracting, best put to rest

Teacher the only potential resource

Assess students' opportunities to resolve

Student or peers have sufficient schema to resolve

Tell students

Initiate an inquiry

No upcoming opportunity to address "properly"

Initiate an inquiry later

Resources to resolve are easily available

Students have now had sufficient learning experiences to resolve

As a way of surfacing students' schema, many teachers are familiar with the classic three-question KWL structure[1] for introducing and then later reviewing a new topic of study. The first question, What do you *Know*? prompts students' consideration of schema (correct or incorrect) they may have related to the topic. The second question, What do you *Want* to know? invites their personal engagement with the topic, whether to learn something new or to clarify a question they have. At the end of the unit of study, the third question, What did you *Learn*? invites students to reflect on new learning, but also to revisit and revise any incorrect or misleading schema that surfaced earlier.

Community college teacher Holly Morris describes using a similar approach with her biology majors. Holly explicitly asks students what confusions as well as what "knowledge" they have about a topic the class is about to investigate:

> A few times during the semester I used a KWL-type approach to begin a new topic. Using the logs, I would ask the class to write what they already knew about the topic, what confused them, and what else they would like to know, and I wrote what they told me on the board. Often, I had them work in small groups to talk about the confusing material. Questions that still remained were discussed by the whole class.

LINK is a similar metacognitive structure that helps students surface, build, and refine their schema across a unit of study. LINK asks students to create a class *List* of what they know (or think they know) about a topic, *Inquire* about "knowledge" classmates have offered, *Note* from memory what they have just learned from their collaborative List and Inquire activities, and then read about the topic and discuss or write about what they now *Know,* including how their schema have changed. Box 8.4 describes the LINK process. High school biology teacher Muthulakshmi Bhavani Balavenkatesan orchestrates all of her Reading Apprenticeship routines within a LINK structure. In Classroom Close-Up 8.3, she describes her approach.

Other ways teachers can surface students' schema when introducing a new text or topic include Give One, Get One (Box 8.5) and Anticipation Guides (Box 8.6). In both of these activities, students surface and record content or topic schema before reading and then return after reading to confirm, add to, or revise their initial thinking.

Building and Revising Schema

Helping students surface schema as a basis for building new schema is something many teachers seem to do almost automatically, whenever an opportunity arises. In Dorothea Jordan's pre-algebra class, her students build their concept

BOX 8.4

LINK (List, Inquire, Note, Know)*

PURPOSE

Through brainstorming and inquiry, students surface schema about a topic. Through reading and discussion (or other processing of new information), they build and revise schema.

PROCEDURE

List

- Give students three minutes to individually list ideas, words, and phrases they associate with a new topic of study.
- Without commenting on students' contributions, compile a class list of ideas.

Inquire

- Invite students to inquire into each other's ideas on the list. Encourage the person who nominated an idea to respond to any questions about it.
- Compile a class list of students' questions to drive the reading and learning.

Note

- Ask students to read one or more texts about the topic and make notes that shed light on the topic—what they think they know and what they wonder.
- It is helpful at this point to look over students' notes, both for accountability and to informally assess students' understanding (and misunderstanding) of the topic.

Know

- Ask students to reflect on how their thinking has changed and why—what they now think they know and questions they still have about the topic.
- As a class, revisit the original list of phrases and questions and identify prior misinformation or misunderstandings and how students' schema have changed as a result of reading and processing the text. Also note lingering confusions and new questions or wonderings prompted by the reading.

* Adapted from Joseph Vaughan and Thomas Estes, in Strategic Teaching and Learning, *California Department of Education, 2000.*

of positive and negative integers by adding to a list of opposites, such as profit and loss, that they have encountered in various word problems during the year. In Classroom Close-Up 8.4, Dorothea's students add the opposites *east* and *west* as a way of building their schema for a number line with zero in the center.

CLASSROOM CLOSE-UP 8.3
LINK Is the Hook

Muthulakshmi Bhavani Balavenkatesan is a third-year teacher of biology at a large comprehensive high school; her classes typically enroll forty students. Two years ago she was introduced to Reading Apprenticeship. Her students now routinely Talk to the Text, discuss with a partner what they are wondering and learning, and make group presentations summarizing what they have learned. LINK is the organizing structure for all of students' work. In this interview, Bhavani describes how her classroom has changed:

"I've been doing Reading Apprenticeship since last year. The majority of the students take it very seriously. I show them my freshman students' scores for the three years that I've been teaching here. The first year I had no Reading Apprenticeship strategies at all. Comparatively, the CST (California Standards Test) scores have gone up dramatically. I also have the lowest failure rate from all the bio teachers. I've shown students the evidence. I tell them constantly, 'The only thing I've done differently is these strategies, and I want you to take them seriously.'"

Her students begin the year with partner reading, Talking to the Text, and collaborative discussion—to counter what Bhavani finds are limitations of traditional reading and seatwork. "I feel when students just write notes out of the book, they're not retaining it. I showed them a videotape of my three-year-old daughter trying to read a book. She does a lot of Talking to the Text, asking clarifying questions. I told them, 'This is the way we learn, talking to each other. But we kind of stray away from it as the years go by, so I want us to return to that because I know you'll do a lot more learning by talking to each other.'"

All the talk in Bhavani's classroom begins with LINK. "I love the LINK," she says, "the way it hooks them into what we're studying."

After surfacing students' schema and questions, Bhavani has students work with partners to read, Talk to the Text, discuss, and complete a packet developed by the biology department.

Then, to represent what they have learned, students work in small groups creating collaborative posters that they present to the class. Groups are responsible for different portions of the reading.

"That's how my lecture goes now," she says. "Instead of me talking, it's them talking. I might add a few examples here and there, but it's more me being a moderator. I'm using LINK now for every unit because I really feel it goes so well."

When introducing key concepts about which students have little or no schema, or for which prior knowledge is dominated by misunderstandings, metacognitive prompts can help students focus on how their understanding grows, changes, and coheres over time as they read. All people develop misconceptions—and relinquish them with difficulty. Explicit prompts like those in Box 8.7 help students hold a metacognitive conversation with themselves as a route to revisiting and perhaps relinquishing misconceptions. By also making a record of their learning process, students are able to easily refresh their understanding and appreciate themselves as agents of their own learning.

BOX 8.5

Give One, Get One

PURPOSE

Before starting to study a subject that students are likely to know something about, having them surface the knowledge they already have and share it with classmates increases the knowledge in the room. Give One, Get One gives students an opportunity to show what they know and primes them to make connections to new schema.[2]

PROCEDURE

- Have students fold a piece of paper lengthwise to form two columns and write "Give One" at the top of the left column and "Get One" at the top of the right column.

- Ask students to individually brainstorm a list in the left column of all the things they already know about the topic they will be studying.

- Have them talk to two or three other students about what is on their lists, adding any new ideas they think are correct to their "Get One" column.

- Once everyone has given and gotten information, have the whole class discuss the information students have listed.

- Again, have students add any new information they get from this discussion in the right-hand column of their lists.

- If any information is in doubt, alert students to try to clarify it as they read and learn more.

MALCOLM X	
Give One	**Get One**
He was shot during a speech	<u>Assassinated</u> during a speech
~~He freed slaves~~	Born in 1925
Famous African American	He argued for Black Power
He was a Muslim	
He spent time in jail.	Became a Muslim in jail
~~Wrote an autobiography~~	Alex Haley wrote <u>The Autobiography of Malcolm X</u> after interviewing him

BOX 8.6

Anticipation Guides

PURPOSE

Statements that anticipate content in a text can serve to surface students' related schema and give them a purpose for reading—to check their predictions against the understanding they develop as they read (see the example that follows).

Anticipation Guides can be designed as discussion starters for content that may support varied interpretations or to draw attention to important content that requires specific evidence.

PROCEDURE

- Prepare five or six statements for students to respond to that relate to ideas they will encounter in the text.
- Ask students to individually agree or disagree with each statement and be prepared to justify their responses.
- Give pairs or small groups a few minutes to compare their reasoning.
- Ask students to read the text, keeping in mind the need to find supporting evidence for their responses to the "anticipation" statements.
- Have pairs or groups review the evidence that confirms or disconfirms their original ideas.

Anticipation Guide: "Food Production in Plants"	Agree	Disagree	Evidence from the Text and Elsewhere
1. Sunshine is absorbed through the leaves of plants.			
2. Photosynthesis is a chemical released by plants.			
3. Plants need carbon dioxide.			
4. Sunlight is food for plants.			
5. Plants absorb food through their roots.			

When students will be reading about key concepts over time and/or in different texts, a metacognitive note taker such as Monitoring Conceptual Change in Box 8.8 can be a help. Students complete a new note taker after every significant reading assignment. By the end of a health unit on obesity, for example, students might have a set of several note takers on obesity, on risk, and on calories, each demonstrating how their understanding of these concepts grew and changed. This graphic evidence of how they build understanding contributes to students' sense of their power as learners and provides a review of their learning.

CLASSROOM CLOSE-UP 8.4

Is West Positive or Negative?

At least a third of the students in Dorothea Jordan's middle school math class are learning English as well as pre-algebra. For a unit about positive and negative integers, the class is creating a list of word pairs that signal opposites in word problems. In the following excerpt, Dorothea introduces a new word problem by referring students to the schema they already have for solving problems involving positive and negative integers. She also invites them to predict how opposites might be part of a problem titled "Nurse."

Teacher: The most important thing we do in this class is make connections to what we've done prior. So let's go over what we've been doing with positive and negative integers. Look over here. Ravinder, what are these?

Positive	Negative
Win	Lose
Profit	Loss
Deposit	Withdraw
Up	Down
Above	Below
Rise	Fall
Increase	Decrease
Gain	Lose
Ascend	Descend

Ravinder: Opposites.

Teacher: They're opposites. How do they help us in our problem solving?

Ravinder: Use them for clue words.

Teacher: Okay, we have our clue words. Here's a new problem: "Nurse." Based on that title and what we've been studying for the last two or three weeks, this isn't going to be about squares, right? What's it going to be about?

Class: Integers . . . Doctors . . . Negative and positive . . . A girl doctor—a nurse.

Teacher: Based on what we've been studying.

George: How many people go to the hospital sick, and how many people go out not sick.

Raul: How many stitches or something.

Teacher: What would be the opposite of giving stitches?

Raul: Taking them out.

Dacia: How many rooms she goes to.

Teacher: And what would be the opposite of that?

Dacia: How many rooms she doesn't go to.

Teacher: Now, we have a bunch of predictions. Here's our new problem. *(She reads aloud the posted text)*

> The new nurse on the fourth floor of the hospital had a really really busy busy day. First it was the patient in the middle room of that floor, who wanted somebody to look at a red spot on her big toe, which was in a cast. Then the patient three rooms farther down at the east end of the hall rang . . . the nurse had to go to the pantry, which was five rooms back to the west . . . By that time . . . four more rooms to the east . . . two more rooms toward the east . . . How many rooms were there on the fourth floor?

Tomas: It's a hard problem because they're talking about east and west and how many doors to the right and left, different places they're going.

Teacher: Okay, what else is hard about this?

Chehra: He's helping a lot of people and you don't know who they are.

Teacher: So there's a lot of information. Right now I want you to read through it and I want you to start Talking to the Text, writing yourself some notes, pulling out some information. I'm going to walk around and see if you need any help.

BOX 8.7

Tracking Concept Development

By intentionally tracking their changing understanding of a key concept, students become metacognitive about how they build knowledge. Prompts like those in the tables shown here are most profitably used to help students focus on key concepts or commonly misunderstood concepts.

Key concept	My understanding before reading	New ideas and examples from the reading	My revised understanding	How I arrived at this understanding
Trade	Trade means to swap. I give you something in exchange for something you give me.	Free trade is an economic theory. "Free trade occurs when people are able to import goods without government interference."	In a country such as Nicaragua, where people have few opportunities for employment, free trade could be useful. The country could have access to things that it otherwise couldn't afford.	Rereading the article on free trade, reading a second article on free trade, and talking with my group.

What I thought I knew	What I know now	How I know it

My prior knowledge (schema)	What I read in the text	My revised schema

BOX 8.8

Monitoring Conceptual Change

Students keep track on a note taker of evolving understanding about significant concepts over a unit of work, completing a new record of their changing understanding after each reading assignment or new text.

Monitoring Conceptual Change: Calorie (1 of 3)

1. Write my ideas about *calorie* before reading:

2. Make revisions to what I wrote above that wasn't quite right (cross out or adjust wording).

3. Write additional ideas I got from the reading:

Exploring Different Types of Knowledge

Preface

This book deals with the intensive campaign of the militant suffragists of America [1913–1919] to win a solitary thing—the passage by Congress of the national suffrage amendment enfranchising women. It is the story of the first organized militant, political action in America to this end . . .

It is my sincere hope that you will understand and appreciate the martyrdom involved, for it was the conscious voluntary gift of beautiful, strong, and young hearts . . .

This book contains my interpretations, which are of course arguable. But it is a true record of events.

Doris Stevens.
New York, August, 1920.

This excerpt is from the preface of *Jailed for Freedom*, suffragist Doris Stevens's first-person account of the militant struggle to finally secure passage of the Nineteenth Amendment. Cindy Ryan's grade 9 academic literacy class is about to read a chapter from Stevens's book, but first they will discuss the preface in a small, student-led seminar. Their teacher has analyzed the preface, considering the schema challenges and opportunities that students will encounter. By sorting these into particular types of knowledge, Cindy can more easily see where she wants to help focus students' attention:

- Knowledge about a *topic* [rights; American women's fight for the vote]

- Knowledge about *text structure and genre* [preface to a book; first-person account]

- Knowledge about *language* [punctuation: dash to set off definition; word families: suffragist-suffrage, martyr-martyrdom, argue-arguable; synonyms: suffrage-enfranchising, campaign-political action]

- Knowledge about *disciplinary discourse and practices* [claims and evidence; sourcing; historical contextualization]

BOX 8.9

Types of Knowledge

These overlapping categories provide a way to think about the challenges and opportunities a given text provides: What will students know and need to know? How might their learning experiences be focused?

Knowledge of Content and the World	Knowledge of Texts	Knowledge of Language	Knowledge of Disciplinary Discourse and Practices
A learned and lived knowledge base	Text genres and text structures; visuals; formatting features	Words and morphology; syntax and text signals	The particular ways members of a subject area community communicate and think

---

In Classroom Close-Ups 8.5 and 8.6, Cindy's students demonstrate what they know and what they grapple with in order to understand this text. In previous lessons they have been building related topic schema about human rights and First Amendment rights and have watched a movie scene of suffragettes picketing the White House. They have studied primary and secondary sources. They use word-learning strategies daily. And they have practiced historical contextualization.

The knowledge categories used by Cindy and presented in this chapter are broad and overlapping (see Box 8.9). For example, some educators might prefer to sort "genre" into the disciplinary category rather than the texts category. Sometimes "words" will seem more salient in the content category than in the language category. These distinctions are not important for our purposes here: analyzing the knowledge challenges and opportunities of a text.

Student Learning Goals in the knowledge-building dimension (see the Assessment Appendix) are organized by the categories in Box 8.9, by discipline. Many Reading Apprenticeship teachers introduce these knowledge-building goals after students have experienced a number of them and can recognize how much they already know about building schema and disciplinary knowledge. Individual Talking to the Text with the set of knowledge-building goals, along with partner sharing and class discussion, alert students to how much they are accomplishing. At the end of a course, if students return to this list of goals, they should be pleased to recognize how much they have learned.

Building Content and World Knowledge

Because students build new knowledge about a topic relative to how much they already know about it, many teachers supplement a primary text about particular content with other texts, photographs, illustrations, films, animations, examples and metaphors, labs and experiential approaches, and so forth to provide students with many layers of related experience and information. (Chapter Five discusses this abundance of schema-building resources in terms of "extensive

---

CLASSROOM CLOSE-UP 8.5

"It's Like the NAACP or the Black Panthers"

In the student-led seminar in Cindy Ryan's grade 9 academic literacy class, Leander leads his classmates in discussing and clarifying the preface to *Jailed for Freedom*, a first-person account of American women's fight for the right to vote. One student's confusion about "political action" is clarified by schema offered by a peer:

Leander: (Reading from the preface) "It is the story of the first organized militant, political action in America to this end." Keep going?

Sean: Stop right there. I'm confused.

Kevin: It's the story of the first organization to like take action—

Leander: Towards . . .

Kevin: Yeah, like towards what's gone wrong. They protested and stuff. It's like the NAACP or the Black Panthers or something. They just came together to fight against something, to change America, I guess.

CLASSROOM CLOSE-UP 8.6
"She Was a First Person"

When students in Cindy Ryan's academic literacy class reach the last sentence in the book preface, they conclude their student-led discussion by building schema both about the purpose of a preface and the disciplinary practice of sourcing a text.

(In the course of their discussion, they also use language schema to explore the definition of "arguably.")

Leander: (Reading the last sentence) "This book contains my interpretations, which are of course arguable. But it is a true record of events." Interpret means to . . .

Kevin: The way you understand something.

Leander: You could say, "This book is my understanding, which of course is arguable."

Kevin: Everybody got their different opinions—arguable. So it's not like this is the only truth, it's like there's more than one truth.

Sean: It says it's a true record of events.

Mariah: I think the person who wrote this knows that you will probably argue about what he's talking about, so that's why he put—

Tony: It's a she.

Mariah: She put "arguably" in the sentence.

Sean: Cause you might think different from her.

Mariah: When she started with this thing, she said, "This book contains," so basically she was saying that somebody might argue about it or it can cause an argument.

Tony: So she wants to argue about it, I guess.

Mariah: No, she knows that what she wrote about—

Kevin: My interpretation. So that's basically the way she understands. She wrote it up the way she understood it. You might of understood it a different way from the way she understood it.

Sean: So that's her opinion.

Teacher: But you guys also pointed out "a true record of events," and no one's talked about that.

Sean: It say true because it say 1920.

Thomas: That's when the Nineteenth Amendment—

Kevin: That's when the story really happened. It wasn't fictional or made up. It really did happen.

Teacher: I need you all to look at the setting now, that she gives us at the end:

> Doris Stevens.
> New York, August, 1920.

Tony: August, 1920.

Leander: That's the date when women got the right to vote.

Sean: That's when they passed the law for women to vote.

Tony: So she's actually viewing it with her own eyes.

Sean: I think she was there when it all happened.

Tony: She might have been actually one of the people or whatever.

Kevin: Yeah, she was a reporter or something.

Tony: Or one of the people.

Sean: I think she witnessed it and she wrote about it.

Kevin: She was there. It's like she was a first person, so she really knows what happened.

reading.") The connections that students make across such texts and experiences help them clarify, consolidate, and elaborate content knowledge.

To build her developmental English students' schema about themes and big ideas in their assigned reading, community college instructor Nancy Ybarra uses vertical text sets of varying genres and levels of difficulty.[3] For example, students explore nonviolence as a strategy for achieving social justice with a memoir by one of the nine African American students who first integrated Little Rock High School and theoretical essays by Martin Luther King Jr. and Mahatma Gandhi. As Nancy explains, text sets such as these allow her students to enrich their schema about important concepts:

> In addition to the memoir *Warriors Don't Cry*, students are making connections with two documents by Gandhi and Martin Luther King Jr. I bring in short but challenging readings that give students an opportunity to "unpack" academic prose. The more complex readings are related to central themes in the simpler reading, in this case the memoir, which helps students establish a schema for the more difficult reading.

As well as the rich layers of content resources and experiences teachers can provide, other students in a class are an important source of content knowledge. When Nancy's students work in small groups, a posted reminder helps them refer to the Reading Apprenticeship strategies they can use for building schema and solving problems:

- Discuss your "schema" for reading this text.
- Share knowledge you have about this topic.
- Help each other with new vocabulary or difficult passages.
- Read specific passages from the text that support your point of view.
- Summarize or paraphrase key passages.
- Pose questions about what you have read.
- Connect this reading to other texts or previous class discussions.

In Cindy Ryan's academic literacy class, students' sharing of schema is constant. Collaboration is expected and is important to students' learning. During the student-led seminar of the book preface referred to earlier, one student's confusion is immediately cleared up by another student's nimble example, constructed from his knowledge of the world (see Classroom Close-Up 8.5).

Building Knowledge of Texts

When making sense of text, readers draw on not only their content knowledge and knowledge of the world, but also their knowledge of genre and text structure: Is this narrative or informational text? Is it an essay or a report? Is it a mathematical formula or a chemical solution? Experienced readers also know to look for text features that highlight important ideas—in subheads, illustrations, or glossaries, for example. Through multiple experiences reading a wide variety of texts for different purposes, students are able to broaden their schema about text, building useful knowledge and strategies to bring to all their interactions with text.

Many teachers have students preview a text as a matter of course, to determine its type, purpose, and text features. Then, alert to its purpose, students can be more strategic in how to focus their reading. Rita Jensen makes sure that before her middle school ELD students read a new text, they surface schema about genre and what that means for how they will approach the particular assignment. In the following example, when she gives students a new poem to preview, she is explicit about the importance of recognizing that they have schema about poems (and newspaper articles and essays) that will help them:

> I'm going to be giving you a new poem today. I want you to take a look at
> the title, the author, the kind of structure it is. I'm not giving you a newspaper
> article, I'm not giving you an essay, so you already know that. But if you didn't
> know that, you would have to figure that out right off the bat, wouldn't you?

When Cindy Ryan's academic literacy students discussed the contents of Doris Stevens's preface (presented earlier), they had not yet learned the structure or purpose of a preface. Only when they reached the end of it, with a little probing by their teacher, did they figure it out. Classroom Close-Up 8.6 shows how these understandings unfold, including students' excitement in recognizing that they were reading a first-person, primary source.

For many students, informational text poses the most problems. Often, students need practice analyzing how it works. For example, when students know they can identify common informational text structures—such as compare and contrast, cause and effect, and analysis—they should also know they can organize their thinking about what they are reading accordingly and so more easily remember it.

Gina Hale's seventh graders explicitly explore the various text structures in their history textbook over the course of the year. With their teacher's support, students discover that different text structures suggest different reading and note-taking strategies. In Classroom Close-Up 8.7, Gina's class begins to develop a chart that helps them visualize different text structures (and take notes strategically).

Text features (such as the subheadings that gave Gina's students their lists of reasons for the fall of Rome) are another way for students to unpack informational text. Such headings, graphs, illustrations, photos and captions, and highlighted vocabulary may seem to be obvious meaning markers for experienced readers, but students must be apprenticed to their usefulness. Many students

CLASSROOM CLOSE-UP 8.7
"That Looks Like a T-Chart!"

Whenever Gina Hale's diverse seventh graders start a new chapter in their history textbook, they first spend some time previewing the text and predicting what it will be about. Gina's goal is that students will become familiar not only with the helpfulness of text features such as the headings and captions that serve to highlight big ideas, but also with the markers and patterns within text that signal how information is organized.

It is the first week of school, and "The Fall of Rome" is the first chapter in the textbook. Students previewed it the previous day, and today Gina intends to introduce the idea of text structure. She begins with a question to the class:

"So, what is this chapter about?"

"The Fall of Rome!" students respond in a chorus.

"So, is it *a story* about how Rome fell, or an explanation, or . . . How is it organized?" Despite students' previewing work the previous day, they are clearly stumped. Gina reminds students that they had noticed an oddly formatted introductory paragraph the day before. "Does the introduction offer any clues about the way the chapter is organized? Read it with your partner and see what you find out."

Partners begin reading and Gina moves around the room, listening. Stopping with one pair, she points to a line in the book and asks Murad to read it again. "There were many reasons for the fall of Rome. The empire was plagued by internal and external problems, including . . ." Murad's partner Wen is excited, "So, this is about *all* the reasons!"

Murad agrees and notices that there were two kinds of reasons: internal and external.

In a class discussion, Murad and Wen share their discovery. Gina asks, "So if I wanted to take notes, make a list of the reasons, how could I start?"

"You gotta have two lists," Murad offers.

"Okay, so how should I set this up?" Gina begins writing across the top of a blank transparency: "Many reasons for the fall of Rome."

"You know, one for internal and one for external."

Gina adds columns labeled "Internal Problems" and "External Problems."

As students call out different problems, she begins to record their ideas.

"That looks like a T-chart!" Doris observes.

Gina draws in the missing lines for a T-chart. "Let's all do that," she says, "make a T-chart so we can begin organizing two lists of information as we read.

(Continued)

read right past these text markers, failing to recognize them as clues to meaning. Hani, a recent immigrant to the United States, first read past a reference to "Figure 25.16" in Chapter Twenty-Five of her high school chemistry textbook and then interpreted the phrase as a mathematics problem involving "figuring out" the relationship of the numbers 25 and 16. In Classroom Close-Up 8.8, Hani's inexperience in reading the visuals of science is a reminder of the instruction and practice many students may need to understand these particular types of text.

As skilled readers of such texts, teachers of science may take for granted that visual models in the textbook are self-explanatory. Yet few students have been explicitly taught to made sense of such visuals. Hani's misunderstandings are more common than teachers may think!

In the following example, ninth grader Rosa reads a textbook paragraph about the treatment of children in totalitarian states and immediately relates it to a photo and caption on the same page. She has been explicitly taught

Any predictions about where to find information for each list?"

"Under the subheadings!" several students suggest.

"Let's see if that works," Gina nods.

Later, students use their T-chart notes as they write their first essay: "Reasons for the Fall of Rome."

With each new chapter, students preview the text they are about to read and make predictions about the content and how the content is organized. On a class poster, they assign note-taking graphics to the different text structures and add the specific language, or signal words, that clue them into the text structure. Next to the T-chart, for example, Gina has recorded Murad and Wen's clue from the text: "There were many reasons."

For a new chapter that is structured chronologically, students organize notes around timelines and explore time-related signal words. Another chapter is organized around definitions and examples, and the class generates tree-charts and finds signal words and punctuation that signal embedded definitions or examples. For a chapter that compares two feudal empires, the class tries out Venn diagrams and identifies signal words such as similarly, in comparison, and by contrast.

Over time, students' previewing and predicting becomes more purposeful and reliable. They take more useful notes, knowing they will need them for tests and writing assignments and projects.

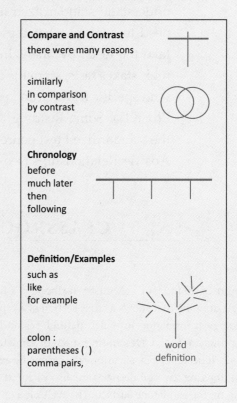

to look for the connections between text and nearby photographs and other graphics:

> (*Reading from her textbook*) "Totalitarian states such as Nazi Germany, the Soviet Union, and communist China took over complete control of children's education. Young people were often enrolled in special camps or movements such as the Hitler Youth. Children were even turned against their own parents, told to spy on them, and given an award for turning them in to the authorities."
>
> (*Stopping to look at a photograph*) The picture, I guess, has to do with that. The picture shows, it says, "Very young Soviets were taught to view Stalin as a benevolent father figure." So I guess that ties in with the reading.

To prepare her physics students to get the most out of the embedded meaning markers in their textbook, high school teacher Nicci Nunes hands out a specific text-previewing assignment along with the textbook in her course.

She asks students to investigate how different text features help to organize the text and why they might be useful to students (see Box 8.10).

Like textbooks, standardized tests are a genre with a specialized structure and conventions particular to schooling. Students benefit from explicit help to understand standardized tests as a kind of text. To build test schema, students need to explore what these tests are all about, rather than only practice and take the tests. By analyzing text passages and test items similar to those on high-stakes tests, students can take a metacognitive approach to tests as a genre with specific features and purposes that they can understand and negotiate (see Box 8.11). Some Reading Apprenticeship teachers combine an exploration of the standardized test genre with a review of students' knowledge of Question-Answer Relationships (see the discussion of QAR in Chapter Seven).

CLASSROOM CLOSE-UP 8.8
Go Figure

Figure 25.16 in Hani's chemistry textbook is a technical drawing that shows a cross-section of a typical geological formation in which natural gas and oil deposits are found. Descending strata of sandstone, shale, limestone, gas, oil, and water are pictured. In the drawing, two oil derricks are also pictured, sitting on the sandstone surface. The well pipe of one derrick reaches down into the gas deposit; the pipe of the other derrick reaches even deeper, into oil.

Hani remarked first of all that as she read her chemistry textbook, the reference to Figure 25.16 was unclear: "I thought it said *figure* something, of all these different numbers [25.16]. Now I'm not sure what it is."

When prompted to find and look at the figure, which she had ignored, Hani responded, "They're describing what they all are. Each step, like they're saying, maybe this is sandstone, or something like that."

In science, figures can display a conceptual model rather than represent a real entity, and the making of models is a key literacy skill in the discipline. Hani described the model of an oil derrick on various strata of earth in Figure 25.16 as a place she could visit: "Let's say if I got there, if I was there, in real life, whatever, I would know what it is, what the machine is, how it works, how the oil and gas, where they're at."

Building Knowledge of Language

In classrooms where students have learned to be metacognitive about their reading processes, their practice thinking about their thinking makes it natural for them to treat language as an object of thought, to be metalinguistic as well as metacognitive. With a focus on thinking about language, students learn to identify and analyze patterns in how words, sentences, paragraphs, and related paragraphs work—and then apply them. Over time, they build greater fluency with a broader range of language patterns, as well as a disposition to reflect on and analyze unfamiliar words and novel syntax. They gain greater control of academic English.

BOX 8.10

Previewing a Physics Textbook

Nicci Nunes does not assume that her high school physics students have mastered how to get the most out of their physics textbook. Early in her course, she assigns small groups to investigate the *purpose* of the various text features in their book.

1. With your group, look through Chapter Four of your physics textbook. Write a list of all the different types of things that you find. (Examples: sections, features, a picture above the title of the chapter.)

2. Discuss your list with the others in your group. Make additions if you hear something you missed.

3. With your group, read through your list again, and for each item, discuss and answer these questions:

    – Why is this part included in the book?

    – What is it useful for? (Example: The picture at the beginning of the chapter is put there to try to interest the reader in the subject as well as give the reader an idea of what he or she will be learning in the chapter.)

4. Recently I gave you a couple of reading assignments. First, I asked you to read sections 4–1 through 4–3 and to answer some questions.

    – How did you go about it? Was there anything about the way the book is organized and presented that helped you?

    – How did you read the visuals?

5. In the second assignment, I asked you to read section 4–4 and to look at the example problems.

    – How did you go about it? Was there anything about the way the book is organized and presented that helped you?

    – How did you read the visuals?

6. Thinking about everything you have discussed today, make a list of the types of things you think people should do when they are reading a physics book to help them understand the material. (Example: Whenever you see an equation, write it on a note card and make sure you know what each symbol stands for and what the equation is used for.)

7. Look over your list from step 6.

    – Which techniques will you try when you read sections 4–5 and 4–6?

    – Why did you pick those techniques?

8. What did you learn from looking at the textbook?

    – Was this activity useful?

    – Do you think it will help you read the textbook?

    – Do you think it will help you learn physics better?

BOX 8.11

Standardized Test Schema

PURPOSE

When students understand the standardized test as a genre and investigate its particular structural properties, the form becomes less threatening: they have schema for dealing with test directions, passages, and questions.

PROCEDURE

1. Pass out sample test directions, passages, and questions.

2. Work with students to surface and build their schema about standardized tests. Invite discussion of their experiences taking the tests, and help students build schema about the purpose of such tests.

3. Think Aloud to model approaching the directions and one passage and its questions.

4. Ask partners to work together on another passage and questions, using either Think Aloud or Talking to the Text.

5. Invite volunteers to describe what they did, with a focus on their process (rather than on the right answer).

6. As a class, look closely at the question and what the reader has to do to find the answer. This is a good time to review Question-Answer Relationships (see Chapter Seven).

7. Ask small groups to analyze additional test passages, questions, and answers, using QAR strategies and explaining what they needed to do to find the answers.

8. Have the class generate a test-specific Reading Strategies List: a Test-Taking Strategies List.

For the students in Cindi Davis Harris's community college developmental English class, "metalinguistics" became one of their most important vocabulary words, one they put to work in a daily routine of chunking sentences, using knowledge of word forms or morphology, and keeping records in reading journals of instances when using their metalinguistic knowledge helped them understand the text they were reading (see Classroom Close-Up 8.9).

Even charged with teaching a vocabulary course that included a predetermined list of words, Cindi Davis Harris did not view vocabulary learning as an activity focused on learning particular words. She taught students how to be word learners. The massive amounts of input needed to acquire knowledge of particular words argues against any other approach; by some research estimates it takes at least seven meaningful encounters with the same word in different contexts to learn that word. Students could never acquire the amount of vocabulary they need from explicit instruction alone. They need to learn word-learning strategies and how to acquire vocabulary during extensive reading. It

CLASSROOM CLOSE-UP 8.9
"This Word Jumped Out at Me"

Community college teacher Cindi Davis Harris saw her assignment to teach the English department's two-credit developmental vocabulary course, with its required vocabulary list, as an opportunity to teach more than a list of words. She designed a course that devotes significant class time to increasing students' linguistic and metalinguistic awareness.

Cindi modeled and asked students to use the following strategies:

Chunking. Break longer sentences and, often, words into smaller parts, and especially focus on transitional words or phrases.

Annotating (Talking to the Text). Use your knowledge of word parts (roots, suffixes, and prefixes) as one means to increase comprehension; use your knowledge of word forms and parts of speech as one means to increase comprehension.

Reading Journals. Record where you notice using your knowledge of word parts and word forms and why it matters, and also record evidence from the text that supports your hypothesis regarding the main idea of the text.

These became daily metacognitive and metalinguistic practices. In Cindi's assessment, it was this "routine" that, aside from the particular content, "caused learning."

At the end of the course, Cindi reports, "Students' final reflections seem to suggest that they are developing a deeper knowledge of their own mental process when they read, as well as developing a tool kit of problem-solving strategies for when they get stuck."

The following excerpts from Cindi's students' reflections indicate how important it is *not* to take students' language knowledge for granted. Help comes at many levels. Some students may never have realized they could break words into smaller meaningful parts:

Fatima: It is good to break up a word and think about it.

Christina: Breaking down words helped me make sense of the meanings of words better.

One student provided a concrete example of how she put her new schema about language to work:

Dawn: I found the word "longevity." This word jumped out at me. The article says, "Can sports records really continue to fall indefinitely? Records based on *longevity* certainly can." So I thought the word meant, "a long time."

is through "incidental" learning of new words from context that students gain the greatest amount of vocabulary growth, by far.

Word-learning strategies give students an important boost to their "incidental" learning of new words. Developing a Word-Learning Strategies List with students helps them to surface and share ways to approach unfamiliar vocabulary. Building such a list is an opportunity as well for students to build the habit of thinking metacognitively and metalinguistically about vocabulary. The Reading Strategies List (see Chapter Four) developed in most Reading Apprenticeship classrooms will naturally include a few word-learning strategies, which can be transferred to a Word-Learning Strategies List to get it started. Then, as students find themselves using different approaches to understanding new words, these strategies can be added to the list.

BOX 8.12

Word Detectives

When students approach unknown words *metacognitively and metalinguistically*, they become "word detectives" and ask themselves a number of questions that help them decide how to proceed:

- How well do I need to know this word to understand this text?
- Is this a word I've often seen before (in this unit, in this subject) and need to learn?
- Do I recognize any word parts that I can use to help define this word (roots, affixes)?
- Does the context provide any clues?
- Is the word followed by an example or description that can help?
- Do commas, parentheses, or dashes set off a definition?
- Is there a family of related words being used repeatedly that can orient me to the meaning?
- Does information from the dictionary make sense in this context?
- Do I know enough about this word to go on?

Teaching students to become effective word learners begins with teaching them to be "word detectives" and make judgments about the words they need to learn. Not all unfamiliar words can or should be the focus of deliberate attention, but because many students have a tendency to read past unfamiliar words, the first step is supporting students to monitor their comprehension. For example, when a group of three girls in Will Brown's Introduction to Chemistry class claim they had no problems with the text they just read, all the same, Will asks them to pick out a few words they may have "read past." The girls stall, so Will suggests the term "substantially" from the text. Because they cannot explain its use, Will advises them of the importance of being aware of choosing to read past unfamiliar words:

> Sometimes you might let words like that go, but I want you to bring that to a conscious level. I want you to make to a conscious decision whether to skip a word or not.

Once students are deliberately noticing unfamiliar words, they must decide whether a particular word seems important to understand, whether there are any morphological or textual clues they can use to figure it out, and whether, if they must resort to the dictionary, the given meaning makes sense. Box 8.12 lists the questions students can ask themselves about how or whether to persist in defining an unfamiliar word.

As word detectives, students often decide they are able to move on without arriving at a precise definition of an unfamiliar word. However, if they (or the teacher) determine that a word is a "survival word," their comprehension of the text is unlikely to survive without developing a sound definition of the word.

The approach to survival words used by academic literacy teachers Christine Cziko and her ninth-grade teaching colleagues included small-group as well as teacher identification of survival words. With a focus on survival words, students came to understand that they could comprehend a passage without understanding every word, that there were some words they simply could not afford to skip, and that in a group or the class not everyone experienced the same words as survival words, so they could help each other out.

Because word knowledge, like comprehension itself, is not an all-or-nothing proposition, Christine and her colleagues developed a graphic organizer to help students recognize that even a minimal amount of familiarity with a word may be enough if there are other clues in the surrounding context (see Box 8.13).

As discussed earlier, the schema students surface may not automatically aid comprehension and the building of new schema. Sometimes misleading or tangential schema leap to the fore. Part of students' introduction to schema should include anti-examples that highlight the importance of remaining metacognitive about using schema and asking, "Is this making sense?" (See, for example, Classroom Close-Up 8.10.)

When students identify a word as a survival word and feel that they have no idea what it means, a helpful approach to understanding it may well be to see whether they can find meaning clues within the word itself. Knowing how prefixes, suffixes, and root words combine is a powerful tool for vocabulary development.

CLASSROOM CLOSE-UP 8.10
How Did Marx Get That Skateboard?

Students in Anthony Linebaugh's grade 9 academic literacy class are preparing to read an article about the practice of cigar factory workers in the late nineteenth and early twentieth century hiring a "reader," someone they paid to read aloud to them as they worked. In addition to newspapers and popular literature, the readers read from the writings of progressive and radical thinkers of the time.

The historical and political context is unfamiliar to students, so Anthony has them talk with a partner about six "survival words" that will be important to their understanding of this long-lost custom.

Students also rate each word; for example, "I have seen the word but I don't know what it means," or "I know the word but I don't use it."

Serena and her partner are considering the word "radical." "I don't know," Serena says. Then she brightens, "With those skaters! Like 'radical dude.' Okay, I know the meaning but I don't use the word."

Serena has perfectly good teenage schema for radical, but as she reads about cigar factory workers, she will need to enlarge and then refocus it to understand radical in a context that includes Marx but not skateboarders.

BOX 8.13

Survival Words

PURPOSE

As all readers know from experience, they are often somewhat familiar with a word, even if they cannot define it specifically. Similarly, even when they do not have prior knowledge of a word, they may be able to derive its meaning from context. Rating word familiarity gets this idea across to students and helps them explore and expand their vocabularies.

PROCEDURE

- From a text students will be reading, choose several key words that may trip students up, or use a list of survival words that students have generated. The list should not exceed five or six words.
- Provide or have students create a graphic organizer, such as the sample below, that lists the survival words.
- Have students work in pairs or small groups to discuss and rate each word. Explain that students will have individual ratings, based on their individual familiarity with the word.
- Bring the class together to develop shared understandings that students will need in their reading of the assigned text.

Text: "Reign of the Reader"

Survival Word	A	B	C	D	Meaning/Information
Cuba					
Florida					
reign					
radical					
solidarity					
revolution/ revolutionary					

KEY: **A** = I've never seen the word before. **B** = I've seen the word, but I don't use it. **C** = I know the meaning, but I don't use the word. **D** = I know the meaning, and I use the word.

By having students investigate morphologically related words to identify what such words may have in common, teachers support them to recognize patterns within words and to search for meaning in the patterns they find. Box 8.14 provides examples of investigations students can undertake.[4] Not all words lend themselves to this kind of word analysis, but students should

BOX 8.14

Word Pattern Investigations

PURPOSE

"Playing" with word parts is a way for students to recognize that many unknown words have meaningful chunks that can be added up to a meaningful whole. Investigations such as those described here alert students to a first line of attack when faced with an unknown word. Morphology is hardly foolproof, but it is second only to repeated incidental exposure (as in extensive reading) for adding to students' word knowledge.

PROCEDURE

1. Create investigations that ask students to deduce the meaning of a prefix or suffix by adding it to a given set of words or roots. For example:

   Add the same word part to different words or roots. Investigate how the meaning changes.
   When you join the prefix re- to each of these words, what happens?

do	join	organize	tell

2. Challenge small groups to create and exchange similar investigations.

3. Create investigations that ask students to identify and deduce the meaning of a root from a wide set of words that all contain the root. For example:

   Investigate words with a common root and how their meanings are related.
   What might the common word part mean in the following words?

inspection	spectacle	speculate	spectrum
specter	inspector	disrespect	spectator
spectrum	inspect	spectacular	respect

4. Challenge small groups to create and exchange similar investigations.

5. Begin a class list of word affixes and roots. Ask groups to nominate word parts and their meanings based on their investigations.

6. Ask students to be on the lookout for new examples for the class list.

understand that when faced with an unfamiliar word, it's always worth looking for a familiar root or affix and, if possible, building from there.

Another word-learning strategy that should be automatic for students is that of using context. Cloze passages can be used to highlight for students the assist available from context. Teachers Christine Cziko and Lori Hurwitz created cloze passages for their academic literacy students by selecting passages from text the class was reading and omitting important words whose meaning could be gathered from the surrounding context. Their goal was to build students'

CLASSROOM CLOSE-UP 8.11

Investigating a Watery Context

Millions of years ago, marine life settled on the ocean floors and became buried in ocean sediments. Heat, pressure, and the action of bacteria changed this residue into petroleum and gas, which are two important fossil fuels.

When Matthew, a grade 11 chemistry student, read the passage above, on hydrocarbons and fossil fuels, he defined *marine*, in the first line, as "people from the army."

Once prompted, however, he ventured another idea that supported his comprehension of the passage: "I know it's another definition for it, though.

"I'm thinking, like fish, fishes and stuff. I started thinking of Marine World. And I was like, Marine World, so it had to be the fish, the fishes and stuff. Then I guess they got old and died.

"And then the fossils and stuff . . . I'm thinking they got buried up under the dirt. I guess they, as they got buried, it say heat and pressure, I guess the heat and pressure changed, changed they body."

comprehension skills generally as well as their vocabulary. Students "solved" the passages by supplying plausible terms for the missing words. By comparing their solutions with the original, students gathered confidence in their ability to use available clues to understand difficult text and the words that contribute to the challenge. Box 8.15 describes another way to use cloze passages, by supplying target vocabulary options.

Vocabulary difficulty often arises when students encounter familiar words used in unfamiliar ways. By being metacognitive, they can recognize these situations and use context to understand the intended meaning of a familiar but now troublesome word. In Classroom Close-Up 8.11, a high school chemistry student employs this kind of contextual redefinition when he realizes there's more than one way to understand "marine world."

When students are encouraged to identify "collisions" between their understanding of a word like *marine* and its appearance in a specific (in this case, scientific) context, this metalinguistic awareness can alert them to new, discipline-specific word meanings. A simple *contextual redefinition* note taker (Box 8.16) can train students to notice their metalinguistic process when such collisions occur. Matthew, for example, might document his contextual redefinition of *marine*.

Science text is loaded with common words that have different or very precise meanings in a scientific context. For example, students' everyday understanding of words like *food, carbohydrate, protein,* and *fat* will not be sufficient to understand scientific discourse about digestion.

BOX 8.15

Clozing the Gap

Cloze passages highlight for students how text hangs together. When selected words are replaced with blanks, students learn that they can use context to fill in the blanks. They experience yet another way to be text problem solvers. To focus students explicitly on vocabulary, teachers sometimes provide a set of vocabulary options for students to select from (see the example that follows). Any use of cloze passages should be accompanied by a metacognitive conversation about why certain words, concepts, or parts of speech are appropriate solutions for a given blank.

EXCERPT FROM "HOW TO MARK A BOOK," BY MORTIMER ADLER*

There are two ways in which you can own a book. The first is the _____ right you establish by paying for it, just as you pay for clothes and furniture. But this act of purchase is only the _____ to possession. Full ownership comes only when you have made it a part of yourself, and the best way to make yourself a part of it is by writing in it. An _____ may make the point clear. You buy a beefsteak and transfer it from the butcher's icebox to your own. But you do not own the beefsteak in the most important sense until you _____ it and get it into your bloodstream. I am arguing that books, too, must be _____ in your bloodstream to do you any good.

prelude	property	illustration	absorbed	consume	illusion

*Source: The Mercury Reader, Pearson Custom Publishing, 2000, p. 1.

BOX 8.16

Contextual Redefinition

When familiar words don't make sense in a particular context, students need to be able to discard or refine the meaning that doesn't make sense to figure out a different meaning that does. A *contextual redefinition* note taker can help students get into the habit of checking whether a familiar word needs a new meaning.

I saw	I Thought
(a word i can define one way but that doesn't make sense in this context)	(this word also means something different; this is what i think it means here, and why)
marine: like a soldier or army person	marine: something to do with oceans, things that live in the sea — "marine life settled on ocean floors"

Although most vocabulary learning is not the product of deliberate word instruction, there are times when teachers choose individual words to teach explicitly. Criteria for making this decision a productive one should include some of the following:[5]

- The word is a "high-frequency" or an "academic vocabulary" word and therefore highly useful to students.

- The word is important to the lesson at hand (a concept related to the theme of the lesson or unit, an important word for understanding the gist of the text, and so on).

- The word is one that students are unlikely to learn on their own (a new and difficult concept, a word for which the text does not give adequate context or explanation, or the like).

- The word is likely to be interesting to students.

- The word serves as a basis for building some kind of generative vocabulary knowledge (illustrates prefix, suffix, spelling patterns, roots, and so on, or serves as an example for word-learning strategies).

In Classroom Close-Up 8.12, grade 9 English teacher Keren Robertson has been very deliberate about choosing to teach the word "justification." Her first considerations are that the word is highly useful and conceptually significant. To give students experience hearing and using it in authentic contexts, she scaffolds their understanding in two contexts, one with a historical basis and the other in terms of literary character motivation.

Teachers often think of academic language as synonymous with difficult vocabulary, but academic texts are full of complex sentences in which multiple concepts and ideas depend on conjunctions, transition words, and other syntactic features to indicate the relationships between concepts and ideas. Without processing these relationships, students cannot understand academic language. Schema for the role of transition words and other conventions that point to relationships between parts of sentences, sentences, and paragraphs are crucial for navigating academic text. Community college teacher Cindi Davis Harris had this reinforced for her when she overheard the confusion that two of her developmental English students were having because of the word "then":

> Richard, who considered himself a strong reader in my class, and fellow student José were reading from a novel in which there are multiple time and perspective shifts. At one point Richard noticed that he was confused by these sentences, which he read aloud to José:

> "'He had no experience as a fighter or a prisoner. . . . Then he
> went to war and was captured by the Germans.'"
>
> Richard objected: "How could he say that he has no experience being
> a prisoner, then that he gets captured. So he *has* experience. That doesn't
> make sense!"
>
> Noticing the word "then" was essential to recognizing the time shift
> between the character reflecting on the moment in the present, and what
> had happened to him in the past. As I pointed it out, Richard somewhat
> sheepishly admitted, "Oh, I missed that." We had a short conversa-
> tion about how those little words matter and I shared how when some-
> thing doesn't seem right in a text, I go back and look to see if I missed a
> transitional word or phrase. For the rest of the course, he would refer to that
> conversation.

Essentially, Cindi's advice to her student Richard was to be a "sentence detective." When sentences don't fit together, missed or misunderstood text signals, such as transition words, are often to blame. Box 8.17 highlights questions that sentence detectives can ask to help sort out meaning relationships within and among sentences.

Teachers of the first cohort of Reading Apprenticeship students introduced the idea of text signals as signposts through a text, and they had students practice finding them in a variety of different texts. Students realized how much they already knew about text signals and how useful they can be. When students practiced finding and using text signals in sample passages from SAT exams, even the teachers were surprised at the number of text signals in these dense informational passages.

Gina Hale's seventh graders (who demonstrate in Classroom Close-Up 8.7 how signal words support their comprehension of text structure) created traffic signs that combined signal words and familiar signage. The words "but" and "however," for example, were represented by a stop sign and the U-turn symbol, meaning readers should stop and go the other way. As Gina notes, "The process of generating these signs for tracking the moves of informational text is at least as helpful for students as the completed and posted signs. It's the metacognitive conversation about why you need a stop sign *and* a U-turn symbol that reminds students how powerful their thinking is."

Other text signals that students often breeze past or misread are referents and their antecedents. Pronouns and other referents (such as relative clauses) are the cause of many reading confusions when students have not learned how to track down antecedents. Rather than deliver formal grammar lessons,

CLASSROOM CLOSE-UP 8.12

Justifying Focus-Word Instruction

Keren Robertson's grade 9 English students are used to their teacher's vocabulary routine. They know that whenever they deal with a focus word, it will enlarge their understanding of a key theme or other big idea in work they are doing. Today, Keren introduces the word "justification." Acknowledging that some students may have heard of it before, she begins by inviting them to use the word in a sentence. Nathan volunteers:

Nathan: The outcome of the events was justification for the means.

Teacher: Anybody want to make an educated guess what the word means?

Anna: A reason why something.

Teacher: What kind of reason? A terrible reason?

Anna: A good reason.

Teacher: A reason why it's okay. Richard.

Richard: There was no justification why Richard wasn't elected captain of his crew.

Teacher: Justification is a good reason for doing something.

Kyu: It's *not* necessarily a good reason.

Teacher: Well, a good reason in your own eyes. Kyu clarified, right? So, can I justify something with good reasons for me that aren't necessarily good reasons?

Kyu: Yes.

Having had her definition refined by Kyu, Keren relates *justification* to a documentary about the bombing of Hiroshima and Nagasaki that students are about to continue watching from the previous day (the documentary relates to students' upcoming reading in *The Martian Chronicles*, in which Earth devolves into nuclear war).

Teacher: The reason I want us to watch this last five minutes has to do with the word *justification*. They are going to have a final interview with the soldiers that were on the plane that dropped the bombs. They're going to ask them the question,

"What do you think now? Do you feel justified for what you've done?" I want you to pay attention to their answers.

When the filmed interviews end, students talk with a partner about how the men involved in dropping the atomic bombs seemed to feel about it. Then Keren opens a class discussion:

Teacher: When you think about the dropping of the bomb on Hiroshima, what did you expect the pilots to say about it?

Jen: That they had nightmares.

Teacher: Why do we expect them to say that they had nightmares?

Jen: Because it is horrendous.

Teacher: Why do we feel it's horrendous?

Jen: So many died.

Brady: Because you'd be responsible for all the deaths.

Teacher: You'd be responsible for all the deaths, or you might *feel* responsible, right?

Julia: Because we know what ended up happening later, really.

Teacher: And how do they feel now?

Julia: They don't really regret it.

Teacher: How did they justify to themselves: "No, I don't have any nightmares"?

Lauren: That they were following out orders, being obedient, doing what they were supposed to do.

Anna: They ended the war quickly, so they saved a lot more lives.

Steven: 'Cause that's what wars do, they destroy.

Teacher: Not exactly the cheeriest subject to look at, but pretty important for us to think about and to learn.

Next, Keren refers students to their reading notes from the previous night's homework in *The Martian Chronicles*. She asks partners to find

(*Continued*)

one example of someone who justified his or her destructive behavior. She then invites students to share their examples with the whole class. Nathan begins:

Nathan: Sam Parkhill says to his wife on page 135 on the bottom—

Teacher: Everyone to page 135.

Nathan: (Reading from the book) "'I'm sorry what happened,' he said. He looked at her and then away. 'You know it was purely the circumstances of Fate.'"

Teacher: What's his motivation? So what's he saying?

Nathan: It wasn't really his fault, like that it *had* to happen.

Teacher: One way that people justify their destructive behavior is thinking that what?

Tim: It was meant to be.

Sarah: Mine was similar to Nathan's, and it's on page 136 . . .

Given the important connections students are able to make, elaborate on, and apply to the concept of *justification,* the class time devoted to developing deep understanding of this focus word could likely be termed *well* justified.

BOX 8.17

Sentence Detectives

When students approach confusing sentences or groups of sentences *metacognitively* and *metalinguistically,* they become "sentence detectives." Beyond particular vocabulary that may be challenging, they look for transition words and other signals in the text that point to directions the text is taking and *relationships* between words and sentences. Questions asked by sentence detectives include the following:

- How can I use punctuation to chunk a confusing sentence?
- What are the transition words within and between sentences? Have I accounted for how they signal meaning?
- Are any specific referents unclear? If I substitute the words I think are their antecedents, do they make sense?

---

many Reading Apprenticeship teachers invite students to nominate confusing sentences or paragraphs for class investigation. Using reciprocal modeling, teachers can then work with students through the detective work that reveals who's who and what's what and how a reader can know. (Box 8.18 shows a sample passage nominated for sentence detective practice.)

Students need frequent and multiple kinds of word detective and sentence detective practice that promotes taking a metacognitive and metalinguistic

BOX 8.18

Sentence Detective Practice

PURPOSE

Students often overlook the clues that can help them solve reading confusions that arise from the relationships signaled in and among sentences. Reciprocal modeling can alert students to the kinds of clues they can employ as "sentence detectives."

PROCEDURE

1. Invite students to nominate a sentence or passage that is confusing for reasons other than vocabulary, in particular.

2. On a display that all can see, write the sentence(s) and alternate with students identifying punctuation, transition words, other signal words, and referents that are a source of confusion or illumination.

3. Facilitate discussion of students' metacognitive and metalinguistic deductions.

4. Give partners an opportunity to continue to practice being sentence detectives.

5. Bring the class back together to discuss students' ideas.

Sample Text: Preamble to the Declaration of Independence

> **We** hold **these** truths to be self evident, **that** all men are created equal, **that they** are endowed by **their** Creator with certain unalienable Rights, **that** among **these** are Life, Liberty and the pursuit of Happiness.

approach to text. Although the strategies students learn to incorporate are inherently valuable, even more valuable are students' accumulating experiences of themselves as problem solvers. As Michele Lesmeister reports, in her adult GED class, students love the power that their new knowledge of language affords them:

> A spark of energy came from the class when students "found" language structures previously studied in a new passage. One student would say, "That appositive phrase is giving us a definition," and another would chime in, "Bye-bye, dictionary, I got it by myself and from the text."

Building Knowledge of Disciplinary Discourse and Practices

As students progress through the grades, the disciplinary discourse and practices they encounter become increasingly specialized. They are expected to read and use disciplinary language in ways that are closer and closer approximations of the ways that particular academic communities use text. Yet these discipline-particular reasons to read and ways with words are rarely explicit for students. What would it mean for teachers to apprentice students to the disciplinary practices they value—the texts, tasks, reasoning practices, and motivations for working in particular ways? In academic disciplines and in virtually any area of learning, practitioners of the discipline read and reason and communicate with colleagues by speaking and writing about their work. How can teachers design students' academic experiences to support them to begin to engage in the discipline, use texts for disciplinary purposes, and learn ways of thinking, speaking, and writing about texts that reflect disciplinary practices and values?

Reasoning processes, interpretive practices, ways of engaging, and the terrain of ideas, activities, literacy tasks, texts, and genres—all vary across and within disciplinary traditions. As students encounter these new forms, purposes, and processing demands, their teachers must make visible to students how literacy operates within their particular academic disciplines. Teachers will need to demystify discipline-based literacy practices, making explicit the tacit reasoning processes, strategies, and discourse rules that shape successful readers' and writers' work in a discipline.

The inquiry stance that develops in Reading Apprenticeship classrooms can be applied specifically to engage students in the nature of a discipline: Why do people study history or science or literature or mathematics? What beliefs and values are embodied? How can these be explored, argued, tested, or proved? How is knowledge, or questions about knowledge, communicated in a disciplinary community? How does knowledge develop?

Understanding that disciplines have particular beliefs, values, and practices, students can appreciate why they might be interested in learning how a discipline works. Understanding that members of a disciplinary community have developed particular strategies to explore and test those beliefs, students can appreciate these as tools that improve their success. Knowing that disciplinary texts take a range of particular forms, students can identify and use those forms to organize their thinking as literate members of a disciplinary community.

The tasks students engage in while reading course materials shape their understanding and appreciation of the discipline they are learning. When teachers regularly ask students to answer questions at the end of a chapter from a textbook in history, students learn that history is a body of information about particular people and events, rather than an interpretive effort to build a continually evolving understanding of the past. In science, depending on the tasks students are assigned, they may learn that science is a body of already established knowledge rather than an ongoing process of gathering and inter-preting evidence to explain the natural and designed or technical worlds. When teachers play the movie version of a piece of literature without engag-ing students in reading the literary language, students learn that literary study is about getting the plot of a story rather than understanding the artful con-struction and aesthetic impact of literary texts. And when teachers limit their use of math texts to problem sets for students to work, students learn that math is about fluent computation and algorithms. They are unlikely to gain an appreciation of the broader enterprise of mathematics as a conceptual sys-tem with internal consistency and rules of reasoning, nor of its utility in the world for identifying patterns, modeling complex interactions, and providing insight or predictions.

The tasks that teachers ask students to do with disciplinary texts there-fore should be focused to help students uncover and engage in disciplinary practices and ways of communicating. Some texts may be especially well suited for one disciplinary purpose but not another, so in addition to the deep knowledge teachers need about the content of a text, they need to understand how to scaffold students' understanding of a text's features as discipline-based communication.

To help students recognize their progress in learning about disciplinary practices and discourse, teachers can orient them to goals designed to make explicit how the disciplinary community carries out and communicates about its academic work. Such goals give students a way to reflect on what they are learning and to monitor their apprenticeship. In the following section of this chapter (and in the Assessment Appendix), we include examples of such goals and what they may look like in practice.

Reading Apprenticeship Goals in Science

Michael Kelcher, who teaches chemistry in community college, considered his instructional approach typical: to lecture. And he wasn't happy about it. Not only were his students missing out on the inquiry stance that defines the discipline of science, but they also weren't learning the core content in their textbook:

> I had been teaching for a long time doing what most of us do—stand and lecture. I was getting the same results over and over. Really strong students can survive, but many students were not learning. I told my stu-dents, "You guys are going to need to read the textbook. We're not doing lecture anymore."
>
> Students look at us as wizards who are able to digest information and spit it back to them in an easily digestible way. I try to tell them that nobody can do that—it requires significant effort on their part.

> So I started modeling Think Aloud, Talking to the Text, various
> things to get students to be more active readers, to think about what
> they're thinking about when they're reading, or why they aren't under-
> standing. Are they asking questions? Developing expectations? Are they
> giving themselves enough time? I want them to become better aware of
> what it is that they are reading—you don't read a chemistry text the way
> you read a novel.

Michael's new self-defined job description is to apprentice his students to the discipline of science, not lecture to them *about* science. Ideally, Michael's chemistry students learn the role of inquiry and monitoring conceptual change in testing and advancing science ideas. They encounter multiple and varied print and electronic texts ranging from traditional, encyclopedic textbooks to trade journals and science reports, numerical equations, visual and physical models of atoms and molecules, and conventional systems for denoting chemical bonding such as Lewis dot structures, chemical equations, and drawings of atomic structures. Even laboratory equipment and the phenomena explored in the lab require reading and interpretation. In such a classroom environment, inexperienced academic readers are apprenticed, over time and in multiple ways, to the literacy practices of science and to the reasoning processes that support and sustain science inquiry.

These experiences and processes can be stated in terms of student goals for building knowledge about science (see Box 8.19).

BOX 8.19

Student Goals: Building Knowledge of the Discipline of Science

In a science classroom, students learn about the discipline of science and themselves as readers, users, and consumers of science by way of the following discipline-specific goals.

SCIENTIFIC DOCUMENTS

I know how to read and/or represent scientific content and ideas in diverse scientific documents: reports, data tables and graphs, illustrations and other visuals, equations, textbooks, and models.

SCIENTIFIC TEXT

I know to look for the predictable ways science text is structured: classification and definition, structure and function, process and interaction, claim and evidence, and procedure.

I know that visuals and numerical representations are particularly powerful ways to convey complex scientific text and ideas.

(Continued)

Because I know that science text is often tightly packed with new terms and ideas, I preview and reread it, and I chunk and restate the chunks in familiar language to keep track of the gist as I read.

Because science textbooks often use passive voice, I know to restate sentences in active voice to keep track of the subject and action.

Because science textbooks often use complex sentence constructions, I know to find the logical connecting words between ideas.

SCIENTIFIC LANGUAGE

I know that when familiar terms are used in unfamiliar ways, I can redefine them in context to clear up confusion.

I know that using scientific names and labels is a shortcut for communicating precisely about scientific processes and structures.

SCIENTIFIC SOURCING

I source a science document, set of data, or piece of evidence as a step in evaluating its authority or reliability.

SCIENTIFIC INQUIRY

Knowing that scientific inquiry involves cycles of questioning, making observations, and explaining and evaluating observations helps me read science investigations and describe my own.

SCIENTIFIC EVIDENCE

I know that scientific claims must be supported by evidence that is carefully collected, evaluated, and reported so that others can judge its value.

SCIENTIFIC EXPLANATION

I can write a scientific explanation that makes a claim about observations of the natural world and convincingly defends the claim with evidence.

SCIENTIFIC CORROBORATION

I know that corroborating findings in science is a way to find out how likely they are to be true.

SCIENTIFIC UNDERSTANDING

I know that for scientific understanding to evolve, science moves forward using best evidence and information, even though these may be proved incomplete or wrong in the future.

CONCEPTUAL CHANGE

I monitor my schema to decide whether compelling evidence about scientific claims changes my personal understanding of the natural world.

SCIENTIFIC IDENTITY

I am aware of my evolving identity as a reader, user, and consumer of science.

Reading Apprenticeship Goals in History

Gayle Cribb invites her high school history students into her disciplinary community by providing the literacy support that makes it possible not only to read history texts but also to "do history":

> We solve problems of unfamiliar vocabulary or vocabulary used in unfamiliar ways, syntax uncommon in our contemporary context, references we do not yet know, and our own interest, motivation, and stamina. Historical conversations about point of view, the occasion and purpose of documents, the reliability of sources, historical context, and causality and historiography flow out of this work. As students engage documents, their questions emerge. They notice contradictions, bump into their own sets of moral standards, revisit other texts, wonder about implications for today's world, and develop historical empathy. Deeper issues and thinking seem to emerge naturally from these text-based conversations. It's almost as if, when students get close enough to history, they are able to think historically.

Gayle's students take on the work of reading history as disciplinary apprentices. They are apprenticing to the texts, tasks, reasoning practices, and motivations for working in the particular ways of historians.

The processes of apprenticing students into the discipline of history are represented in Box 8.20, a set of student goals for building disciplinary knowledge.

In Classroom Close-Up 8.13, from Gayle Cribb's mainstream history class, students—including her special needs students—employ several of the student goals for "Building Knowledge of the Discipline of History": they understand the nature of a primary source document, use historical schema to consider how language may change over time, and use historical contextualization to understand a particular workplace during the Industrial Revolution.

CLASSROOM CLOSE-UP 8.13

Historians All

Gayle Cribb has several English learners and special needs students in her mainstream high school U.S. history class. Here she describes a discussion of a primary source from the Industrial Revolution in which three of these "special" students—Ineko, Harry, and Austin—enable the others to learn from them—socially, cognitively, and as disciplinary thinkers:

"We were studying various vignettes from workplaces of the time, and one was a sweatshop.

Groups had a paragraph, and they were Talking to the Text and trying to work it out. There was a phrase 'a stint of work on the sewing machine.' So one of the big questions was what was a 'stint.' Somebody thought it meant time because of this, this, and this context clue. Ineko, a Japanese exchange student, had looked it up [on her electronic translator] and said it was a unit of time.

(*Continued* on page 279)

BOX 8.20

Student Goals: Building Knowledge of the Discipline of History*

In a history classroom, students learn about the discipline of history and themselves as readers of and actors in history by way of the following discipline-specific goals.

HISTORICAL DOCUMENTS AND ARTIFACTS

I know how to identify and use diverse types of historical documents and artifacts.

PRIMARY AND SECONDARY SOURCES

I know the differences between primary sources and secondary sources.

DOCUMENT SOURCING

I "source" a document or account to evaluate its credibility and point of view by identifying who wrote it, when, why, and for what audience.

DOCUMENT CORROBORATION

I compare documents or accounts to look for evidence that what is written is credible and to find other points of view or perspectives.

CHRONOLOGICAL THINKING

I know how to order events and assess their duration and relationships in time.

HISTORICAL SCHEMA

I actively work to build my schema about particular times and places and how they differ—the geography, people, customs, values, religions, beliefs, languages, technologies, and roles of men, women, children, and minority groups.

HISTORICAL CONTEXTUALIZATION

I use my historical schema to understand what it was like in times and places that I cannot personally experience.

HISTORICAL CAUSE AND EFFECT

I use my understanding of cause and effect to identify historical relationships and impacts.

HISTORICAL RECORD AND INTERPRETATION

I understand that history is a combination of what can be observed, how it is observed, what can be interpreted, and how it is interpreted.

HISTORICAL IDENTITY

I am aware of my evolving identity as a reader of and actor in history.

*The 1995 Bradley Commission on History in Schools and the work of educational psychologist Sam Wineburg have been important influences on these disciplinary goals.

(*Continuation* of Close-Up 8.13)

"Another student pointed at her and burst out, 'You can't use electronic devices in the classroom. That's against the school rules. That's not fair.' So then we took that on and talked about it. We talked about differences—differences in need—and what was it like for Ineko to read the textbook every day. She was writing Japanese characters above practically every word. What did it mean for her to read something in English? Was this a fair tool, and was it unfair to them? What would be an equivalent tool they could use?

"We looked in the dictionary. The definition was similar, about a measurement of time.

"Someone said, 'Well, I thought it was a pile of clothes.' So we talked about whether that was a possibility and asked did it make sense in context. And then Harry [a student who rebuilt a Model T that he drives and who knows all about farm machinery from the nineteenth century] said, 'When was that dictionary written?' So we checked the copyright. Then he said, 'That's how we use it now, but that might not be

what it means in 1900, when this is from. It changes, how people use words over time.'

"Then each group talked about which was the *best* definition, given all of that. They each were to write an individual position—it means this because of that. Several students wanted to know, 'But what's the right answer?' I said, 'There isn't a right answer. All of this thinking is really good thinking, and you have to decide for yourself which you think is the best definition for this piece.'

"At that point Austin [a student who initially believed he would fail in a college prep history class due to his learning differences] said, 'I actually think it's both, and the reason is a pile of clothes takes time to do the work on, and so actually a pile of clothes is a measurement of time.' Everybody went, 'Oh, yeah . . . !'

"Afterwards, I thought, elements of that discussion were very disciplinary. If a group of history graduate students were talking about that primary source, they could have had the same conversation about the word 'stint.'"

Reading Apprenticeship Goals in Literature

In April Oliver's high school AP Literature and Composition classroom, students read to understand the art, craft, and varied purposes of literature.

As April's students discuss the novel *Invisible Man* (Classroom Close-Up 8.14), they demonstrate many of the practices of literary readers. They recognize and discuss literary themes, conceptualize literature as commentary, attend to (but don't fully understand) the narrative voice and its relationship to the authorial voice, and participate in literary inquiry by making evidence-based inferences and interpretations and responding to those of their classmates.

The literary practices demonstrated by April's students are among those described as disciplinary student goals for apprenticeship into the literary community in Box 8.21.

BOX 8.21

Student Goals: Building Knowledge of the Discipline of Literature

In a literature classroom, students learn about the discipline of literature and themselves as readers and writers of literary forms by way of the following discipline-specific goals.

LITERARY GENRES

I can identify and use diverse literary genres and subgenres. I use my knowledge of genres and subgenres to predict how ideas are organized.

LITERARY THEMES

I recognize universal literary themes—such as good versus evil, ideal versus flawed behavior, and psychological growth and change—and how to trace their development.

LITERARY STRUCTURES

I understand how different literary structures—such as plot, stanza, and act—organize and contribute to the meaning of a piece of literature.

LITERARY COMMENTARY

I recognize how literature may incorporate or promote social, historical, economic, political, and cultural commentary, either transparently or through figuration such as irony, allegory, and symbolism.

LITERARY MOVEMENTS

I can identify how a piece of literature is affected by literary movements such as transcendentalism, romanticism, realism, and feminism.

NARRATIVE VOICE

I understand narrative voice (first-person, third-person, third-person omniscient, unreliable narrator) and authorial voice, including relationships between author and narrator.

LANGUAGE CHOICES

I can identify and use imagery, tone, dialogue, rhythm, and syntax to shape meaning.

LITERARY INQUIRY

I understand that literature invites inference and interpretation within and across texts and experiences. I offer and also consider others' evidence-based inferences and interpretations.

LITERARY IDENTITY

I am aware of my evolving identity as a reader and writer of literary forms.

CLASSROOM CLOSE-UP 8.14
"There Is Always a Deeper Meaning"

Students in April Oliver's grade 12 AP Literature and Composition class are reading Ralph Ellison's 1953 novel *Invisible Man*. For homework, they have read an article conceptualizing six aspects of alienation. In small groups assigned to different chapters of the novel, students are now discussing quotes from their chapter that illustrate concepts about alienation and how the narrator is changing or growing. They are also generating questions to use when they disperse to new groups, where each member of the new group will be an "expert" on a different chapter and will lead the discussion of that chapter.

In the following excerpt from one group's discussion of Chapter Eight, students are being deliberately apprenticed into a disciplinary community that knows how to read and discuss literature by citing evidence, incorporating ideas such as alienation and individual responsibility into consideration of theme and character development, and exploring various roles of the novel, including as social and cultural commentary and "lessons" to live by.

Steve: On page 164, a quarter of the way down, "Of course you couldn't speak that way in the South. The white folks wouldn't like it, and the Negroes would say that you were putting on. But here in the North I would slough off my southern ways of speech. Indeed, I would have one way of speaking in the North and another in the South." So this goes into like how he changes himself, to put it in terms of the article, he socially and culturally estranges himself and is thus alienated. 'Cause he changes his speech.

Christopher: It's like he is culturally estranged.

Julia: And socially.

Christopher: He's pretty smart, I think. His like language and stuff.

Julia: He's not unintelligent.

Steve: He's very unintelligent.

Christopher: You think he's unintelligent?

Julia: I think he's kind of naïve, but I don't think he's unintelligent.

Christopher: Intelligent, but naïve. Kind of drives me nuts.

Julia: But it's kind of hard to blame him, too. He gets so much conflicting advice.

Christopher: Yeah.

Steve: I have no pity for him, though, 'cause he has no sense of self.

Julia: That's something I wrote down, too. He calls himself "invisible man" but doesn't do anything about it. It's pretty clear he doesn't appreciate [being invisible], but he doesn't do anything about it.

Christopher: It's kind of weird to think about, like why?

Julia: So a discussion question could be like, Why doesn't he do anything about his invisibility?

Christopher: So, do you guys think this book is more about society, or just him, or like blacks or something in this time period?

Maribel: I think it's supposed to be about society. That is why we are reading it in English. There's supposed to be a larger message.

Julia: I think that is an interesting question, though. Because even though it is supposed to be a commentary about society, he's very egocentric, for lack of a better word. He talks about himself and his own invisibility a lot, but he doesn't really

(Continued)

seem to talk about if anybody else feels like that or if anybody else has the same situation.

Students return to scanning the text.

Maribel: On page 170 he says, "My doubts grew. Perhaps all was not well. I remained in my room all the next day. I grew conscious that I was afraid; more afraid here in my room than I had ever been in the South." He's like just sitting in his room scared of what's going to happen next. He's almost like a kid, you know.

Julia: That could be part of the commentary, though, that the black people can't properly be themselves and they're always confined to this childish behavior or whatnot because society has alienated them.

Steve: No, 'cause if you look at the other people, like Bledsoe, who's in a position of power, and he's black, so I don't think it's that.

Julia: Yeah, that's true.

Maribel: We need more discussion questions.

Christopher: Well, I kind of wrote down the questions we had, like, Why is he such a self-estranged dude?

Julia: Is it really the narrator *being* estranged, or is he estranging himself?

Christopher: Is it just me or is most of the books we read here supposed to teach us psychologically or something? I feel like each one has to sort of be like lessons.

Maribel: There is always a deeper meaning.

Reading Apprenticeship Goals in Mathematics

Tim Jones teaches high school algebra and precalculus. He is acutely aware of how literacy interacts with mathematics, and he takes responsibility for helping his students see it as well:

> As the person trying to get students to comprehend a math textbook better, I really have to be a specialist in coming up with strategies to help them address those issues, and then encouraging them to think about how they think about reading and get inside their own heads when they read a textbook. How do they have to switch if they're looking at a history book or a science book? How does that change? And making them aware that when you go to a math textbook, there are some subtle differences and some very large differences in how they have to approach the way they're reading.

Student goals for building knowledge about the discipline of mathematics identify what some of those dispositions look like to a mathematics apprentice reading and doing math (see Box 8.22).

For a perspective on the discipline of mathematics as practiced by some relatively young mathematicians, Dorothea Jordan and her grade 7 pre-algebra class illustrate a number of disciplinary goals, which are represented in Classroom Close-up 8.15.

BOX 8.22

Student Goals: Building Knowledge of the Discipline of Mathematics

In a mathematics classroom, students learn about the discipline of mathematics and themselves as readers and users of mathematics by way of the following discipline-specific goals.

CONCEPTUAL CATEGORIES*

I can identify the purpose for and use different areas of math knowledge such as number, algebra, functions, geometry, statistics and probability, and modeling.

MATHEMATICAL REASONING

I can think interchangeably about a math problem in abstract and quantitative terms. I monitor the reasonableness of the relationship between my abstract and quantitative thinking.

MATHEMATICAL REPRESENTATION

I can read and represent mathematics with words, formulas, and mathematical symbols. I can read and create diagrams, tables, graphs, and flowcharts for mathematical purposes.

MATHEMATICAL LANGUAGE

I understand the precise nature of mathematical language and use it to communicate exactly.

PROBLEM IDENTIFICATION

I can read and identify "the problem" in a math problem.

PROBLEM SOLVING

I make conjectures about and evaluate alternative approaches to a problem and then monitor the reasonableness of a solution approach as it proceeds.

ACCURACY

I understand that in mathematics there may be alternate approaches to a solution, but only one correct answer. I check that the final solution makes sense and all computation is correct.

PATTERN APPLICATION

I look for mathematical structures, approaches, and patterns that I can apply to the solution of new problems.

MATHEMATICAL IDENTITY

I am aware of my evolving identity as a reader and user of mathematics.

*These conceptual categories are drawn from the Common Core State Standards for Mathematical Practice.

CLASSROOM CLOSE-UP 8.15

A Sampling of Mathematics Disciplinary Goals in Pre-Algebra

The majority of Dorothea Jordan's grade 7 transitional mainstream pre-algebra students scored at the "intervention" level on a grade-level math readiness test. Dorothea is firmly convinced that reading is central to students' success in math: "There is a big initiative that all eighth graders will have algebra because algebra is the gatekeeper to success in college. And what I'm finding is that the gatekeeper to success in algebra is literacy."

From classroom observations and interviews with Dorothea, the following sampling of student goals in mathematics can be anchored to students' experience.

Mathematical Representation: Dorothea worked explicitly on academic literacy, helping her students navigate the many texts they encountered in the class. In addition to textbook word problems, students read lengthy supplemental multistep word problems, instructions, rubrics, and computer text, as well as graphs, charts, numerals, and algebraic symbols.

Talking to the Text, which Dorothy modified to include drawing and visual note taking, became an automatic classroom practice. However, knowing what to pay attention to in a word problem before reading it all the way through can be tricky (see the Problem Identification paragraph that follows).

Mathematical Language: In the first weeks of school, Dorothea frequently drew students' attention to the language of math, guiding them in translating conversational English into academic math language and urging greater specificity and precision in students' use of language: "Let's put that in math language. The number of eggs is *unknown*." When her student Chris offered, "Positive is always higher than negative," Dorothea used the phrase "Positive always has higher *value* on the number line." Chris later used parallel language to express a new idea, "Negative always has a lower *value*."

Mathematical Reasoning: Many of Dorothea's students brought with them a view developed from years of too many math worksheets that math is a meaningless, for-school activity. In challenging this view, Dorothea made it a point to bring the real world, and students' experience of it, into the classroom to support understanding. For example, while working on a multistep word problem involving the diameters of a soccer ball and a Ping-Pong ball, she brought a real soccer ball and Ping-Pong ball into the classroom, musing to students, "Why would I want to have a real soccer ball? So it could be another tool, just looking at it."

She elaborated on her reasoning during an interview: "Theoretically these students did not need the props to solve the problem. But one of the goals of doing math is mental math and predicting what the answer will be. If you can't predict what that answer will be, you have no way of monitoring your answer."

In promoting the reciprocity of concrete and abstract thinking, bringing in real balls conveyed the message that math should make sense. Internalizing this message, one of Dorothea's students went to the store the night after the comparative diameters lesson. The next morning Sal brought in his research on the diameter of soccer balls. Using mathematical language, Dorothea thanked him for his *independent confirmation* of their solution.

Problem Identification: Dorothea's students never read mathematics problems without Talking to the Text to identify the key math words and symbols they need to understand in solving the problem. She learned, however, to modify this routine to fit the structure of word problems, which often must be read all the way through before the actual problem begins to take shape. Rene, for example, had marked the phrase *quite a while* on a first read-through of a problem, expecting that it would be important, but later noted that it had not been necessary for solving the problem. After a number of similar incidents, Dorothea concluded that in mathematics reading, students need a complete first read-through of a problem before going back to reread, mark the text, and identify the particular problem to be solved.

Pattern Application: Dorothea noted a tendency for students to attribute success in math to luck or cleverness rather than to knowledge or skill. It was in the context of games that she began to chip away at the mystery of math, thinking aloud about her own decision making, and requiring students to explain the reasoning behind their moves: "Was that a good move? Why?" "Now why did you pick that one? How does that help you?" In addition, Dorothea challenged students to become metacognitive about the implicit theories behind their decisions: "See if you can find a general rule."

Apprenticeship into a Technical Community

As students move closer to professional participation in a career or technical community, apprenticeship can include on-the-job as well as classroom experiences. Pam Williams-Butterfield's nursing assistant students combine reading about professional practices with "doing" nursing. Students concurrently learn on the job and read about their job. As apprentice members of the nursing community, when they read about the treatment of arthritis, for example, they can interrogate the practices they have seen in nursing homes relative to the treatment described in their texts, and vice versa. Classroom Close-Up 8.16 shows a group of nursing assistant students supporting each other in understanding what they have seen practiced in light of the relevant disciplinary text they have been assigned to read.

CLASSROOM CLOSE-UP 8.16

"I Was Making the Connection to the Lady in the Nursing Home"

In a previous class, Pam Williams-Butterfield's nursing assistant students have read about the use of passive-range-of-motion exercises for use with patients who cannot move their joints independently. Today students are reading about arthritis. Partners have discussed the notes they each recorded in metacognitive logs while reading the assignment, and they are now bringing their ideas to a small group.

In a brief visit to one group, we see students mobilize schema from earlier reading and experience, question each other, support each other, read closely to clarify points of confusion, and build on each other's ideas.

Annette: This lady right here *(points to Figure 41–6),* that's what I was talking about, how I was making the connection to the lady in the nursing home. Yeah, her body was just like that, in a fetal position, and that's exactly what happened to her.

So me and Angie were talking about how if they would have performed passive range of motion, maybe she wouldn't end up like that. But then we were reading here that it says you're supposed to immobilize the joint—you can use splints or braces—and that arthritis causes a lot of pain.

So with all of those, it would be kind of hard to perform passive range of motion, because if you have to immobilize it, that means you can't move it, and if you were wearing braces or splints, then you really can't move it.

Gail: No, wait, where does it say that you should immobilize it?

Annette: Under "Treatment." "Joint immobilization where there is pain."

Gail: I just know with arthritis there's a lot of pain, but if you don't use 'em, they get stiffer and worse. So I don't know, it sort of seems like a double-edge sword, huh?

Annette: Exactly. That's what I was trying to say.

Illiana: It says, "Exercise of arthritic joints in warm water—"

Gail: That would be good.

Illiana: Yeah, I think is going to help. *(Reads another bullet)* "Prevention of deformity of contractures." So how you can prevent deformities of contraction? Just doing this: "Exercise arthritic joints in warm water"?

(Continued)

Gail: I think exercising when you can.

Illiana: (Referring to earlier bullet) So how you "Use splints and braces to enable the patient to get the most range of motion"? Do you have any idea? I know when you use splints and braces, you keep the body in the same position. You don't perform any range of motion.

Annette: Yeah, that's what I was thinking. Everything it says to do to prevent it contradicts on the other side. So that's like what we were saying, the double-edged sword.

Illiana: Just like this one, "Medication to relieve pain and reduce the inflammation."

Gail: I think that's a big part of it, medications. And then doing as much as you can—

Illiana: Yeah. When you reduce inflammation, I think you can exercise.

Gail: More.

Carla: It says, "Balance of rest *and* exercise." You've got to try to balance it out.

Pam's nursing students will be admitted to the nursing community depending on their performance in relation to the standards of their chosen profession. Their goals, as student apprentices, are to build specific knowledge through professional discourse and to adopt the practices that define the nursing community. They need to be able to read a range of technical text and to adopt professional practices, much as they demonstrated in Classroom Close-Up 8.16—reading to understand and gain disciplinary knowledge, selecting treatment approaches based on a patient's condition, and questioning practices that appear to ignore a patient's condition. Pam's students have become agents of their own learning and have internalized an inquiry stance that will serve them and their patients well.

■ ■ ■

Not only in the preceding pages focused on disciplinary literacy, but throughout this book, teachers have demonstrated the myriad ways they apprentice their students to reading disciplinary texts and taking up the dispositions and practices of a disciplinary community. In all instances, these teachers have built disciplinary learning on the trust and confidence established through consistent attention to the social and personal dimensions of classroom life. These are classrooms in which the focus on metacognitive conversation has introduced all students to their capacity for engaged academic literacy and a new perspective on what it means to learn.

Notes

1. Ogle, D. M. (1986). A teaching model that develops active reading of expository text. *Reading Teacher, 39*, 564–570.

2. Give One, Get One was developed by Kate Kinsella, initially for use with English learners in college classrooms.

3. Nancy Ybarra created an informative website describing her use of Reading Apprenticeship practices as they relate to four participation structures in her class: sharing personal reading (book talk), individual work, small groups, and class discussion. See http://www.cfkeep .org/html/snapshot.php?id=68198986880667

4. See Bear, D., Invernizzi, M., Templeton, S., & Johnston, F. (2012). *Words their way: Word study for phonics, vocabulary, and spelling instruction* (5th ed.). Upper Saddle River, NJ: Pearson.

5. These criteria were developed by reading researcher and vocabulary expert William Nagy.

Collaborating Beyond the Classroom

IN THESE PAGES, we have shared an approach to academic literacy development that has the potential to reengage secondary and college students as readers and learners—to develop their strategic reading repertoire and control of reading comprehension, and to give all students access to academic texts and literacy practices across the disciplines. We have described the ways many teachers bring this approach to life in their individual classrooms.

The experiences of these teachers and their students highlight the potential of Reading Apprenticeship to turn the tables on instruction-as-usual, putting students in charge of their reading, their learning, and, by extension, their futures. But we are also well aware that a host of complex issues affects how well and how eagerly students read, and teachers' own sense of their capacity to work with students' real needs and diverse abilities. We have focused this book on the work teachers can do, and have done, in their own classrooms to provide differentiated support for students' literacy growth, subject-area learning, and academic identity development.

In addition to the efforts made by individual teachers, collaborative efforts at various professional and community levels are needed to meet students' disparate literacy needs. Our own experience collaborating with teachers to develop and refine Reading Apprenticeship (through the Strategic Literacy Initiative at WestEd) reminds us that communities and networks can have exponentially more effect than can their individual members. As part of this Reading Apprenticeship professional community, we continue to learn from the experiences of educators who are creating school-wide and campus-wide initiatives to help sustain their individual efforts. Many of these colleagues, in concert with others, have also reached into their wider communities for political and material support on behalf of the wide range of students served by their institutions.

In schools, districts, and community colleges around the nation, teachers, administrators, literacy leaders, and community members are taking the following collaborative actions to support the needs of all students within their school communities:

- Integrating Reading Apprenticeship into the academic curriculum across disciplines and grade levels

- Embedding Reading Apprenticeship into professional learning communities and faculty inquiry groups focused on building and sharing models of successful teaching school-wide and campus-wide

- Creating literacy leadership groups focused on analyzing student outcome data and identifying needed areas of support for teachers and students alike

- Developing integrated approaches to support populations of students with particular needs by working across departments within school and campus settings

- Providing additional time and resources for students who need the most help (in secondary schools, this may mean an extended school year or voluntary before- or after-school literacy support; in college communities, this could mean coordinating with the instructional support center staff)

- Investigating "acceleration" alternatives for restructuring the content and duration of remedial, or developmental, literacy programs at the community college level

- Offering transitional courses in Reading Apprenticeship, like the *Reading Apprenticeship Academic Literacy Course,* at key educational junctures—entry to middle school, entry to high school, bridge to college

- Maintaining well-stocked classroom and campus libraries that offer students reading choices linked to the curriculum, including various genres and levels of difficulty

- Reaching out to the wider community to create understanding of and support for educational practices and opportunities that contribute to a more equitable society

Developing and sustaining such support for Reading Apprenticeship is the topic of a companion volume to this book—*Reading Apprenticeship Leaders' Guide: Transforming Disciplinary Teaching and Learning in Schools and Colleges.* In it, we describe our model of inquiry-based professional development and offer descriptions and resources for key professional inquiries designed to build teachers' insights into disciplinary literacy practices, instructional strategies and routines, and students' literacy learning capacities and needs. In addition, drawing on the work of communities of educators across the country, we offer examples of Reading Apprenticeship embedded in and adapted to various school-, district-, college-, and other system-wide contexts. We share resources for building and sustaining professional communities around this work, and the experiences of administrators, literacy leaders, and teams of teachers who have come together to support all of their students' literacy growth.

Our website (www.wested.org/readingapprenticeship) is another resource for teachers and administrators. It offers publications, news, a discussion of Reading Apprenticeship in relation to the Common Core State Standards, and reports about our research studies, as well as a point of communication with us and with the many communities of teachers engaged in Reading Apprenticeship.

We invite you to join with us in the work of preparing students to become more confident and critical readers and thinkers—and, in the process, engaged and lifelong learners.

Assessment Appendix

Interests and Reading Survey

Student Learning Goals

How to Use Student Learning Goals

Student Learning Goals: Science

Student Learning Goals: History

Student Learning Goals: Literature

Student Learning Goals: Mathematics

Monitoring and Assessing Student Work

Monitoring Participation and Contribution to Classroom Learning

Assessing Student Growth

Curriculum-Embedded Reading Assessment (CERA) Guidance and Tools

Guidelines for Administering the CERA

CERA Lesson Plan and Rubric

Sustained Silent Reading+ (SSR+) Assessment Guidance and Tools

Monitoring and Assessing SSR+

Grading SSR+

Tools for Students

What Does a Reading Apprenticeship Classroom Look Like?

Interests and Reading Survey

Part 1: Getting to Know Each Other

1. What is your favorite subject in school? _____

2. What is your favorite pastime or hobby? _____

3. What obligations do you have besides school?

   ☐ Work   If so, how many hours per week? Where _____

   ☐ Sports   If so, what sports? _____

   ☐ Music   If so, what? _____

   ☐ Family (taking care of siblings, chores, etc.) If so, what? _____

   ☐ Community/School Activities If so, please list:

4. What are your talents? Sports? Music? Drawing? Interacting with others? Making friends? Studying? Reading? Other (describe)? Please list:

   _____

5. What is a possible career or occupation you are considering pursuing after completing your education?

6. What kind of writing do you do besides school writing? Letters? Poetry? Notes to people? Journal writing? Email? Other (describe)? What is your favorite kind of writing? Please list:

   _____

7. What is your favorite movie? _____

8. What type of music do you like best? _____

9. Name one of your favorite musicians/musical groups: _____

10. Do you have a favorite poet?   ☐ Yes   ☐ No

    If yes, please tell me who: _____

Part 2: Getting to Know Each Other as Readers

11. How many books are there in your home?

    ☐ 0–10 ☐ More than 10 ☐ More than 25 ☐ More than 50
    ☐ More than 100

12. How many books do you own?

    ☐ 0–10 ☐ More than 10 ☐ More than 25 ☐ More than 50
    ☐ More than 100

13. Does your family get a newspaper regularly? _____

    If yes, what is the name of the newspaper? _____

14. Does your family get any magazines regularly? _____

    If yes, which magazines? _____

15. Is there a computer in your home?   ☐ Yes   ☐ No

    If yes, who uses the computer most often? _____
    For what? (Check *all* the ones that are true)

    ☐ Internet browsing   ☐ email   ☐ business   ☐ school work
    ☐ games   ☐ other (explain) _____

16. Does your family read in a language other than English?   ☐ Yes   ☐ No

    If so, which language(s)? _____

17. Who reads a lot in your home? _____

    What do they read? _____

18. What are some different reasons people read? _____

19. What does someone have to do to be a good reader? (Check only the three
    most important ones.)

    ☐ read aloud well   ☐ read with expression
    ☐ understand what they read   ☐ concentrate on the reading
    ☐ read a lot   ☐ read harder books
    ☐ pronounce all the words correctly ☐ know the meaning of most
    ☐ know when they are having   of the words
       trouble understanding   ☐ use strategies to improve their
    ☐ read different kinds of books   understanding
    ☐ read fast   ☐ other _____
    ☐ enjoy reading

20. Do you think you are a good reader?   ☐ Yes   ☐ No   ☐ It depends

    Explain why:

21. Do you think reading will be important to your future?   ☐ Yes   ☐ No

    Explain why:

22. From what you can remember, learning to read was

    ☐ very easy for you   ☐ easy for you   ☐ hard for you
    ☐ very hard for you

23. Do you read in a language other than English?

    If yes, which language(s)? _____

    In which language do you read best? _____

24. What do you usually do when you read? (Check *all* that describe what you do.)

    □ I read silently.

    □ I look over what I'm going to read first to get an idea of what it is about.

    □ I try to pronounce all the words correctly.

    □ I get distracted a lot while I'm reading.

    □ I ask myself questions about what I'm reading.

    □ I have trouble remembering what I read.

    □ I try to get the reading over with as fast as I can.

    □ I read a section again if I don't understand it at first.

    □ I try to concentrate on the reading.

    □ I try to figure out the meaning of words I don't know.

    □ I read aloud to myself in a quiet voice.

    □ I look up words I don't know in the dictionary.

    □ I picture what is happening in the reading.

    □ I try to read with expression.

    □ I put what I'm reading into my own words.

    □ I try to understand what I read.

    □ I try to read smoothly.

    □ I think about things I know that connect to the reading.

25. What is the best way for you to read?

    □ read silently to myself

    □ read aloud by myself or with a partner

    □ listen to the teacher read in class

    □ listen to other students read in class

26. Do you ever read at home, *other* than for your school assignments?

    □ Yes   □ No

    If yes, what kinds of things do you read? (Check *all* the ones you like to read.)

    □ newspapers   □ information   □ song lyrics   □ how-to books
    □ novels   books   □ cookbooks   □ video game
    □ letters or email □ poetry   □ website pages   □ strategy books
    □ magazines   □ comic books   □ computer   or magazines
                                                manuals

    □ other _____

27. How often do you read, *other* than for your school assignments?

    ☐ every day   ☐ frequently   ☐ once in a while, not often   ☐ never

28. How often do you read at home for school assignments?

    ☐ every day   ☐ frequently   ☐ once in a while, not often   ☐ never

29. How long do you usually read at a time?

    ☐ 1–10 minutes   ☐ 11–30 minutes   ☐ 31–60 minutes
    ☐ more than an hour

30. During the past 12 months, how many books have you read? _____

    How many of these were *not* for school? _____

31. What kinds of books do you like to read? (Check *all* the ones you like to read.)

    ☐ science fiction   ☐ thrillers   ☐ picture books
    ☐ adventure/action   ☐ true-life drama   ☐ comic books
    ☐ horror   ☐ poetry   ☐ romance
    ☐ mysteries   ☐ short stories   ☐ fantasy/myth
    ☐ how-to books   ☐ history   ☐ information books
    ☐ sports   ☐ science/nature   ☐ teen problems
    ☐ (auto)biography   ☐ humor   ☐ none
    ☐ other (describe) _____

32. Which are your three *favorite* kinds of books? (Circle three of the ones you checked in question 31.)

33. Who are your favorite authors? (List as many as you'd like.)

    _____

    _____

    _____

34. How do you choose a book to read? (Check *all* the ones that describe what you do.)

    ☐ look at the book cover   ☐ see how long the book is
    ☐ ask a teacher or librarian   ☐ look for an interesting title
    ☐ pick a book that looks easy   ☐ ask a family member
    ☐ look at the pictures in   ☐ look for a particular author
       the book   ☐ look to see if it has gotten
    ☐ ask a friend or classmate   an award
    ☐ look for books on a particular ☐ look in special displays at the
       subject   library or bookstore
    ☐ read the book cover or jacket   ☐ pick from a best-sellers list

☐ look for books that have been made into movies

☐ read a few pages

☐ look for particular kinds of books (drama, horror, etc.)

☐ look for books about my culture

☐ I have no method of choosing a book

☐ look for books I've heard about

☐ other (describe) _____

35. Do you ever talk with a friend or someone you live with about something you have read?

☐ almost every day   ☐ once or twice a week

☐ once or twice a month   ☐ never or hardly ever

36. Do you borrow books from friends, family members, or teachers?

☐ almost every day   ☐ once or twice a week

☐ once or twice a month   ☐ never or hardly ever

37. Do you borrow books from the school or public library?

☐ almost every day   ☐ once or twice a week

☐ once or twice a month   ☐ never or hardly ever

38. In general, how do you feel about reading?

Part 3: Final Reflections

39. Write any comments or concerns you have about this class.

40. What do you hope to achieve in this class?

Thank you for completing this survey. I will use your answers to help guide my teaching.

Student Learning Goals

Student Learning Goals let students in on all the ways they can expect their reading and learning to grow in a Reading Apprenticeship classroom. They also allow the teacher and students to monitor growth.

How to Use Student Learning Goals

The learning goals are organized in sets that parallel the dimensions of the Reading Apprenticeship framework.

Social Dimension:
Collaborating in a Community of Readers and Writers Goals

These goals may be introduced as a set after the Setting Norms for Learning activity (Box 3.4); for example, with students invited to highlight those they intend to focus on.

Personal Dimension:
Building Personal Engagement Goals

This set of goals may be introduced after the Personal Reading History activity (Box 3.9); for example, with students invited to highlight those they intend to focus on.

Metacognitive Conversation:
Making Thinking Visible Goals

This short set of goals may be introduced after students have been introduced to metacognition with non-reading activities that illustrate their ability to think about their thinking (see Chapter Four, particularly Box 4.2 and Classroom Close-Up 4.1).

Cognitive Dimension:
Using Cognitive Strategies to Increase Comprehension Goals

After students have been introduced to a number of the reading strategies, it may be effective for them to read over the list of cognitive goals, Talk to the Text (annotate the list with their questions and ideas), and notice how many of these goals they are already working on and which ones they are curious about.

Knowledge-Building Dimension:
Knowledge-Building Goals

As with the cognitive goals, these are best introduced with a Talk to the Text activity after students have experienced a number of them, so that they can be impressed with those they have already learned and anticipate others.

Customized learning goals are provided for four subject areas: science, history, literature, and mathematics. In each subject area, the set of goals is the same in the social and personal dimensions and for metacognitive conversation. The learning goals vary somewhat by subject area in the cognitive dimension and are entirely discipline-specific in the knowledge dimension.

If students have selected goals to focus on, from time to time they will want to reflect on how successfully they are meeting their goals and perhaps focus on new goals.

At the end of a course, students can select a small subset of goals (for example, two in each of the five categories) in which they think they have made progress—progress that they can document with early and later work samples, or with metrics like the amount of time they are able to stay focused on their reading or the number of pages they are able to complete now, compared with at the beginning of the course.

Students may also enjoy simply checking off *all* the goals they feel they have accomplished or grown in using. Teachers report that the goals make students feel successful (and even surprised by how much they have learned).

Student Learning Goals: Science

Collaborating in a Community of Readers and Writers

Contributing to Our Community	I contribute to maintaining a classroom community that feels safe, where everyone is able to take risks and grow.
Collaborating Effectively	I work with partners and groups in ways that are both respectful and risk-taking.
Participating Thoughtfully	I make my thinking count in discussions, as a speaker and a listener. I share my reading confusions and understandings to get and give help. I listen and learn from the reading confusions and understandings of others.
Building a Literacy Context	I understand and use the shared literacy vocabulary of our classroom.
Being Open to New Ideas	I appreciate and evaluate alternative viewpoints.
Developing a Literacy Agenda	I read to understand how literacy opens and closes doors in people's lives.
Sharing Books	I talk about books I am reading to involve others in what the books have to offer.
Writing to Communicate	I write to communicate my ideas to others.

Building Personal Engagement

Knowing My Reader Identity	I am aware of my reading preferences, habits, strengths, weaknesses, and attitudes—my Reader Identity.
Practicing	I put effort into practicing new reading strategies so that they become automatic.
Digging In	I am increasing my confidence and persistence for digging into text that seems difficult or boring.
Building Silent Reading Fluency	I read more smoothly and quickly, so I get more pages read.
Building Oral Reading Fluency	I read aloud more fluently and expressively.
Increasing Stamina	I set and meet stretch goals to read for longer and longer periods.
Increasing Range	I set and meet stretch goals for extending the range of what I read.
Choosing Books (SSR+)	I use tools I have learned for choosing a book that's right for me.
Taking Power	I read to understand how *what* I read applies to me and gives me power.
Reflecting on My Evolving Reader Identity	I reflect in discussions and in writing on my growth as a reader—my evolving Reader Identity.
Writing to Reflect	I use writing to step back and think about what I am learning.

Making Thinking Visible

Monitoring	I monitor my reading processes and identify problems.
Repairing Comprehension	I know what strategies to use to get back on track.
Talking to Understand Reading	I talk about my reading processes to understand them better.
Writing to Understand Reading	I write about my reading processes to understand them better.

Using Cognitive Strategies to Increase Comprehension: Science

Setting a Reading Purpose	I set a purpose for reading a text and keep it in mind while I read.
Choosing a Reading Process	I vary my reading process to fit my reading purpose.
Previewing	I preview text that is long or appears to be challenging, to mobilize strategies for dealing with it.
Identifying and Evaluating Roadblocks	I identify specific reading roadblocks and decide what to do.
Tolerating Ambiguity	I tolerate ambiguity or confusion in understanding a text while I work on making sense of it.
Clarifying	I work to clear up a reading confusion—whether it is a word, a sentence, an idea, or missing background information that I need to find.
Using Context	I use context to clarify confusions by reading on and rereading.
Making Connections	I make connections from texts to my experience and knowledge.
Chunking	I break difficult text into smaller pieces to better understand the whole.
Visualizing	I try to see in my mind what the author is describing. I read and represent scientific content and ideas in drawings, graphs, flow charts, and other visuals.
Using Mathematics	I read and create numerical representations to help clarify complex scientific text and ideas.
Questioning	I ask myself questions when I don't understand. I ask myself questions about the author's idea, story, or text, and I know where to find the answers—whether in my mind, the text, other texts, other people, or a combination of these. I ask inquiry questions when something I read makes me want to know more. I take a "convince me" stand and ask questions about the evidence presented to support a scientific claim.
Predicting	I use what I understand in the reading to predict what might come next.
Organizing Ideas and Information	I use graphic organizers to sort out ideas or items of information to see how they are related.

Paraphrasing	I restate a sentence or an idea from a text in my own words.
Getting the Gist	I read and answer in my own words the question, "What do I know so far?"
Summarizing	I boil down what I read to the key points.
Sequencing	I order events in time to understand their relationships. I keep track of how scientific processes unfold.
Comparing and Contrasting	I make comparisons to identify similarities and differences.
Identifying Cause and Effect	I find conditions or events that contribute to or cause particular outcomes.
Using Evidence	I use evidence to build and support my understanding of texts and concepts.
Rereading	I reread to build understanding and fluency.
Writing to Clarify Understanding	I write about what I think I know to make it clearer to myself.

Building Knowledge: Science

Mobilizing Schema	I use my relevant networks of background knowledge, or schema, so that new information has something to connect to and is easier to understand.
Building and Revising Schema	I add to and revise my schema as I learn more.
Synthesizing	I look for relationships among my ideas, ideas from texts, and ideas from discussions.
Writing to Consolidate Knowledge	I use writing to capture and lock in new knowledge.

Building Knowledge . . . About Text: Science

Text Structure	I use my knowledge of text structures to predict how ideas are organized. I know to look for the predictable ways science text is structured: classification and definition, structure and function, process and interaction, claim and evidence, and procedure. I know that visuals and numerical representations are particularly powerful ways to convey complex scientific text and ideas.
Text Features	I use my knowledge of text features like headings and graphics to support my understanding.
Text Density	Because I know that science text is often tightly packed with new terms and ideas, I preview and reread it. Because I know that science text is often tightly packed with new terms and ideas, I chunk and restate the chunks in familiar language to keep track of the gist as I read.
Point of View	I use my understanding that authors write with a purpose and for particular audiences to identify and evaluate the author's point of view.

Building Knowledge . . . About Language: Science

Word Analysis	I use my knowledge of word roots, prefixes, and suffixes to figure out new words.
Referents	I use my knowledge of pronouns and other referents to find and substitute the word that a pronoun or other word is standing for.
Signal Words and Punctuation (Text Signals)	I use my knowledge of signal words and punctuation to predict a definition, results or conclusions, examples, sequence, comparison, contrast, a list, or an answer. I know to look for the text signals that go with different scientific text structures.
Contextual Redefinition	I know that when familiar terms are used in unfamiliar ways, I can redefine them in context to clear up confusion.
Sentence Structure	I use my knowledge of sentence structure to help me understand difficult text. Because science textbooks often use passive voice, I know to restate sentences in active voice to keep track of the subject and action. Because science textbooks often use complex sentence constructions, I know to find the logical connecting words between ideas.
Word-Learning Strategies List	I use strategies to learn new words in the texts I read.

Building Knowledge . . . About the Discipline of Science

Scientific Documents	I know how to read and/or represent diverse scientific documents: reports, data tables and graphs, illustrations and other visuals, equations, textbooks, and models.
Scientific Sourcing	I source a science document, set of data, or piece of evidence as a step in evaluating its authority or reliability.
Scientific Labels	I know that using scientific names and labels is a shortcut for communicating precisely about scientific processes and structures.
Scientific Inquiry	Knowing that scientific inquiry involves cycles of questioning, making observations, and explaining and evaluating observations helps me read science investigations and describe my own.
Scientific Evidence	I know that scientific claims must be supported by evidence that is carefully collected, evaluated, and reported so that others can judge its value.
Scientific Explanation	I can write a scientific explanation that makes a claim about observations of the natural world and convincingly defends the claim with evidence.

Scientific Corroboration	I know that corroborating findings in science is a way to find out how likely they are to be true.
Scientific Understanding	I know that for scientific understanding to evolve, science moves forward using best evidence and information even though these may be proved incomplete or wrong in the future.
Conceptual Change	I monitor my schema to decide whether compelling evidence about scientific claims changes my personal understanding of the natural world.
Scientific Identity	I am aware of my evolving identity as a reader and consumer of science.

Student Learning Goals: History

Collaborating in a Community of Readers and Writers

Contributing to Our Community	I contribute to maintaining a classroom community that feels safe, where everyone is able to take risks and grow.
Collaborating Effectively	I work with partners and groups in ways that are both respectful and risk-taking.
Participating Thoughtfully	I make my thinking count in discussions, as a speaker and a listener. I share my reading confusions and understandings to get and give help. I listen and learn from the reading confusions and understandings of others.
Building a Literacy Context	I understand and use the shared literacy vocabulary of our classroom.
Being Open to New Ideas	I appreciate and evaluate alternative viewpoints.
Developing a Literacy Agenda	I read to understand how literacy opens and closes doors in people's lives.
Sharing Books	I talk about books I am reading to involve others in what the books have to offer.
Writing to Communicate	I write to communicate my ideas to others.

Building Personal Engagement

Knowing My Reader Identity	I am aware of my reading preferences, habits, strengths, weaknesses, and attitudes—my Reader Identity.
Practicing	I put effort into practicing new reading strategies so that they become automatic.
Digging In	I am increasing my confidence and persistence for digging into text that seems difficult or boring.
Building Silent Reading Fluency	I read more smoothly and quickly, so I get more pages read.
Building Oral Reading Fluency	I read aloud more fluently and expressively.
Increasing Stamina	I set and meet stretch goals to read for longer and longer periods.
Increasing Range	I set and meet stretch goals for extending the range of what I read.
Choosing Books (SSR+)	I use tools I have learned for choosing a book that's right for me.
Taking Power	I read to understand how *what* I read applies to me and gives me power.
Reflecting on My Evolving Reader Identity	I reflect in discussions and in writing on my growth as a reader—my evolving Reader Identity.
Writing to Reflect	I use writing to step back and think about what I am learning.

Making Thinking Visible

Monitoring	I monitor my reading processes and identify problems.
Repairing Comprehension	I know what strategies to use to get back on track.
Talking to Understand Reading	I talk about my reading processes to understand them better.
Writing to Understand Reading	I write about my reading processes to understand them better.

Using Cognitive Strategies to Increase Comprehension: History

Setting a Reading Purpose	I set a purpose for reading a text and keep it in mind while I read.
Choosing a Reading Process	I vary my reading process to fit my reading purpose.
Previewing	I preview text that is long or appears to be challenging, to mobilize strategies for dealing with it.
Identifying and Evaluating Roadblocks	I identify specific reading roadblocks and decide what to do.
Tolerating Ambiguity	I tolerate ambiguity or confusion in understanding a text while I work on making sense of it.
Clarifying	I work to clear up a reading confusion, whether it is a word, a sentence, an idea, or missing background information that I need to find.
Using Context	I use context to clarify confusions by reading on and rereading.
Making Connections	I make connections from texts to my experience and knowledge.
Chunking	I break difficult text into smaller pieces to better understand the whole.
Visualizing	I try to see in my mind what the author is describing.
Listening for Voice	I listen for the author's voice to help me engage with a text.
Questioning	I ask myself questions when I don't understand. I ask myself questions about the author's idea or text, and I know where to find the answers—whether in my mind, the text, other texts, other people, or a combination of these. I ask inquiry questions when something I read makes me want to know more.
Predicting	I use what I understand in the reading to predict what might come next.
Organizing Ideas and Information	I use graphic organizers to sort out ideas or items of information to see how they are related.
Paraphrasing	I restate a sentence or an idea from a text in my own words.

Getting the Gist	I read and answer in my own words the question, "What do I know so far?"
Summarizing	I boil down what I read to the key points.
Sequencing	I order events in time to understand their relationships.
Comparing and Contrasting	I make comparisons to identify similarities and differences.
Identifying Cause and Effect	I find conditions or events that contribute to or cause particular outcomes.
Using Evidence	I use evidence to build and support my understanding of texts and concepts.
Rereading	I reread to build understanding and fluency.
Writing to Clarify Understanding	I write about what I think I know to make it clearer to myself.

Building Knowledge: History

Mobilizing Schema	I use my relevant networks of background knowledge, or schema, so that new information has something to connect to and is easier to understand.
Building and Revising Schema	I add to and revise my schema as I learn more.
Synthesizing	I look for relationships among my ideas, ideas from texts, and ideas from discussions.
Writing to Consolidate Knowledge	I use writing to capture and lock in new knowledge.

Building Knowledge . . . About Text: History

Text Structure	I use my knowledge of text structures to predict how ideas are organized.
Text Features	I use my knowledge of text features like headings and graphics to support my understanding.
Point of View	I use my understanding that authors write with a purpose and for particular audiences to identify and evaluate the author's point of view.

Building Knowledge . . . About Language: History

Word Analysis	I use my knowledge of word roots, prefixes, and suffixes to figure out new words.
Referents	I use my knowledge of pronouns and other referents to find and substitute the word that a pronoun or other word is standing for.
Signal Words and Punctuation (Text Signals)	I use my knowledge of signal words and punctuation to predict a definition, results or conclusions, examples, sequence, comparison, contrast, a list, or an answer.

Contextual Redefinition	I know that when familiar terms are used in unfamiliar ways, I can redefine them in context to clear up confusion.
Sentence Structure	I use my knowledge of sentence structure to help me understand difficult text.
Word-Learning Strategies List	I use strategies to learn new words in the texts I read.

Building Knowledge . . . About the Discipline of History

Historical Documents and Artifacts	I know how to identify and use diverse types of historical documents and artifacts.
Primary and Secondary Sources	I know the differences between primary sources and secondary sources.
Document Sourcing	I source a document or account to evaluate its credibility and point of view by identifying who wrote it, when, why, and for what audience.
Document Corroboration	I compare documents or accounts to look for evidence that what is written is credible and to find other points of view or perspectives.
Chronological Thinking	I know how to order events and assess their duration and relationships in time.
Historical Schema	I actively work to build my schema about particular times and places and how they differ—the geography, people, customs, values, religions, beliefs, languages, technologies, and roles of men, women, children, and minority groups.
Historical Contextualization	I use my historical schema to understand what it was like in times and places that I cannot personally experience.
Historical Cause and Effect	I use my understanding of cause and effect to identify historical relationships and impacts.
Historical Record and Interpretation	I understand that history is a combination of what can be observed, how it is observed, what can be interpreted, and how it is interpreted.
Historical Identity	I am aware of my evolving identity as a reader of and actor in history.

Student Learning Goals: Literature

Collaborating in a Community of Readers and Writers

Contributing to Our Community	I contribute to maintaining a classroom community that feels safe, where everyone is able to take risks and grow.
Collaborating Effectively	I work with partners and groups in ways that are both respectful and risk-taking.
Participating Thoughtfully	I make my thinking count in discussions, as a speaker and a listener. I share my reading confusions and understandings to get and give help. I listen and learn from the reading confusions and understandings of others.
Building a Literacy Context	I understand and use the shared literacy vocabulary of our classroom.
Being Open to New Ideas	I appreciate and evaluate alternative viewpoints.
Developing a Literacy Agenda	I read to understand how literacy opens and closes doors in people's lives.
Sharing Books	I talk about books I am reading to involve others in what the books have to offer.
Writing to Communicate	I write to communicate my ideas to others.

Building Personal Engagement

Knowing My Reader Identity	I am aware of my reading preferences, habits, strengths, weaknesses, and attitudes—my Reader Identity.
Practicing	I put effort into practicing new reading strategies so that they become automatic.
Digging In	I am increasing my confidence and persistence for digging into text that seems difficult or boring.
Building Silent Reading Fluency	I read more smoothly and quickly, so I get more pages read.
Building Oral Reading Fluency	I read aloud more fluently and expressively.
Increasing Stamina	I set and meet stretch goals to read for longer and longer periods.
Increasing Range	I set and meet stretch goals for extending the range of what I read.
Choosing Books (SSR+)	I use tools I have learned for choosing a book that's right for me.
Taking Power	I read to understand how *what* I read applies to me and gives me power.
Reflecting on My Evolving Reader Identity	I reflect in discussions and in writing on my growth as a reader—my evolving Reader Identity.
Writing to Reflect	I use writing to step back and think about what I am learning.

Making Thinking Visible

Monitoring	I monitor my reading processes and identify problems.
Repairing Comprehension	I know what strategies to use to get back on track.
Talking to Understand Reading	I talk about my reading processes to understand them better.
Writing to Understand Reading	I write about my reading processes to understand them better.

Using Cognitive Strategies to Increase Comprehension: Literature

Setting a Reading Purpose	I set a purpose for reading a text and keep it in mind while I read.
Choosing a Reading Process	I vary my reading process to fit my reading purpose.
Previewing	I preview text that is long or appears to be challenging, to mobilize strategies for dealing with it.
Identifying and Evaluating Roadblocks	I identify specific reading roadblocks and decide what to do.
Tolerating Ambiguity	I tolerate ambiguity or confusion in understanding a text while I work on making sense of it.
Clarifying	I work to clear up a reading confusion, whether it is a word, a sentence, an idea, or missing background information that I need to find.
Using Context	I use context to clarify confusions by reading on and rereading.
Making Connections	I make connections from texts to my experience and knowledge.
Chunking	I break difficult text into smaller pieces to better understand the whole.
Visualizing	I try to see in my mind what the author is describing.
Listening for Voice	I listen for the author's voice or the voices of characters to help me engage with a text.
Questioning	I ask myself questions when I don't understand. I ask myself questions about the author's idea, story, or text, and I know where to find the answers—whether in my mind, the text, other texts, other people, or a combination of these. I ask inquiry questions when something I read makes me want to know more.
Predicting	I use what I understand in the reading to predict what might come next.
Organizing Ideas and Information	I use graphic organizers to sort out ideas or items of information to see how they are related.
Paraphrasing	I restate a sentence or an idea from a text in my own words.

Getting the Gist	I read and answer in my own words the question, "What do I know so far?"
Summarizing	I boil down what I read to the key points.
Sequencing	I order events in time to understand their relationships.
Comparing and Contrasting	I make comparisons to identify similarities and differences.
Identifying Cause and Effect	I find conditions or events that contribute to or cause particular outcomes.
Using Evidence	I use evidence to build and support my understanding of texts and concepts.
Rereading	I reread to build understanding and fluency.
Writing to Clarify Understanding	I write about what I think I know to make it clearer to myself.

Building Knowledge: Literature

Mobilizing Schema	I use my relevant networks of background knowledge, or schema, so that new information has something to connect to and is easier to understand.
Building and Revising Schema	I add to and revise my schema as I learn more.
Synthesizing	I look for relationships among my ideas, ideas from texts, and ideas from discussions.
Writing to Consolidate Knowledge	I use writing to capture and lock in new knowledge.

Building Knowledge . . . About Text: Literature

Text Structure	I use my knowledge of literary genres and subgenres to predict how ideas are organized.
Text Features	I use my knowledge of text features such as chapter titles, stage directions, and dialogue to support my understanding.
Point of View	I use my understanding that authors write with a purpose and for particular audiences to identify and evaluate the author's point of view.

Building Knowledge . . . About Language: Literature

Word Analysis	I use my knowledge of word roots, prefixes, and suffixes to figure out new words.
Referents	I use my knowledge of pronouns and other referents to find and substitute the word that a pronoun or other word is standing for.
Signal Words and Punctuation (Text Signals)	I use my knowledge of signal words and punctuation to predict a definition, results or conclusions, examples, sequence, comparison, contrast, a list, or an answer.

Contextual Redefinition	I know that when familiar terms are used in unfamiliar ways, I can redefine them in context to clear up confusion.
Sentence Structure	I use my knowledge of sentence structure to help me understand difficult text.
Word-Learning Strategies List	I use strategies to learn new words in the texts I read.

Building Knowledge . . . About the Discipline of Literature

Literary Genres	I can identify and use diverse literary genres and subgenres.
Literary Themes	I recognize universal literary themes—such as good versus evil, ideal versus flawed behavior, and psychological growth and change—and I know how to trace their development.
Literary Structures	I understand how different literary structures—such as plot, stanza, and act—organize and contribute to the meaning of a piece of literature.
Literary Commentary	I recognize how literature may incorporate or promote social, historical, economic, political, and cultural commentary, either transparently or through figuration such as irony, allegory, and symbolism.
Literary Movements	I can identify how a piece of literature is affected by literary movements such as transcendentalism, romanticism, realism, and feminism.
Narrative Voice	I understand narrative voice (first-person, third-person, third-person omniscient, unreliable narrator) and authorial voice, including relationships between author and narrator.
Language Choices	I can identify and use imagery, tone, dialogue, rhythm, and syntax to shape meaning.
Literary Inquiry	I understand that literature invites inference and interpretation within and across texts and experiences. I offer and also consider others' evidence-based inferences and interpretations.
Literary Identity	I am aware of my evolving identity as a reader and writer of literary forms.

Student Learning Goals: Mathematics

Collaborating in a Community of Readers and Writers

Contributing to Our Community	I contribute to maintaining a classroom community that feels safe, where everyone is able to take risks and grow.
Collaborating Effectively	I work with partners and groups in ways that are both respectful and risk-taking.
Participating Thoughtfully	I make my thinking count in discussions, as a speaker and a listener. I share my reading confusions and understandings to get and give help. I listen and learn from the reading confusions and understandings of others.
Building a Literacy Context	I understand and use the shared literacy vocabulary of our classroom.
Being Open to New Ideas	I appreciate and evaluate alternative viewpoints.
Developing a Literacy Agenda	I read to understand how literacy opens and closes doors in people's lives.
Sharing Books	I talk about books I am reading to involve others in what the books have to offer.
Writing to Communicate	I write to communicate my ideas to others.

Building Personal Engagement

Knowing My Reader Identity	I am aware of my reading preferences, habits, strengths, weaknesses, and attitudes—my Reader Identity.
Practicing	I put effort into practicing new reading strategies so that they become automatic.
Digging In	I am increasing my confidence and persistence for digging into text that seems difficult or boring.
Building Silent Reading Fluency	I read more smoothly and quickly, so I get more pages read.
Building Oral Reading Fluency	I read aloud more fluently and expressively.
Increasing Stamina	I set and meet stretch goals to read for longer and longer periods.
Increasing Range	I set and meet stretch goals for extending the range of what I read.
Choosing Books (SSR+)	I use tools I have learned for choosing a book that's right for me.
Taking Power	I read to understand how what I read applies to me and gives me power.
Reflecting on My Evolving Reader Identity	I reflect in discussions and in writing on my growth as a reader—my evolving Reader Identity.
Writing to Reflect	I use writing to step back and think about what I am learning.

Making Thinking Visible

Monitoring	I monitor my reading processes and identify problems.
Repairing Comprehension	I know what strategies to use to get back on track.
Talking to Understand Reading	I talk about my reading processes to understand them better.
Writing to Understand Reading	I write about my reading processes to understand them better.

Using Cognitive Strategies to Increase Comprehension: Mathematics

Setting a Reading Purpose	I set a purpose for reading a text and keep it in mind while I read.
Choosing a Reading Process	I vary my reading process to fit my reading purpose.
Previewing	I preview text that is long or appears to be challenging, to mobilize strategies for dealing with it.
Identifying and Evaluating Roadblocks	I identify specific reading roadblocks and decide what to do.
Tolerating Ambiguity	I tolerate ambiguity or confusion in understanding a text while I work on making sense of it.
Clarifying	I work to clear up a reading confusion, whether it is a word, a sentence, an idea, or missing background information that I need to find.
Using Context	I use context to clarify confusions by reading on and rereading.
Making Connections	I make connections from texts to my experience and knowledge.
Chunking	I break difficult text into smaller pieces to better understand the whole.
Visualizing	I try to see in my mind what the text is describing. I read and create numerical representations to help clarify complex mathematical text and ideas.
Questioning	I ask myself questions when I don't understand. I ask myself questions about the text, and I know where to find the answers—whether in my mind, the text, other texts, other people, or a combination of these. I ask inquiry questions when something I read makes me want to know more.
Predicting	I use what I understand in the reading to predict what a reasonable answer might be.
Organizing Ideas and Information	I use graphic organizers to sort out ideas or items of information to see how they are related.
Paraphrasing	I restate a sentence or an idea from a text in my own words.
Getting the Gist	I read and answer in my own words the question, "What do I know so far?"

Summarizing	I boil down what I read to the key points.
Sequencing	I order the steps in solving a problem.
Comparing and Contrasting	I make comparisons to identify similarities and differences.
Identifying Cause and Effect	I find conditions or events that contribute to or cause particular outcomes.
Using Evidence	I use evidence to build and support my understanding of texts and concepts.
Rereading	I reread to build understanding and fluency with mathematical language and processes.
Writing to Clarify Understanding	I write about what I think I know to make it clearer to myself.

Building Knowledge: Mathematics

Mobilizing Schema	I use my relevant networks of background knowledge, or schema, so that new information has something to connect to and is easier to understand.
Building and Revising Schema	I add to and revise my schema as I learn more.
Synthesizing	I look for relationships among my ideas, ideas from texts, and ideas from discussions.
Writing to Consolidate Knowledge	I use writing to capture and lock in new knowledge.

Building Knowledge . . . About Text: Mathematics

Text Structure	I use my knowledge of text structures to predict how ideas are organized.
Text Features	I use my knowledge of text features like headings and graphics to support my understanding.
Text Density	Because I know that mathematics text is often tightly packed with new terms and ideas, I preview and reread it. Because I know that mathematics text is often tightly packed with new terms and ideas, I chunk and restate the chunks in familiar language to keep track of the gist as I read.

Building Knowledge . . . About Language: Mathematics

Word Analysis	I use my knowledge of word roots, prefixes, and suffixes to figure out new words.
Referents	I use my knowledge of pronouns and other referents to find and substitute the word a pronoun or other word is standing for.
Signal Words and Punctuation (Text Signals)	I use my knowledge of signal words and punctuation to predict a definition, results or conclusions, examples, sequence, comparison, contrast, a list, or an answer.

Contextual Redefinition	I know that when familiar terms are used in unfamiliar ways, I can redefine them in context to clear up confusion.
Sentence Structure	I use my knowledge of sentence structure to help me understand difficult text.
Word-Learning Strategies List	I use strategies to learn new words in the texts I read.

Building Knowledge . . . About the Discipline of Mathematics

Conceptual Categories*	I can identify the purpose for and use different areas of math knowledge such as number, algebra, functions, geometry, statistics and probability, and modeling.
Mathematical Reasoning	I can think interchangeably about a math problem in abstract and quantitative terms. I monitor the reasonableness of the relationship between my abstract and quantitative thinking.
Mathematical Representation	I can read and represent mathematics with words, formulas, and mathematical symbols. I can read and create diagrams, tables, graphs, and flowcharts for mathematical purposes.
Mathematical Language	I understand the precise nature of mathematical language and use it to communicate exactly.
Problem Identification	I can read and identify "the problem" in a math problem.
Problem Solving	I make conjectures about and evaluate alternative approaches to a problem and then monitor the reasonableness of a solution approach as it proceeds.
Accuracy	I understand that in mathematics there may be alternate approaches to a solution, but only one correct answer. I check that the final solution makes sense and all computation is correct.
Pattern Application	I look for mathematical structures, approaches, and patterns that I can apply to the solution of new problems.
Mathematical Identity	I am aware of my evolving identity as a reader and user of mathematics.

*These conceptual categories are drawn from the Common Core State Standards for Mathematical Practice.

Monitoring and Assessing Student Work

In Reading Apprenticeship, assessment focuses on students' effort and growth. We describe here ways that teachers can monitor and assess these. In addition, students benefit from taking responsibility for assessing their own effort and growth, with a rubric or other form of self-assessment.

Monitoring Participation and Contribution to Classroom Learning

Students' participation and contribution to classroom learning are important parts of a Reading Apprenticeship class. Students should understand that their participation is valued and expected. A seating chart can be used, for example, to note participation and substantive contributions to class work and discussion for each student.

By checking your records regularly, you can get a quick snapshot of which students are (and are not) participating. Being reminded of students who are not participating is a prompt to use deliberate strategies to distribute participation among your students so that everyone benefits from the class and has opportunities to demonstrate growth. (See Box 3.5, Scaffolding Academic Conversation, for ideas.)

Participation Log

Mark the seating chart for each student who participates productively in these ways:

☐ Came to class prepared with materials and work

☐ Contributed to climate of safety and respect

☐ Worked productively and collaboratively with others

☐ Encouraged the participation of others

Discussion Log

Monitor partner and small group work, SSR+ debriefings, and whole class discussions for each of the following items, and mark the seating chart for each substantive contribution a student makes:

☐ Talked about reading and thinking processes

☐ Shared reading confusions and understandings to give or get help

☐ Used the shared vocabulary of the classroom

☐ Listened and responded to others during the conversation

☐ Made a thoughtful contribution to the conversation

☐ Engaged with alternative viewpoints in respectful ways

☐ Talked about books to involve others in what the books have to offer

Discussion Record

Periodically monitor partner and small group work, collecting examples of the substantive contributions each student makes. Keep these in a Discussion Record for each student and use the records in assessment conferences. Record examples in the categories for the preceding Discussion Log.

Assessing Student Growth

When teachers talk about changes they notice in their classrooms and their students' reading as a result of their work with Reading Apprenticeship, many lament that "all" they have as proof is stories and "anecdotal" evidence. "I know it's working, but I don't have test scores or anything."

The work students do in Reading Apprenticeship classrooms constitutes a rich source of information about their growth over time. This section presents some ideas for collecting and comparing student work samples of your choosing to get a concrete sense of how your students are growing.

Use one (or more) of the ideas offered here to evaluate your students' progress and growth and to demonstrate to colleagues, parents, and students themselves what impact literacy work is having in your classroom. You may want to use the Student Learning Goals (earlier in this appendix) as a reference.

In general, whatever data you collect, it is helpful to

☐ Choose a subgroup of students to focus your attention on.

☐ Collect data samples from similar tasks at different points in the year. Look for changes over time.

☐ Compare data regularly and note trends. Use this information to design supports that help increase on-task behavior.

☐ Create regular opportunities for students to look at this data with you, with partners, and in small groups, and to discuss and write about what changes they see over time in themselves and each other.

Think Aloud

☐ Record a subgroup of students' comments during Think Aloud as you move and monitor groups in the classroom. Keep these records, and compare excerpts across the year. Records can be scripted by you in notebooks or recorded on audiotape or videotape. When comparing samples, ask yourself, "Are my students' Think Alouds getting longer, more complex? Is there evidence that students are more engaged, reading with better stamina, using more strategies, and so forth?"

☐ Have students use a metacognitive bookmark (Box 4.7) as they listen to each other, marking the reader's and listener's name and the date on the bookmark. Compare bookmarks over time.

☐ Have students talk about and reflect on what they notice about their own and others' Think Aloud experiences. Make notes or records of these conversations.

Pre- and Post-Reading Surveys and Reading Histories

☐ Give pre- and post-Interests and Reading Surveys and/or Personal Reading History assignments. (The survey and reading histories are described in Chapter Three; the Interests and Reading Survey itself is in this appendix.) Collect and save the pre-survey so that you and students can compare it to the post-survey.

☐ Compare survey items or reading histories and look for evidence of growth in particular areas of focus. What evidence is there that students are reading more, spending more time reading, or reading more broadly, with better engagement and comprehension, less frustration, more use of strategies, and so on?

☐ Ask students to look at their pre- and post-surveys or reading histories, discuss them with a partner, and then write reflectively about what changes they notice.

Talking to the Text

☐ Collect samples over time, and compare.

☐ Focus the task on a particular literacy strategy that is challenging (questioning, for example) and have students Talk to the Text using that literacy strategy (for example, writing all the questions that come to mind). Do this before and after instruction in that particular literacy strategy (such as learning the QAR strategy). Compare samples.

☐ Give pre and post Curriculum-Embedded Reading Assessments (CERA) and compare. (See the CERA section of this appendix.)

☐ Have students respond to their peers' Talking to the Text, looking for evidence of particular strategies you have taught.

☐ Save samples of work from early in the year and later in the year, pass them back, and ask students to talk and write about what they notice about their reading and Talking to the Text.

Reading Task Behavior

- ☐ Collect observations regularly and look for trends over time.

- ☐ During silent reading tasks or responses, keep an attendance list in front of you, glance around the room at regular intervals (for example, every three minutes), and quickly mark each student (or particular students you are focusing on) for on- or off-task behavior. Time how long it takes students to begin a task. Time how long students engage in reading and/or writing responses to reading.

- ☐ Count the number of students using reading supports (sticky notes, highlighters, logs, and so on). Note who is and who is not.

- ☐ Note who finishes first and last or rereads. Compare students' individual patterns.

- ☐ Note who responds or participates during group discussions.

- ☐ Note who is reading what. Are students' individual selections and preferences changing? Are these more complex, more difficult, or longer? Do they extend genres?

- ☐ Ask students to regularly reflect, orally or in writing, on their level of attention and engagement. Discuss focusing engagement strategies as well as risk factors for inattention and how to deal with them. Have students write about learning to deal with inattention and lack of engagement. Ask them to design action plans for dealing with difficult, boring, or confusing texts and challenging reading environments.

- ☐ Time how long students will remain in discussion about readings in pairs or small groups. Notice whether or not the length of discussion and time on task increases over the year.

Metacognitive Logs and Other Written Work

- ☐ Is there evidence of interaction with the text? Does the writing specifically connect to the text the student is reading? Is the student making a variety of connections to the text, such as text to self, text to world, and text to text?

- ☐ Where do the student's responses map onto the Student Learning Goals?

- ☐ Compare the student's work over time on comparable assignments. You may want to include the student in the decision about which assignments or pages to assess.

- ☐ Have students make their own assessments about growth over time on particular Student Learning Goals. Ask students to select comparable earlier and later assignments or pages, describe why the selections were made, and explain how they demonstrate growth on a particular learning goal or goals.

SSR+ Metacognitive Logs

☐ Compare samples from different times in the year. Note changes in the number of pages read (fluency), time spent reading (stamina), length of responses (engagement in task), depth and complexity of responses (comprehension and/or engagement), range in complexity or choice of reading (any increase in sophistication or difficulty), and range in selected responses.

☐ Have students invent new metacognitive prompts for the logs.

☐ Ask students to look at early samples and current samples and discuss with a small group what they see. Then ask them to reflect individually in writing about what they notice.

Rubric for Student Self-Assessment of Collaborative Work

Students often need help understanding what is required of them in collaborative group work. A rubric such as this one, adapted from a self-assessment rubric that team teachers Allie Pitts and Andrew Hartig provide their high school students, focuses students on their responsibility for the work of the group as a whole.

	Beginning	Approaching	Meeting	Exceeding
Uses Time	Student rarely or never makes effective use of collaboration time.	Student often makes effective use of collaboration time.	Student makes effective use of collaboration time and sometimes facilitates others' participation.	Student makes effective use of collaboration time and facilitates others' participation.
Contributes Ideas	Student's comments are mostly off task.	Student's comments are mostly on task and sometimes move the conversation forward.	Student's comments are on task and often move the conversation forward.	Student's comments are on task, thoughtful, and consistently move the conversation forward.
Listens	Student is not respectful and/or does not listen to others.	Student is respectful but does not demonstrate active listening.	Student is respectful and usually demonstrates active listening.	Student is respectful and consistently demonstrates active listening through body language and tone of voice.
Participates	Student participates only if asked, or refuses to participate.	Student participates, but sometimes needs to be asked.	Student usually participates without being asked.	Student consistently participates without being asked.
Encourages Others	Student discourages others from participating and/or dominates.	Student sometimes encourages others to participate and does not dominate.	Student usually encourages others to participate and does not dominate.	Student consistently encourages others to participate and does not dominate.

Curriculum-Embedded Reading Assessment (CERA) Guidance and Tools

The Curriculum-Embedded Reading Assessment (CERA) is a formative assessment that measures literacy growth. The CERA offers teachers a rich picture of students' awareness of their reading processes and abilities to make sense of regular classroom reading materials.

Guidelines for Administering the CERA

Most students will be unfamiliar with a reading assessment that asks them to report on their own reading processes in both internal and external metacognitive conversations. Teachers find that explaining the CERA rationale and routine to students is an important first step.

How Is the CERA Administered?

The assessment can be given in one class period or less. Because it is not timed, teachers can adjust its timing to meet the needs of their students.

1. *Introduce the Assessment:* Explain the role of literacy in your classroom.

2. *Individual Reading:* Students read a piece of text and Talk to the Text (annotating the text with their responses and reading processes).

3. *Individual Writing:* Students respond to a series of prompts about the piece and their reading processes.

4. *Whole Class Metacognitive Conversation:* The class discusses reading and problem-solving processes and adds to the class Reading Strategies List.

5. *Scoring:* The teacher scores the student work using the CERA rubric.

6. *Using the Data:* The teacher sets new literacy instruction goals based on the data.

7. *Self-Assessment:* Students may reflect on their CERA work and set personal literacy goals.

How Often Is the CERA Administered?

You may give a CERA for your own purposes. The amount of time between the pre-assessment and post-assessment will depend on what the teacher hopes to learn. For example, a CERA might be given at the beginning and end of a year, grading period, or unit:

- Per year, to assess long-term growth.

- Per grading period, to gauge progress on academic literacy goals.

- Per unit or even a single week of instruction, when a new literacy strategy is introduced and practiced. For example, if the focus for that period of time has been asking and answering questions about reading, the CERA can be administered to see how well students are using this technique.

Text Selection and Question Development

Select a short, self-contained passage (a page or less) from a textbook, a supplementary text, or core curricular materials. For example, you might choose the introduction to a chapter, a primary source document, or a piece of literature from an anthology. The text should be representative of the content and challenge level of regular course materials that you use but should not be something you will actually assign either in class or for homework.

Students answer different kinds of questions on the CERA. A set of Individual Writing Prompts is included, and teachers also customize a few (four to six) comprehension questions that will provide a good snapshot of students' understanding of the specific text selected for students to read.

Materials and Preparation

Make a copy of the text for each student. Leave plenty of blank space around the text for note making. Also reproduce the writing prompts for students.

CERA Lesson Plan and Rubric

1. Introducing the assessment

- Give the first CERA early in the year, prior to significant instruction in metacognitive conversation, and then periodically as you deem necessary, to monitor student growth throughout the year.

- Before giving the CERA, establish purposes for supporting and assessing literacy growth. Explain that this assessment is designed to give you information that will help you teach students to become stronger readers in the discipline. Explain that the class will complete assessments like this periodically, as you monitor their progress and growth.

- Ask students to do their best. To elicit their best work, it can help to assure them that you will grade their effort and evidence of their literacy growth. Explain the overall process: they will read and annotate a piece of text and then respond to a set of questions at the end.

2. Individual reading (ten to twenty minutes, depending on the text)

- Have students write their names on both the text and the questions, and ask them to use pen for their writing.

- Ask students to read the text silently and individually and Talk to the Text. If you have not introduced the Talking to the Text routine, explain that you want them to mark the text and make notes about their reading—for example, to underline words and write in the margins any questions, comments, clarifications, and predictions they have.

- If students finish early, ask them to go back over their writing and see whether they want to add any other reflections, comments, questions, and confusions.

3. Individual writing (about ten minutes)

- Ask students to respond to the written prompts (in pen) when they finish reading and Talking to the Text.

- Encourage students to write a good summary that shows what they understood of the reading.

- Be sure to explain that their answers to the questions after the summary will help you see what is confusing about the text and what they know how to do to make sense of texts as they read. Encourage students to take time to respond thoughtfully to the questions so that you can learn about them as readers. It can be helpful to assure students that you will grade this on effort and thoughtful answers that help you understand how they approach reading.

4. Whole class metacognitive conversation (five to fifteen minutes)

- Ask students to review their Talking to the Text and responses to the questions and choose one or two things to share.

- Invite students to share something they noticed about their reading—something they figured out, a confusion or a challenge in the reading. (You may need to model an example or two from your own reading.)

- You might ask:

  What did you mark or comment on in the text?

  What did you do there? What was going on in your thinking?

  How did doing that help your reading?

- Add to the class Reading Strategies List (or introduce the term "metacognition" and start a Reading Strategies List now if this is the class's first metacognitive conversation.)

- Take a moment to appreciate students for sharing their thinking. Explain that this is one of many conversations that will help you learn how to help them become stronger readers of the discipline over the year.

- You might offer students a minute or two to write a brief reflection on what they learned from the CERA process and discussion.

5. Assessing student work

- Use the descriptors in the CERA Rubric to assess students' academic literacy.

6. Using the data to set and adjust literacy instruction goals

- Once you have a sense of what your students know how to do as they read, you can begin to set instructional goals. For example:

  Many students begin by not marking the page much at all. It will be difficult to see what they know how to do as they approach reading. The first step for students on this end of the rubric is to learn to Talk to the Text and make their thinking visible to you and to themselves.

  For students who are marking the text, you will want to assess the breadth of their repertoire of strategies and knowledge (about the content and the world, text, language, and disciplinary practices) that support reading.

- With this information, you can consider next steps for modeling and practicing reading processes.

- As you gather data from new CERAs, you can adjust your disciplinary literacy goals and instruction to respond to students' changing abilities and needs, helping them to develop disciplinary reading habits that will support stronger comprehension and growing independence over time.

7. Self-assessment

- You might offer students an opportunity to read their work, review the rubric, and set literacy goals. You may also want to share your observations about their strengths and literacy instructional goals for the next period of time.

Curriculum-Embedded Reading Assessment (CERA) Individual Writing Prompts

Please respond to the following questions (in pen).

Part I. Summary

1. In your own words, write a short summary (one or two sentences) of this piece.

Part II. Reading Process

2. What kinds of things were happening in your mind as you read this?

3. What did you do that helped you to understand the reading?

4. What questions or problems do you still have with this piece?

Part III. Self-Assessment

5. How easy or difficult was this piece for you? (circle one)

   pretty easy   not too hard   pretty hard   too hard

6. How well would you say you understood this piece?

Part IV. Comprehension Questions *(teacher to supply for the given text)*

7.

8.

9.

10.

Curriculum-Embedded Reading Assessment (CERA) Rubric

Overview	Noticing Reading	Focusing on Reading	Taking Control of Reading
Evidence of student's overall control of reading processes	Few or no marks on the page along with vague responses to process questions and confused answers to comprehension questions. Teacher gains little insight into student's reading process, what is confusing, or how to support the student.	Marks on the page and responses to questions give insight into student's reading process and comprehension. Teacher gathers important information about problems student encountered and next steps for supporting the student.	Substantial marking on the page and elaborated answers to questions give detailed information about student's reading process and comprehension. Teacher is able to develop rich ideas for instruction and how to support student's reading comprehension.

Metacognitive Conversation	Noticing Reading	Focusing on Reading	Taking Control of Reading
Student writes about reading process to monitor comprehension and get back on track	**ANNOTATIONS ON THE TEXT** Few or no marks to give evidence of strategic or thoughtful reader interaction with the text; for example: • Sparse underlining with no written comments. • Whole paragraphs highlighted with no indication of important ideas or questions. • Marks limited to a single type of interaction, such as underlining unfamiliar words.	Marking indicates some reader interaction with the text; for example: • Some limited strategic marks focused on one or more strategies, such as making connections, asking questions. • Comments in margins are generalized responses, such as "boring," "cool," or "me too." • Comments and marks identify specific problems, such as "What?" connected to a highlighted section.	Marking indicates substantial reader-text interactions focused on problem solving and building understanding; for example: • A variety of marks for varying purposes, such as highlights, circles, underlines. • Strategic marking of main ideas, text signals. • Purposeful comments that clarify, ask and answer questions, make connections, summarize.
	RESPONSES TO CERA QUESTIONS Summary misses the main idea or indicates confusions, yet student indicates text was "easy" and he or she understood it "well."	Summary indicates identification of the main ideas.	Summary indicates understanding of the main ideas and may connect to larger themes.
	Process responses offer little evidence of strategic reading; for example, the response is vague, no problems or confusions are identified, strategies are vague—"I just read it."	Process responses indicate some evidence of what is seen in the marking and annotating; for example, student thought about what a key term meant.	Process responses use literacy vocabulary to specifically describe reading processes.
	Taken together, responses suggest student is unaware of reading difficulty.	Taken together, responses indicate an awareness of roadblocks and processes. Student identifies at least one comprehension problem either solved or unsolved.	Taken together, responses demonstrate student is aware of confusions and able to apply strategies to get back on track.

Using Cognitive Strategies	Noticing Reading	Focusing on Reading	Taking Control of Reading
Student uses strategies to focus on reading and take control: *Setting reading purpose* *Choosing reading process* *Previewing* *Identifying and evaluating roadblocks* *Tolerating ambiguity* *Clarifying* *Using context* *Making connections* *Chunking* *Visualizing* *Listening for voice* *Questioning* *Predicting* *Organizing ideas and information* *Paraphrasing* *Getting the gist* *Summarizing* *Using evidence*	**ANNOTATIONS ON THE TEXT** Few or no marks give evidence of strategic interaction with the text.	Specific areas of the text are marked and commented on as roadblocks or confusions.	Marks and comments connect to one another; for example, an underline of a key term is connected to a definition; a section underlined is related to a summary note or question.
	Marks, if any, indicate a single strategy, such as underlining only key words or highlighting everything indiscriminately.	Marks indicate the use of one or more literacy strategies but may not lead to solutions. Marks may appear "practiced." For example, many questions are asked but not all seem useful, purposeful, or strategic, and few are answered.	Multiple strategies are in use, possibly signaling student's attempt to resolve a persistent confusion.
	Comments, if any, indicate general confusion or reactions—such as "Huh?" or "Why am I reading this?"—and do not draw attention to specific problems to be solved.	Comments focus on the text and reader response, but not on identifying roadblocks and problems.	Comments clarify problems or answer questions posed by student.
	RESPONSES TO CERA QUESTIONS Summary does not clearly demonstrate comprehension.	Summary identifies main ideas.	Summary clearly states main ideas, which may also be marked in the text.
	Process responses do not identify roadblocks or problems to solve.	Process responses relate to marks and annotations on the text and describe at least one strategy used or problem solved.	Process responses relate to marks and annotations on the text and demonstrate the use of multiple strategies to solve problems.
	Taken together, responses indicate student is unable to use strategies to get back on track.	Self-assessment demonstrates understanding of challenges and how to get back on track.	Self-assessment demonstrates understanding of main ideas and awareness of how reading problems were solved.

Building Knowledge	Noticing Reading	Focusing on Reading	Taking Control of Reading
Student mobilizes, builds, and revises schema about: *Content and the world* *Texts* *Language* *Disciplinary discourse and practices*	**ANNOTATIONS ON THE TEXT** Marks indicate little or no attention to developing word knowledge; for example, student highlights all long words, or words—such as proper nouns—that do not interfere with comprehension.	Marks indicate a focus on understanding; for example, student highlights words that have importance for comprehension of the big ideas in the text.	Marks indicate several strategies for word learning and attention to syntax and context clues; for example, in addition to words, context clues are highlighted; margin notes indicate word analysis.
	No indication that student is reading beyond word level to attend to sentence and context clues.	Some indication that student is reading beyond word level and attending to sentence and context clues.	Student reads beyond word level, attending to range of sentence and context clues.
	RESPONSES TO CERA QUESTIONS Responses indicate student is not connecting to background knowledge to understand the author's ideas or themes.	Responses indicate some relevant background knowledge to understand the author's ideas or themes.	Responses indicate ample background knowledge to understand the author's ideas and themes.
	Summary reflects limited schema about the author's ideas or theme; for example, "This was about reading and how he hated it."	Summary reflects general understanding and unelaborated referencing of the author's ideas; for example, "This is about how going to jail made him want to learn how to read."	Summary reflects strong understanding and references the author's ideas and themes; for example, "Learning to read may have been the most important turning point in his life."
	Either responses indicate no attention to word learning and language, or responses to language are generalized; for example, "It had lots of hard words."	Student may describe clarifying a difficult word or phrase.	Process responses indicate ways that student learned new words or solved complex syntax problems. Student may use new vocabulary from the text in his or her summary in ways that reflect understanding.
	Process responses do not reference text structures or signals as guides to reading.	Process responses indicate awareness of text structures or signals; for example, student references the introduction.	Process responses indicate use of text structures and signals to solve problems and build understanding of the text; for example, "I figured out that it had two different parts when she said 'All that changed when . . .'"

Sustained Silent Reading+ (SSR+) Assessment Guidance and Tools

Teachers have an important role in helping students establish SSR+ routines. They also monitor and grade students' SSR+ work, making their expectations and grading criteria explicit. Students' responsibilities include setting reading goals and monitoring and assessing their reading behaviors and growth in SSR+.

Monitoring and Assessing SSR+

Monitoring student engagement in reading during SSR+ is critical, especially in the beginning of the year when you are establishing routines and expectations with the class. Many students will need help finding books that engage them and building the stamina to read for longer and longer periods of time. By monitoring students closely each time they start a new book, you will be able to focus your attention on conferring with students who need the most help getting into a book and staying with it.

Keeping Track of Student Reading Behaviors

Use a seating chart or class roster to monitor student reading behavior during SSR+. To begin each SSR+ session, have your own SSR+ book out and open as students come into the room. When the bell for class rings, who is reading? Scan the room and place a small check mark next to the names of those students who are reading (or not). While you and the students are reading, look up at regular intervals (no less than every two minutes to begin) to check students' engagement with reading. Record who is reading (or not). Repeat this throughout SSR+ time. These records will enable you to zero in on students who are having trouble engaging, as well as to grade participation in SSR+.

Be aware, however, that students can stop reading to think or reflect momentarily yet still be engaged in their book. To double check your judgments about students who are or are not engaged in SSR+ reading, you will need to talk with students regularly about their books and review their metacognitive logs.

	9/8 On task at:						9/9 On task at:					
	bell	+2m	+2m	end	On-task	Time	bell	+2m	+2m	end	On-task	Time
Student A	✓	✓	✓		3	4/5	✓	✓			2	4/6
Student B		✓			1	2/5			✓		1	1/6
Student C		✓	✓		2	4/5	✓	✓	✓	✓	4	6/6
Student D	✓	✓	✓	✓	4	5/5	✓	✓	✓		3	4/6

Checking and Responding to Metacognitive Logs

Use a simple check system to record completion of page and minute record-keeping. For the log entries, you might want to differentiate +, ✓, and − for good, adequate, and missing/inadequate.

Respond to log entries to encourage students' efforts to be metacognitive rather than simply summarizing or retelling their reading for the day. Write comments, ask questions, or make suggestions that help students focus on their reading processes.

Over time, use your comments to nudge students in the direction of more elaborate responses and problem solving. Increase expectations for number, length, or complexity of the log prompts that they use.

Grading SSR+

Part of making sure that SSR+ benefits students will mean holding them accountable for their independent reading and their growth as readers. Grades can signal what you value and are a way to reward the reading behaviors you are hoping to increase. At the same time, grades must be used carefully so they do not erode any students' low reading confidence or increase their reluctance to read.

Rewarding Effort

Award credit for students' completion of expectations for SSR+. Use criteria such as the following:

- Coming to class with SSR+ books and materials
- Reading during SSR+ time
- Completing SSR+ metacognitive log entries
- Participating in whole class and small group conversations about books
- Reading for SSR+ homework as assigned or needed
- Completing one book per month, or at least two hundred pages (for most students)
- Completing reflection letters as assigned
- Completing a book project for each book read
- Making progress toward personal reading goals

Rewarding Growth and Progress

Give students credit for increasing their pages read and time on task. Also award credit for students' progress toward any other individual reading goals. Giving credit for meeting goals underscores the importance of working toward a goal and making progress over time.

Reading goals are based on your own observations and records as well as the students' individual SSR+ logs and reflections. Not all students may be able to read two hundred pages a month, for example, but students who steadily increase how much they read should be recognized for their perseverance and progress. Credit for progress toward the goals places the emphasis on the student continuously improving as a reader. This is, in the end, what the SSR+ program is about.

Tools for Students

The following pages include tools students can use for keeping track of their SSR+ goals and reflections: Setting SSR+ Goals, SSR+ Reflections, and SSR+ Reflection Letter.

Setting SSR+ Goals

Please look over your metacognitive log entries.

What do you notice about how long you read?

What do you notice about how many pages you read?

What do you notice about the metacognitive log prompts you used?

Did you use any new strategies to solve reading problems or to reflect on what you read?

Are you ready to try a new author or a new genre?

What reading goals would you like to set and reach in the next month? Here are some of the areas of SSR+ in which you may want to set goals:

Stamina
Fluency
Metacognitive log prompts
Using strategies
Book choice
Other

SSR+ Reflections

1. How have you been feeling during SSR+ time over the past month?

2. What book are you reading?

3. What kind of book is it?

4. Tell me one thing you like about this book:

5. Have you finished your SSR+ book?　☐ Yes　☐ No

6. If not, how close are you to finishing your book?

Look back over your metacognitive log for the past month to answer these questions:

7. How many pages do you usually read during SSR+?

8. How many minutes of SSR+ time do you usually spend reading?

9. Which metacognitive log prompts have you used?

10. Which metacognitive log prompts have you not used yet?

11. Is there anything that is particularly hard for you in SSR+? What help would you like from me?

SSR+ Reflection Letter

Write a letter to your teacher. This letter should be at least one page long and include the following information:

About the Book

- Give the title, author, and a brief summary of the book's plot.

- Choose one character you like or dislike most in the book. Describe the character and explain why you feel this way.

- How does this book compare with other books you have read so far in this course?

- Would you recommend this book to a friend? Why or why not?

About Yourself as a Reader

- What, if anything, are you noticing about yourself as a reader that is different from the way you read at the beginning of this course? Are your interests, skills, or habits changing in any way?

- What, if anything, is surprising you?

- Did you meet any of the reading goals you set for yourself last month? Which ones? Why do you think that is so?

What Does a Reading Apprenticeship Classroom Look Like?

Teachers can use this snapshot of a Reading Apprenticeship classroom as a reflection tool, for lesson planning, and with colleagues for peer observations. It can also serve as a guide for administrators' classroom walk-throughs. Three characteristics of a Reading Apprenticeship classroom are paramount: a focus on comprehension, a climate of collaboration, and an emphasis on student independence.

A Focus on Comprehension

- Reading Apprenticeship is embedded in subject area learning: students develop strategies, identify and use text features, build topic knowledge, and carry out discipline-based activities while reading course-related materials.

- The work of comprehending reading materials takes place in the classroom; the teacher scaffolds the learning and serves as model and guide.

- The work of comprehending is metacognitive; how readers make sense of text is as important as what sense they make of it.

A Climate of Collaboration

- Class members draw on each other's knowledge, serving as resources to make sense of text together.

- Class members respect and value problem-solving processes: classroom norms support risk taking, sharing knowledge and confusion, and working together to solve comprehension problems.

- Grouping arrangements support collaboration and inquiry: students work independently, in pairs, in small groups, and as a class, depending on the task and the text.

- A shared vocabulary to describe reading processes and text features is evident in classroom talk, materials in use, and materials on display.

An Emphasis on Student Independence

- Students are agents in the process of reading and learning: they actively inquire into text meaning, their own and others' reading processes, the utility of particular reading strategies, and their preferences, strengths, and weaknesses as readers.

- Students are expected and supported to read extensively: course- related materials are available on various levels, and accountability systems are in place to ensure that students read large quantities of connected text.

- Over time, students are expected and able to do more reading, make more sophisticated interpretations, and accomplish more work with texts with less support from the teacher during class time.

Other Things to Notice

Reading Apprenticeship classrooms can also be recognized by a number of other classroom characteristics, including how materials and student groupings are used, the types of learning activities students undertake, and the roles of the teacher, students, and classroom talk in the learning environment.

Materials

- What materials are present? How are they being used?

- What kind of work is displayed in the classroom? On the walls? On the board?

- What do these displays indicate about how reading is approached and the role it plays in the class?

Groupings

- How is the classroom arranged?

- What kinds of groupings are students in as they carry out classroom tasks?

- What do these arrangements offer students as learning environments?

Tasks and Activities

- What activities are the teacher and students engaged in?

- What activities seem to be routine in this classroom?

- Who is doing the work of reading and comprehending?

Teaching and Learning Roles

- What roles do the teacher and students play in classroom activities?

- Does the teacher model, guide, and collaborate in comprehension as well as give instructions, assign, and question students?

- Do students pose questions and problems as well as respond to questions about course readings?

- Do all members of the classroom community collaborate in comprehension, share their knowledge and experience, inquire?

Classroom Talk

- What does the teacher say—to the class, to small groups, to individual students?

- What do the students say—to the teacher, to each other?

- What do the teacher and the class talk about?

- What kind of language is being used?

List of Downloadable Resources

Many of the resources in this book are available to be downloaded from the Reading Apprenticeship website: www.wested.org/RA. Permission is given for individual classroom teachers to reproduce these for classroom use. No other reproduction of these materials is permissible. (See explicitly the copyright page of this volume.)

The documents in this list may be downloaded at http://www.wested.org/cs/ra/print/docs/ra/pub.htm.

Chapter Two

The Reading Apprenticeship Framework Graphic

Chapter Three

Research About Education and Economic Power

Confused? Fix-Up Steps

Chapter Four

Metacognitive Bookmark

Metacognitive Reading Log Template

Metacognitive Reading Log: Pair Work

A Metacognitive Funnel

Chapter Five

Reflective Reading Logs and Evaluation Rubric

Chapter Six

My Genre Preferences

SSR+ Metacognitive Log Template

Sample Metacognitive Log Prompts

Discussion Prompts for Debriefing SSR+ Reading

Chapter Seven

Evaluating Roadblocks

Clarification Chart

Diagram Dialogues

QAR Introduction: David Woke Up Late

How Are My Predictions Doing?

Reciprocal Teaching Role Cards in Science

Chapter Eight

Word Detective Bookmark

Sentence Detective Bookmark

Assessments

Interests and Reading Survey

Student Learning Goals: Science

Student Learning Goals: History

Student Learning Goals: Literature

Student Learning Goals: Mathematics

Rubric for Student Self-Assessment of Collaborative Work

Curriculum-Embedded Reading Assessment (CERA) Rubric

Setting SSR+ Goals

SSR+ Reflections

SSR+ Reflection Letter

What Does a Reading Apprenticeship Classroom Look Like?

WestEd and the Strategic Literacy Initiative

WESTED IS A NATIONAL nonprofit research, development, and service agency that creates research-based improvements in learning policy and practice. For more than forty years, WestEd has worked to solve problems across the fields of education, health, labor, child welfare, and other disciplines related to learning and human development.

WestEd is home to the Strategic Literacy Initiative (SLI), which is the developer of Reading Apprenticeship and a nationally recognized leader in literacy professional development and research.

Through Reading Apprenticeship, SLI serves educators in middle school, high school, and college with a research-based and research-tested approach that promotes students' engagement and achievement in subject area literacy.

SLI researchers regularly contribute to the field of adolescent and adult literacy with publications in professional books and journals, including the *American Educational Research Journal,* the *Journal of Adolescent and Adult Literacy,* and the *Handbook of Adolescent Literacy Research.*

About the Authors

RUTH SCHOENBACH is codirector of WestEd's Strategic Literacy Initiative (SLI). For over twenty-five years she has developed programs, curricula, and professional development to help secondary and college students become more successful readers and writers. As coauthor of the first edition of *Reading for Understanding*, her work launched an international movement of educators who use Reading Apprenticeship approaches in their schools and classrooms. She earned an education master's in teaching, curriculum, and learning environments from the Harvard Graduate School of Education.

CYNTHIA GREENLEAF is SLI's other codirector and a coauthor of the first edition of *Reading for Understanding*. She directs the research program of SLI, including multiyear experimental studies of the impact of Reading Apprenticeship on teachers' practice and students' academic literacy and dispositions for learning. Her research has been published widely in professional books, peer-reviewed journals, and periodicals for teachers and administrators. She received a doctorate in language and literacy education from the University of California, Berkeley.

LYNN MURPHY is director of materials development for SLI. She contributes product development and communications expertise to SLI's print and video materials. She has worked previously as director of materials development for Developmental Studies Center and as a communications specialist, an editor of education newsletters, and a journalist.

Subject Index

Name Index